Artificial Intelligence and Society 5.0

The artificial intelligence-based framework, algorithms, and applications presented in this book take the perspective of Society 5.0 – a social order supported by innovation in data, information, and knowledge. It showcases current case studies of Society 5.0 in diverse areas such as healthcare, smart cities, and infrastructure.

Key Features:

- Elaborates on the use of big data, cyber-physical systems, robotics, augmented-virtual reality, and cybersecurity as pillars for Society 5.0.
- Showcases the use of artificial intelligence, architecture, frameworks, and distributed and federated learning structures in Society 5.0.
- Discusses speech recognition, image classification, robotic process automation, natural language generation, and decision support automation.
- Elucidates the application of machine learning, deep learning, fuzzy-based systems, and natural language processing.
- Includes case studies on the application of Society 5.0 aspects in educational, medical, infrastructure, and smart cities.

This book is intended especially for graduate and postgraduate students, and academic researchers in the fields of computer science and engineering, electrical engineering, and information technology.

Emerging Technologies: Research and Practical Applications

Series Editors:

Aryan Chaudhary
Chief Scientific Advisor, Bio Tech Sphere Research, India

Raman Chadha
Chandigarh University, Punjab

Forthcoming Books:

Artificial Intelligence and Society 5.0
Issues, Opportunities, and Challenges
Edited by Vikas Khullar, Vrajesh Sharma, Mohit Angurala, Nipun Chhabra

For more information about the series, please visit: https://www.routledge.com/
Emerging-Technologies/book-series/CRCCHETRPA

Artificial Intelligence and Society 5.0

Issues, Opportunities, and Challenges

Edited by
Vikas Khullar, Vrajesh Sharma, Mohit Angurala,
and Nipun Chhabra

CRC Press
Taylor & Francis Group
Boca Raton London New York

CRC Press is an imprint of the
Taylor & Francis Group, an **informa** business
A CHAPMAN & HALL BOOK

Front cover image: metamorworks/Shutterstock

First edition published 2024
by Chapman & Hall / CRC Press
2385 NW Executive Center Drive, Suite 320, Boca Raton FL 33431

and by Chapman & Hall / CRC Press
4 Park Square, Milton Park, Abingdon, Oxon, OX14 4RN

Chapman & Hall / CRC Press is an imprint of Taylor & Francis Group, LLC

© 2024 selection and editorial matter, Vikas Khullar, Vrajesh Sharma, Mohit Angurala, and Nipun Chhabra; individual chapters, the contributors

ISBN: 978-1-032-50075-1 (hbk)
ISBN: 978-1-032-50141-3 (pbk)
ISBN: 978-1-003-39705-2 (ebk)

DOI: 10.1201/9781003397052

Typeset in Palatino
by Deanta Global Publishing Services, Chennai, India

Contents

About the Editors..vii
Contributors...ix
Preface...xiii

1   Introduction and Role of Society 5.0 in Human-Centric Development......................1
    Mohit Angurala and Vikas Khullar

2   AI Architectures and Technologies for Raising Society 5.0...9
    Tejinder Kaur

3   Disruptive Technologies and Sustainable Development Goals for Society 5.0......17
    Kiran Deep Singh, Prabhdeep Singh, Ankit Bansal, Gaganpreet Kaur, and Rishu Chhabra

4   Use of Big Data Architecture in Society 5.0...27
    Naresh Kumar Trivedi and Vinay Gautam

5   Ethics and Regulations of AI in Society 5.0...37
    Priyanshu Rawat, Prerna, and Prabhdeep Singh

6   Opportunities and Challenges in AI Society 5.0...49
    Vikas Khullar, Mohit Angurala, and Sangeetha Annam

7   Emergence of AI in Education: A Way Forward for Societal Development.............56
    Shivani Malhan, Rekha Mewafarosh, Shikha Agnihotri, and Divya Gupta

8   Applications and Use of AI in e-Commerce: Opportunities and Challenges
    in Society 5.0...69
    Nitish Kumar Ojha, Archana Pandita, Nikhil VP, and Edip Senyurek

9   AI-Based Machine Learning and Deep Learning Smart Electricity Grids for
    Society 5.0..96
    Prabhjot Kaur and Anand Muni Mishra

10   Securing Smart Grids Using Machine Learning Algorithms.................................103
    Moushumi Das, Vandana Mohindru Sood, Kamal Deep Garg, and Sushil Kumar Narang

11   Energy Management in IoT-Enabled Smart Grid: A Review 118
    Vrinda Vritti, Kamal Deep Garg, Vandana Mohindru Sood, and Sushil Kumar Narang

12   E-Healthcare and Society 5.0..133
    Rishu Chhabra and Saravjeet Singh

13 Role of Disruptive Technologies in the Smart Healthcare
    Sector of Society 5.0 143
    Prerna, Prabhdeep Singh, and Devesh Pratap Singh

14 Agriculture in Society 5.0 154
    Meenakshi Aggarwal, Vikas Khullar, and Nitin Goyal

15 Personalized Navigation System in Society 5.0 163
    Saravjeet Singh and Rishu Chhabra

16 Role of Geospatial Technology in the Development of Society 5.0 176
    Sangeetha Annam

17 Application of Machine Learning for IoT Security:
    A Step Toward Society 5.0 184
    *Swapnil Morande, Veena Tewari, Mohit Kukreti, Aarti Dangwal, Tahseen Arshi, and
    Amitabh Mishra*

18 Emerging Trends in Cybersecurity Challenges with Reference to Pen
    Testing Tools in Society 5.0 196
    *Gaganpreet Kaur, Bharathiraja N., Kiran Deep Singh, Veeramanickam M.R.M., Ciro
    Rodriguez Rodriguez, and Pradeepa K.*

19 Role of Delay-Sensitive Smart Health Framework Using Nature-Inspired
    Load Balancer in Society 5.0 213
    Navneet Kumar Rajpoot, Prabhdeep Singh, and Bhaskar Pant

20 Performance Comparison of AODV, DSDV, and DSR Routing Protocols in
    Wireless Sensor Networks 221
    *Shiva Mehta, Mankaj Mehta, Devesh Bathla, Prashant Chauhan, Ruhi Sarangal, and
    Aarti Dangwal*

21 Enhancing Rating and Learning through Clustering in Artificial Intelligence 239
    Ekta and Varsha

22 Aquatic Weed Mining Using Artificial Intelligence 246
    *Aviraj Datta, Lubhan Cherwoo, Htet Ne Oo, Nagendra Prabhu, Saurav Kumar,
    Anupma Sharma, and Amol P. Bhondekar*

Index 267

About the Editors

Vikas Khullar is currently working as Associate Professor at the Department of Computer Science and Engineering, the Chitkara University Institute of Engineering and Technology, Chitkara University, Rajpura, Punjab, India. He has 15 years of experience in research and academia. Dr. Khullar has completed his Ph.D. in Computer Science and Engineering. During his Doctorate dissertation, he had developed new and unique assistive technologies with the use of machine learning and deep learning along with the Internet of Things (IoT) and embedded hardware. He has published more than 80 publications. His major findings are published in reputed/indexed journals with significant impact factors. He has filed patents to tackle most social and commercial problems. He has acted as a team leader and has organized several international/national conferences, short-term courses, faculty development programmes, seminars, and webinars. At present, he is working in the field of Intelligent Internet of Things in Society 5.0, Assistive Technologies for Neurological Disorders, Federated Learning, and Trusted Artificial Intelligence.

Mohit Angurala is currently working as Associate Professor at the Apex Institute of Technology in Chandigarh University, Gharuan, Mohali, Punjab, India. He completed his Ph.D. in Computer Science and Engineering from I.K. Gujral Punjab Technical University, Kapurthala, Punjab, in 2021. He has completed his Master of Technology in Computer Science and Engineering, in 2014, from the Punjab Institute of Technology, PTU Main Campus, Kapurthala, Punjab. In addition to this, he has obtained Master's degree (MBA in distance) in Human Resources from Guru Nanak Dev University, Amritsar. He did his Bachelor of Technology in Information Technology, in 2011, from the Beant College of Engineering and Technology, Gurdaspur, Punjab. Recently, he has completed his advanced certification in machine learning and deep learning from IIIT Bangalore. His areas of interest include energy management in wireless sensor networks, topology management, modulation, network security, optics, and the Internet of Things. He has a total of 44 international publications in his records. He has published four book chapters and one international book as well. He has got four patents for his research studies, out of which three are filed and one has already been granted. He is serving as an editorial board member and reviewer for many reputed international journals like Web of Science, Scopus, and many others of high repute.

Vrajesh Sharma is working as an Incharge Computer Centre/System Manager at Panjab University Swami Sarvanand Giri Regional Centre, Hoshiarpur, which is an off-campus establishment of Panjab University, Chandigarh. He has obtained his Ph.D. from I.K. Gujral Punjab Technical University, Jalandhar, in the field of Cloud Computing. He has a multifaceted personality and his major areas of interest include Cloud Computing, Computer Networks, and Network Security and Firewalls with a specialization in the field of Scheduling Algorithms in Cloud Computing. He completed his Bachelor of Science from Panjab University, Chandigarh, and obtained Master of Computer Applications (with Hons) from Punjab Technical University, Jalandhar. His employment history includes over 18 years of qualitative technical experience in Industry, Educational Institutes/College, and University. He holds two patents and has published over 18 papers/articles in reputed journals (indexed in SCIE, ESCI, Web of Science, and Scopus), international conferences and national seminars, and book chapters, in total. For his research and contributions in the field of priority-based scheduling algorithms for optimizing the performance of Cloud Computing, he has received the InSc Research Excellence Award in the year 2020. He has been a member of the Technical Program Committees, a Resource Person for Webinars, Seminars, and Conferences, and he has also delivered various Expert Talks in Colleges and at All India Radio, Jalandhar. He has filed three patents.

Nipun Chhabra is currently working as Associate Professor at SEDA-E, GNA University in Phagwara, Punjab, India. She has obtained her Ph.D. from I.K. Gujral Punjab Technical University, Kapurthala, Punjab, India. She has completed her Master of Computer Applications (with Hons) from Punjab Technical University, Jalandhar, Punjab, and Bachelor of Computer Applications from Guru Nanak Dev University, Amritsar. In addition to this, she has qualified National Eligibility Test (UGC-NET) for teachers and her major areas of interest include Cloud Computing, Deduplication, and Security Issues in Cloud Computing. She has published over 18 papers/articles in reputed journals (indexed in SCIE, ESCI, Web of Science, and Scopus), international conferences/national seminars, and two chapters in books. She has over 18 years of qualitative teaching experience, and she has been a member of various academic and research committees. She has filed two patents.

Contributors

Meenakshi Aggarwal
Chitkara University Institute of
    Engineering and Technology
Chitkara University
Punjab, India

Shikha Agnihotri
Institute of Management Studies
Ghaziabad

Mohit Angurala
Apex Institute of Technology
Chandigarh University
Gharuan, Mohali, Punjab, India

Sangeetha Annam
Chitkara University Institute of
    Engineering and Technology
Chitkara University
Punjab, India

Tahseen Arshi
American University of Ras al-Khaimah
United Arab Emirates

Ankit Bansal
Chitkara University Institute of
    Engineering and Technology
Chitkara University
Punjab, India

Devesh Bathla
Chitkara Business School
Chitkara University
Punjab, India

Amol P. Bhondekar
Central Scientific Instruments
    Organisation
Chandigarh, India

Prashant Chauhan
Chitkara University Institute of
    Engineering and Technology
Chitkara University
Punjab, India

Lubhan Cherwoo
Central Scientific Instruments
    Organisation
Chandigarh, India

Rishu Chhabra
Chitkara University Institute of
    Engineering and Technology
Chitkara University
Punjab, India

Aarti Dangwal
Chitkara Business School
Chitkara University
Punjab, India

Moushumi Das
Chitkara University Institute of
    Engineering and Technology
Chitkara University
Punjab, India

Aviraj Datta
International Crops Research Institute for
    the Semi-Arid Tropics
India

Ekta
Lovely Professional University
Phagwara, India

Kamal Deep Garg
Chitkara University Institute of
    Engineering and Technology
Chitkara University
Punjab, India

Vinay Gautam
Chitkara University Institute of
    Engineering and Technology
Chitkara University
Punjab, India

Nitin Goyal
Central University of Haryana
India

Divya Gupta
Department of CSE
Chandigarh University
Mohali, India

Pradeepa K.
Department of CSE
SMCET
Kalayarkoil, India

Gaganpreet Kaur
Chitkara University Institute of
    Engineering and Technology
Chitkara University
Punjab, India

Prabhjot Kaur
Chitkara University Institute of
    Engineering and Technology
Chitkara University
Punjab, India

Tejinder Kaur
Chitkara University Institute of
    Engineering and Technology
Chitkara University
Punjab, India

Vikas Khullar
Chitkara University Institute of
    Engineering and Technology
Chitkara University
Punjab, India

Mohit Kukreti
University of Technology and Applied
    Sciences
Ibri, Oman

Saurav Kumar
Central Scientific Instruments
    Organisation
Chandigarh, India

Veeramanickam M.R.M.
Chitkara University Institute of
    Engineering and Technology
Chitkara University
Punjab, India

Shivani Malhan
Chitkara Business School
Chitkara University
Punjab, India

Mankaj Mehta
Chitkara Business School
Chitkara University
Punjab, India

Shiva Mehta
Chitkara University Institute of
    Engineering and Technology
Chitkara University
Punjab, India

Rekha Mewafarosh
Shri Ram Institute of Management and
    Technology
Kashipur, Uttarakhand

Amitabh Mishra
University of Technology and Applied
    Sciences
Ibri, Oman

Anand Muni Mishra
Chitkara University Institute of
    Engineering and Technology
Chitkara University
Punjab, India

Swapnil Morande
University of Naples
Italy

Bharathiraja N.
Chitkara University Institute of
    Engineering and Technology
Chitkara University
Punjab, India

Sushil Kumar Narang
Chitkara University Institute of
    Engineering and Technology
Chitkara University
Punjab, India

Nitish Kumar Ojha
Amity University, Noida
Noida, India

Htet Ne Oo
Chitkara University Institute of
    Engineering and Technology
Chitkara University
Punjab, India

Prerna
Department of Computer Science &
    Engineering Graphic Era (Deemed to be
    University)
Dehradun, India

Archana Pandita
Amity University, Dubai
Dubai, UAE

Bhaskar Pant
Department of Computer Science &
    Engineering Graphic Era (Deemed to be
    University)
Dehradun, India

Nagendra Prabhu
University of Kerala
India

Ciro Rodriguez Rodriguez
Universidad Nacional Mayor de
    San Marcos
Lima, Peru

Navneet Kumar Rajpoot
Department of Computer Science &
    Engineering Graphic Era (Deemed to be
    University)
Dehradun, India

Priyanshu Rawat
Department of Computer Science &
    Engineering Graphic Era (Deemed to be
    University)
Dehradun, India

Ruhi Sarangal
Chitkara Business School
Chitkara University
Punjab, India

Edip Senyurek
Vistula University
Warsaw, Poland

Anupma Sharma
Central Scientific Instruments
    Organisation
Chandigarh, India

Devesh Pratap Singh
Department of Computer Science &
    Engineering Graphic Era (Deemed to be
    University)
Dehradun, India

Kiran Deep Singh
Chitkara University Institute of
    Engineering and Technology
Chitkara University
Punjab, India

Prabhdeep Singh
Department of Computer Science &
    Engineering Graphic Era (Deemed to be
    University)
Dehradun, India

Saravjeet Singh
Chitkara University Institute of
    Engineering and Technology
Chitkara University
Punjab, India

Vandana Mohindru Sood
Chitkara University Institute of
    Engineering and Technology
Chitkara University
Punjab, India

Veena Tewari
University of Technology and Applied
    Sciences
Ibri, Oman

Naresh Kumar Trivedi
Chitkara University Institute of
    Engineering and Technology
Chitkara University
Punjab, India

Nikhil V.P.
University of Stirling
Ras al-Khaimah, UAE

Varsha
Lovely Professional University
Phagwara, India

Vrinda Vritti
Chitkara University Institute of
    Engineering and Technology
Chitkara University
Punjab, India

Preface

Human civilizations have claimed for many golden eras as per the prevalent societal standards and have always dreamt of a society that balances all the facets that contribute towards quality of life. Thus, a society that caters to human-centric development, either economically or morally, by addressing its problems and integrating the innovations of the fourth industrial revolution, such as cyberspace and physical space, is an aim for many developed/developing countries. Evolution and advancements in various societies all over the globe are non-monolithic by their very own nature, but the technology and Internet are narrowing down the gaps between them. In this era, the modern-day human-centric society (Society 5.0) is progressing towards self-reliant and automatic systems; thus, the idea of intelligent decision-making by considering cyber-physical systems for human-centric automation is paving the path for Society 5.0.

The overall focus of this book is on contemporary and advanced artificial intelligence (AI) techniques and methods, by enabling intelligent Internet of Things, cloud analytics, big data analytics, etc., to develop the frameworks and applications for Society 5.0. In this book, diverse AI techniques, including machine learning, deep learning, reinforcement learning, etc., are considered as a base for the Society 5.0-specific applications. This book covers most of the aspects of AI in Society 5.0 including the introduction of Society 5.0, the role of AI in Society 5.0, various architectures and frameworks, big data analytics in Society 5.0, intelligent Internet of Things (IoT) for Society 5.0, and other novel learning paradigms. Society 5.0 is application-specific; hence, the challenging domain case studies, including educational, medical, industrial, developmental, infrastructural, and cases for smart cities, etc., have been focused in this book. At the end of the book, the chapters related to issues, challenges, and future work in Society 5.0 are added.

The first section of this book focuses on the introductory roles of AI in Society 5.0. In this section, authors have contributed bridge-establishing chapters for AI for societal concerns and majorly included terms are technological architectures for Society 5.0, disruptive technologies for sustainability goals, ethics, opportunities, challenges, etc. The second section of this book focuses on the application/utilization of AI for the development of Society 5.0. This section delivers insights of practical applications of AI in diverse human-centric domains, including education, commerce, energy management, healthcare, agriculture, and so on. In the third section, this book emphasizes on futuristic requirements and the scope of AI in Society 5.0 for development in the domain of personalized navigation with privacy, geospatial technology for remote sensing, AI-based IoT for intelligent sensing, cybersecurity to handle cyber challenges, operating system concerns, and sensor network management.

"The rise of the human race is limited without futuristic imaginations." With this thought, this book is written. For the development of this book, the authors have contributed their level best and this book could be considered a step forward for the development of human-centric society.

1

Introduction and Role of Society 5.0 in Human-Centric Development

Mohit Angurala and Vikas Khullar

1.1 Introduction

Society 5.0 has become a popular idea for human society's future. The Japanese government invented it to describe a society that incorporates modern technology like artificial intelligence (AI), Internet of Things (IoT), and robots into daily life. Society 5.0 aims to establish a human-centred, technologically advanced society that prioritises individual and community well-being. It uses technology to better society and quality of life. Technology improves healthcare, transportation, education, and agriculture in Society 5.0. AI and IoT can monitor and forecast illnesses for earlier detection and treatment.

Society 5.0 promotes sustainability and environmental protection. To decrease trash and increase recycling, it promotes renewable energy and a circular economy. However, Society 5.0 may have drawbacks. Automation and AI might eliminate employment. More data collection and processing may harm privacy and security. Despite these concerns, Society 5.0 offers a promising future for human society that could improve lives worldwide. Governments, corporations, and people must maximise the benefits of Society 5.0 while minimising its drawbacks. Society 5.0 merges digital and physical technologies to create a human-centred society. It was debuted in Japan in 2016 and has garnered global interest.

1.2 The Origins of Society 5.0

Industrial Revolution advances in manufacturing and production led to Society 5.0. Society 1.0 involved physical labour and subsistence life. Society 2.0 introduced equipment and mass manufacturing, whereas Society 3.0 used computers and automation. Society 4.0, often known as the Fourth Industrial Revolution, integrates digital and physical technologies. The Internet of Things, AI, and sophisticated robots define this stage. Society 5.0 focuses on human-centric technology-physical world convergence. This suggests that technology should serve people and society rather than just achieving profit or efficiency.

DOI: 10.1201/9781003397052-1

1.3 The Need for Human-Centric Development

As the globe faces environmental deterioration, socio-economic inequity, and ageing populations, human-centric development becomes more important. Society 5.0 seeks to solve these issues by prioritising human needs and ideals. Society 5.0 merges digital and physical technologies to create a human-centred society. The Industrial Revolution-era idea prioritises human wants and ideals to solve society's problems.

1.4 The Importance of Data in Society 5.0

Society 5.0 is the fifth stage of human society's growth when digital technology and AI alter how people live, work, and interact. Data drives innovation, prosperity, and social change today. Society 5.0 values data. Data powers the digital economy, from AI algorithms and machine learning (ML) models to virtual assistants and driverless cars. It might change everything from healthcare and education to transportation and energy management. Digital devices and systems generate massive volumes of data that may enhance decision-making, optimise resource utilisation, and establish new business models and services. It can address climate change, poverty, and disease outbreaks. Data-driven innovation in Society 5.0 will only succeed if we address its ethical, legal, and social ramifications. This involves preserving personal privacy and data security and prohibiting discriminatory or harmful data usage. In conclusion, data powers Society 5.0's sustainable, egalitarian, and successful future. We must also be aware of data-use hazards and take proactive steps to mitigate them.

1.5 The Benefits of Human-Centric Development

Human-centric development prioritises user demands, values, and experiences. This strategy emphasises understanding and empathising with consumers, incorporating them in design, and iterating and improving depending on their input. Human-centric development has several benefits. First, it may improve products and services to satisfy user wants, increasing consumer happiness and loyalty. Developers may learn what features and functions are most essential and how to optimise the product for usability and accessibility by incorporating consumers in the design process. Second, human-centric development promotes innovation and distinction. Developers can find new chances and solutions by understanding consumer demands. This can develop unique goods and markets.

Human-centred development also helps society. Developers may improve inclusiveness and equity by prioritising user requirements regardless of background or ability. This can improve access and social inclusion.

1.6 The Challenges of Implementing Human-Centric Development

Human-centred development puts people first. It empowers people to engage in growth and realise their potential. Implementing human-centric development to enhance people's lives is difficult. Changing development practitioners' mindsets is a major problem of human-centric development. Government agencies and foreign organisations have traditionally led development through top-down policies and programmes. This strategy has overlooked the needs and ambitions of the people it serves, resulting in disappointing development outcomes. Development practitioners must change their thinking to enable people to engage in development and establish policies and programmes that meet their needs to implement human-centric development.

Resources and capacity are another issue. Human-centric development requires financing, technological knowledge, and institutional backing. Human-centric development is challenging in developing nations due to limited resources and capacity. Governments and international organisations must invest in local institutions and communities to engage in development and execute specific programmes. Human-centred development can be hindered by politics. Political instability, corruption, and poor governance hinder progress in many nations. These challenges can impede human-centric development by restricting involvement, resources, and responsibility. Human-centred development requires addressing these political issues. Finally, cultural and societal conventions might hinder human-centric growth. Cultural and social norms affect development programme attitudes and behaviour. These standards might restrict participation, resources, and development programmes. Development practitioners must collaborate with local communities to understand cultural and social norms and construct culturally relevant programmes to address these difficulties.

Finally, human-centric development is difficult. These problems may be overcome by changing mindsets, investing in resources and capacity building, resolving political issues, and engaging with local people to understand their cultural and social norms. Human-centric development encourages individuals to engage in development and realise their potential, notwithstanding the limitations.

1.7 The Importance of Ethics in Society 5.0

Ethics governs a person's actions and decisions. It shapes and sustains society. Ethics is even more important in Society 5.0, the fifth stage of human society, which integrates modern technology. In Society 5.0, new technologies like artificial intelligence, big data, and the Internet of Things have greatly enhanced the power and influence of individuals and organisations, making ethics crucial. These technologies can reshape society, yet also raise ethical issues. Artificial intelligence can create autonomous weaponry, which creates ethical considerations. Ethics in Society 5.0 helps divide the advantages of modern technology fairly. Without ethics, these technologies may favour a minority and leave others behind. Social upheaval and inequality might result.

Society 5.0 ethics also fosters trust between people and organisations. Society 5.0, where people and organisations are more linked, needs trust. Ethical behaviour builds trust and credibility, fostering cooperation and collaboration. Society 5.0 ethics also encourages creativity and innovation. Ethical people and organisations take chances and try new things, which can lead to breakthrough discoveries. Innovation drives economic and social progress in Society 5.0.

Finally, Society 5.0 principles emphasise sustainability and environmental responsibility. As sophisticated technologies influence society, people and organisations must consider their impact on the environment and future generations. Ethical behaviour promotes sustainability and a more ecologically conscious society. In conclusion, ethics is crucial in Society 5.0. Ethical behaviour promotes trust, credibility, innovation, creativity, sustainability, and environmental responsibility. To improve society, people and organisations must prioritise ethics in their decision-making and behaviour.

1.8 Addressing Ethical Challenges in Society 5.0

Society 5.0, powered by AI, IoT, and blockchain, is the latest human society. These advances raise several ethical issues that must be addressed to make Society 5.0 fair and just for all. Data privacy is a major ethical concern. Society 5.0 collects and analyses personal data at unprecedented levels. This raises worries about firms or governments misusing this data and the need for tougher privacy legislation.

Automation and AI might displace employees and increase economic inequality. This raises problems about the government's responsibility in protecting employees' rights and providing education and training to adapt to new technology. Technology's effects on mental health are also an issue. Digital platforms are connected to anxiety, despair, and loneliness. This has led to proposals for more platform regulation and mental health-promoting technology.

Society 5.0's ethical issues include autonomous weaponry, AI prejudice, and technology's influence on democracy and political institutions. Governments, industry, academia, and civic society must collaborate to solve these problems. Ethical frameworks and norms will be required to be imposed to share technology's advantages and minimise hazards. Additionally, citizens should be more involved in shaping Society 5.0's policies and regulations and educated about technology's risks and benefits. In conclusion, Society 5.0 has several ethical issues that must be addressed to build a fair and just society that benefits everybody. There is no *one* answer to these difficulties, but a collaborative, multifaceted strategy that incorporates all stakeholders is crucial to maximising technology's advantages and minimising its hazards.

1.9 Architectures, Protocols, Hardware Devices, Implementation Structures, Edge Devices, Cloud Systems, FOG Systems, Wireless Sensor Networks

Society 5.0 is a sustainable future society with enhanced digital technology [1, 2]. This Society integrates cyber-physical system (CPS) with social infrastructure, which helps residents in many ways. The architecture of Society 5.0 is discussed below.

Architectures: Edge devices, fog systems, cloud systems, and wireless sensor networks (WSNs) form Society 5.0's layered architecture. Layered design simplifies technology integration and data sharing.

Protocols: Society 5.0 uses many protocols to communicate data between systems. These protocols include Wi-Fi, Bluetooth, Zigbee, Ethernet, and CAN.

Hardware: Society 5.0 uses sensors, actuators, and embedded systems. These gadgets send physical data to the cloud for processing.

Implementation Structures: Society 5.0 needs intelligent transportation systems, smart buildings, and smart grids. These interwoven structures help Society run smoothly.

Edge Devices: Society 5.0 relies on edge devices to gather and analyse data from the physical world before transmitting it to the cloud. Smartphones, wearables, and sensors are examples.

Cloud Systems: Society 5.0 relies on cloud systems to store and analyse large volumes of device data. These systems analyse data using big data analytics, machine learning, and AI.

FOG Systems: Fog systems bring cloud and edge computing power and storage to edge devices. Data processing and cloud transmission are quicker.

WSNs: Society 5.0 collects physical data via wireless sensor networks. Many small sensors wirelessly communicate in these networks.

Society 5.0 has a sophisticated architecture of hardware, communication protocols, implementation frameworks, and computer systems. These systems must be integrated to run society smoothly and achieve their aims.

1.10 Big Data, Blockchain, Cyber-Physical Systems, Robotics, Augmented-Virtual Reality, and Cybersecurity as Pillars for Society 5.0

Society 5.0 envisions a sustainable and thriving society where technology is interwoven into all aspects of life [3]. This Society relies on Big Data, Blockchain, Cyber-Physical Systems, Robotics, Augmented-Virtual Reality, and Cybersecurity. In this chapter, we examine how these technologies contribute to Society 5.0 through medicine development.

Big Data: Social media, e-commerce platforms, and IoT gadgets create vast amounts of data daily. In Society 5.0, Big Data improves decision-making, predicts trends, and finds patterns that enhance healthcare. Big Data can find novel therapeutic targets and evaluate medication efficacy in drug development. Researchers can find therapeutic targets and understand disease genetics by analysing big genomic databases.

Blockchain: Blockchain can securely store and transport data. Blockchain fosters industry trust and transparency in Society 5.0. Blockchain can trace medication supply chains transparently and securely in drug development. This can prevent counterfeit pharmaceuticals and ensure that patients receive safe and effective treatments.

Cyber-Physical Systems: CPS mixes physical and digital components to build intelligent and autonomous systems. In Society 5.0, CPS creates smart cities, intelligent transportation networks, and other autonomous technologies to better people's lives [4]. CPS may be used to establish autonomous drug discovery systems that swiftly find and evaluate therapeutic candidates for efficacy and safety.

Robotics: Robot design, building, and operation. In Society 5.0, robots do risky or demanding tasks. Robotics can automate medication production and quality control in drug development. This ensures constant, high-quality medication production.

Augmented Reality/Virtual Reality: AR/VR technologies replicate or improve the actual world with digital information. Immersive AR/VR experiences boost education, entertainment, and healthcare in Society 5.0. AR/VR may simulate medication interactions and instruct healthcare personnel on new medicines and technologies.

Cybersecurity: Protecting computer systems and networks from unauthorised access and assaults. Cybersecurity is vital to technological safety in Society 5.0. Cybersecurity protects patient data and medication development procedures against cyberattacks.

Thus, Society 5.0 relies on Big Data, Blockchain, Cyber-Physical Systems, Robotics, Augmented-Virtual Reality, and Cybersecurity. These technologies can enhance drug discovery, guarantee that patients obtain safe and effective treatments, and improve global healthcare results.

1.11 Role of AI Technologies and Algorithms in Society 5.0

Society 5.0 relies on AI and algorithms that analyse and interpret massive volumes of data for policymaking and decision-making. AI helps create smart systems that boost productivity in numerous industries. Society 5.0 uses AI and algorithms in these ways [5].

Healthcare: AI algorithms and technology diagnose ailments, design treatment strategies, and monitor patient health. AI algorithms can spot problems in medical photos that doctors may overlook. AI can analyse patient data to identify health hazards and customise treatment approaches. Telemedicine, which allows patients to get healthcare remotely, also uses AI.

Mobility: Smart transport systems improve mobility and alleviate traffic congestion using AI technology and algorithms. AI systems can analyse traffic data to forecast congestion and suggest alternate routes for drivers. Autonomous cars employ AI to decrease human-caused accidents.

Infrastructure: Smart cities employ AI to improve efficiency and minimise energy use. AI can analyse energy use to create energy-efficient buildings and infrastructure. AI algorithms can also monitor traffic flow, garbage management, and other urban services using sensor and camera data.

Energy: AI-powered smart energy systems cut energy use and boost efficiency. AI can analyse energy use trends to create energy-efficient home and building systems [6]. AI systems can optimise renewable energy performance and cut costs by analysing data.

Disaster Prevention: AI algorithms forecast and avert calamities. AI systems can anticipate storms, floods, and earthquakes by using meteorological data. AI can also analyse sensor data to avert fires and explosions.

Thus, AI technologies and algorithms are crucial to Society 5.0. AI technologies process, analyse, and understand massive volumes of data, which aids policymaking and decision-making. AI helps create smart systems that boost productivity in numerous industries. Healthcare, transportation, infrastructure, energy, and catastrophe avoidance must include AI technology and algorithms to advance society.

1.12 Intelligent Internet of Things Technologies for Development of Society 5.0

Connecting things to the Internet and allowing them to interact has made our daily life more convenient and efficient. As we go towards Society 5.0, where technology is more intertwined with society, we must evaluate not just convenience but also how intelligent IoT technologies may benefit society.

AI and ML-based intelligent IoT systems make data-driven judgements [7]. Intelligent IoT solutions may enhance productivity, cut costs, and solve complicated issues in numerous sectors by merging enormous IoT device data with AI and ML. Intelligent IoT technology can change healthcare. The sector is under pressure to improve care delivery due to an ageing population and rising demand. Intelligent IoT devices can remotely monitor patients' vital signs and discover health issues before they become critical, thus reducing hospital admissions and enhancing patient outcomes. Intelligent IoT technology can increase transportation safety and efficiency. Autonomous cars can utilise IoT sensors to interact with other vehicles and alter speed and direction to avoid collisions. IoT sensors can also optimise traffic flow and alleviate congestion, saving time and carbon emissions.

Intelligent IoT solutions enhance production efficiency and save costs. Manufacturers may prevent downtime by monitoring equipment performance with sensors. IoT sensor data may also optimise manufacturing and quality control. Energy management is another example of smart IoT use. Energy suppliers may identify energy waste in buildings and residences using IoT devices and offer solutions [8]. IoT sensors can optimise energy distribution to lower costs and assure a reliable supply [9, 10].

Intelligent IoT technologies raise data privacy and security concerns. More Internet-connected gadgets mean more data breaches and cyberattacks. Organisations must safeguard and comply with data privacy laws. Thus, intelligent IoT technologies can transform industries and society. IoT devices, AI, and ML provide data-driven decision-making, efficiency gains, cost savings, and complicated issue solving. However, organisations must consider the risks and use these technologies responsibly and securely. Intelligent IoT technology will shape Society 5.0.

1.13 Conclusion

AI, IoT, and Big Data will make Society 5.0 increasingly linked. This society is anticipated to be efficient, productive, sustainable, and focused on solving social issues via innovation. With 5G networks, blockchain, and quantum computing, Society 5.0 may witness even more technological advances. However, concerns about privacy, security, and employment arise as society digitises. Therefore, policymakers, business leaders, and citizens must work together to distribute Society 5.0's benefits fairly and equitably.

Society 5.0 aims to improve society by integrating technological advances into people's lives. It stresses the need of developing technologies and systems that prioritise human dignity and well-being over efficiency and production. Society 5.0 strives to establish a sustainable and inclusive society by putting humans at the centre of technical breakthroughs. This guarantees that technical advances improve people's lives rather than merely progressing.

References

1. F. Montori, L. Bedogni, and L. Bononi, "A collaborative Internet of Things architecture for smart cities and environmental monitoring", *IEEE Internet Things J.*, vol. 5, no. 2, pp. 592–605, Apr. 2018.

2. Y. Harayama, "Society 5.0: Aiming for a new human-centered society", *Hitachi Rev.*, vol. 66, no. 6, pp. 556–557, 2017.

3. F. Cugurullo, "Exposing smart cities and eco-cities: Frankenstein urbanism and the sustainability challenges of the experimental city", *Environ. Plann. A: Econ. Space*, vol. 50, no. 1, pp. 73–92, 2018.

4. J. Cotta, M. Breque, L. De Nul, and A. Petridis, "Industry 5.0: Towards a sustainable, human-centric and resilient European industry", European Commission Research and Innovation (R&I) Series Policy Brief, 2021.

5. A. Deshpande, C. Guestrin, S. R. Madden, J. M. Hellerstein, and W. Hong, "Model driven data acquisition in sensor networks", *Proceedings of the 13th International Conference on Very Large Data Bases*, vol. 30, no. 1, pp. 588–599, 2004.

6. E. G. Carayannis, J. Draper, and B. Bhaneja, "Towards fusion energy in the industry 5.0 and society 5.0 context: Call for a global commission for urgent action on fusion energy", *J. Knowl. Econ.*, vol. 12, no. 4, pp. 1891–1904, 2021.

7. Y. Lu, "Industry 4.0: A survey on technologies, applications and open research issues", *J. Ind. Inf. Integr.*, vol. 6, pp. 1–10, 2017.

8. V. Roblek, M. Mesko, M. P. Bach, O. Thorpe, and P. Sprajc, "The interaction between internet, sustainable development, and emergence of society 5.0", *Data*, vol. 5, no. 3, pp. 80/1-27, 2020.

9. M. Singh, R. Kumar, D. Tandon, P. Sood, and M. Sharma, "Artificial Intelligence and IoT based Monitoring of Poultry Health: A review", *2020 IEEE International Conference on Communication, Networks and Satellite (Comnetsat)*, Batam, Indonesia, pp. 50–54, 2020, doi: 10.1109/Comnetsat50391.2020.9328930.

10. D. Gupta, S. Wadhwa, and S. Rani, "On the role of named data networking for IoT content distribution", *2021 6th International Conference on Communication and Electronics Systems (ICCES)*, Coimbatore, India, pp. 544–549, 2021, doi: 10.1109/ICCES51350.2021.9488946.

2

AI Architectures and Technologies for Raising Society 5.0

Tejinder Kaur

2.1 Introduction

The integration of artificial intelligence (AI) into Society 5.0 has the potential to revolution-ize several industries and domains (Afuah et al., 2019). For example, in healthcare, AI can be used to develop personalized treatment plans, diagnose diseases, and monitor patient health (Aguilera et al., 2007) in agriculture, AI can be used to predict weather patterns, optimize crop yields, and monitor soil conditions. In education, AI can be used to person-alize learning, improve student engagement, and automate administrative tasks (Aguinis et al., 2011). Finally, there is a concern about the potential misuse of AI, such as the devel-opment of autonomous weapons. The following chapters will delve deeper into specific AI architectures and technologies, as well as their applications and ethical considerations. This book aims to provide a comprehensive overview of AI in Society 5.0 and explore its potential to create a sustainable and equitable society (Balzarova et al., 2012).

This chapter provides an overview of AI architectures and technologies that are being used to raise Society 5.0.

2.2 AI Architectures

AI architectures refer to the design and structure of AI systems, which are composed of several components, including data, algorithms, models, and hardware. These compo-nents work together to enable AI systems to perform specific tasks, such as recognizing objects in images, translating languages, or playing games.

There are several AI architectures that are being used to build AI systems that can be used to raise Society 5.0. One of the most popular AI architectures is the deep learn-ing architecture, which is based on artificial neural networks that can learn from large amounts of data (Carroll et al., 2010). Deep learning has been used to build AI systems that can recognize images, speech, and text with high accuracy. Another popular AI architec-ture is the reinforcement learning architecture, which is based on training AI agents to learn from their interactions with the environment. Reinforcement learning has been used to build AI systems that can play games, control robots, and optimize complex systems.

DOI: 10.1201/9781003397052-2

These architectures can be categorized into several types, each with its own strengths and weaknesses. In this chapter, we will discuss some of the most popular AI architectures that are being used today (Crifo et al., 2015).

2.2.1 Feedforward Neural Networks

They are composed of several layers of interconnected nodes, with each node performing a simple mathematical operation on the inputs it receives (Dahlsrud et al., 2008). The output of each node is then passed on to the nodes in the next layer until the final output is produced (Crifo et al., 2015). Feedforward neural networks (FNNs) are commonly used in image and speech recognition tasks (Crifo et al., 2015).

2.2.2 Reinforcement Learning (Crifo et al., 2015)

Reinforcement learning (RL) is a type of AI architecture that is used to learn optimal decision-making strategies in complex environments. RL involves an agent that interacts with an environment and receives rewards or penalties based on its actions. The goal of the agent is to learn a policy that maximizes its long-term rewards. RL is commonly used in robotics, game playing, and control systems.

In conclusion, AI architectures are essential for building effective AI systems. In the following chapters, we will delve deeper into these AI architectures and their applications in Society 5.0 (Gelfand et al., 2017).

2.3 AI Technologies

In addition to AI architectures, there are several AI technologies that are being used to raise Society 5.0. These technologies enable AI systems to process intelligent decisions and interact with humans in a natural way. In this chapter, we will discuss some of the most important AI technologies that are being used today (Gelfand et al., 2017).

Deep learning (DL) algorithms are designed to learn multiple layers of representations of the input data, which enables them to learn complex features and make accurate predictions. DL is used in applications such as image and speech recognition, natural language processing (NLP), and autonomous driving (Gelfand et al., 2017).

NLP algorithms are designed to analyze the structure and meaning of text or speech and generate responses that are appropriate to the context. NLP is used in applications such as chatbots, virtual assistants, and sentiment analysis (Hofman et al., 2017).

Computer vision (CV) is a type of AI technology that enables machines to analyze and interpret visual information. CV algorithms are designed to recognize patterns and objects in images or video and make intelligent decisions based on the input. CV is used in applications such as autonomous driving, surveillance, and quality control (Hofman et al., 2017).

Robotics is a field that combines AI with mechanical engineering and electronics to create machines that can perform physical tasks. Robots are designed to interact with the environment and perform tasks that are too dangerous or too difficult for humans. Robotics is used in applications such as manufacturing, healthcare, and agriculture.

In conclusion, AI technologies are critical for building effective AI systems that can improve people's quality of life and address societal challenges. In the following chapters, we will delve deeper into these AI technologies and their applications in Society 5.0 (Hubert et al., 2010).

Unsupervised learning algorithms are used to identify patterns in unlabeled data. Unlabeled data is data that does not have a specific outcome associated with it. Unsupervised learning algorithms are often used for clustering and anomaly detection. One example of an unsupervised learning algorithm that could be used in Society 5.0 is a clustering algorithm. A clustering algorithm can be used to group similar items together based on their characteristics. This could be used in a variety of applications, such as customer segmentation or identifying groups of people with similar health risks (Jensen et al., 2000).

2.4 Application of AI in Society 5.0

AI is a critical component of this vision, as it enables making intelligent decisions in real time. In this chapter, we will discuss some of the most promising applications of AI in Society 5.0 (Kassin et al., 2017). AI algorithms can analyze medical images, genomic data, and electronic health records to identify patterns and make predictions about patient health. AI can also be used to develop new drugs and treatments and to monitor patients in real time (Kassin et al., 2017).

2.4.1 Transportation

AI is already being used in transportation to improve safety, reduce congestion, and enhance the driving experience. In the future, AI-powered transportation systems could enable seamless and efficient travel between cities and even countries (Kish-Gephart et al., 2017).

2.4.2 Education and Study

AI can also be used to develop new educational content and tools such as intelligent tutoring systems and educational games (Lins et al., 2017).

2.4.3 Agriculture

AI can help improve the efficiency and sustainability of agriculture by enabling precision farming techniques.

2.4.4 Smart Cities

AI can be used to create smarter and more efficient cities by enabling real-time monitoring and optimization of infrastructure and services. AI algorithms can analyze data from sensors, cameras, and other sources to detect problems, such as traffic congestion, air pollution, and water leaks, and take action to address them (Lins et al., 2017).

In conclusion, AI has the potential to transform every aspect of society in the coming years by enabling machines to process and analyze vast amounts of data and make intelligent decisions in real time, In the following chapters, we will discuss some of the technical and ethical considerations that must be taken into account when developing AI systems for Society 5.0 (Lins et al., 2017).

2.5 Ethical Considerations for AI in Society 5.0

AI systems have the potential to improve people's lives in many ways, but they can also have unintended consequences and raise ethical concerns. In this chapter, we will discuss some of the most important ethical considerations for AI in Society 5.0 (Lin's et al., 2017).

2.5.1 Privacy and Security

AI systems often process large amounts of personal data, such as medical records, financial information, and location data. AI systems must also be designed with strong security features to prevent data breaches and cyberattacks.

2.5.2 Transparency and Explainability

AI systems should ensure transparency and explainability, especially when they make decisions based on complex algorithms and data (Lin's et al., 2017).

2.5.3 Accountability and Responsibility

AI systems can have unintended consequences or make mistakes, which can lead to harm or negative outcomes.

2.5.4 Human-Centered Design

AI systems should be designed with human-centered principles in mind so that they are aligned with human values, preferences, and needs. This includes designing AI systems that are accessible and inclusive for all people, and that prioritize the well-being and safety of humans (Metaxas et al., 2014).

In conclusion, ethical considerations are an important aspect of AI development and deployment in Society 5.0. In the following chapters, we will discuss some of the technical considerations for developing AI systems for Society 5.0.

2.6 Future Directions for AI in Society 5.0

In this chapter, we will discuss some of the most promising future directions for AI in Society 5.0.

2.6.1 Human–Machine Collaboration

One of the most promising directions for AI in Society 5.0 is the development of human–machine collaboration. Rather than replacing human workers with machines, AI can be used to augment human capabilities and enable more efficient and effective collaboration between humans and machines. This can lead to improved productivity, innovation, and creativity.

2.6.2 Augmented Reality

Another promising direction for AI in Society 5.0 is the development of augmented reality applications that combine virtual and physical environments. AI algorithms can be used to analyze and interpret the real world and to generate virtual content that is seamlessly integrated with the physical environment. This can enable new forms of education, entertainment, and communication.

2.6.3 Cognitive Computing

Cognitive computing is a new paradigm for AI that is focused on mimicking human cognitive abilities, such as perception, reasoning, and decision-making. Cognitive computing systems use advanced algorithms and natural language processing to understand and respond to human queries and requests. This can enable more natural and intuitive interactions between humans and machines (Rego et al., 2017).

2.6.4 Quantum Computing

Quantum computers have the potential to solve problems that are currently intractable for classical computers, such as simulating complex systems and factoring large numbers. Quantum computing could have significant implications for AI in Society 5.0, enabling new forms of machine learning and optimization (Rego et al., 2017).

2.6.5 Neuromorphic Computing

This can enable more efficient and flexible machine learning, as well as new forms of perception and reasoning (Rego et al., 2017). By considering these future directions for AI in Society 5.0, we can anticipate the potential impact of AI on society and prepare for its implementation in a responsible and ethical manner.

2.7 Implementation Challenges for AI in Society 5.0

While AI has the potential to revolutionize many aspects of society, there are also significant implementation challenges that must be addressed. In this chapter, we will discuss some of the most important implementation challenges for AI in Society 5.0.

2.7.1 Data Quality and Availability

One of the biggest challenges for AI in Society 5.0 is the availability and quality of data. It is important to ensure that AI systems are trained on high-quality, diverse, and representative data in order to avoid biased outcomes (Kumar Sachdeva et al., 2022).

2.7.2 Regulatory Frameworks

There are currently few established frameworks for regulating the use of AI, and many questions remain about issues such as liability, transparency, and accountability.

2.7.3 Ethical Considerations

As discussed in Chapter 5, there are a number of ethical considerations that must be taken into account when developing and deploying AI systems. These considerations can be complex and multifaceted (Shen et al., 2016).

2.7.4 Workforce Adaptation

The widespread use of AI in Society 5.0 is likely to have significant impacts on the workforce, with many jobs being automated or significantly changed. It is important to ensure that workers are prepared for these changes, with training and education programs that enable them to adapt and take advantage of new opportunities (Shen et al., 2016). In conclusion, AI has the potential to transform society in many positive ways, but there are also significant implementation challenges that must be addressed. By considering these challenges and developing strategies to address them, we can ensure that AI is used in a responsible and ethical manner and that its benefits are shared by all members of society.

2.8 Case Studies in AI Implementation in Society 5.0

In this chapter, we will examine some case studies of AI implementation in Society 5.0. These examples illustrate the potential benefits and challenges of AI in different domains and provide insights into best practices for AI implementation.

2.8.1 Medical

One example of this is the use of AI in medical imaging, where deep learning algorithms can analyze medical images and provide automated diagnoses. Another example is the use of AI-powered chatbots to provide patients with personalized health advice and support (Shen et al., 2016).

2.8.2 Education

One example of this is the use of AI-powered educational games and simulations, which can provide engaging and interactive learning experiences (Shen et al., 2016). However, the implementation of AI in education also raises important ethical considerations, such as the potential for AI systems to reinforce biases or perpetuate inequality, and the need for transparency and accountability in educational decision-making.

2.8.3 Finance

AI has significant potential to improve financial services by enabling more accurate risk assessments and personalized financial advice (Shen et al., 2016).

2.8.4 Transportation

AI has the potential to transform transportation by enabling more efficient and sustainable transportation systems and improving safety and security (Shiroishi et al., 2018).

AI-powered traffic management systems can optimize traffic flow and reduce congestion. Another example is the use of AI algorithms to detect and prevent accidents and other safety incidents (Shiroishi et al., 2019).

2.9 Conclusion

In our discussion, we have explored the various AI architectures and technologies that are driving the development of Society 5.0. We have discussed the potential applications of AI in different domains, including healthcare, education, finance, and transportation, and the ethical considerations and implementation challenges that must be addressed to ensure the responsible and effective use of AI.

AI has the potential to transform our society in significant ways, by enabling more personalized and efficient services, improving decision-making and problem-solving, and addressing some of the most pressing societal challenges. However, its implementation must be guided by ethical principles and considerations to ensure that it is used in a manner that benefits all members of society and does not perpetuate existing inequalities or biases.

As we continue to develop and implement AI technologies in Society 5.0, it is important that we prioritize transparency, accountability, and inclusivity, and work to build trust and confidence in AI systems among all stakeholders. By doing so, we can realize the full potential of AI to create a more sustainable, equitable, and prosperous society for all. Machine learning algorithms, deep learning algorithms, natural language processing algorithms, and reinforcement learning algorithms all have the potential to be powerful tools for promoting social progress, economic growth, and sustainability. Policymakers and developers must take a proactive approach to address the risks and challenges associated with the use of AI, ensuring that algorithms are trained on diverse and representative data sets. By taking a proactive and inclusive approach to the development and implementation of AI algorithms, we can harness their potential to create a better future for all.

References

Afuah, A. (2019), *Business Model Innovations: Concepts, Analysis, and Cases*, Taylor and Francis, New York.

Aguilera, R.V., Rupp, D.E., Williams, C.A. and Ganapathi, J. (2007), "Putting the S back in corporate social responsibility: A multilevel theory of social change of organizations", *Academy of Management Review*, Vol. 32, No. 3, pp. 836–863.

Aguinis, H. (2011), "Organizational responsibility: Doing good and doing well", in Zedeck, S. (Ed.), *APA Handbook of Industrial and Organizational Psychology*, Vol. 3, American Psychological Association, Washington, DC, pp. 855–879.

Balzarova, M. and Castka, P. (2012), "Stakeholders' influence and contribution to social standards development: The case of multiple stakeholder approach to ISO 26000 development", *Journal of Business Ethics*, Vol. 111, No. 2, pp. 265–279.

Carroll, A. and Shabana, K. (2010), "The business case for corporate social responsibility: A review of concepts, research and practice", *International Journal of Management Reviews*, Vol. 12, No. 1, pp. 85–105.

Crifo, P. and Forget, V. (2015), "The economics of corporate social responsibility: A firm-level perspective survey", *Journal of Economic Surveys*, Vol. 29, No. 1, pp. 112–130.

Dahlsrud, A. (2008), "How corporate social responsibility is defined: An analysis of 37 definitions", *Corporate Social Responsibility and Environmental Management*, Vol. 15, No. 1, pp. 1–13.

European Commission (EC). (2017), *Germany: Industrie 4.0*, Digital Transformation Monitor, European Commission, Brussels.

Gelfand, M.J., Aycan, Z., Erez, M. and Leung, K. (2017), "Cross-cultural industrial organizational psychology and organizational behavior: A hundred-year journey", *Journal of Applied Psychology*, Vol. 102, No. 3, pp. 514–529.

Hofman, P., Moon, J. and Wu, B. (2017), "Corporate social responsibility under authoritarian capitalism: Dynamics and prospects of state-led and society-driven CSR", *Business and Society*, Vol. 56, No. 5, pp. 651–671.

Hubert, A. (2010), *Empowering People, Driving Change: Social Innovation in the European Union*, Bureau of European Policy Advisers, Brussels.

Jensen, M. (2000), "Value maximization and the corporate objective functions", in Beer, M. and Nohria, N. (Eds.), *Breaking the Code of Change*, HSB Press, Boston, pp. 37–57.

Kassin, S., Fein, S. and Markus, H. (2017), *Social Psychology*, Cengage Learning, Belmont.

Kish-Gephart, J., Treviño, L., Chen, A. and Tilton, J. (2019), "Behavioral business ethics: The journey from foundations to future", in Wasieleski, D. and Weber, J. (Eds.), *Business Ethics, Business and Society 360*, Emerald, Bingley, pp. 3–34.

Lins, K., Servaes, H. and Tamayo, A. (2017), "Social capital, trust, and firm performance: The value of corporate social responsibility during the financial crisis", *The Journal of Finance*, Vol. 72, No. 4, pp. 1785–1824.

Metaxas, T. and Tsavdaridou, M. (2014), "Green CSR practices: An European approach", *International Journal of Environment and Sustainable Development*, Vol. 13, No. 3, pp. 261–283.

Rego, A., Cunha, M.P. and Polonia, D. (2017), "Corporate sustainability: A view from the top", *Journal of Business Ethics*, Vol. 143, No. 1, pp. 133–157.

Sachdeva, R.K., Garg, T., Khaira, G.S., Mitrav, D. and Ahuja, R. (2022), "A systematic method for lung cancer classification", *2022 10th International Conference on Reliability, Infocom Technologies and Optimization (Trends and Future Directions) (ICRITO)*, Noida, India, pp. 1–5, doi: 10.1109/ICRITO56286.2022.9964778.

Sachdeva, R.K., Bathla, P., Rani, P., Kukreja, V. and Ahuja, R. (2022), "A systematic method for breast cancer classification using RFE feature selection", *2022 2nd International Conference on Advance Computing and Innovative Technologies in Engineering (ICACITE) (2022)*, pp. 1673–1676, doi: 10.1109/ICACITE53722.2022.9823464.

Shen, J. and Benson, J. (2016), "When CSR is a social norm: How socially responsible human resource management affects employee work behavior", *Journal of Management*, Vol. 42, No. 6, pp. 1723–1746.

Shiroishi, Y., Uchiyama, K. and Suzuki, N. (2018), "Society 5.0: For human security and well-being", *Computer*, Vol. 51, No. 7, pp. 91–95.

Shiroishi, Y., Uchiyama, K. and Suzuki, N. (2019), "Better actions for society 5.0: Using AI for evidencebased policy making that keeps humans in the loop", *Computer*, Vol. 52, No. 11, pp. 73–78.4.

3

Disruptive Technologies and Sustainable Development Goals for Society 5.0

Kiran Deep Singh, Prabhdeep Singh, Ankit Bansal,
Gaganpreet Kaur, and Rishu Chhabra

3.1 Introduction

Disruptive technologies and sustainable development goals (SDGs) are two crucial elements in realizing Society 5.0. Disruptive technologies refer to innovations that transform and disrupt the traditional way of doing things. The combination of disruptive technologies and sustainable development goals has the potential to create a sustainable and thriving Society 5.0 (Vinet and Zhedanov 2011).

3.1.1 Industry 4.0 vs. Society 5.0.

Society 5.0 is a super-intelligent society, whereas Industry 4.0 is centered on constructing smart industries. Table 3.1 shows Industry 4.0 vs. Society 5.0 in developed countries (Mourtzis, Angelopoulos, and Panopoulos 2022).

Whereas Industry 4.0 focuses on implementing cyber-physical systems in the industrial sector, Society 5.0 aspires to do the same for all of society (Carayannis, Draper, and Bhaneja 2021). Germany's High-tech Strategy 2020 Action Plan and Japan's fifth Science and Technology Basic Plan lay out ambitious goals for the future of technology and its influence on society; these goals are referred to as "Industry 4.0" and "Society 5.0," respectively. They include a top-down, state-led strategy with input from private enterprises, scholarly institutions, and public sectors and the utilization of Internet of Things (IoT)-related technologies, artificial intelligence (AI), and big data analysis. It's important to note that the two perspectives do not coincide 100 percent.

3.1.2 Sustainable Concept of Society 5.0

Although the Society 5.0 model was created for Japan, its components apply to any country. As a result, adjusting the concept while focusing on the parts related to industrial development is crucial (Peraković et al. 2020). The Europeans have long been at the forefront of adopting the Industry 4.0 approach, but it is narrow in its scope. Society 5.0, on the other hand, is equally concerned with the social realm.

Figure 3.1 presents a significant shifting of paradigm from Society 4.0 to Society 5.0. It represents the vision of a human-centric society that integrates technological advancements with the needs of individuals and communities. The core of Society 5.0 is the idea of

TABLE 3.1

Industry 4.0 vs. Society 5.0 in Developed Countries

	Design Methodology	Scope and Objectives	Identified Key Phrases
Industry 4.0	– Action plan for developed countries focusing on high-tech strategies -Implementing the strategic initiative	– Smart industry/factory – Focused on manufacturing, production, assembly, supply chain, etc.	– Artificial intelligence – Internet of Things – Cloud computing – Cyber-physical system – Mass customization
Society 5.0	– Basic plan for science and technology – Comprehensive science, technology, and innovation	– Society as a whole – Super-smart society	– An advanced degree of convergence between cyberspace and the real world – Human-centered culture

using advanced technologies. For example, using smart home systems, people can control their home appliances remotely, thereby saving energy and reducing costs. Healthcare can be made more accessible and personalized through health sensors and wearables, monitoring vital signs and providing real-time feedback to doctors and patients. Autonomous vehicles can reduce traffic congestion, accidents, and carbon emissions. The aim is to create a seamless, connected environment that makes life easier, more efficient, and more enjoyable for everyone (Karpunina et al. 2021).

Society 5.0 has a human-centered approach. The focus is on creating solutions tailored to the needs of individuals and communities rather than the other way around. Technology is not used for its own sake but to address people's real problems. For instance, advanced assistive devices can help people with disabilities to live more independently and participate fully in society (Gladden 2019). Social robots can provide

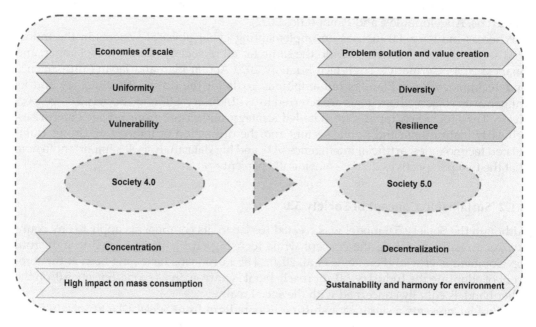

FIGURE 3.1

Significant shift from Society 4.0 to Society 5.0.

companionship and support for older people who may be isolated or lonely. Online education platforms can make learning more accessible and inclusive for people of all ages and backgrounds.

3.2 Background

Society 5.0 is a concept that the Japanese government developed as part of their plan for the future of their society. One key area where data is available is the adoption of advanced technologies (Deguchi et al. 2020). According to a report by the World Economic Forum, Japan has the world's highest density of industrial robots, with 303 robots per 10,000 employees (Nair, Tyagi, and Sreenath 2021). According to a report by Deloitte, Japan has one of the highest life expectancies in the world, and the government is investing in digital health technologies to address the challenges of an aging population. The report cites examples such as telemedicine, which enables patients to access medical consultations remotely, and mobile health apps, which can help people manage chronic conditions.

Another area where Society 5.0 has a potential impact is the environment and sustainability. The government of Japan has set ambitious targets for reducing carbon emissions, and there are efforts to leverage advanced technologies to achieve these goals. For example, the International Energy Agency report highlights the potential of smart grids, which use real-time data to optimize energy use and reduce emissions. The report also notes the importance of integrating renewable energy sources. In the area of social inclusion, there are also some indicators of progress toward the goals of Society 5.0 (Ciasullo et al. 2022). A report by the Japan International Cooperation Agency highlights efforts to promote universal access to education, including online education platforms and initiatives to support disadvantaged students. The report also notes the importance of assistive devices and social robots for promoting the well-being of elderly and disabled people.

3.3 Disruptive Technologies for Society 5.0

Developing novel architectures is critical to realizing the vision of Society 5.0. By leveraging the power of the IoT, blockchain technology, AI, edge computing, and cloud computing, we can create a more sustainable, efficient, and equitable society that promotes the well-being of all its members. However, to achieve this vision, we must address the challenges associated with these architectures and ensure that their development and deployment are ethical, transparent, and participatory. Several novel architectures can serve as the groundwork for Society 5.0. By leveraging the power of the IoT, blockchain technology, AI, edge computing, and cloud computing, we can create a human-centric society that promotes sustainable development and improves the quality of life for all (Singh and Sood 2020). It may require new policies and regulations to ensure that the benefits of these architectures are shared equitably across society and that they do not exacerbate existing social and economic inequalities.

Society 5.0 uses advanced technologies to address societal challenges and promote sustainable development. The role of disruptive technologies in SDGs while processing data systematically and information extraction is presented in Figure 3.2. The development of novel architectures is critical to realizing this vision. In this context, several promising architectures can serve as the groundwork.

3.3.1 Internet of Things

In Society 5.0, the IoT can create smart cities, improve healthcare, and enhance transportation systems. For example, by deploying sensors and other IoT devices throughout a city, it is possible to monitor traffic patterns, identify areas of congestion, and optimize traffic flow (Singh and Sood 2021). Similarly, the IoT can monitor patient health remotely in the healthcare sector and provide real-time feedback to doctors and other healthcare professionals.

3.3.2 Blockchain

Blockchain is a distributed ledger technology that allows multiple parties to securely and transparently record and track transactions. In the context of Society 5.0, blockchain can be used to create more transparent and secure systems. For example, blockchain can track the supply chain of goods and services, ensuring that products are ethically and sustainably sourced. Blockchain can also create more secure and transparent voting systems, enabling citizens to participate more directly in the democratic process (Schär 2021).

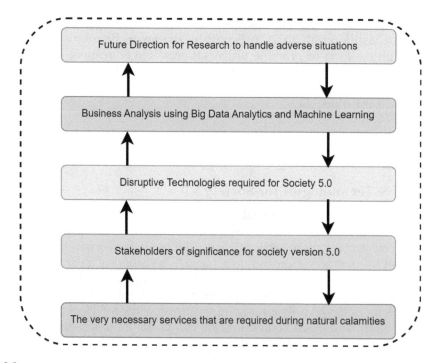

FIGURE 3.2

Role of disruptive technologies in sustainable development goals while processing data systematically and information extraction.

3.3.3 Artificial Intelligence

Artificial intelligence is another architecture that is essential to Society 5.0. AI can analyze vast amounts of data and develop predictive models for various applications. For example, AI can predict health risks in the healthcare sector and develop personalized treatment plans (Khullar et al. 2022a) (Khullar 2014). In the transportation sector, AI can be used to optimize traffic flow and reduce congestion. AI can also be used to develop intelligent virtual assistants and chatbots that can support and assist users.

3.3.4 Edge Computing

It is another architecture that is relevant to Society 5.0. Edge computing refers to processing data at the network's edge by reducing latency and improving the performance of applications (Sood and Singh 2019) (Sood and Deep Singh 2021). In Society 5.0, edge computing can be used to develop real-time applications that require low latency, such as self-driving cars and other autonomous systems. Edge computing can also be used to process data from IoT devices, enabling real-time decision-making in various applications.

3.3.5 Cloud Computing

Finally, cloud computing is another architecture that is critical to Society 5.0. Cloud computing delivers services, including servers, storage, and applications, over the Internet. In the context of Society 5.0, cloud computing can be used to create scalable, flexible, and cost-effective systems (Deep Singh 2019). Cloud computing can also provide access to advanced analytics tools and AI algorithms, enabling organizations to develop innovative solutions to complex problems.

3.3.6 Big Data

The increasing availability of big data is transforming industries and societies, allowing organizations to understand their customers and operations better. In the context of Society 5.0, big data can be used to inform decision-making, personalize services, and optimize resource use (Prabhat and Khullar 2017).

3.3.7 Cyber-Physical Systems

Cyber-physical systems (CPS) also integrate physical and cyber components to enable new automation, optimization, and control forms. In the context of Society 5.0, CPS can be used to optimize industrial and logistical processes, increase efficiency and productivity, and improve the overall quality of life. For example, CPS can enable smart manufacturing, where machines can self-diagnose and fix problems, reducing downtime and improving productivity (R. Kaur et al. 2021).

3.3.8 Robotics

In the context of Society 5.0, robotics can be used to automate and optimize industrial and logistical processes and provide new forms of support and assistance to individuals (P. Kaur and Singh 2019). For example, robotics can automate the manufacturing process, increase efficiency and productivity, and provide elderly and disabled people with assistance in their daily lives.

3.3.9 Augmented/Virtual Reality

Augmented Reality/Virtual Reality (AR/VR) is a technology that can be used to create new forms of education, training, and entertainment and provide new forms of support and assistance to individuals (Sood and Singh 2018). For example, AR/VR can provide immersive and interactive training experiences, improving training effectiveness and reducing the risks associated with dangerous or complex tasks.

3.3.10 Cybersecurity

Cybersecurity protects computers, networks, and data from unauthorized access, theft, and damage. In the context of Society 5.0, cybersecurity is critical to ensuring the safe and responsible use of technology and protecting individuals and society from the potential risks of cyberattacks and data breaches. Cybersecurity can also protect critical infrastructure, such as energy grids, water supplies, and transportation systems from cyberattacks that could disrupt or disable essential services (Singh 2021).

3.4 Impact of Integrated Disruptive Technologies on the Sustainable Development Goals

The sustainable development goals (SDGs) were conceived with an all-encompassing concept of sustainable development to help both people and the natural world. Achieving sustainability requires incorporating aspects of human progress, the economy, technological advancements, resource management, land and water use, and alterations to the natural environment. It will be difficult to accomplish such ambitious aims, especially considering the unprecedented and incalculable degree of uncertainty. A qualitative study to provide directions for achieving Sustainable Development Goals (SDGs) or to provide a starting point to achieve maximum effectiveness (Carayannis, Draper, and Bhaneja 2021; Kasinathan et al. 2022).

This research explicitly analyzes disruptive technologies' role in pursuing the sustainable development goals (SDGs). In particular, introducing disruptive technology has several reverberative impacts that may be felt throughout the SDG framework. Disruptive technologies have a variety of applications and may be found in practically all sectors; nevertheless, the majority of the advantages favorable to sustainability are accomplished through the development of two primary areas, namely, Industry 5.0 and Society 5.0. The establishment of intelligent metropolitan areas and rural communities would be supported by the successful completion of Industry 5.0 and Society 5.0. Still, it also needs assistance from other domains, such as the political, economic, and security domains as well as investment and societal acceptability. Figure 3.3 illustrates the impact of integrated disruptive technologies on the sustainable development goals. Overall, the role of disruptive technologies has the potential to encompass the whole SDG framework.

The initial financial commitment required for such a massive transformation is one of the major obstacles that must be overcome. Despite this, the shift toward more disruptive technologies is unavoidable, given the current course of technological advancement. The only thing that is taken into consideration is how quickly the implementation will take place and the benefits it will offer over time (Khullar et al. 2022b).

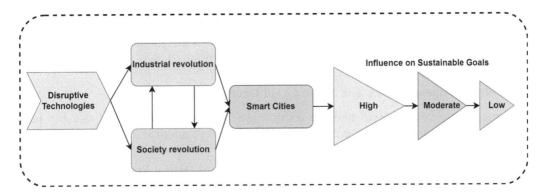

FIGURE 3.3
Impact of integrated disruptive technologies on the sustainable development goals.

3.5 Challenges

As we progress toward the realization of Society 5.0, several challenges must be addressed to ensure the development of a sustainable, equitable, and inclusive society. Some of the major challenges to the realization of Society 5.0 are discussed in the following sections.

3.5.1 Data Privacy and Security

Data privacy and security are critical challenges for the realization of Society 5.0. With the vast amount of data generated by IoT devices and other sources, there is a risk that this data could be misused, manipulated, or stolen. It could lead to a breach of personal privacy, financial losses, and other negative consequences and enforce standards for data privacy and security.

3.5.2 Interoperability

It is critical to enable the sharing and analysis of data across different platforms and to ensure that data can be used to drive new insights and innovations.

To address the interoperability challenge, it is necessary to develop new standards and protocols that enable seamless communication and data exchange between different systems and devices (Kasinathan et al. 2022). It includes the development of new data formats, communication protocols, and other tools to ensure that data can be shared and analyzed seamlessly and efficiently.

3.5.3 Sustainability

Sustainability is a critical challenge for realizing Society 5.0, as it seeks to promote sustainable development through technology and innovation. It requires the development of architectures and systems that minimize energy consumption and carbon emissions, promote renewable energy sources, and optimize IT infrastructure (Bui and Tseng 2022).

3.5.4 Ethical and Responsible Use of AI and Other Emerging Technologies

As AI and other emerging technologies become increasingly integrated into our lives, ensuring they are used ethically and responsibly is essential.

3.5.5 New Business Models and Value Chain Development

It means that companies will need to rethink how they do business and develop new approaches to meet the changing needs of consumers and society.

3.5.6 Inclusive and Equitable Access to Technology and Digital Resources

For Society 5.0 to be truly inclusive and equitable, everyone must have access to technology and digital resources. It means that efforts must be made to bridge the digital divide and ensure all individuals have access to the tools and resources needed to participate in the digital economy (Khullar et al. 2022b).

3.5.7 Overcoming Barriers to Digital Literacy and Digital Skills Development

In addition to ensuring that all individuals have access to technology and digital resources, addressing barriers to digital literacy and skills development is important. It includes addressing the digital divide and ensuring that individuals have the skills and knowledge they need to participate in the digital economy.

3.5.8 Addressing the Digital Divide and Promoting Universal Access to Technology and Digital Resources

The digital divide is a critical challenge for the realization of Society 5.0, as it represents a significant barrier to the participation of many individuals in the digital economy.

3.6 Conclusion

Disruptive technologies and sustainable development goals are crucial components for realizing Society 5.0. Combining disruptive technologies, such as IoT, AI, blockchain, cybersecurity, robotics, and AR/VR, can help achieve several SDGs. Therefore, it is essential to develop policies and strategies that promote the integration of these technologies into Society 5.0 and ensure that they align with the SDGs. However, integrating these technologies into our daily lives also presents significant challenges. Developing and adopting these technologies will require significant investments in infrastructure, education, and research and development. Additionally, the implementation of these technologies must be done in a way that ensures ethical and responsible use and minimizes potential risks to individuals and society.

References

Bui, Tat Dat, and Ming Lang Tseng. 2022. "Understanding the Barriers to Sustainable Solid Waste Management in Society 5.0 Under Uncertainties: A Novelty of Socials and Technical

Perspectives on Performance Driving." *Environmental Science and Pollution Research International* 29(11): 16265–93. https://doi.org/10.1007/s11356-021-16962-0.

Carayannis, Elias G., John Draper, and Balwant Bhaneja. 2021. "Towards Fusion Energy in the Industry 5.0 and Society 5.0 Context: Call for a Global Commission for Urgent Action on Fusion Energy." *Journal of the Knowledge Economy* 12(4): 1891–904. https://doi.org/10.1007/s13132-020 -00695-5.

Ciasullo, Maria Vincenza, Francesco Orciuoli, Alexander Douglas, and Rocco Palumbo. 2022. "Putting Health 4.0 at the Service of Society 5.0: Exploratory Insights from a Pilot Study." *Socio-Economic Planning Sciences* 80. https://doi.org/10.1016/j.seps.2021.101163.

Deep Singh, Kiran. 2019. "Role of Optical Network in Cloud/Fog Computing." In *Telecommunication Systems - Principles and Applications of Wireless-Optical Technologies*. IntechOpen. https://doi.org /10.5772/intechopen.84404.

Deguchi, Atsushi, Chiaki Hirai, Hideyuki Matsuoka, Taku Nakano, Kohei Oshima, Mitsuharu Tai, and Shigeyuki Tani. 2020. "What Is Society 5.0?" *Society 5.0: A People-Centric Super-Smart Society*: 1–23. https://doi.org/10.1007/978-981-15-2989-4_1.

Gladden, Matthew E. 2019. "Who Will Be the Members of Society 5.0? Towards an Anthropology of Technologically Posthumanized Future Societies." *Social Sciences* 8(5). https://doi.org/10.3390 /socsci8050148.

Karpunina, Evgeniya K., Irina V. Kosorukova, Alexander A. Dubovitski, Gulnaz F. Galieva, and Eleonora M. Chernenko. 2021. "State Policy of Transition to Society 5.0: Identification and Assessment of Digitalisation Risks." *International Journal of Public Law and Policy* 7(4): 334–50. https://doi.org/10.1504/IJPLAP.2021.118895.

Kasinathan, Padmanathan, Rishi Pugazhendhi, Rajvikram Madurai Elavarasan, Vigna Kumaran Ramachandaramurthy, Vinoth Ramanathan, Senthilkumar Subramanian, Sachin Kumar, et al. 2022. "Realization of Sustainable Development Goals with Disruptive Technologies by Integrating Industry 5.0, Society 5.0, Smart Cities and Villages." *Sustainability (Switzerland)* 14(22). https://doi.org/10.3390/su142215258.

Kaur, Prabhjot, and Kulvinder Singh. 2019. "Detection of Heart Diseases Using Machine Learning and Data Mining." *International Journal of Computer and Applications* 178(31): 34–40. https://doi .org/10.5120/ijca2019919183.

Kaur, Rupinder, Prabh Deep Singh, Rajbir Kaur, and Kiran Deep Singh. 2021. "A Delay-Sensitive Cyber-Physical System Framework for Smart Health Applications." In *Advances in Clean Energy Technologies: Select Proceedings of ICET 2020*: 475–86. https://doi.org/10.1007/978-981-16-0235 -1_38.

Khullar, Vikas. 2014. "A Framework to Design and Implement University Information Security Policy." In *MultiTrack Conference on Sciences, Engg and Technical Innovations* 1: 269–71.

Khullar, Vikas, Harjit Pal Singh, Yini Miro, Divya Anand, Heba G. Mohamed, Deepali Gupta, Navdeep Kumar, and Nitin Goyal. 2022a. "IoT Fog-Enabled Multi-Node Centralized Ecosystem for Real Time Screening and Monitoring of Health Information." *Applied Sciences (Switzerland)* 12(19): 9845. https://doi.org/10.3390/app12199845.

Mourtzis, Dimitris, John Angelopoulos, and Nikos Panopoulos. 2022. "A Literature Review of the Challenges and Opportunities of the Transition from Industry 4.0 to Society 5.0." *Energies* 15(17). https://doi.org/10.3390/en15176276.

Nair, Meghna M., Amit Kumar Tyagi, and N. Sreenath. 2021. "The Future with Industry 4.0 at the Core of Society 5.0: Open Issues, Future Opportunities and Challenges." *2021 International Conference on Computer Communication and Informatics, ICCCI 2021*. https://doi.org/10.1109/ ICCCI50826.2021.9402498.

Peraković, Dragan, Marko Periša, Ivan Cvitić, and Petra Zorić. 2020. "Information and Communication Technologies for the Society 5.0 Environment." *Researchgate.Net*. https://doi.org/10.37528/ftte /9788673954318/postel.2020.020.

Prabhat, Anjuman, and Vikas Khullar. 2017. "Sentiment Classification on Big Data Using Naïve Bayes and Logistic Regression." *2017 International Conference on Computer Communication and Informatics, ICCCI 2017*. https://doi.org/10.1109/ICCCI.2017.8117734.

Schär, Fabian. 2021. "Decentralized Finance: On Blockchain-and Smart Contract-Based Financial Markets." *Federal Reserve Bank of St. Louis Review* 103(2): 153–74. https://doi.org/10.20955/r .103.153-74.

Singh, Kiran Deep. 2021. "Securing of Cloud Infrastructure Using Enterprise Honeypot." In *Proceedings - 2021 3rd International Conference on Advances in Computing, Communication Control and Networking, ICAC3N 2021,* 1388–93. https://doi.org/10.1109/ICAC3N53548.2021.9725389.

Singh, Kiran Deep, and Sandeep K. Sood. 2020. "5G Ready Optical Fog-Assisted Cyber-Physical System for IoT Applications." *IET Cyber-Physical Systems: Theory and Applications* 5(2): 137–44. https://doi.org/10.1049/iet-cps.2019.0037.

Sood, Sandeep K., and Kiran Deep Singh. 2021. "Identification of a Malicious Optical Edge Device in the SDN-Based Optical Fog/Cloud Computing Network." *Journal of Optical Communications* 42(1): 91–102. https://doi.org/10.1515/joc-2018-0047.

Sood, Sandeep K., and Kiran D. Singh. 2018. "An Optical-Fog Assisted EEG-Based Virtual Reality Framework for Enhancing E-Learning through Educational Games." *Computer Applications in Engineering Education* 26(5): 1565–76. https://doi.org/10.1002/cae.21965.

Sood, Sandeep K., and Kiran Deep Singh. 2019. "SNA Based Resource Optimization in Optical Network Using Fog and Cloud Computing." *Optical Switching and Networking* 33: 114–21. https://doi.org/10.1016/j.osn.2017.12.007.

Vinet, Luc, and Alexei Zhedanov. 2011. "A 'Missing' Family of Classical Orthogonal Polynomials." *Journal of Physics A: Mathematical and Theoretical* 44(8): 1–8. https://doi.org/10.1088/1751-8113 /44/8/085201.

4

Use of Big Data Architecture in Society 5.0

Naresh Kumar Trivedi and Vinay Gautam

4.1 Introduction

Big data refers to the massive volume of structured and unstructured data that is generated every day, which is too large and complex to be processed by traditional data management tools. The term big data was first coined in the late 1990s and has since become a buzzword in the world of technology and business. In today's digital world, data is being generated at an unprecedented rate, with an estimated 2.5 quintillion bytes of data being created every day.

Big data can come from a variety of sources, including social media, online transactions, and machine-generated data from sensors and devices. The data generated from these sources is diverse and includes text, images, videos, and audio files. The sheer volume of data that is generated daily makes it a challenge to process and analyze, but it also represents a massive opportunity for organizations to gain valuable insights into their operations and customers.

One of the biggest challenges of big data is its sheer volume, which makes it difficult to process and manage using traditional data management tools. This is where big data technologies come into play, including Hadoop, Spark, and NoSQL (Not Only SQL) databases. These technologies are designed to handle the massive scale of data, enabling organizations to process, store, and analyze large amounts of data in a cost-effective and efficient manner [1].

Big data also presents a challenge in terms of its velocity or the speed at which data is generated. The velocity of big data is increasing, making it necessary for organizations to have real-time processing capabilities to keep up with the fast-paced flow of data. This is why big data technologies have evolved to support real-time processing, such as Apache Storm and Apache Flink.

Another challenge of big data is its variety, or the diversity of data types and formats that it comes in. The variety of data types and formats makes it difficult to integrate and analyze, requiring organizations to use specialized tools and techniques to manage and process the data. This is where tools such as Apache Hive, Apache Pig, and Apache Spark come into play, enabling organizations to process and analyze diverse data types and formats.

Big data has the potential to provide valuable insights into various aspects of an organization, including customer behavior, market trends, and operational efficiency. For example, by analyzing customer data, organizations can gain insights into customer preferences and buying habits, which can be used to inform marketing and sales strategies. Similarly,

DOI: 10.1201/9781003397052-4

analyzing operational data can help organizations identify inefficiencies and optimize their processes, leading to increased efficiency and cost savings.

Despite the many benefits of big data, there are also challenges associated with its use. One of the biggest challenges is data privacy and security, as organizations need to ensure that sensitive data is protected and secure. This is particularly important in industries such as finance and healthcare, where sensitive information must be kept confidential. Additionally, organizations must ensure that their big data initiatives are following data protection regulations, such as the European Union's General Data Protection Regulation (GDPR) [2].

In conclusion, big data represents a massive opportunity for organizations to gain valuable insights and improve their operations. However, it also presents challenges in terms of volume, velocity, and variety, which require organizations to adopt specialized tools and techniques to manage and process the data. While big data initiatives can provide significant benefits, organizations must also ensure that they are in compliance with data protection regulations and take measures to protect sensitive data.

4.2 Big Data Architecture

Big data architecture refers to the design and components of a big data solution that enables organizations to process, store, and analyze large volumes of data. The architecture of big data solutions is typically designed to be scalable, flexible, and able to handle the volume, velocity, and variety of data that is generated.

Here are some of the most common big data architectures:

1. **Lambda Architecture**: This architecture is a design pattern for big data processing that combines batch and real-time processing to provide a complete, accurate, and up-to-date view of the data. It provides a way to handle both the batch processing of historical data and the real-time processing of incoming data, which allows for the creation of a single, unified view of data that is updated in near real time.

   The Lambda architecture consists of three main components:

   a. **Batch Layer**: This layer processes large volumes of historical data and updates the data store. This layer is responsible for maintaining an immutable, centralized repository of all data and is used to provide a complete and accurate view of the data.

   b. **Speed Layer**: This layer handles incoming data in real time and provides a near real-time view of the data. This layer is responsible for handling the data that arrives too quickly to be processed by the batch layer and is used to provide a real-time view of the data.

   c. **Serving Layer**: This layer provides a unified view of the data by combining the results of the batch and real-time processing layers. This layer is responsible for serving the results to the end users and is used to provide a complete, accurate, and up-to-date view of the data.

   The Lambda architecture allows for the processing of both batch and real-time data, which provides a more complete view of the data. The batch layer provides a complete view of the data by processing all historical data, while the real-time layer provides a near real-time view of the data by handling incoming data in real time. The serving layer combines the results of the batch and real-time processing to provide a unified view of the data.

In conclusion, the Lambda architecture is a powerful design pattern for big data processing that combines batch and real-time processing to provide a complete, accurate, and up-to-date view of the data. It provides a way to handle the processing of both large volumes of historical data and incoming real-time data, which allows for the creation of a single, unified view of the data that is updated in near real-time [3].

2. **Kappa Architecture**: This architecture is a design pattern for big data processing that focuses on the real-time processing of incoming data. Unlike the Lambda architecture, which separates batch and real-time processing into two separate systems, the Kappa architecture combines batch and real-time processing into a single system. This design pattern is well-suited for use cases that require low latency and high-throughput processing of data.

The Kappa architecture consists of three main components:

a. **Data Ingestion**: This component is responsible for capturing and storing incoming data. The data is typically stored in a distributed data store, such as Apache Kafka or Amazon Kinesis, which allows for the parallel processing of data.

b. **Real-Time Processing**: This component is responsible for processing incoming data in real time. The real-time processing component uses a stream processing framework, such as Apache Flink or Apache Spark Streaming, to process the data. The processed data is then stored in a data store for further analysis.

c. **Serving Layer**: This component is responsible for serving the processed data to end users. The serving layer can use a data store, such as Apache Cassandra or Amazon S3, to store the processed data, or it can use a data serving layer, such as Apache Druid or Apache Superset, to serve the data to end users.

The Kappa architecture is designed to handle the processing of incoming data in real time and is well-suited for use cases that require low latency and high-throughput processing of data. Unlike the Lambda architecture, which separates batch and real-time processing into two separate systems, the Kappa architecture combines batch and real-time processing into a single system, which reduces complexity and simplifies the processing of data.

In conclusion, the Kappa architecture is a design pattern for big data processing that focuses on the real-time processing of incoming data. It combines batch and real-time processing into a single system and is well-suited for use cases that require low latency and high-throughput processing of data. The Kappa architecture simplifies the processing of data by reducing the complexity of the architecture and providing a more streamlined approach to big data processing [4].

3. **Hadoop Architecture**: This architecture is based on the Hadoop ecosystem, which includes components such as Hadoop Distributed File System (HDFS), MapReduce, and Hive. Hadoop is designed for large-scale batch processing of data and is well-suited for use cases that involve large volumes of data.

Hadoop is an open-source software framework for distributed storage and processing of large datasets. It is designed to scale from a single node to thousands of nodes, each offering local computation and storage.

The core components of the Hadoop architecture are as follows:

a. **Hadoop Distributed File System (HDFS)**: This is the storage layer of Hadoop, and it is responsible for distributing large data sets across multiple nodes in a cluster. The data is divided into smaller blocks and stored on different nodes, and these blocks are replicated for fault tolerance.

b. **MapReduce**: This is the processing layer of Hadoop, and it is responsible for performing parallel processing on large data sets. It consists of two main components: the Map task, which filters and sorts the data, and the Reduce task, which aggregates the results.

c. **Yet Another Resource Negotiator (YARN)**: This is the resource management layer of Hadoop, and it is responsible for allocating resources such as CPU and memory to the applications running on the cluster.

d. **Hadoop Common**: This is a set of common utilities that support the other Hadoop modules. It includes libraries and utilities required by other modules, as well as scripts for starting and stopping the Hadoop cluster.

e. **Hadoop Ozone**: This is an object store for Hadoop that provides scalable and performant storage for big data workloads.

These components work together to provide a highly scalable and flexible architecture for storing and processing big data. Hadoop is often used in combination with other big data technologies such as Apache Spark and Apache Storm to provide a complete solution for big data processing and analysis [5].

4. **Spark Architecture**: This architecture is based on the Apache Spark platform, which is designed for fast, in-memory processing of data. Spark is well-suited for use cases that involve real-time processing and can handle both batch and real-time data processing.

Apache Spark is an open-source, distributed computing system designed for large-scale data processing. It was designed to be fast and flexible while providing a unified programming model for batch processing, interactive queries, and stream processing.

The core components of the Spark architecture are as follows:

a. **Spark Core**: This is the foundation of the Spark architecture, and it contains the basic functionality of Spark, including the Resilient Distributed Datasets (RDDs), task scheduling, and the Spark Application Programming Interface (API).

b. **Spark SQL**: This component allows users to run SQL-like queries on structured data and supports reading data from a variety of sources, including Hive, Avro, Parquet, and JSON.

c. **Spark Streaming**: This component allows for real-time processing of data streams, making it possible to process data as it is generated in near real-time. It integrates with a variety of data sources, including Kafka, Flume, and Kinesis.

d. **Spark MLlib**: This is the machine learning library for Spark, and it provides a wide range of algorithms for data mining and machine learning tasks, including regression, classification, clustering, and recommendation systems.

e. **Spark GraphX**: This component provides a graph processing API for Spark and allows users to perform graph computations on large-scale graph data.

In addition to these core components, Spark also provides many libraries and APIs for working with data, including SparkR (for R programming), Spark Cassandra Connector (for connecting to Cassandra databases), and Spark on Mesos (for running Spark on Mesos clusters).

The Spark architecture is designed to be highly scalable and can handle data processing needs ranging from small to big data, making it a popular choice for organizations of all sizes. Additionally, Spark's in-memory computing capability makes it much faster than traditional MapReduce-based systems, making it ideal for data processing and analysis tasks that require low-latency access to large data sets.

5. **NoSQL Architecture**: This architecture is designed for use cases that involve unstructured data and require a flexible data model. NoSQL databases, such as MongoDB and Cassandra, are well-suited for this type of architecture, as they are designed to handle large volumes of unstructured data.

NoSQL, or "Not Only SQL," is a term used to describe a class of databases that are designed for large-scale data processing and storage. Unlike traditional relational databases, NoSQL databases are designed to handle unstructured, semi-structured, or structured data without using a fixed schema. This makes them well-suited for handling big data, where the volume, velocity, and variety of data can be challenging for traditional relational databases.

NoSQL databases come in several different types, including:

a. **Document Databases**: These databases store data as documents, and each document can have different fields and structures. Examples of document databases include MongoDB and Couchbase.

b. **Column-Family Databases**: These databases store data as columns instead of rows and are optimized for fast data retrieval. Examples of column-family databases include Apache Cassandra and Hbase.

c. **Key-Value Databases**: These databases store data as key-value pairs, with the key being a unique identifier for the data and the value being the data itself. Examples of key-value databases include Redis and Riak.

d. **Graph Databases**: These databases store data as nodes and edges in a graph, making them well-suited for handling relationships between data. Examples of graph databases include Neo4j and Amazon Neptune.

Regardless of the specific type, NoSQL databases share several common characteristics, including:

- **Distributed Architecture**: NoSQL databases are designed to be highly scalable, and typically run on clusters of commodity hardware.

- **Flexible Data Modeling**: NoSQL databases allow for dynamic and flexible data modeling, making it easy to handle changing data requirements.
- **High Performance and Availability**: NoSQL databases are designed for high performance and availability, making them well-suited for handling big data.
- **Base partitioning and indexing**: NoSQL databases support partitioning and indexing, which helps to improve performance and scalability.

In conclusion, NoSQL databases provide a flexible and scalable architecture for handling big data and are well-suited for a variety of use cases, including real-time analytics, content management, and e-commerce [6].

6. **Microservices Architecture**: This architecture is based on the microservices design pattern, which involves breaking down an application into small, independent components that can be developed and deployed independently. This architecture is well-suited for use cases that involve real-time processing and can handle both batch and real-time data processing.

Microservices architecture is a software design pattern that involves breaking a large, monolithic application into smaller, independent services that can be developed, deployed, and scaled independently. This approach to software development is particularly well-suited for big data applications, as it allows for greater flexibility, scalability, and resilience.

In a microservices architecture, each microservice is responsible for a specific, well-defined business capability. Microservices communicate with each other over APIs and can be written in different programming languages and technologies. This allows for greater innovation and faster time-to-market, as different teams can work on different parts of the system independently.

The key components of a microservices architecture for big data are:

a. **API Gateway**: This component acts as the entry point for all client requests and route requests to the appropriate microservice. It also provides security, monitoring, and rate-limiting capabilities.

b. **Microservices**: These are the individual components that make up the system, each responsible for a specific business capability. They are designed to be small, autonomous, and loosely coupled, allowing for greater flexibility and scalability.

c. **Service Registry**: This component maintains a list of all microservices and their current status and helps the API gateway route requests to the appropriate microservice.

d. **Data Store**: This component is responsible for storing the data generated by the microservices. It can be a traditional relational database, a NoSQL database, or a data lake.

e. **Monitoring and Logging**: This component is responsible for monitoring the performance and availability of the microservices and logging events for troubleshooting and analysis.

f. **Load Balancer**: This component distributes incoming requests across multiple instances of a microservice, helping to ensure that the system remains highly available and scalable.

The microservices architecture allows for greater flexibility in big data processing, as different microservices can be developed, deployed, and scaled independently. It also provides for greater resilience, as a failure in one microservice will not impact the rest of the system. Additionally, the use of APIs and a loosely coupled architecture makes it easier to integrate with other systems and technologies [7].

4.3 Big Data Architecture and Industry 4.0

In conclusion, the architecture of a big data solution depends on the specific use case and requirements of an organization. Some of the most common big data architectures include Lambda, Kappa, Hadoop, Spark, NoSQL, and Microservices. Organizations must choose the architecture that is best suited to their specific use case, taking into consideration factors such as volume, velocity, and variety of data, as well as processing and storage requirements.

Big data architecture can play an important role in supporting the implementation of Industry 4.0, also known as the Fourth Industrial Revolution or "Smart Factory." The use of big data and advanced analytics can help companies to better understand and optimize their operations and make informed decisions about the use of technology and automation.

Some of the ways big data architecture can help to implement Industry 4.0 include:

1. **Real-Time Monitoring and Predictive Maintenance**: Big data architecture can be used to collect and process large amounts of sensor data from manufacturing machines and equipment, enabling real-time monitoring and predictive maintenance. This can help companies to identify and address potential issues before they become major problems, improving reliability and reducing downtime.
2. **Optimized Supply Chain Management**: Big data can be used to track and analyze data from suppliers, logistics providers, and customers, providing a complete view of the supply chain and enabling companies to optimize processes and improve efficiency.
3. **Personalized Customer Experience**: Big data can be used to analyze customer behavior and preferences, allowing companies to personalize the customer experience and better understand their needs.
4. **Improved Decision-Making**: Big data can provide companies with real-time insights into their operations, enabling them to make informed decisions about the use of technology and automation, and to continuously improve processes and efficiency.
5. **Advanced Analytics**: Big data architecture provides the infrastructure needed to store and process large amounts of data, enabling companies to use advanced analytics techniques, such as machine learning and artificial intelligence, to gain insights into their operations and make data-driven decisions.

In conclusion, big data architecture can play a crucial role in supporting the implementation of Industry 4.0 by providing the infrastructure and capabilities needed to collect, process, and analyze large amounts of data in real time. This can help companies to improve their operations, make informed decisions, and stay ahead in a rapidly evolving technological landscape [8, 9].

4.4 Big Data Architecture and Society 5.0

Society 5.0 refers to a proposed new stage of human society that is being enabled by the development of advanced technologies such as artificial intelligence, robotics, and the Internet of Things (IoT). The term was first introduced by the Japanese government and refers to a society that leverages technology to address social and economic challenges, such as an aging population, declining birth rates, and environmental problems.

Society 5.0 aims to create a more sustainable and equitable society by integrating digital and physical systems in ways that support human well-being, while also promoting economic growth and social development. This is achieved using cutting-edge technologies that are designed to enhance human life, such as smart cities, autonomous vehicles, and wearable devices.

While Society 5.0 is seen as a positive development by many experts, it also raises important ethical and societal questions around issues such as privacy, security, and the role of humans in a world increasingly dominated by technology. Despite these challenges, the hope is that Society 5.0 will bring about a more harmonious and balanced world, where people are empowered to live healthier and more fulfilling lives.

Big data plays a critical role in Society 5.0, as it provides the information and insights needed to make informed decisions about complex problems, such as healthcare, energy, and transportation. By collecting and analyzing large amounts of data from various sources, such as social media, sensors, and IoT devices, organizations can gain insights into patterns, trends, and relationships that would be difficult to detect using traditional methods.

In Society 5.0, big data can be used to optimize systems and processes in various industries, such as healthcare, where data can be used to develop personalized treatments and improve overall patient outcomes. In transportation, big data can be used to optimize traffic flow, reduce emissions, and increase safety. In agriculture, big data can be used to improve crop yields, reduce waste, and make the food production process more sustainable.

However, big data also raises important ethical and privacy concerns in Society 5.0. The vast amounts of data being collected and analyzed raise questions about who owns and controls the data, as well as how it is used and protected. It is essential that data privacy and security be considered as an integral part of the development of big data technologies so that people's rights and privacy are respected in the age of Society 5.0.

In conclusion, big data is an essential component of Society 5.0 and holds the potential to improve many aspects of society, from healthcare to transportation. However, it is important to address the ethical and privacy concerns that arise from big data and ensure that technology is used for the benefit of all people [10].

4.5 Challenges in Implementing Society 5.0 with Big Data

The implementation of Society 5.0 using big data presents several significant challenges that must be addressed to realize its full potential. These challenges can be broadly categorized into three areas: technical, societal, and ethical.

Technical Challenges: One of the primary technical challenges is ensuring the accuracy and reliability of the data being collected and analyzed. With big data, the sheer volume and variety of data can lead to data quality issues, such as missing values, outliers, and irrelevant information. This can result in incorrect or misleading insights and decision-making. To mitigate this, organizations must invest in data quality control processes and technologies that can help to ensure the reliability of the data being used.

Another technical challenge is the complexity of data analytics and machine learning algorithms used to process and analyze the data. These algorithms are often highly specialized and require significant technical expertise to implement and maintain. In addition, the interpretation of the results generated by these algorithms can be difficult, and it is essential that organizations have access to experts who can interpret the results and apply them to real-world problems.

Societal Challenges: Society 5.0 and big data have the potential to create a more sustainable and equitable society, but they also raise important societal questions about the role of technology in society and the future of work. The widespread use of automation and artificial intelligence may displace certain jobs, leading to a loss of income for some workers and increased inequality.

Another societal challenge is the potential for big data to reinforce existing biases and discrimination. Algorithms that use big data can perpetuate the biases present in the data, leading to discriminatory outcomes, such as racial and gender-based discrimination. To mitigate this, organizations must take steps to ensure that their algorithms are transparent, auditable, and free from biases.

Ethical Challenges: The collection and use of big data raise important ethical questions about privacy and the protection of personal information. The vast amount of data being collected and analyzed can reveal sensitive information about individuals, such as their health status, financial status, and personal preferences. This raises questions about who owns and controls the data, as well as how it is used and protected.

Another ethical challenge is the potential for big data to be used for malicious purposes, such as cybercrime, political manipulation, and psychological manipulation. To mitigate this, organizations must implement robust security measures to protect the data and ensure that it is used for legitimate purposes only [11].

In conclusion, the implementation of Society 5.0 through big data presents several technical, societal, and ethical challenges that must be addressed to realize its full potential. Addressing these challenges requires a multidisciplinary approach that involves experts from the fields of technology, sociology, ethics, and law. By working together, we can ensure that the benefits of big data and Society 5.0 are realized while minimizing the risks and negative impacts.

References

1. Furht, B., Villanustre, F., Furht, B., & Villanustre, F. (2016). Introduction to big data. In: *Big Data Technologies and Applications.* Springer, Cham, (pp. 3–11). https://doi.org/10.1007/978-3-319 -44550-2_1
2. Abu-Salih, B., Wongthongtham, P., Zhu, D., Chan, K. Y., Rudra, A., Abu-Salih, B., ... Rudra, A. (2021). Introduction to big data technology. In: *Social Big Data Analytics: Practices, Techniques, and Applications.* Singapore: Springer, (pp. 15–59). https://doi.org/10.1007/978-981-33-6652-7_2
3. Hasani, Z., Kon-Popovska, M., & Velinov, G. (2014). Lambda architecture for real time big data analytic. In: *ICT Innovations 2014 Web Proceedings* (pp. 133–143). ISSN 1857-7288.

4. Roukh, A., Fote, F. N., Mahmoudi, S. A., & Mahmoudi, S. (2020). Big data processing architecture for smart farming. *Procedia Computer Science, 177,* 78–85.

5. Awaysheh, F. M., Alazab, M., Gupta, M., Pena, T. F., & Cabaleiro, J. C. (2020). Next-generation big data federation access control: A reference model. *Future Generation Computer Systems, 108,* 726–741.

6. Meier, A., & Kaufmann, M. (2019). *SQL & NoSQL Databases.* Berlin/Heidelberg: Springer Fachmedien Wiesbaden.

7. Zhelev, S., & Rozeva, A. (2019, November). Using microservices and event driven architecture for big data stream processing. In *AIP Conference Proceedings* (Vol. 2172, No. 1, p. 090010). AIP Publishing LLC.

8. Jiang, D., Wang, Y., Lv, Z., Qi, S., & Singh, S. (2019). Big data analysis-based network behavior insight of cellular networks for industry 4.0 applications. *IEEE Transactions on Industrial Informatics, 16*(2), 1310–1320.

9. Yüksekbilgili, Z., & Çevik, G. Z. (2018). With respect to industy 4.0 an analysis on Turkey's current and future state. *Finans Ekonomi Ve Sosyal Araştırmalar Dergisi, 3*(2), 422–436.

10. Gladden, M. E. (2019). Who will be the members of Society 5.0? Towards an anthropology of technologically posthumanized future societies. *Social Sciences, 8*(5), 148.

11. Shiroishi, Y., Uchiyama, K., & Suzuki, N. (2018). Society 5.0: for Human Security and Well-Being. *IEEE Computer, 51*(7), 91–95.

5

Ethics and Regulations of AI in Society 5.0

Priyanshu Rawat, Prerna, and Prabhdeep Singh

5.1 Introduction: Background and Driving Forces

Artificial intelligence (AI) has advanced quickly in the last several decades, and its influence on our lives has grown significantly. AI technologies have already changed how we work and live, and they can completely reshape sectors like banking, healthcare, and transportation. At the same time, there are rising worries about AI's ethical ramifications and the need for rules to guarantee its responsible development and use as society becomes more integrated with AI. The study of the ethical issues surrounding the design, development, and use of AI systems is one way that the area of AI ethics aims to alleviate these worries. Investigating these concerns entails looking at privacy, prejudice and fairness, transparency, accountability, and the effect of AI on society. To guarantee that AI is utilized responsibly and ethically, legislation for AI must be developed. In this chapter, we will discuss the moral and legal issues that arise when AI is developed and used in Society 5.0, a hypothetical society where technology development is based on people. The potential for AI to reinforce pre-existing social prejudices, the need for openness in AI decision-making processes, and the ethical ramifications of AI in healthcare have all been covered in our discussion of the numerous ethical and regulatory concerns AI brings. Also, we have looked at the shortcomings and difficulties of the current legal frameworks for AI and Society 5.0, including the Global Data Protection Regulation (GDPR) and the Japanese Society 5.0 program. We have also explored the necessity for international collaboration in developing AI rules and recommendations for new or revised regulations for AI and Society 5.0, including the AI Act put out by the European Union (EU). We have also looked at case studies and best practices for the ethical development and implementation of AI, including successful AI applications in self-driving vehicles, healthcare, and climate change. We have also covered the best practices for incorporating ethical considerations and legal requirements into the design and use of AI and the significance of including various stakeholders and conducting continuing evaluations of AI systems [1].

As a result, various stakeholders must continue to pay attention to the complex ethical and legal issues raised by AI in Society 5.0. It is crucial to prioritize ethical issues and create acceptable regulatory frameworks as AI technologies continue to advance and are more fully integrated into society. By doing this, we can ensure that AI is created and used in a way that benefits society as a whole while preserving moral standards and safeguarding people's rights.

5.2 Ethical Considerations for Society 5.0

With the world advancing toward a highly technological and interconnected future, the concept of Society 5.0 has gained popularity, which aims to blend technology with human-centered development. However, it is crucial to contemplate emerging technologies' ethical implications and potential social impacts during their development and usage in our daily lives. In this chapter, we will examine the ethical concerns that must be considered while establishing and executing Society 5.0 and emphasize the significance of establishing ethical guidelines to ensure the sustainable growth of our society.

5.2.1 Ethics and Its Significance for AI

As AI technologies become increasingly prevalent in our daily lives and with the development of Society 5.0, it is critical to consider the ethical implications of their use. AI systems can have far-reaching effects on individuals, communities, and society, making it necessary to address potential ethical concerns and develop guidelines to ensure that these technologies are used responsibly and ethically. One major ethical concern related to AI is bias. AI algorithms are only as objective as the data they are trained on, and if that data is biased, the algorithms themselves will be biased as well. This can seriously affect hiring, lending, and law enforcement, where biased algorithms can perpetuate existing social inequalities. Another ethical issue is transparency. Many AI systems are complex and difficult to understand, making it difficult for individuals to know how decisions are made or hold those responsible for their actions. As AI increasingly integrates into critical systems like healthcare and transportation, these systems must be transparent and understandable to ensure public trust. Real-world examples of the ethical implications of AI can be seen in cases like the use of facial recognition technology by law enforcement, which has been criticized for its potential to perpetuate racial profiling and infringe on privacy rights [2].

Additionally, AI-powered predictive policing systems have been criticized for their potential to reinforce existing biases in the criminal justice system. As we continue to develop and integrate AI into Society 5.0, we must prioritize ethical considerations and work to mitigate potential negative impacts. This can include developing ethical guidelines for AI development and use, ensuring transparency in decision-making processes, and actively working to address issues like bias and privacy concerns.

5.2.2 Ethical Concerns in AI for Society 5.0

With the rapid advancement of AI technologies, there are growing concerns about the ethical implications of their use in Society 5.0. AI has the potential to significantly impact society and shape our future, making it important to consider the ethical issues that arise from its use. Privacy, bias and fairness, transparency, and accountability are among the major ethical concerns related to AI for Society 5.0.

5.2.2.1 Privacy

Privacy protection is one of the most significant ethical concerns with AI in Society 5.0. As AI algorithms process and analyze vast amounts of data, there is an increased risk of privacy violations. This risk is particularly significant in healthcare, where AI-powered systems process sensitive patient information. It is important to establish ethical guidelines and regulations to protect privacy while still allowing for the benefits of AI technology.

For example, in 2018, it was revealed that the political consulting firm Cambridge Analytica had obtained the personal data of millions of Facebook users without their consent, which was later used for political advertising. This raised concerns about personal data privacy in the era of big data and AI. In 2020, Zoom's video conferencing app faced criticism for its data privacy practices, including sharing user data with third-party services without user consent (Figure 5.1).

The value of privacy protection in using AI technology is acknowledged by Society 5.0. It underlines the significance of including ethical issues in developing and using AI systems to protect users' privacy. To solve privacy issues, Society 5.0 encourages the employment of privacy-preserving technologies like differential privacy and federated learning, which enable data analysis while protecting individual privacy [3].

5.2.2.2 Bias and Fairness

Another important ethical concern is bias and fairness in AI. AI systems are only as unbiased as the data they are trained on. If the data is biased, the AI systems will also be biased. This bias can significantly impact Society 5.0, particularly regarding employment, education, and criminal justice systems. It is crucial to develop ethical guidelines for ensuring fairness in developing and deploying AI systems.

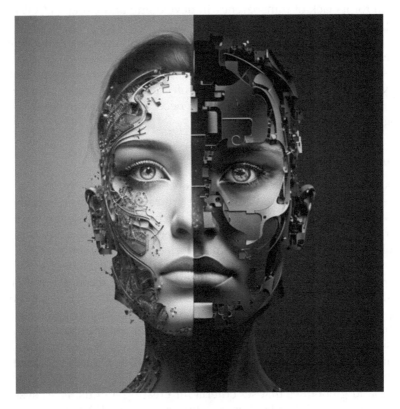

FIGURE 5.1
The intersection of humanity and AI (generated by Midjourney).

For example, in 2018, Amazon's AI-based hiring tool was criticized for showing bias against women in recruiting. The tool was trained on resumes submitted to the company over a 10-year period, which were mostly from men, leading to bias in the AI's recommendations. In 2020, a study found that several facial recognition algorithms were racially biased, with higher error rates for people of color. This raised concerns about the use of such technology by law enforcement agencies.

Regarding fairness and prejudice, Society 5.0 acknowledges that biased data or algorithms may impact AI systems, leading to unjust treatment or choices. Society 5.0 encourages the use of various datasets and the creation of impartial algorithms to assure fairness and eliminate prejudice. For users to comprehend how AI systems arrive at their decisions, it also underlines the need for openness and explicability in AI decision-making [4].

5.2.2.3 Transparency

Transparency is another important ethical concern related to AI in Society 5.0. AI systems can be complex and difficult to understand, making determination of how they arrive at certain decisions difficult. This lack of transparency can lead to distrust and ethical concerns. To address this, it is important to establish standards for transparency in AI systems, including the ability to explain how decisions are made.

For example, in 2019, Google was criticized for not being transparent enough about its data collection practices. The company was accused of secretly collecting users' location data even if the "Location History" setting was turned off. In 2020, the UK government faced criticism for its lack of transparency in developing and using its COVID-19 contact tracing app [5].

To ensure that consumers are aware of how AI systems function and what data they utilize, Society 5.0 encourages openness in developing and using AI systems. Moreover, Society 5.0 supports adopting open-source technology to advance accountability and transparency in AI decision-making. To guarantee that AI systems are utilized ethically and responsibly, Society 5.0 also highlights the necessity for human supervision in using AI technology.

5.2.2.4 Accountability

Finally, accountability is an important ethical concern for AI in Society 5.0. As AI systems become more integrated into our daily lives, it is crucial to establish accountability for their actions. This includes ensuring that AI systems are held responsible for any negative consequences of their actions and that there are mechanisms to address any issues.

For example, in 2018, Uber faced criticism for its lack of accountability after a self-driving car owned by the company hit and killed a pedestrian in Arizona. The incident raised questions about the safety of autonomous vehicles and the accountability of companies developing them. In 2020, Facebook faced criticism for its lack of accountability in moderating hate speech on its platform, leading to a boycott by several major advertisers.

Accountability is a key component in guaranteeing the appropriate and moral development and use of AI in Society 5.0. Establishing distinct lines of accountability and ensuring people and organizations are held responsible for their choices and their actions are part of it.

Regulations and guidelines that set criteria for creating and using AI systems are one method to assure responsibility. For instance, Europe's General Data Protection Regulation (GDPR) mandates that businesses seek customers' express agreement before collecting and using their personal information. This makes it possible for people to hold companies responsible if their privacy rights are violated since they know how their data is used [6].

5.3 Regulatory Frameworks for Society 5.0

Regulations have a significant impact on how society and technology progress. Regulatory frameworks are required in the case of Society 5.0 to ensure that technology development is balanced with societal needs and the defense of individual rights. Although they are still being developed, the legal underpinnings for Society 5.0 are already in place. To address ethical problems and ensure that technology is used to benefit society as a whole, the Japanese government, for instance, has developed the Society 5.0 program. In addition to government measures, business associations and nongovernmental organizations are working to create moral standards and best practices for Society 5.0. These principles guarantee that technology is created and utilized in a way consistent with human-centered values. They address various topics, including privacy, bias and fairness, transparency, and responsibility. The IEEE Global Initiative on Ethics of Autonomous and Intelligent Systems, created in 2016, is a noteworthy illustration of these initiatives. The goal of this program is to create ethical norms and guidelines for the creation and use of autonomous and intelligent systems. It brings together specialists from academia, business, and government [7].

5.3.1 Overview of Existing Regulations and Guidelines for AI and Society 5.0

A legislative framework is required to safeguard the ethical and responsible development and deployment of AI technologies, given their fast expansion in Society 5.0. Many organizations and governments throughout the globe have proposed and put into effect several policies and recommendations in recent years. One example of such a legal framework is the General Data Protection Regulation (GDPR) of the European Union, which became effective in 2018. It contains provisions for the right to access personal data, the right to be forgotten, and the right to data portability, in addition to outlining precise guidelines for collecting, processing, and using personal data. Under the GDPR, people will have control over their data, and businesses will be held responsible for how they handle it. The OECD Guidelines on AI, published in 2019, are another regulatory framework [8]. These recommendations provide a set of standards for AI's moral and responsible development and stress the significance of openness, responsibility, and human-centric principles. They also emphasize the need for ongoing monitoring and assessment of AI systems to ensure they are consistent with societal norms and not prejudice any one group.

Moreover, several nations have created rules and laws for Society 5.0 and AI. For instance, the "Basic Concept of Society 5.0," which explains the government's goal for a human-centric society and the role of technology in attaining it, is a part of Japan's Society 5.0 idea. The idea highlights the value of privacy protection and openness and contains rules for AI's moral development and use. The basis for the appropriate and moral development of these technologies is provided by the laws and policies that already exist for AI and Society 5.0. To ensure that these frameworks continue to be applicable and successful in advancing human-centric ideals and defending individual rights, assessing and adapting them as AI develops regularly will be crucial.

5.3.2 Challenges and Limitations of Current Regulatory Frameworks

The laws controlling AI and Society 5.0 confront many difficulties and restrictions like any other legal system. The rapid speed of technology innovation, which often exceeds regulators' capacity to keep up, is one of the biggest problems. This may result in out-of-date or ineffectual rules that do not consider recent developments or new issues.

The lack of globally standardized AI legislation is another issue that might lead to considerable differences between various areas or nations. Because of this, it may be difficult for companies and organizations that operate in several locations to comprehend their duties or even to comply with rules.

The efficiency of regulatory systems in ensuring compliance and dealing with infractions is another area of concern. For instance, in certain situations, fines or other punishments could not be enough to discourage wrongdoers. In contrast, in other situations, regulatory authorities might not have the resources or power necessary to implement legislation.

The Cambridge Analytica scandal, in which the personal information of millions of Facebook users was obtained without their consent, and the use of facial recognition technology by American law enforcement agencies, which has drawn criticism for its potential to uphold bias and violate privacy rights, are two examples of the difficulties and limitations of current regulatory frameworks in real-world settings. These and other instances demonstrate the need for strong and efficient regulatory frameworks to keep up with the quickly changing environment of AI and Society 5.0 [9].

5.3.3 Proposals for New or Updated Regulations for AI and Society 5.0

Novel and revised legislation that can address these technologies' ethical and societal ramifications is urgently needed as the development of AI technology progresses. This section will cover some suggestions for new or modified laws governing AI and Society 5.0.

The notion of ethical AI certification is one of the most important suggestions for new rules. Similar to the safety certificates already necessary for many consumer items, this certification would serve the same purpose. It would include evaluating AI systems independently by a third party to ensure they adhere to moral principles and do not endanger human safety or well-being. Several organizations and professionals have strongly supported this idea, and other nations have even begun putting such certification schemes into place.

Another suggestion is to develop new legislative frameworks that provide more responsibility and transparency in using AI technology. For instance, some experts have advocated mandating that businesses and organizations using AI reveal the data and methods they use to create these systems. This might assist in avoiding any ethical transgressions or biases by enabling more inspection and monitoring of these technologies.

In addition, some experts have suggested that new rules should emphasize encouraging the creation of AI systems that are more human-centered. The development of AI systems that emphasize human values and well-being, such as those that promote privacy and openness, may be encouraged in this way. Also, there have been suggestions for new laws that would oblige businesses and organizations to incorporate a wider range of stakeholders and viewpoints in creating AI systems.

Notwithstanding these suggestions, the present frameworks for regulating AI and Society 5.0 still face substantial obstacles and restrictions. Given the wide diversity of AI applications and use cases, one important obstacle is designing effective policies across many businesses and sectors. There are also worries about the possibility of regulatory capture, in which the interests of the sectors that regulatory bodies are supposed to control may become too influential.

The debate around face recognition technology and the use of AI in employment procedures are two real-world examples of the difficulties and constraints of present legislative systems. While there have been worries about possible biases and ethical transgressions in both situations, there is no established regulatory structure to deal with these problems [10].

5.3.4 International Cooperation and Harmonization of Regulations for AI and Society 5.0

There is a growing need for new or revised legislation to ensure that AI and related technologies are used responsibly and ethically as their development and usage continue to grow. This section will cover some suggestions for new or modified laws governing AI and Society 5.0.

One suggestion is to create a comprehensive international framework for AI's moral and responsible use. For instance, the European Commission has made recommendations for trustworthy AI that emphasize human-centered values and include ideas like openness, responsibility, and privacy. Moreover, these rules provide suggestions for putting these concepts into action.

Another suggestion is to create an AI regulatory organization to control the development and use of AI technology. This would include creating certification procedures to ensure AI systems adhere to moral and security requirements before being made available to the general public. The National Institute of Standards and Technology (NIST) in the United States has created a framework to monitor and reduce the risks connected with AI systems.

Likewise, some have suggested developing laws for AI technology that are industry-specific. For instance, there are issues with the use of AI in medical decision-making and the need for legislation to guarantee patient safety and ethical standards in the healthcare sector. Guidelines for developing and regulating AI-based medical devices have previously been released by the US Food and Drug Administration (FDA).

Notwithstanding these suggestions, it would not be easy to implement new or revised legislation for AI and Society 5.0. The speed of technological growth is a problem since this can make it difficult for regulatory authorities to keep up with new advances. The lack of global agreement on AI's ethical and governing principles is another problem.

However, others contend that too rigid rules may hinder innovation and restrict the potential advantages of AI technology. A complex and continuing process of finding the ideal balance between regulation and innovation calls for continual coordination between regulators, lawmakers, and business leaders [11].

5.4 Case Studies and Best Practices

The field of AI and Society 5.0 is rapidly advancing, and with this progress comes the need for ethical guidelines and regulatory frameworks to ensure that AI development and deployment are aligned with the needs and values of society. While there have been instances where AI has been used unethically, there have also been successful examples of ethical AI development and deployment. This section will explore case studies and best practices that demonstrate the importance of integrating ethics and regulations into AI development and deployment. We will examine real-world examples of both the challenges and successes in implementing ethical guidelines and regulatory frameworks and discuss best practices for integrating these considerations into the development and deployment of AI. Additionally, we will reflect on the lessons learned and future directions for the field of AI and Society 5.0.

5.4.1 Real-World Examples of Ethical and Regulatory Challenges in AI and Society 5.0

It is crucial to consider the ethical and regulatory problems that come with AI as it plays a significant role in Society 5.0. We would look at some actual instances of these problems in this part and the recommended solutions.

The possibility of prejudice is one of the main ethical issues with AI in Society 5.0. For instance, it has been shown that face recognition software has greater mistake rates for individuals with darker skin tones, which might result in inaccurate identifications and possibly injure innocent individuals. When the American Civil Liberties Union (ACLU) evaluated Amazon's facial recognition software, Recognition, in 2018, it discovered that 28 members of Congress were mistakenly matched to mugshot photographs, with representatives of color seeing a disproportionately high number of false matches. This raises important concerns regarding the possible abuse of face recognition technology, especially concerning police enforcement [12].

The problem of privacy is a further illustration of an ethical conundrum in AI and Society 5.0. After being exposed in 2018, Cambridge Analytica was found to have collected millions of Facebook users' personal information without their knowledge and used it to target political ads during the 2016 US presidential election. This highlighted concerns about how Internet corporations utilize personal data and the need for stricter laws to safeguard people's privacy.

In addition to these ethical difficulties, regulatory difficulties must be resolved. For instance, the European Commission published ethical principles for creating and using AI in 2019. Nevertheless, many experts have criticized these principles as too flimsy and toothless. To guarantee that AI is created and deployed responsibly and ethically, there is a need for greater rules and monitoring.

The absence of a global agreement on AI rules is another problem. Various nations' methods of governing AI vary, which may cause ambiguity and inconsistency. For instance, China has come under fire for using AI for social control and surveillance, while the United States has been under fire for having no laws governing the creation and use of AI.

There have been several suggestions for new or revised rules for AI and Society 5.0 to address these issues. New AI legislation, for instance, is being considered by the EU and would clearly define the conditions for the AI system's accountability, transparency, and human supervision. The Algorithmic Accountability Act of 2019 was implemented in the United States as a requirement for businesses to evaluate and reduce bias in their AI systems [13].

5.4.2 Successful Cases of Ethical AI Development and Deployment

While there have been various instances where AI has been used unethically, there have also been examples of successful and ethical AI development and deployment. These cases demonstrate that it is possible to design and use AI in a manner that is beneficial to society while still adhering to ethical principles.

One such example is Google's use of AI to improve healthcare outcomes. In 2018, Google partnered with a hospital in India to develop an AI system that could predict medical events such as heart attacks, strokes, and other cardiovascular events. The system was trained on a dataset of over 250,000 medical records, and it could predict such events with an accuracy rate of 90%. The system identified patients at risk of medical events earlier, allowing for timely intervention and treatment. The system was designed with ethical considerations, such as ensuring patient privacy and informed consent.

Another example is the use of AI to combat climate change. Microsoft has developed an AI tool that can analyze vast amounts of data to identify areas where energy efficiency can be improved. The tool uses machine learning algorithms to analyze energy usage patterns and identify areas where energy consumption can be reduced. This has led to significant energy savings for businesses and organizations that use this tool. This tool was designed with ethical considerations in mind, such as ensuring that the data used is accurate and that the tool is transparent in its recommendations [14].

A third example is the use of AI to improve the safety of self-driving cars. Companies like Tesla and Waymo have been using AI to develop self-driving cars that can navigate roads safely and efficiently. These companies have designed their AI systems with ethical considerations in mind, such as ensuring that the cars are programmed to prioritize the safety of passengers and pedestrians. The use of AI in self-driving cars has the potential to significantly reduce the number of car accidents caused by human error.

It is important to note that successful ethical AI development and deployment cases are not limited to large corporations. Small- and medium-sized enterprises (SMEs) have also demonstrated the ability to develop ethical AI solutions that benefit society.

One example is the use of AI in precision agriculture. A Canadian company, Farmers Edge, has developed an AI system that analyzes data from sensors in agricultural fields to provide farmers with insights into crop yields, soil conditions, and other important factors. The system helps farmers optimize their use of resources and improve crop yields, which has positive economic and environmental impacts. The system was designed with ethical considerations, such as ensuring that the data used is secure and that farmers have control over their data.

Another example is the use of AI to improve mental healthcare. A UK-based company, Xploro, has developed an AI-powered chatbot that provides children with information and support related to their medical treatments. The chatbot uses natural language processing to interact with children in a friendly and engaging manner. The system has been shown to reduce anxiety and improve knowledge retention among children undergoing medical treatment. The system was designed with ethical considerations, such as ensuring that children's privacy is protected and that the chatbot is accessible to all children regardless of their language or literacy level.

Overall, these instances show that developing and deploying ethical AI is feasible and has a good influence on society. AI may be developed and used in a way that is beneficial to all parties by taking ethical values like openness, privacy, and fairness into account [15].

5.4.3 Best Practices for Integrating Ethics and Regulations into AI Development and Deployment in Society 5.0

Prioritizing ethics and rules in creating and using AI is crucial as technology develops and is incorporated into many facets of society. The following are some best practices for incorporating morality and laws into the creation and use of AI:

Please Include Various Stakeholders: It is crucial to engage various stakeholders, including ethicists, legal professionals, politicians, and representatives from groups impacted by AI, to guarantee that AI research and deployment are ethical and inclusive.

Incorporate Transparency: Ensuring that AI is created and used responsibly requires openness. Developers need to explain the judgments made by AI systems and be open about the data and techniques employed in such systems.

Perform Extensive Testing and Validation: To guarantee that AI systems are dependable, accurate, and secure, rigorous testing and validation are required. Developers should test in actual settings and track the effectiveness of AI systems over time.

Emphasize Privacy and Security: While developing AI systems, developers should keep privacy and security in mind to preserve users' privacy and security. This involves putting policies like data encryption and access restrictions in place.

Create Accountability: Developers should establish responsibility while developing and deploying AI systems. This entails establishing distinct lines of accountability for the choices made by AI systems and procedures for correcting any damage these systems may have caused [16].

5.4.4 Lessons Learned and Future Directions for Ethics and Regulations in Society 5.0

It is crucial to reflect on the lessons gained from earlier ethical and legal difficulties and consider the future paths for enhancing AI research and deployment as the use of AI becomes more pervasive in Society 5.0.

The value of incorporating a variety of stakeholders in the creation and use of AI is one of the most important lessons discovered. This comprises ethicists, legal professionals, lawmakers, and representatives from groups that AI may have an impact on, as was previously indicated. AI engineers may better comprehend the possible effects of their technology and create it in a manner that is moral, inclusive, and advantageous to society by including various viewpoints.

Another lesson is the need to continue to monitor and assess AI systems. When AI systems are used in practical contexts, it is critical to regularly examine their effectiveness and identify any possible moral or legal dilemmas. This covers methods for obtaining input from users and impacted groups and continuous testing and validation of AI systems.

As we advance, numerous ways exist to strengthen the rules and ethics of AI in Society 5.0. The creation of uniform ethical frameworks for AI is one approach. These frameworks may provide an agreed-upon set of moral principles and recommendations for AI developers, which might assist in guaranteeing that AI is created and used in a manner that is compatible with moral standards [17].

The creation of legal frameworks that are specially adapted to AI is another possible option. As was already established, the unique ethical and legal issues that AI presents may not be sufficiently addressed by the current regulatory frameworks. Thus, creating new regulatory frameworks specially designed to deal with these difficulties is necessary.

A constant effort must be made to educate the public and raise awareness about AI ethics and laws. This includes public awareness efforts to assist and inform the general public on AI's possible hazards and advantages, as well as training programs for AI developers, policymakers, and other stakeholders [18].

5.5 Conclusion

In conclusion, the development and deployment of AI in Society 5.0 present a range of ethical and regulatory challenges. The potential benefits of AI are significant, but there is also the potential for harm if it is not developed and used ethically. This chapter has explored various aspects of AI ethics and regulation, including privacy, bias, transparency, accountability, and the human-centered approach to AI development. We have also examined the existing regulatory frameworks for AI and the challenges and limitations of these frameworks.

While there have been instances of AI being used unethically, there have also been examples of successful and ethical AI development and deployment. These cases demonstrate that it is possible to design and use AI in a manner that is beneficial to society while still adhering to ethical principles. In particular, involving diverse stakeholders in the development and deployment of AI is crucial for ensuring that AI is developed and used ethically and inclusively.

There are also best practices that organizations can follow to integrate ethics and regulations into AI development and deployment. These include incorporating ethical considerations into the design of AI systems, ensuring transparency and accountability in AI systems, and involving diverse stakeholders in developing and deploying AI.

Looking to the future, it is clear that ethical and regulatory considerations will continue to be crucial as AI continues to be developed and deployed in Society 5.0. It will be important for policymakers, researchers, and organizations to continue to work together to develop regulatory frameworks that promote ethical and inclusive AI development and deployment. The development of AI presents a significant opportunity to improve society. Still, it is crucial that it is developed and used in a beneficial and inclusive manner for all.

Furthermore, as AI technology advances, it is important to prioritize ethics and regulations in its development and deployment. By doing so, we can ensure that AI is used in a manner that benefits society and respects human rights and values. The key is to balance innovation and regulation to encourage continued development while ensuring that it is done responsibly and ethically.

In conclusion, integrating AI into Society 5.0 can potentially transform our world for the better. However, it is essential that we approach this integration with caution and that we prioritize ethical considerations and regulatory frameworks in its development and deployment. This chapter has discussed the ethical challenges and opportunities presented by AI in Society 5.0, the importance of value alignment and a human-centered approach to AI development, and the regulatory frameworks and best practices that can help ensure that AI is used ethically and responsibly. By learning from the successes and failures of past efforts, we can work toward a future where AI and Society 5.0 work in harmony to create a better world for all.

References

1. Angurala, M., Bala, M. and Bamber, S.S., 2022. Wireless battery recharging through UAV in wireless sensor networks. *Egyptian Informatics Journal*, 23(1), pp. 21–31.

2. Khullar, V., Singh, H.P., Miro, Y., Anand, D., Mohamed, H.G., Gupta, D., Kumar, N. and Goyal, N., 2022. IoT fog-enabled multi-node centralized ecosystem for real time screening and monitoring of health information. *Applied Sciences*, 12(19), p. 9845.

3. Wong, A., 2021. Ethics and regulation of artificial intelligence. In *Artificial Intelligence for Knowledge Management: 8th IFIP WG 12.6 International Workshop, AI4KM 2021, Held at IJCAI 2020, Yokohama, Japan, January 7–8, 2021, Revised Selected Papers 8* (pp. 1–18). Springer International Publishing.

4. Carayannis, E.G. and Morawska-Jancelewicz, J., 2022. The futures of Europe: Society 5.0 and Industry 5.0 as driving forces of future universities. *Journal of the Knowledge Economy, 3*, pp. 3445–3471. https://doi.org/10.1007/s13132-021-00854-2

5. Fukuda, K., 2020. Science, technology and innovation ecosystem transformation toward society 5.0. *International Journal of Production Economics*, 220, p. 107460.

6. Rousi, R.A., Saariluoma, P.O. and Nieminen, M., 2022. AI for a humane society 5.0-governance AI ethics editorial. *Frontiers in Computer Science, 6*, p. 153.

7. Schoitsch, E., 2020. Towards a resilient society-technology 5.0, risks and ethics. *28th Interdisciplinary Information Management Talks: Digitalized Economy, Society and Information Management, IDIMT 2020*, pp. 403–412.

8. Šoša, I., 2023. Education made easy with lab-on-a-chip, or one tool--mass-spectrometry-based techniques, OMICS 2.0 and society 5.0.

9. Oktradiksa, A., Bhakti, C.P., Kurniawan, S.J. and Rahman, F.A., 2021. Utilization artificial intelligence to improve creativity skills in society 5.0. In *Journal of Physics: Conference Series* (Vol. 1760, No. 1, p. 012032). IOP Publishing.

10. Ellitan, L., 2020. Competing in the era of Industrial Revolution 4.0 and society 5.0. *Jurnal Maksipreneur: Manajemen, Koperasi, dan Entrepreneurship*, 10(1), pp. 1–12.

11. Minchev, Z. and Boyanov, L., 2018, October. Future digital Society 5.0: Adversaries & opportunities. In *International Conference on Application of Information and Communication Technology and Statistics in Economy & Education (ICAICTSEE), Bulgaria, DOI* (Vol. 10).

12. Hamdani, N.A., Herlianti, A.O. and Amin, A.S., 2019, December. Society 5.0: Feasibilities and challenges of the implementation of fintech in small and medium industries. In *Journal of Physics: Conference Series* (Vol. 1402, No. 7, p. 077053). IOP Publishing.

13. Beniiche, A., Rostami, S. and Maier, M., 2022. Society 5.0: Internet as if people mattered. *IEEE Wireless Communications*, 29(6), pp. 160–168.

14. Huang, S., Wang, B., Li, X., Zheng, P., Mourtzis, D. and Wang, L., 2022. Industry 5.0 and Society 5.0—Comparison, complementation and co-evolution. *Journal of Manufacturing Systems, 64*, pp. 424–428.

15. Islam, A., Islam, M., Hossain Uzir, M.U., Abd Wahab, S. and Abdul Latiff, A.S., 2020. The panorama between COVID-19 pandemic and Artificial Intelligence (AI): Can it be the catalyst for Society 5.0. *International Journal of Scientific Research and Management*, 8(12), pp. 2011–2025.

16. Mohan, N., Singla, R., Kaushal, P. and Kadry, S. eds., 2021. *Artificial Intelligence, Machine Learning, and Data Science Technologies: Future Impact and Well-Being for Society 5.0*. CRC Press.

17. Veeramanickam, M.R., Khullar, V., Salunke, M.D., Bangare, J.L., Bhosle, A.A. and Ingavale, A., 2022, December. Streamed incremental learning for cyber attack classification using machine learning. In *2022 2nd International Conference on Innovative Sustainable Computational Technologies (CISCT)* (pp. 1–5). IEEE.

18. Angurala, M., Bala, M., Bamber, S.S., Kaur, R. and Singh, P., 2020. An internet of things assisted drone based approach to reduce rapid spread of COVID-19. *Journal of Safety Science and Resilience*, 1(1), pp. 31–35.

6

Opportunities and Challenges in AI Society 5.0

Vikas Khullar, Mohit Angurala, and Sangeetha Annam

6.1 Introduction

Society 5.0 has several smart grid uses. Security is another draw for researchers worldwide. Cybersecurity safeguards computers, networks, and devices from theft, damage, and unauthorised access. Hackers, fraudsters, and even workers pose cybersecurity risks. As more data is stored and transmitted digitally, the scope of cybersecurity is vital. Cybersecurity includes encryption, firewalls, and antivirus software. Cybersecurity experts analyse risk and manage threats.

6.2 Challenges in Society 5.0

Society 5.0 envisions integrating technology into all aspects of life to improve people's lives. Technology integration creates new cybersecurity problems. Cybercriminals can attack increasingly connected gadgets. Artificial intelligence (AI) and machine learning (ML) may potentially be used for attack, posing new cybersecurity issues.

Society 5.0 faces privacy difficulties, ethical dilemmas relating to AI and automation, and the possibility of increasing inequality if certain groups cannot access or profit from new technology. Cybersecurity is more important in Society 5.0. Communication, finance, transportation, and healthcare are becoming increasingly dependent on technology as technology improves. Hacking, data breaches, and identity theft become more likely due to this dependence on technology. Thus, cybersecurity measures must protect individuals, businesses, and governments from cyberattacks.

Cybersecurity in Society 5.0 includes personal data protection. Digital technologies are storing massive amounts of personal data. Cybercriminals can profit from this sensitive data. Thus, encryption, firewalls, and other security protocols are needed to protect this data.

In Society 5.0, electricity grids, transportation networks, and healthcare facilities are interconnected and dependent on technology. Cyberattacks on these facilities might cause physical injury and death due to their interconnection. Thus, these infrastructures must be protected using strong cybersecurity systems. Society 5.0 requires cybersecurity. As technology evolves and our reliance on it grows, cyberattacks must be prevented. Personal data, essential infrastructure, and cybersecurity standards must be protected. These actions are the only way to ensure that technology provides benefits without causing hazards. Society

5.0 needs technology solutions, regulatory frameworks, and education and awareness programmes to ensure cybersecurity.

Society 5.0, the next stage of human progress, will incorporate modern technology
into daily life. Society 5.0 will leverage linked gadgets and networks to enhance social
operations. Cyberattacks and risks rise with device and network connectivity. The sheer
quantity of Internet-connected gadgets in Society 5.0 makes accomplishment of network
security difficult. Smartphones, computers, automobiles, appliances, and medical gadgets are some of the Internet-connected gadgets. Cyberattack danger increases with these
Internet-connected products. Each device is a possible hacker-entry point to the network
and to sensitive data.

Network complexity complicates Society 5.0 network security. Society 5.0 will use
sophisticated, linked networks to integrate gadgets and systems. Complexity makes
it hard to find and fix network vulnerabilities and to detect and respond to cyberattacks. AI and ML in Society 5.0 also pose network security issues. Cyberattacks must
be prevented since AI and ML systems make conclusions using enormous volumes of
data. Cybercriminals might exploit AI and ML systems to harm people or organisations. Cloud computing is another Society 5.0 network security issue. Cloud computing
lets companies use storage and processing power online. Cloud computing provides
not only cost savings and flexibility but also new security threats. Cloud data is prone
to data breaches; thus, organisations must verify that their cloud service providers have
proper security measures.

In Society 5.0, mobile devices pose a major network security risk. Mobile devices with
sensitive personal and financial data are especially vulnerable to cyberattacks. Mobile
devices routinely access business networks, increasing the danger of a cyberattack. In
Society 5.0, network security must be proactive. From smartphones to cloud infrastructure, this requires strong network security. This involves teaching people how to use
secure passwords and avoid dubious links and downloads. Society 5.0 uses AI and ML
to secure networks. These systems can identify and respond to cyberattacks in real time,
thereby helping organisations keep ahead of developing risks. AI and ML may automate
security procedures like threat detection and response, thereby relieving human security
personnel. Society 5.0 has substantial network security issues, but proactive security measures and new technology can solve them. Network security is crucial to protecting our
personal and financial data and Society 5.0's key infrastructure as we incorporate technology into every area of our life.

6.3 Ethics for Sustainable Development of Society 5.0

Society 5.0 uses AI, IoT, and robots to make society more sustainable and inclusive. In
this new technology era, Society 5.0's sustainability depends on ethical issues and laws.
Society 5.0's fast technological improvement has created a demand for ethical development
and use of AI, IoT, and robots. To guarantee that AI, IoT, and robots are developed ethically,
Society 5.0 must evaluate their possible effects on ethical issues such as privacy, security,
accountability, openness, and human rights. Society 5.0 prioritises privacy. The Internet of
Things (IoT) and AI are collecting a greater amount of personal data. For ensuring privacy,
this data must be maintained and utilised properly. It is also crucial that people can regulate, and opt out of, data collecting.

Security is also ethical. Security threats rise as technology becomes more interconnected. These systems must be secure to withstand assaults. Transportation, energy, and healthcare infrastructure require security systems. Ethics also need accountability and openness. As the use of AI and robots increases, popular, fair, and impartial application of AI and robots is crucial. Algorithms and data must be transparent. These technologies must also be held accountable. This involves making individuals and organisations accountable for the detrimental effects of these technologies.

Finally, human rights matter ethically. As technology becomes more widespread, human rights must be upheld. These technologies should not discriminate based on race, gender, or financial background.

6.4 Regulations for Sustainable Development of Society 5.0

Society 5.0 needs regulations to survive. These technologies must be regulated to meet social goals. Regulating these technologies ensures safe and ethical use. Society 5.0 regulates safety, sustainability, and social responsibility. Society 5.0 prioritises safety regulations. AI, IoT, and robots used in critical infrastructure create safety hazards. These technologies must safeguard people and the environment. This demands strict safety requirements. Society 5.0 also regulates environmental sustainability. As these technologies become more popular, environmental sustainability must be ensured, that is, reducing greenhouse gas emissions and wastes and promoting the circular economy. These technologies must also be environmentally friendly.

Finally, regulation requires social responsibility. As technology becomes more embedded into society, it must fit with values and aims. The development and usage of these technologies must be regulated to meet society's demands. These technologies must not harm society. Society 5.0 needs ethics and laws for survival. Ethical concerns guarantee that these technologies match with social values and aspirations, while laws assure safe and responsible use of technologies.

6.5 Challenges and Opportunities of Implementing Trustworthy AI in Society 5.0

AI has changed healthcare, transportation, education, and finance. AI has raised ethical and societal issues including prejudice, privacy, and security in several domains. Trustworthy AI – transparent, ethical, and responsible AI systems – addresses these challenges. Society 5.0, which integrates AI and other digital technologies to solve social problems and improve well-being, requires trustworthy AI [1, 2]. This article examines trustworthy AI in Society 5.0 and its difficulties and prospects.

Society 5.0 uses digital technology to create a sustainable, inclusive, and affluent society for humans. AI is supposed to help solve societal issues including healthcare, education, and climate change. AI must be trustworthy to solve these problems. Trustworthy AI can boost public confidence in AI systems, which is necessary for the broad adoption of AI systems. Trustworthy AI can handle ethical and societal issues including prejudice, privacy, and security. If trained on biassed data or designed with biassed assumptions, AI systems can be biassed. Trustworthy AI systems are transparent, explainable, and bias-free [2]. Trustworthy AI ensures that AI systems are created with privacy and security in mind and comply with relevant legislation and standards.

Trustworthy AI in Society 5.0 is difficult. Trustworthy AI requires AI, ethics, legal, and social science specialists [2]. Experts may have various goals and viewpoints, making this difficult. Implementing trustworthy AI may be costly and time-consuming, especially for small and medium-sized enterprises (SMEs) that may not have the means to spend on AI research and development. Trustworthy AI in Society 5.0 also offers great prospects [3]. Trustworthy AI lets developers experiment with novel AI systems without sacrificing ethics and transparency, while fostering innovation and creativity. By accommodating varied user demands and tastes, trustworthy AI may promote social inclusion and diversity.

Society 5.0 needs trustworthy AI. Trustworthy AI can assist in addressing ethical and societal issues related to AI while boosting public confidence in AI technologies. Trustworthy AI in Society 5.0 demands a multidisciplinary approach, which might be difficult and expensive for SMEs. Trustworthy AI in Society 5.0 opens doors to innovation, social inclusion, and diversity.

6.6 Society 5.0's Digital Twin Challenges and Opportunities

Engineering, manufacturing, and healthcare are using digital twins. Digital twins can change society outside these businesses [4–6]. Digital twins can alter society on Society 5.0, the Japanese vision for the future. This chapter examines how digital twins can change Society 5.0. Digital twins simulate tangible items, processes, or systems. We can monitor, analyse, and optimise these digital copies by simulating their behaviour and reaction with real-time data [7]. Digital twins have been present for decades, but the Internet of Things (IoT), Artificial Intelligence(AI), and Big Data have made them more prominent in Industry 4.0 and beyond [8, 9]. In Society 5.0, digital twins might change how we build, manage, and maintain complex systems and infrastructure. Society 5.0 envisions a sustainable, human-centred society that integrates the digital and physical worlds. It differs from agricultural, industrial, information, and automation-based societies. Society 5.0 uses cutting-edge technology to solve the problems of ageing populations, climate change, and resource depletion. It imagines a world where data-driven decision-making unites people, technology, and the environment. Digital twins can help realise Society 5.0. They can simulate and optimise buildings, transportation networks, energy grids, and cities. We can monitor these systems in real time, foresee problems, and optimise their efficiency and sustainability by constructing digital twins. Digital twins can simulate traffic flow and optimise transportation routes or can model a building's energy use and discover opportunities for improvement.

Digital twins provide data-driven decision-making. Data from physical systems and their digital analogues may reveal how those work and suggest improvements. This can improve resource allocation, maintenance scheduling, and system upgrades. Digital twins allow us to simulate scenarios and strategies before executing them in the real world. Society 5.0 may redesign, run, and maintain complex systems and infrastructure using digital twins. Real-time insights and data-driven decision-making may help us build a more sustainable, efficient, and human-centred society. Digital twins will be employed in smart buildings, cities, healthcare, and education as this technology matures. Society 5.0 strives towards sustainability and inclusivity. AI, IoT, and robots will be incorporated into all parts of life as per Society 5.0's vision. These technologies will solve the problems in this society, including an ageing population, climate change, and urbanisation. Digital twins simulate physical items, processes, and systems. They may model and test real-world scenarios to identify possible issues. This technology may be used in infrastructure, resources, healthcare, and education.

Finally, digital twins boost schooling. They may be used to develop virtual models of complicated systems so that students can safely explore and learn those systems. Students may customise their learning with this technology. Thus, digital twins can solve society's biggest problems and transform Society 5.0. Digital twins can develop virtual models of real-world events in resource management, healthcare, and education to predict and prevent issues. Digital twins can make society more sustainable, inclusive, and efficient.

6.7 Related Discussions

Society 5.0 integrates developing technology to support sustainable development, economic progress, and social harmony in the future. Digital twins can enable Society 5.0. Digital twins may replicate and optimise the behaviour and performance of actual objects, processes, and systems. Manufacturing, healthcare, transportation, and urban planning use digital twins. Digital twins in Society 5.0 present various issues that must be addressed.

Society 5.0 digital twins face data management issues initially. Digital twins need lots of data, including sensor data, historical data, and simulation data. Complex data management systems are needed to collect, store, and process such data. Digital twins need data from numerous sources with diverse forms, protocols, and standards. Therefore, digital twins need interoperability and data integration to provide meaningful insights and predictions.

Standards and rules are Society 5.0's second digital twin challenge. Digital twins are a novel technology; hence, there are no guidelines for their creation, implementation, and operation. Lack of rules and laws can cause digital twins to perform inconsistently and raise ethical and legal difficulties relating to data ownership, privacy, and responsibility. Thus, Society 5.0 requires a regulatory framework for safe and ethical digital twin use. Humans are Society 5.0's third digital twin challenge. Digital twins optimise and automate complicated systems and processes, but they need human oversight. Digital twins' real-time feedback and recommendations may influence human behaviour and decision-making. Thus, digital twins in Society 5.0 must align with human values, goals, and aspirations. This requires user-friendly interfaces, training programmes, and governance frameworks with diverse stakeholders.

Cost and scalability are Society 5.0's fourth digital twin challenges. Digital twins are expensive to develop and install, especially for small and medium businesses (SMBs). Digital twins also require high-performance processing and networking infrastructure, which may not be accessible everywhere. Thus, Society 5.0 requires cost-effective and scalable digital twin adoption solutions. Industry, academia, and government must collaborate to create open-source platforms, shared data repositories, and creative business models that lower entry barriers.

Society 5.0's digital twin issues are complicated. They demand a comprehensive strategy that incorporates technological, social, economic, ethical, and legal concerns. Technology developers, governments, corporations, civil society organisations, and individuals must collaborate to solve these problems. We must collaborate to make Society 5.0's digital twins sustainable, inclusive, and affluent. Digital twins simulate physical items, processes, and systems. IoT, AI, and ML are used to produce real-time digital copies of physical assets. Digital twins can improve industrial productivity, forecast equipment breakdowns, and many more. Digital twins will shape Society 5.0.

Society 5.0 integrates AI, IoT, and robots to build a sustainable, human-centred society. Digital twins can improve system efficiency, foresee and avoid breakdowns, and monitor and control physical assets in real time. Smart city applications of digital twins in Society 5.0 are promising. Planners and politicians may utilise digital twins to develop virtual city models to simulate alternative situations and make better judgements. Digital twins can simulate traffic flow, air quality, and other effects of a new building or infrastructure project. This data can optimise project design and reduce negative effects. Power grids, water systems, and transportation networks may be monitored and optimised using digital twins. Operators may monitor these systems in real time and make modifications to increase efficiency and prevent breakdowns by constructing a virtual model. A digital twin of a power system can discover possible failure sites and avoid blackouts.

Digital twins are improving production efficiency and cost. Engineers may optimise manufacturing process design and discover bottlenecks and inefficiencies by constructing a virtual model. This data can be used to optimise the process and cut costs. Personalised treatment with digital twins might revolutionise healthcare. Doctors may monitor patient health in real time by developing a digital twin. This may be used to create patient-specific treatment strategies. Digital twins, like any technology, create privacy and security problems. Digital twins capture a lot of data, which might be misused. Hackers might influence physical assets or systems using digital twins [10].

Thus, digital twins could transform how we design, build, and manage physical assets and systems. Digital twins and IoT security will help Society 5.0 become sustainable and human-centred [11, 12]. To reap the benefits of digital twins without endangering people or society, privacy and security must be addressed.

6.8 Conclusion

Society 5.0, where technology is incorporated into every element of society, poses new cybersecurity issues. Cybersecurity protects devices, networks, and systems from theft, damage, and unauthorised access. Antivirus, firewalls, and encryption are cybersecurity essentials. Cybersecurity experts analyse risk and manage threats. Society 5.0 faces privacy problems, ethical challenges around AI and automation, and the possibility of growing inequality if certain people cannot access or profit from new technology. Cybersecurity involves protecting personal data. Society 5.0 is the stage of human progress when modern technology is integrated into daily life. Society 5.0 must secure personal data, key infrastructure, and cybersecurity standards. This needs technology solutions, legislative frameworks, and education and awareness programmes to ensure that individuals and organisations understand the risks and take proper precautions.

References

1. A. Bilberg and A. A. Malik, "Digital twin driven human–robot collaborative assembly", *CIRP Annals*, vol. 68, pp. 499–502, 2019.
2. C. Mandolla, A. M. Petruzzelli, G. Percoco and A. Urbinati, "Building a digital twin for additive manufacturing through the exploitation of blockchain: A case analysis of the aircraft industry", *Computers in Industry*, vol. 109, pp. 134–152, Aug. 2019.
3. O. Elijah, T. A. Rahman, I. Orikumhi, C. Y. Leow and M. N. Hindia, "An overview of Internet of things (IoT) and data analytics in agriculture: Benefits and challenges", *IEEE Internet of Things Journal*, vol. 5, pp. 3758–3773, 2018.
4. V. Kharchenko and O. Illiashenko, "Concepts of green IT engineering: Taxonomy principles and implementation", in *Green IT Engineering: Concepts Models Complex Systems Architectures, Studies in Systems, Decision and Control*, Cham: Springer, vol. 74, pp. 3–19, 2017.
5. O. Potii, O. Illiashenko and D. Komin, "Advanced security assurance case based on ISO/IEC 15408", in *Theory and Engineering of Complex Systems and Dependability. DepCoS-RELCOMEX 2015, Advances in Intelligent Systems and Computing*, vol. 365, pp. 391–401, 2015.
6. Y. Zheng, S. Yang and H. Cheng, "An application framework of digital twin and its case study", *Journal of Ambient Intelligence and Humanized Computing*, vol. 10, no. 3, pp. 1141–1153, Jun. 2018.
7. W. Kritzinger, M. Karner, G. Traar, J. Henjes and W. Sihn, "Digital twin in manufacturing: A categorical literature review and classification", *IFAC-PapersOnLine*, vol. 51, no. 11, pp. 1016–1022, 2018.
8. A. Coraddu, L. Oneto, F. Baldi, F. Cipollini, M. Atlar and S. Savio, "Data-driven ship digital twin for estimating the speed loss caused by the marine fouling", *Ocean Engineering*, vol. 186, Aug. 2019, 1–14.
9. X. Zhang, X. Wei, C. X. J. Ou, E. Caron, H. Zhu and H. Xiong, "From human-AI confrontation to human-AI symbiosis in Society 5.0: Transformation challenges and mechanisms", *IT Professional*, vol. 24, no. 3, pp. 43–51, 1 May–June 2022, doi: 10.1109/MITP.2022.3175512.
10. M. Fukuyama, "Society 5.0: Aiming for a new human-centered society", *Jpn. Spotlight*, vol. 1, pp. 47–50, 2018.
11. A. Kumar and I. Sharma, "CNN-based approach for IoT intrusion attack detection", *2023 International Conference on Sustainable Computing and Data Communication Systems (ICSCDS)*, Erode, India, 2023, pp. 492–496, doi: 10.1109/ICSCDS56580.2023.10104967.
12. D. N. Malleswari, D. N. Rao, P. Vidyullatha, G. S. P. Ghantasala, R. Sathiyaraj and Yogesh, "Enhanced SS-FIM algorithm for high utility uncertain itemsets", *2022 IEEE 2nd International Conference on Mobile Networks and Wireless Communications (ICMNWC)*, Tumkur, Karnataka, India, 2022, pp. 1–5, doi: 10.1109/ICMNWC56175.2022.10031871.

7

Emergence of AI in Education: A Way Forward for Societal Development

Shivani Malhan, Rekha Mewafarosh, Shikha Agnihotri, and Divya Gupta

7.1 Introduction to Artificial Intelligence

The potential of Artificial Intelligence (AI) in teaching has amplified over the years and is discussed in political debates all over the world [30]. As Artificial Intelligence literacy has gained popularity, it becomes important for educators to start the journey of exploring Artificial Intelligence, which was confined to computer science laboratories initially. It has become imperative for educators and administrators to use Artificial Intelligence in teaching and to adopt this technology so that it can be beneficial for the students.

Previously, research on artificial intelligence in the education sector was confined to scientists, primarily to computers; however, in the last decade, it has become an area of commercial interest as well [5, 50, 53]. The use of Artificial Intelligence in the education sector is growing as there are 30 multimillion-dollar-funded corporations of Artificial Intelligence in Education (AIED) across the world, and this number is about to become around US$ 20 billion within the next five years [11]. Many commercial systems of AI developed for education, which are known as tutoring systems and which are intelligent, provide more automotive and adaptive instructions.

A link has been found between Artificial Intelligence and Science related to cognition [10], and it means that Artificial Intelligence systems have been built on architectures that are cognitive. These cognitive architectures have further been based on the idea of the human brain as the processor of information. The capacity related to solving of problems depends on the knowledge structures, which are present in the mind of humans [25].

AIED will navigate society toward Society 5.0. The term Society 5.0 was proposed by Japan in the 5th Science and Technology Basic Plan as a futuristic view of society. Society 5.0 will lead society toward economic development by overcoming the various problems and challenges prevalent in society by integrating technology, decision support systems, and physical factors present in the environment. With Society 5.0, technology can be integrated with the education sector through AI applications, intelligent decision support systems, and technology. Creating a society by integrating technology into daily life prepares skill sets for the coming generation to play their futuristic roles.

DOI: 10.1201/9781003397052-7

7.2 Definition of Artificial Intelligence

Artificial Intelligence refers to the things that are done through technology that otherwise could have been done by human intelligence [31]. Many Artificial Intelligence scientists and philosophers have proposed that Artificial Intelligence research can even find out how the human mind works. Artificial Intelligence refers to systems that are machine-based and that through various sets of objectives make various predictions, decisions, and recommendations, which further influence the real and virtual environment. Mostly these systems operate in an autonomous way and adapt certain behaviors after learning the context [43].

This definition is beneficial in various ways [19]. Firstly, it will not emphasize data but data-driven Artificial Intelligence techniques like neural networks and deep learning. Secondly, it considers human perspectives as it draws various predictions and recommendations on the basis of the objectives predefined by the system designer and the time of the design of the system.

7.3 Types of Artificial Intelligence

Artificial Intelligence is broadly classified into data-driven Artificial Intelligence and knowledge-based Artificial Intelligence.

7.3.1 Data-Driven Artificial Intelligence

In last decade, data-driven Artificial Intelligence had a crucial role for robotics and computer vision. With the help of a given set of large data, the computer prepares a model, which optimizes its predictions. It is based on the simple principle that the computer program makes the predictions, but if the predictions are wrong in the training phase, then it adjusts the program's behavior to minimize the error. Moreover, if the predictions made by the program are correct, then it adapts the behavior in such a way that the same predictions are made with higher probability.

The main problem associated with this is that the system needs to adjust its behavior and it is difficult to do so. It adjusts its behavior by using simple calculus methods. The change in the system output will take place if the parameters of the system are changed. For every parameter of the system, the direction of maximum change is known as the gradient. The parameters of the system can be improvised so that the system starts making predictions that are good. Many Artificial Intelligence systems can have parameters that can be adjusted, for example, Open AI's GPT-3 language model [4].

The inspiration behind the development of a computer system that can learn was the brain [36]. Artificial networks of neurons consist of neurons, which are computations with input and output systems where the system of a particular neuron is associated with the input of another neuron. Even a complex neural network is a linkage of an input and output system. Many Artificial Intelligence systems with multilayers have millions of connections among their computational neurons (Figures 7.1 and 7.2).

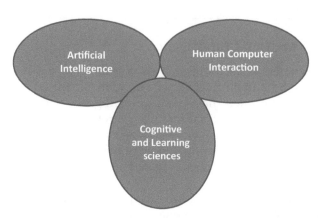

FIGURE 7.1
Artificial intelligence in education.

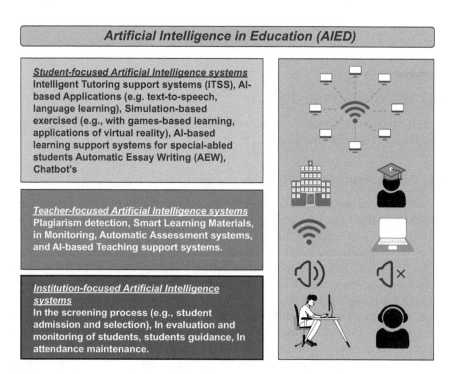

FIGURE 7.2
Comprehensive model of Artificial Intelligence systems in education.

7.3.2 Knowledge-Based Artificial Intelligence

The knowledge-based AI applications play a significant and imperative impact in the education sector [41]. The domain model in knowledge-based Artificial Intelligence contains a conceptual model that defines the study. Therefore, this has its application in education, but in the real world, the domain models are very expensive. These domain models are easy to develop in physics and mathematics, as they comprise a closed formal world. The knowledge-based intelligent tutoring system (ITS) is successful in subjects like physics, mathematics, etc. The knowledge-based Artificial Intelligence systems derive their knowledge from the conceptual structures made by humans. So, in knowledge-based Artificial Intelligence, a computer has been used as a text-processing machine or a simple programmed calculation. The knowledge-based Artificial Intelligence systems use an inference engine rather than an algorithm to derive their data.

7.4 Technical Aspects of Artificial Intelligence

Artificial Intelligence-aided education includes innovative learning tools, intelligent education, predictive analysis, and data analysis. It is imperative as it aids the learning process [43]. Intelligent education systems provide various instructions and feedback for teachers and students. These systems use various Artificial Intelligence technologies like machine learning to increase the efficiency of learning. Several techniques are incorporated in Artificial Intelligence systems for acquiring knowledge, that is, understanding and learning processes that are based on the concepts drawn from machine learning, data mining, and knowledge models.

7.5 AI Education Model

In an AI learning system, the learner model is important for improvising independent learning capabilities. Learners' thinking is analyzed, and their learning abilities are assessed. Then it is mapped with the knowledge to assess users' knowledge mastery. Learning modeling establishes various connections between the results of learning and certain factors that include resources and teaching behaviors.

The knowledge model creates the structure map related to knowledge, which includes detailed contents of learning that includes expert knowledge. The combination of the learning model and knowledge model provides various rules to access knowledge and provides instructions to tailor strategies and actions related to teaching.

7.6 AI in Education

AIED refers to Artificial Intelligence in education and its applications. For the purpose of this chapter, AIED tools are categorized as student-focused AIED, teacher-focused AIED, and institution-focused AIED [18].

7.6.1 Student-Focused Artificial Intelligence

Student-focused AIED refers to AI-assisted devices meant to support students in learning and knowledge-sharing processes. Often AIED includes tools and techniques that were not designed to aid students. However, due to their user-friendly features and wide acceptability, these tools, for example, Google Docs, drives, and sheets, are used as AI-assisted tools for students [13]. Further, social networking sites such as WhatsApp [49] and YouTube [52] have been extensively used as AIED tools by students.

These tools are referred to be repurposed for education and learning. Covid-19 had been a great push for the use of AIED in education, specifically for students. This chapter focuses on elaborating few of the AIED systems for students, which are briefed below.

7.6.1.1 Intelligent Tutoring System

ITS refers to an AI-based system that is a step-by-step guide to run structured objects in complex subjects. It is composed of numerous information, activities, puzzles, quizzes, and discussion forums. The student is guided to follow certain steps to engage in different activities, and his or her responses are captured as data points by the computer system. These attempts are then reflected in the faculty's dashboard to record and monitor the student's performance and progress. Gooru Navigator is the most popular and commonly used AI-based ITS, which acts as a Google map for education and learning [40].

7.6.1.2 AI-Assisted Applications

AI-assisted applications are widely available on online play stores and are meant to serve the needs of learners. SayHi app is an AI-assisted application that translates language based on the requirement of the learner [38]. Photomath is another example of an AI-assisted application, which helps students in solving complex mathematical problems.

However, the use of AI-assisted applications undermines learning in students by providing them with readymade solutions to problems [48]. Thus, the positive contribution of AI-assisted applications is still questionable (Table 7.1).

7.6.1.3 AI-Assisted Simulations

AI-assisted simulation refers to a digital simulated learning environment, which includes reality that is virtual (VR), reality related to augmentation (AR), and gamification tools. AI-assisted AR creates 3D models of organic molecules to impart a better understanding of the subject to students in the case of Chemistry subject [3]. Google has designed numerous AR and VR pertaining to different education contexts. Additionally, the use of AI game-based learning is a modern attempt to engage students in the learning process [26].

7.6.1.4 AI to Support Specially Abled Students

Many of the student-focused AIEDs such as ITS have been further extended to provide support to specially abled students with some learning disabilities [2]. This research on

TABLE 7.1

Major Scenarios in Artificial Intelligence and Key Technologies

Scenarios in AI-based education systems	AI techniques
Assessment of students and schools	Adaptive learning method and personalized learning approach
Grade system and evaluation of exams	Image recognition and prediction system
Personalized intelligent	Learning analytics and data mining
Smart school	Face recognition and space recognition
Online and mobile remote education	Real-time analysis and edge computing

AI-based robotics for educating autistic students has been a booming area of study [1]. Certain AI applications are utilized in translating text to speech to serve students with disabilities.

7.6.1.5 Automatic Essay Writing

Essay writing has been a major component of assessment in the education system to date. GPT-3 is one example of an AI-based platform, which provides easy online content for essay writing [14]. There are certain organizations operating commercially and offering automatic essay writing (AEW) tools to students, although the content generated by AEW is found to be superficial and nonsensical in certain cases [29].

7.6.1.6 Chatbots

AI-assisted chatbots are widely used in educational contexts these days [24, 34]. Chatbots provide ongoing support and guidance to students pertaining to assignments, accommodation, etc. Ada is one of the common chatbots designed by IBM Watson [23] and is extensively used in the education sector. Another AI-assisted chatbot for virtual teaching assistants is used to answer students' queries in classrooms automatically without any human intervention [12]. Chatbot provides great support to online educational institutes, especially where the number of students is large. However, the functioning of chatbot relies on the inbuilt database, and anything that is not covered in the database will not be answered by chatbot in that case [18].

7.6.2 Teacher-Focused Artificial Intelligence

As we have discussed in the section on student-focused Artificial Intelligence, students use the intelligent tutoring system. In this system, the student gains knowledge through the system itself, but the teacher needs to track the performance of the student as well. This is possible with a new approach using augmented reality in which glasses are worn by the teachers and the teachers are able to superimpose dashboard-like systems just to check what the student is doing [20]. This is although a solution to a problem caused by the Artificial Intelligence system only. Most of the dashboard-enabled AI systems and ITS are student-focused, but the teacher-focused Artificial Intelligence systems consist of six major possibilities, which are classroom monitoring, plagiarism detection, Artificial Intelligence teaching assistants, automatic assessment, smart curation of learning material, and classroom orchestration.

7.6.2.1 Classroom Monitoring

Many commercially available Artificial Intelligence computer systems are available that help in classroom-based monitoring of the students. One of the artificial systems helps in analyzing the focus of the students when they are in class. It tries to analyze if the student is paying attention to what the teacher is discussing [27]. In another application, students are required to wear electroencephalography (EEG) headsets, which allow the teacher to map the brain activity of the students so that they can track their attentiveness in class [35]. For instance, the US-based company, BrainCo provides a system that monitors the brain activity of its pupils, and the data is presented on the dashboard. The system helps in analyzing the brain activity of all the students [33].

Many such headsets are used in Chinese schools where the mental activity of the students is being monitored by the teachers and parents [15]. However, the usage of these systems is controversial as it is not certain that they will be able to do what they claim to do [44]. On the contrary, the Chinese teachers feel that these headbands have made the students more disciplined and focused on their studies. They have started paying more attention in the class and have started working even harder [46]. Many Artificial Intelligence-assisted systems also monitor the movement of the students in the campus area, content downloaded from learning platforms, what they buy from the cafeteria, and much more.

7.6.2.2 Plagiarism Detection

Plagiarism software is increasingly being used by teachers and researchers. These software use machine learning methods, and their usage has increased drastically in the last decade. The main leader among plagiarism-checking software is Turnitin [42].

In this age of information overload, there is no dearth of content on the Internet. There are many Artificial Intelligence systems that help in finding quality data over the network, and this can be helpful to teachers. Research tools, such as X5GON, and commercial tools, such as Clever Owl, are helpful in finding quality content on the Internet [51, 6]. These tools are really insightful for the faculty as well as the researchers as they help them to increase their knowledge and share the same with the students. Also, they help in scraping the web and finding the queries of the teachers.

7.6.2.3 Automotive Summative Assessment

Artificial Intelligence system of automotive summative assessment is helpful to teachers as it helps in evaluating students' assignments and homework [45]. This automated assessment is also known as auto-grader and is also a well-known research area to study. Some of the automotive summative assessment tools claim to assess the marks of the student with ninety percent accuracy [22], although the assessment of the student marks that are at high stake remains controversial.

7.6.2.4 AI Teaching and Assessment Assistant

All AIED reduces the teacher's time and effort, allowing them to concentrate on their functional roles-related work [39, 17]. The Artificial Intelligence assistant helps in enhancing the teacher's expertise and skill sets. This commercial tool helps students in their assessment practices [14]. It can help the teacher to add phrases to the checked and marked assessments, and these can be reused. Here the teacher is assessing the student, not the Artificial Intelligence system.

7.6.2.5 Classroom Orchestration

It refers to the management of various activities by the teacher for a group of individuals or the whole class that includes curriculum, time, assessment, space, and energy [8]. Past research asserts that classroom orchestration will help teachers in managing well and disseminating imperative information and knowledge in the classroom.

7.6.3 Institution-Focused Artificial Intelligence

Educational institutions have gradually accepted Artificial Intelligence as an effective tool for automating several functions like admission, evaluation, course planning, scheduling, timetable, financial planning, etc. Algorithmic decision-making (ADM) is becoming very important in all walks of life. AI and algorithmic decision-making applications in education have increased manifold because they can efficiently process a large amount of data, and this data helps in improved decision-making. Some major functions where the AI applications are increased are as follows:

7.6.3.1 In Admissions

Admission and the criteria associated with AI are a crucial function for any institute or university. The AI-based decision support systems and technologies provide the decision support system by generating, processing, and presenting the processed information in making the decision regarding the screening of students. These intelligent support systems aid in the admission and selection of students in higher education. The intelligent support systems have received positive feedback from the decision-makers. The application and use of intelligent decision support systems (IDSS) are also suited to the institute or university decision [47].

In higher education, the AI-based system helps in the mining of relevant data, and these decision support systems and applications will make robust the mechanism of admission and screening of students. This will provide decision support by generating, synthesizing, and processing relevant information to improve the qualitative factors in education scenarios [46].

7.6.3.2 Attendance-Record maintenance

Artificial Intelligence-based face detection-based techniques gained popularity during and after the Covid-19 pandemic. A systematic learning architecture on this technology is developing fast and gaining momentum. This technology will help in designing an efficient and robust mechanism for monitoring the attendance of students [37].

7.6.3.3 Automated Assessment Systems

Traditional and manual evaluations require time, patience, and effort from evaluators. Automated assessment techniques are becoming one of the most prominent and promising applications of AI for educational institutions [32]. Automated assessment systems provide brief feedback and guidance to students to improve their knowledge and skills.

These scoring algorithm systems are designed in such a manner that these can meet the needs of students and teachers in various tasks, for example, writing exams, assignments, and other tasks that are usually performed by the student and evaluated by the teacher. Assessment systems provide a support system to faculties to lessen their workload as well as to help them to focus on research and other important work to extend their academic performance. Ideally, these AI-based systems provide support to evaluators as these can help to grade quickly, based on the predefined criteria.

7.6.3.4 Student Support and Guidance

AI-based applications are also growing in use in student support, counseling, and guidance. Institutions utilize machine learning and its algorithm in this function of student support and guidance. AI-based tools help students make course recommendations for their majors, minor subjects, and career pathways—tasks that career counsellors have historically handled. These applications are also guiding and assisting students who are struggling with subjects like chemistry, mathematics, etc. [54].

Educational institutions can use the data about students to support them financially through microloans or advances when they need them at the last minute. AI applications support students through financial aid, as the AI support system is based on predictive analytics that gives early warning to systems.

AI applications are analyzing huge data—academic, nonacademic, and operational—to identify the students who are at the risk of failing or dropping out or dealing with mental health issues.

7.6.3.5 Facial Recognition Applications and Predictive Analytics

AI applications use facial recognition application to capture and monitor students' facial expressions. These systems help faculties in monitoring and tracking students' behavior through their reactions and facial expressions. In this way, AI applications assist faculties to make their strategic plans for better learner outcomes and student engagement.

7.6.3.6 Chatbots

Chatbots are the dialogue-based systems developed through AI-based applications [7]. They are also known as dialogue systems or conversational agents [21]. These AI applications are very helpful in responding to students with a conversational tone. These chatbots assist students in registration, especially for any query residing in the mind of students and their parents. A text-based Chabot system used at Georgia State University called "Pounce" assists students in the registration and admission process and in financial aid and in guiding and counseling them [16]. Chatbots can answer the students' queries about the schedule of their class or support students in mental health issues as well. AI-generated systems remind students about deadlines, to register for classes, to turn in assignments, and to pay their fees. AI-based applications are widely used in detecting plagiarism in assignments [28].

Applications of AI are positively affecting students' and faculty's educational experiences. These applications are aiding individuals in effectively managing the obstacles encountered in the areas of delivery and instructional matters. However, AI cannot be a substitute for human interaction [9]. However, its applications can be of great timesaving and can aid in building strong cognitive mechanisms for educational institutes and for the academic fraternity.

7.7 Future of Artificial Intelligence in Education

Artificial Intelligence used in the sector of education has grown from USD 537.3 million to USD 3.68 billion globally in 2023. Various Artificial Intelligence technologies like machine learning are used in education to increase the performance of various students.

According to the World Economic Firm, it is estimated that by 2025, a large number of firms will adopt technologies like machine learning to enhance learning.

7.8 Challenges

The use of intelligence created artificially in education has opened various opportunities for designing new and innovative activities of learning and developing learning applications that involve technologies, but devising such activities still remains a challenge as it requires a lot of human intervention.

Similarly, the development of intelligent tutorial systems requires computer skills and techniques related to the simulation of human expert intelligence. These problems arise as Artificial Intelligence is totally dependent on technology.

In addition, the problem arises when AI learning systems that have been trained on the students at a particular university in California might not reflect the same level of accuracy for the students in other parts of the country or a different country. Moreover, the system of Artificial Intelligence that has been made for the millennials might not have the same efficacy for the students of other age groups.

7.9 Conclusion

The intervention of Artificial intelligence in teaching will help in increasing the quality of education and will be helpful for teachers and students. This will help in navigating from Society 4.0 to Society 5.0. With Society 5.0, technology can be integrated with the education sector through AI applications, intelligent decision support systems, and technology. Teachers can benefit from the systems that help in assessing the marks of the students and can invest their time in other functional activities that are constructive in nature. They can even assess the mental activity of their students using the EEG technique and find out the attention level of the students in class. Students can take the help of chatbots which will provide them with support and guidance related to assignments, accommodation, and examinations. They can also benefit from smart tutorial systems and asynchronous learning. So, we can say that Artificial Intelligence related to Education is not only an integration of education and AI, but it is also an integration of human knowledge, culture, and cognition. Artificial Intelligence will remain a major technological issue in education for the next many decades.

References

1. Alabdulkareem, A., Alhakbani, N., & Al-Nafjan, A. (2022). A systematic review of research on robot-assisted therapy for children with Autism. *Sensors*, 22(3), 944. https://doi.org/10.3390/s22030944

2. Barua, P. D., Vicnesh, J., Gururajan, R., Oh, S. L., Palmer, E., Azizan, M. M., Kadri, N. A., & Acharya, U. R. (2022). Artificial intelligence enabled personalised assistive tools to enhance education of children with neurodevelopmental disorders—A review. *International Journal of Environmental Research and Public Health, 19*(3), 1192.

3. Behmke, D., Kerven, D., Lutz, R., Paredes, J., Pennington, R., Brannock, E., Deiters, M., Rose, J., & Stevens, K. (2018). Augmented reality chemistry: Transforming 2-D molecular representations into interactive 3-D structures. *Proceedings of the Interdisciplinary STEM Teaching and Learning Conference ,2* (3). DOI: 10.20429/stem.2018.020103.

4. Brown, T. B., Mann, B., Ryder, N., Subbiah, M., Kaplan, J., Dhariwal, P., Neelakantan, A., Shyam, P., Sastry, G., Askell, A., Agarwal, S., Herbert-Voss, A., Krueger, G., Henighan, T., Child, R., Ramesh, A., Ziegler, D. M., Wu, J., Winter, C., & Amodei, D. (2020). *Language Models are Few-Shot Learners.* Cornell University Press. http://arxiv.org/abs/2005.14165

5. Chen, X., Xie, H., Zou, D., & Hwang, G.-J. (2020). Application and theory gaps during the rise of artificial intelligence in education. *Computers and Education: Artificial Intelligence, 1,* 100002. https://doi.org/10.1016/j. caeai.2020.100002

6. Clever Owl. (2022). Clever Owl. https://cleve rowl.educat ion/#about

7. Dignum, V. (2018). Ethics in artificial intelligence: Introduction to the special issue. *Ethics and Information Technology, 20*(1), 1–3.

8. Dillenbourg, P., Zufferey, G., Alavi, H., Jermann, P., Do-Lenh, S., Bonnard, Q., Cuendet, S., & Kaplan, F. (2011). Classroom orchestration: The third circle of usability. In *Computer Support for Collaborative Learning Conference. CSCL2011 Proceedings* (Vol. 1, pp. 510–517). Springer.

9. Dishon, G. (2017). New data, old tensions: Big data, personalized learning, and the challenges of progressive education. *Theory and Research in Education, 15*(3), 272–289.

10. Gardner, H. (1985). *The Mind's New Science: Cognitive Revolution in the Computer Age.* Basic Books.

11. GMI. (2022). *AI in Education Market Size & Share, Growth Forecast 2022–2030.* Global Market Insights Inc. https://www.gminsights.com/industry-analysis/artificial-intelligence-ai-in-education-market

12. Goel, A. K., & Joyner, D. A. (2017). Using AI to teach AI: Lessons from an online AI class. *AI Magazine, 38*(2), 48–59. https://doi.org/10.1609/aimag.v38i2.2732.

13. Google. (2022). Google Drive. Website for Personal Cloud Storage & File Sharing Platform. https://www.google.co.uk/drive/

14. GPT-3. (2020, September 8). A robot wrote this entire article. Are you scared yet, human? *The Guardian.* https://www.theguardian.com/commentisfree/2020/sep/08/robot-wrote-this-article-gpt-3

15. Graide. (2022). Graide. https://www.graide.co.uk/

16. Greenhow, C., Galvin, S., Brandon, D., & Askari, E. (2020). A decade of research on K-12 teaching and teacher learning with social media: Insights on the state-of-the-field. *Teachers College Record: The Voice of Scholarship in Education, 122*(6), 1–7.

17. Guilherme, A. (2019). AI and education: The importance of teacher and student relations. *AI and Society, 34*(1), 47–54. https://doi.org/10.1007/s00146-017-0693-8

18. Holmes, W., & Tuomi, I. (2022). State of the art and practice in AI in education. *European Journal of Education, 57*(4), 542–570. https://doi.org/10.1111/ejed.1253

19. Holmes, W., Porayska-Pomsta, K., Holstein, K., Sutherland, E., Baker, T., Buckingham Shum, S., Santos, O. C., Rodrigo, M. M. T., Cukorova, M., Bittencourt, I. I., & Koedinger, K. (2021). Ethics of AI in education: Towards a community- wide framework. *International Journal of Artificial Intelligence in Education, 32,* 504–526. https://doi.org/10.1007/s40593-021-00239-1

20. Holstein, K., Hong, G., Tegene, M., McLaren, B. M., & Aleven, V. (2018). The classroom as a dashboard: Co-designing wearable cognitive augmentation for K-12 teachers. In *Proceedings of the 8th International Conference on Learning Analytics and Knowledge - LAK '18* (pp. 79–88). Association for Computing Machinery. https://doi.org/10.1145/31703 58.3170377

21. Hrastinski, S., Olofsson, A. D., Arkenback, C., Ekström, S., Ericsson, E., Fransson, G., Jaldemark, J., Ryberg, T., Öberg, L., Fuentes, A., Gustafsson, U., Humble, N., Mozelius, P., Sundgren, M., & Utterberg, M. (2019). Critical imaginaries and reflections on artificial intelligence and robots in postdigital K-12 education. *Postdigit Scientiae Educatia, 1,* 427–445.

22. Hsu, S., Li, T. W., Zhang, Z., Fowler, M., Zilles, C., & Karahalios, K. (2021). Attitudes surrounding an imperfect AI autograder. In *Proceedings of the 2021 CHI Conference on Human Factors in Computing Systems* (pp. 1–15). Association for Computing Machinery. https://doi.org/10.1145/34117 64.3445424

23. Hussain, A. (2017). Ada—Bolton College's latest digital assistant. Blogtext. http://www.aftab-hussain.com/ada.html

24. Hwang, G.-J., & Chang, C.-Y. (2021). A review of opportunities and challenges of chatbots in education. *Interactive Learning Environments*, 1–14. https://doi.org/10.1080/10494820.2021.1952615

25. Koedinger, K. R., Corbett, A. T., & Perfetti, C. (2012). The knowledge- learning- instruction framework: Bridging the science- practice chasm to enhance robust student learning. *Cognitive Science*, 36(5), 757–798. https://doi.org/10.1111/j.1551-6709.2012.01245.x

26. LaPierre, J. (2021, January 18). Educational games and AI. Blogtext. Filament games. https://www.filamentgames.com/blog/educational-games-and-ai/

27. Lieu, J. (2018). Eyes to the front camera: Chinese facial recognition tech targets inattentive students. Blogtext. Mashable. https://masha ble.com/article/Chinese-facial-recognition-class

28. Marcinkowski, F., Kieslich, K., Starke, C., & Lünich, M. (2020, January). Implications of AI (un-) fairness in higher education admissions: The effects of perceived AI (un-) fairness on exit, voice and organizational reputation. In *Proceedings of the 2020 Conference on Fairness, Accountability, and Transparency* (pp. 122–130).

29. Marcus, G., & Davis, E. (2020). GPT-3, bloviator: OpenAI's language generator has no idea what it's talking about. *MIT Technology Review*. https://www.technologyreview.com/2020/08/22/1007539/gpt3-openai-languagegeneratorartificial-intelligence-ai-opinion/

30. Miao, F., & Holmes, W. (2021). *AI and Education: Guidance for Policy-Makers*. UNESCO. https://unesd oc.unesco.org/ ark:/48223/ pf0000376709

31. Minsky, M. (Ed.). (1969). *Semantic Information Processing*. The MIT Press.

32. Murphy, R. F. (2019). Artificial intelligence applications to support k–12 teachers and teaching: A review of promising applications, challenges, and risks. *Perspective*, 1–20. https://doi.org/10.7249/PE315

33. NeuroMaker. (2022). NeuroMaker BCI. NeuroMaker. https://staging4.neuromakerstem.com/neuromaker-bci

34. Pérez, J. Q., & Daradoumis, T., & Puig, J. M. M. (2020). Rediscovering the use of chatbots in education: A systematic literature review. *Computer Applications in Engineering Education*, 28(3). https://doi.org/10.1002/cae.22326

35. Poulsen, A. T., Kamronn, S., Dmochowski, J., Parra, L. C., & Hansen, L. K. (2017). EEG in the classroom: Synchronised neural recordings during video presentation. *Scientific Reports*, 7, 43916. https://doi.org/10.1038/srep43916

36. Rosenblatt, F. (1958). The Perceptron: A probabilistic model for information storage and organization in the brain. *Psychological Review*, 65(6), 386–408.

37. Saraf, I., & Iqbal, J. (2019). Generalized multi-release modelling of software reliability growth models from the perspective of two types of imperfect debugging and change point. *Quality and Reliability Engineering International*, 35(7), 2358–2370.

38. SayHi. (2022). SayHi translate. https://www.sayhi.com/en/translate/. Amazon Inc. Bull, S., & Kay, J. (2010). Open learner models. In R. Nkambou, J. Bourdeau, & R. Mizoguchi (Eds.), *Advances in intelligent tutoring systems* (pp. 301–322). Springer. https://doi.org/10.1007/978-3-642-14363-2_15

39. Selwyn, N. (2019). *Should Robots Replace Teachers?: AI and the Future of Education*. Polity.

40. Songer, N. B., Newstadt, M. R., Lucchesi, K., & Ram, P. (2020). Navigated learning: An approach for differentiated classroom instruction built on learning science and data science foundations. *Human Behavior and Emerging Technologies*, 2(1), 93–105. https://doi.org/10.1002/hbe2.169

41. Tuomi, I. (2018). The impact of artificial intelligence on learning, teaching, and education. European Union Joint Research Centre. Publications Office of the European Union. https://publi cations.jrc.ec.europa.eu/repos itory/ bitst ream/ JRC11 3226/jrc11 3226_jrcb4_the_ impact_of_artif icial_intelligence_on_learn ing_final_2.pdf

42. Turnitin. (2022). Turnitin. https://turni tin.com
43. UNICEF. (2021). Policy guidance on AI for children. Author. https://www.unicef.org/globalin-sight/media/2356/file/unicef-global-insight-policy-guidance-ai-children-2.0-2021.pdf.pdf
44. Rus, V., D'Mello, S., Hu, X., & Graesser, A. (2013, September). Recent advances in conversational intelligent tutoring systems. *AI Magazine*, 34(3), 42–54.
45. Bresfelean, V. P. et al., Towards the development of decision support in academic environments. In *Proceedings of the ITI 2009, 31st International Conference on Information Technology Interface*, June 22–25, 2009, Cavtat, Croatia.
46. Vohra, R. (2011). Intelligent decision support systems for admission management in higher education institutes. *International Journal of Artificial Intelligence & Applications (IJAIA)*, 2(4, October), Available at SSRN: https://ssrn.com/abstract=3663918
47. Wall Street Journal. (2019). How China is using artificial intelligence in classrooms. Video. Author. https://www.youtu be.com/watch ?v=JMLsH I8aV0g
48. Watters, A. (2015, March 12). A brief history of calculators in the classroom. Blogtext. http://hackeducation.com(2015/03/12)/calculators
49. WhatsApp. (2022). WhatsApp. WhatsApp.Com. https://www.whatsapp.com/
50. Williamson, B., & Eynon, R. (2020). Historical threads, missing links, and future directions in AI in education. *Learning, Media and Technology*, 45(3), 223–235. https://doi.org/10.1080/17439884.2020.1798995
51. X5GON. (2022). X5GON. Website. [Artificial Intelligence and Open Educational Resources]. https://www.x5gon.org/
52. YouTube. (2022). YouTube. https://www.youtube.com/
53. Zawacki-Richter, O., Marín, V. I., Bond, M., & Gouverneur, F. (2019). Systematic review of research on artificial intelligence applications in higher education – Where are the educators? *International Journal of Educational Technology in Higher Education*, 16(1), 39. https://doi.org/10.1186/s41239-019-0171-0
54. Zeide, E. (2019). Artificial intelligence in higher education: Applications, promise and perils, and ethical questions (summer 2019). *Educause Review*, 54(3). https://ssrn.com/abstract=4320049

8

Applications and Use of AI in e-Commerce: Opportunities and Challenges in Society 5.0

Nitish Kumar Ojha, Archana Pandita, Nikhil VP, and Edip Senyurek

8.1 Introduction

8.1.1 Brief History

The use of artificial intelligence (AI) in financial services started basically in the late 1950s as reported by John et al. [1] in his research paper. In a university conference at Dartmouth College, when a mathematics professor named McCarthy coined the term "Artificial Intelligence" for the first time, it was hard to believe and to predict the effect of computers on human daily life, specifically in financial services [2]. McCarthy established the fact that after World War II the world is going to see a new field of science. Professor McCarthy and his coauthor Prof. Claude Shannon, in a further paper [3], established the fact that automata subject will be the basis for machine learning (ML) and machine learning will play a key role in major part of automation in every industry by the term "Computational Intelligence or Artificial Intelligence" [1]. If we further study the research papers of that era, then it has been verified and well predicted that statistics will rule over natural language processing, and it is obvious because the logic behind science works. These days, AI is available and implementable everywhere step by step where intelligent activity happens and the human brain can learn that activity. This learning gave a good subject area where AI is completely implemented nowadays, that is, "Planning" [2]. We read reports that Deep Blue had beaten human chess champions just by planning and matching all the rules that are required at a certain point of time in a move. The research moved further and improved more, and a better modeling-based prediction was possible when Prof. Bayes gave the idea of Bayesian theorem by deriving it from conditional probability [3]. Basically, he established the mathematical logic behind common-sense psychology that was also discussed by Prof. McCarthy in his research paper 10 years back [4]. With the help of Bayesian statistics, it became very easy to predict the accurate assessment, which is highly used these days in the automation industry.

8.1.2 Birth of AI-based System for Financial Services

From 1970 to 1980, the evolvement of many mathematical techniques improved AI in many ways, i.e., Prolog language, Artificial Neural Network (ANN), language translation and transliteration, bounded rationality, automated decision-making, etc. [5]. Bounded rationality played a major role in deciding the fate of machine-based models being used for decision-making in financial services for the long term. The breakthrough came when the first "expert systems" machine was launched practically for commercial activities [6]. Considering one example of cost–benefit analysis, humans cannot make optimum decision if not enough information is available, but instead of that, they select an option that fulfills their adequacy criteria as it depends on the cognitive capability of each human mind. "Rationality as optimization," [7] which views decision-making as a process of finding an optimal choice given the available information, is complemented by the idea of bounded rationality. Further research in this way leads to the development of a better decision-making model provided that enough and accurate information is available at the required time [8].

This led to the discovery of the smart financial expert system "Alacrity" in 1987, which was used to interpret financial statements and models. More research studies are being carried out, and they rely on the basic fact that AI excels at formal logic which allows it to select exact algorithms depending on the specific data type we have provided as input [9]. In financial services, the following data types can be analyzed with high accuracy with the help of AI:

1. Numbers
2. Audio
3. Images
4. Texts

Most of the companies working in the field of financial sectors are now very much specific about the data type they process in-house activities [10]. This technology-supported journey has been so much long that till 1990, at least 75% of all the companies listed in the Fortune 1000 were running at least one project involving AI for sure. Finally, at the end of 1990, most companies shifted their research toward the use of AI for better detection of ongoing financial frauds, and for this, previous history of users was of utmost need so that further research for prevention purposes could be done. Thus, AI played a major role in this direction [11], either collection of relevant data or detection of anomalous activity leading to fraud detection. A very common name in this field is Hodgkinson and Walker who made an expert system for making decisions for loan grant facilities to bank customers depending on their previous records of transactions [12].

8.2 Use of AI in Financial Services

Majorly AI is a highly used technology these days in almost all the services and sectors of the financial organization. The focus of AI revolves around two major points:

1. Generation of new areas of market
2. Minimizing the risk factors

8.2.1 Generation of New Areas of Market

AI helps to understand the market better depending on the logic used and the data availability [13]. It leverages the analysis part of planning department while searching the pattern of customers whenever they do any new transaction. These days many recommendation-based systems are easily available on many banking portals, which suggest users where to invest at what rate and for how much long time. Deployment of a machine learning algorithm makes the logic interpretation and inference easy for making any rational decision. Collecting rules, logics, and methods and finding the actual pattern of the users enable companies to understand and analyze their market environment better autonomously toward pre-determined outcomes. In many reports, the World Economic Forum (WEF) has reported many times that almost one out of every three financial companies is using AI to find the new emerging area of growth [14]. One of the major path-breaking technologies being used by banking organizations is eKYC (electronic Know Your Customer form – a type of identity identification form) where people located in remote areas can document and do ID verification irrespective of lack of resources [15]. This improved and helped the economy at a large scale while boosting the transfer of money, to send and receive funds across country borders including foreign exchange too. McKinsey reported in their finding that many obstacles are still there from validation and verification points of view as the software is still like a black box (as it comes from third-party vendor), so supervisory control and privacy are also playing a major challenge [16]. Saving deposits, remittances, digital wallets, online purchases, etc., are some key players considering which AI is being used by banking companies to spread their business in new places. The growth in value and volume of online transactions is increasing at an exponential rate, and this is possible online because of minimizing the digital divide and increasing the customer base [17].

8.2.2 Minimizing the Risk Factors

As the volume of online transactions is increasing, the possibility of attacks is also increasing. The biggest challenges in online transactions in every financial organization are as follows:

1. Fraud and chargeback
2. Multicurrency and payment method issues
3. Technical integration and on-time response
4. Cross-border transaction
5. Technological illiteracy
6. Vulnerable resources
7. Data security

Considering all the above issues, banking organizations are in continuous endeavor to minimize the risk evolved as a throughput of these challenges; however, the war is still not won [18]. Banking organizations are continuously improving their strategy to fight back against the different types of hacks and fraud being reported at their end such as they are using EMV (Europay, Mastercard, and Visa), chip-based ATM cards, email-based OTP (One-Time Password), auto expiry OTP, long number based OTP, by default disabling international transactions, disabling of big transactions, complete deployment of compliance, i.e., PCIDSS (*Payment Card Industry Data Security Standard*), COBIT (Control Objectives for Information and Related Technologies), ISO standard, etc.; however, more has to be done to resolve the issue of risk factors as it reduces the trust of the customers in digital services in financial operations [19].

8.3 Benefits of AI in Financial Services

8.3.1 Trading Algorithms

The adoption of AI in financial services has improved the results a lot and specifically trading operations have really benefitted from AI. The main goal of enhancing and catalyzing the economic process is readily made possible only because of AI. IHC Markit report identifies that in the year 2018, financial organizations were using AI-based technology at least in each sector closing to $41.1 billion, and by the next 10 years, this industry will touch $300 billion. Depending on how it is going to be implemented and the constraints of the environment, AI will have a tremendous effect on the growth of the financial industry. These are many parameters that are easily achievable with the help of AI in financial organizations [20].

8.3.2 Equating the Price Value of New Products

Price optimization is a new field where AI is helping a lot and lots of industries are using the historical data of customers to decide the price of a new commodity-based product, depending on the purchasing capacity of the customer [21]. This value can be adjusted while measuring the competitor's price for the same product. Many statistical analysis-based tools are used for this purpose which works on several parameters for understanding of the market demand, predicting the success of launch, and tracking the sale and upcoming demand in the market [22].

8.3.3 Minimizing the Risk Emerging for New Products

According to the Harvard Business Report, out of 30,000 products launched yearly 95% of products fail in the market. The reason behind this is a lack of prior exhaustive study particularly the risk involved for that product [23]. Financial risk refers to the chances of occurrence of loss, which occurred while delivering the product in this case, and here the major reason behind this loss may be the lack of proper study while making the investment decision. Categorically AI is helping to minimize the following types of risks to any product:

a) **Market Risk**: It is related to the risk that arises because of the change in the dynamics of the market because of certain factors. There are several tools to analyze and minimize the market risk, i.e., QRAFT, KAVOUT, EquBot, Trendspider, Sigmoidal, etc.

b) **Credit Risk**: Most of the insurance sector-related companies are these days using AI exhaustively to understand any substantial risk that occurs to customers as well as in the market affecting the credit of the risk. The most recent example is the case of Adani Group where the credit risk was analyzed by a third-party independent company named Hindenburg Inc., and later on, it became a catastrophic event as market losses swelled to over $100 billion as shelved share sale spook investors [24]. These days financial companies are using AI-based tools and algorithms to understand and analyze credit risk, i.e., heterogeneous algorithms, homogeneous algorithms, individual classifiers, Stacked Average Hill Climbing algorithms (HCEF), Bagging, Random Forest (RF), Boosting Algorithm, etc. [25]. Figure 8.1 represents the algorithms being used in Black Box models in a timeline journey.

c) **Liquidity Risk**: Risk relating to the loss evolved through the inability to settle the payment in a timely manner. Liquidity risk arises mostly because of banks' inability while any threatening factor is there on their financial positions. Many financial organizations are implementing AI-based algorithms through a variety of software according to their need [28]. AI helps not only in a general way but also in many typical case scenarios, i.e., prediction of loss and benefit in next quarters considering the history of liquidity in early quarters when foreign currency balances are falling down, prediction of cash flow in the market while analyzing the previous cash receipts, and calculation of risk in all sectors of a company for over drafting facility when the company has cash surplus. With the help of AI/ML tools, cash flow predictions can be projected easily in a timely manner with accuracy for a short term [29]. By conducting a more in-depth analysis of historical data of users, all stakeholders, different running services, and businesses will be able to predict cash flows more accurately by season or in an emerging region [30]. As a result, the organization will be able to focus less on essential tasks like managing accounts payable, managing the traditional loss, anticipating risk-free and free cash flow closing, and adjusting the payment campaign budget for a long term [31]. AI also helps organization in preventing the mass adoptions of the early customs, which may be risk for a small organization particularly as AI focuses on the relevancy of the services while predicting the benefits and calculating loss. The most common applications being used these days in financial organizations for risk calculation and optimization are SEON fraud fighters, Backstop, Fraud.net 4.0, Socure, Riskalyze, Essential ERM, LogicGate, etc. [32].

d) **Operational Risk**: Many AI-based software are used for optimizing the operational risk too. In a particular scenario, in a banking organization, a customer profile may be risky if he is found to be less educated and nonresident so if he is applying for a car loan then in this case scenario, it is quite easy to model the risk profile of such customer using Shapley value analysis, which is implemented in many AI-based software [33]. Considering the data analysis of many customers, this conclusion was drawn that less professionally educated, younger people with smaller loans are highly risky for car loans while they are less risky for educational loans for a longer time. Table 8.1 depicts the same finding in a separate study conducted by Phaure et al. at Deloitte Inc., UK [34]. The Shapley value analysis works on the selection of several features of the customers while making their profile according to their age, education, and requirement of the specific type of loan.

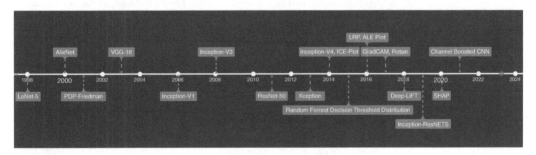

FIGURE 8.1
Timeline of algorithms developed and used in black box approach [26].

TABLE 8.1

Digital Payment Application and Their Parametric Comparison

S. No.	Application	Pros	Cons
1.	Apple Pay	1. Almost all payment functionalities are possible. 2. History-based tracking of payments is available. 3. 3D Security is well integrated and implemented. 4. Data is highly secured in case of any key-loss so inaccessible to others.	1. It is only available for Apple devices. 2. Contactless payment not available at many places makes it less popular. 3. Regular update makes it vulnerable and obsolete for old devices. 4. Not available for bitcoin purchase in many countries.
2.	Cash Pay	1. Available for bitcoin payments. 2. Very good level of security implemented. 3. Not available for international transactions.	1. Not easily compatible with other tools. 2. Commission-based payment mechanism is present. 3. Data storage is not fully transparent.
3.	Dwolla	1. Highly featureful software. 2. Online technical support is readily available. 3. Security mechanism is readily available. 4. Token-based coins are available.	1. Multiple tariff plan is available which makes it quite confusing. 2. Credit card-based linking is not available. 3. Not available in many countries. 4. Class-wise user profile is quite.
4.	Google Play	1. Fully integrated with all your Gmail account. 2. Highly secured application. 3. Highly available as the default application in most Android phones. 4. Fast processing transaction. 5. Customer care is not readily available.	1. Only available for Android-based OS devices. 2. Mostly not unavailable for contactless payment. 3. Not easily integratable with other online payment systems, i.e., BharatPay.
5.	PayPal	1. Smooth Registration mechanism. 2. Customer care mechanism is readily available. 3. Available for most types of devices. 4. Highly secured application and data storage. 5. Available on almost all websites easily and all over the world.	1. Multi-fact-based authentication is not readily available. 2. Customized user profiling is not available. 3. Transaction speed is slow.
6.	Samsung Wallet	1. Comes pre-installed in most of the Galaxy devices. 2. User registration and activation is readily available. 3. Highly fast and secure application. 4. Token-based mapping of currency and its storage available.	1. Works only on Samsung devices. 2. Cannot be recharged with ATM. 3. Mostly available in the tier-1 country.
7.	Venmo	1. Easily available and easily interactable with all platforms. 2. Commission-based payment mechanism is available. 3. Active customer care response is present. 4. Easily connectable with credit card and debit card.	1. Only available in the USA. 2. Commission-based system is highly discouraged. 3. Privacy setting is not transparent.

(Continued)

TABLE 8.1 CONTINUED

Digital Payment Application and Their Parametric Comparison

S. No.	Application	Pros	Cons
8.	Zelle	Freely available. Easy to install and smooth to use. Highly secured and storage mechanism is managed. Double authentication is available making it very secure. Customer care is readily available.	1. Privacy is not transparent. 2. Limitations are there for a particular amount of money for transfer. 3. Tracking is not easily available. 4. User profiling is not available.
9.	Walmart Pay	1. QR code-based transfer is easily integrated. 2. NF-based payment is easily available. 3. Easily available for prepaid and postpaid customers. 4. Customer care is readily available.	1. Credit card integrity is not readily available. 2. Only available in the USA. 3. Only available for payment in Walmart stores.
10.	Amazon Pay	1. Transaction is quite low. 2. Users' data is stored in a secured manner. 3. High level of security is available. 4. Available with almost all departmental stores.	1. Privacy setting is not transparent. 2. Customer care support is not readily available. 3. Integration and implementation is easily available with other tools.

8.3.4 Providing Liquidity to the Organization

Artificial intelligence is changing the components of financial organizations and changing its role into Business Intelligence. AI enhances the liquidity management and timely execution of orders with minimum inclusion of risk and resources [35]. AI led to consolidation and, as a result, illiquidity at times of stress and flash collapses. Large sales, sudden declines because of inherent vulnerability, loss occurring because of competition in the market, increase in online cybersecurity-based attacks, lack of trained employees, etc., are the common issues that arise while searching the liquidity options in any financial organization, and here again AI plays a vital role minimizing all types of risk and issues [36]. Businesses and their related components must be easy to track and manage more assets than ever before in the Internet age. With the proliferation of mobile devices in the office, increasingly complex cloud solutions, generation of high amount of data in an exponential manner on regular interval, license-based software, and more regular updates, maintaining and tracking IT assets has become significantly more difficult [37]. Furthermore, frequent employee turnover poses data security concerns. As per the report published by Investopedia 2022, there are lots of tools available in the market to handle the different issues of liquidity, i.e., one is "asset management," and for these tools, e.g., InvGateAsst, Asset Panda, GoCodes, iVanti, etc., are available that works on AI algorithms and need quality data for the best outcome [38] (Figure 8.2).

8.3.5 Automation of the Routine Process

Automation is the area where AI has hit certainly the most. Whether it is data management or be it product delivery, bias calculation, credit intermediation, impact analysis, participant asset and liability analysis, creditworthiness analysis, finalizing governance and accountability, skill improvement, employee training, integration of new technologies,

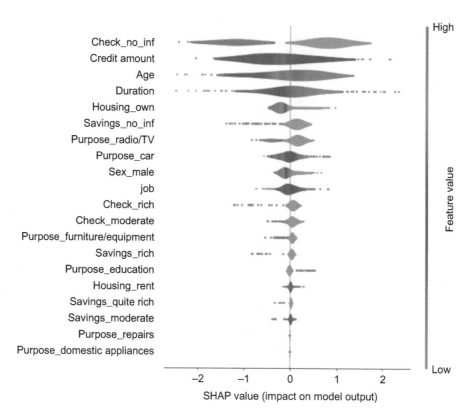

FIGURE 8.2
Shapley value analysis chat for profile identification (source: Deloitte Inc. UK).

i.e., blockchain-based identification of the products and delivery, keeping the integrity of records based on blockchain, managing the data concentration in an emerging area for a new product, or it is use of hedge funds in every domain, AI is being used to automate the traditional customs in this digital era. The second most common effect that is easily observable is that the use of AI by one organization is bringing advantages, and this advantage is acting like catalysis for its other peer group members working in that domain which ultimately drives more and more use of AI technologies at large level for all players in totality [39]. AI understands the unique complexity and the dynamics behind the change from the starting level up to the delivery level considering every individual stakeholder involved in the process inline. AI is leading in front roles in the following ways (Figures 8.3 and 8.4).

a) **Dynamic KYC**: Many KYC applications, i.e., Paytm, Google Pay, PhonePe, Payulater, PayuMoney, and PayU are the common applications that are being used these days and changing the finance world in India as well as the world [40].

b) **Invest Solutions**: Automation is helping a lot while deciding investments these days using AI on most of the banking websites. The following pyramid depicts the strategy required for making the risk profile (Figure 8.3).

c) **Fraud Prevention Mechanism**: Based on several features, i.e., Date, IP address, Location, Credit/Debit card number, Amount, Frequency, and User type, many algorithms are being used for fraud prevention mechanisms through training and testing processes. IP intelligence, device profiling, customer profiling, threat detection, market intelligence, etc., are also important factors for deciding frauds. Common names in this approach are Linear Regression, K-Means, Decision Tree, Bayesian Network, etc. [41].

d) **Wealth Management Software**: Sage Intact, DocuSign, Acorn, Altvia, Morningstar Advisor, RightCapital, SSCAPX, Coverty, Experian Management, Backstop, Naviplan, Charles River Management software, Wealth Block, Angel List Ventures, ECOS, etc., are the common names, which are solely dependent on AI-based algorithms, and these are used in financial companies for wealth management [42].

e) **Digital Wallets**: Paying on the Internet through digital payment systems is quite common these days because of core banking solution technology, which is intrinsically an AI-based mechanism. Digital wallets provide many features to users that make them advantageous, i.e., freedom to keep a small amount of money for online transactions so that in case of any mishappening your big amount of money is safe, easier to pen anywhere irrespective of environment, location, gender, age, amount, availability, etc. Apple Pay, Cash App, Dwolla, Google Pay, PayPal, Samsung Wallet, Venmo, Zelle, Walmart Pay, and Amazon Pay are the common names in this field [43]. As per the report by the Reserve Bank of India (RBI), digital payment-based systems are discouraging people from using less cash-based payments as depicted in Figure 8.4.

f) **Intuitive Payment Systems**: In frictionless payment system which is being achieved by most of the banking organizations in the future, whether it is tax offices, utility payments, or court agencies, all these are possible together and can be implemented and integrated solely with almost all types of the platform irrespective of the language and domain [44]. Table 8.1 presents a comparative statistic of the features and demerits:

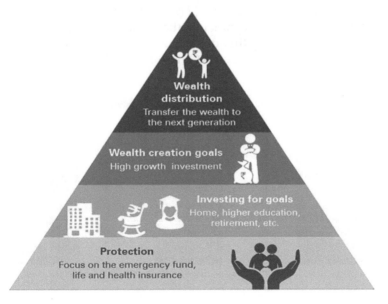

FIGURE 8.3
Automated investment solution recommendation.

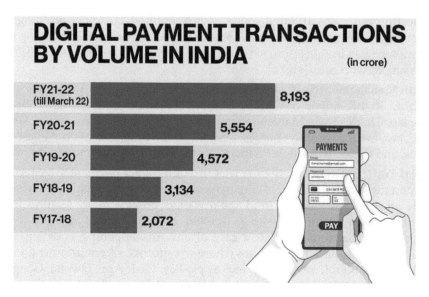

FIGURE 8.4
Digital payment systems growth and comparison with cash payment system (source: Reserve Bank of India, RBI).

8.3.6 Accounting Software

AI is also ruling the accounting finance where multiple applications are using machine learning and artificial intelligence together [27]. Current research projects that "Online Accounting Software" is increasing at an high exponential rate [45]. In fact, the World Economic Forum (WEF), in a separate finding, reported that 43% of financial organizations all over the world expressed a huge reduction in their existing workforce because of the high use of technology, and 41% also expressed that they will go for expansion based only on AI-based technology automation, alternatively, 34% are highly interested in further automation and technology integration in their workforce [46] (Figure 8.5).

The most common software in this domain are Oracle Netsuite, QuickBooks, Sage Intacct, Xero, FreshBooks, Thomson Reuters CS Professional Suite, TrulySmall Accounting,

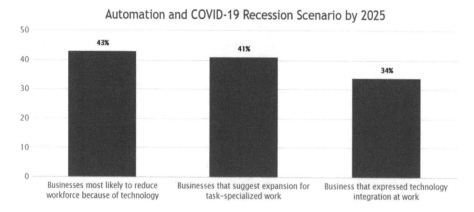

FIGURE 8.5
World Economic Forum report on automation and effect of COVID-19: depiction of automation and recession.

ePromis ERP Cloud, Vic. Ai, Odoo Accounting, AccountsIQ, Serenic Navigator, Kinetic Financial Management by Epicor, ZarMoney, ClearBooks, and many more [47].

8.3.7 End-to-End Banking Solution

Starting with the history of IBM Watson software, end-to-end software has traveled a long journey. According to a recent report by an independent organization named "Global Market Insights USA," the global market size of digital banking is expected to reach more than 12 trillion US dollars in 2026. Today almost all financial organizations have reached a level where any customer can interact with Interactive Voice Response Systems (IVRS) in many languages and users can take advantage of many services which are having AI and ML inbuilt, i.e., generation of password, checking account balance, checking last ten transactions, transfer of fund, updating the registered mobile number, live chat, and many more. Not only direct transactional services but non-transactional services are also being offered by software in the banking sector in a very featureful way, i.e., stock investment advisory, risk management, etc. No one wants to visit a bank in person for their banking needs as most of the services are now available in their mobile app. The most common applications that are readily available in many front-line financial organizations are Temenos, Finastra, Oracle FLEXCUBE, EBANQ, BankWare, Mambu, CorePlus, FIS Profile, Avaloq, Cleartouch, etc. [48].

8.3.8 Lending and Mortgage Software

AI is highly advantageous specifically in wealth management and loan management. AI-based machine learning algorithms are supporting the bank industry in drafting the decision-making policy for granting loan and mortgage [49–51] (Figure 8.6).

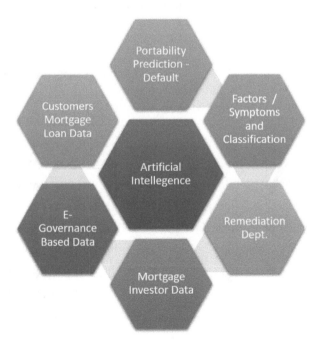

FIGURE 8.6
Depiction of different components of loan management and use of AI.

8.3.9 Point-of-Sale (PoS) Solution

AI-based applications are making life easy even where banking services are not available. In many of the developing countries, banking organizations have not established their ATM so in those remote locations PoS terminal-based technologies are enhancing the banking business and scaling up the merchant's business too [52]. PoS is a single terminal where all retail operations-based transactions are possible only by the use of single authentication, i.e., OTP or biometric authentication [53]. The Reserve Bank of India reports in its dedicated study of OTP authentication, as shown in (Figure 8.7).

RBI PoS terminal is leveraging the banking services in the following domain.

- Employee Management
- Customer Relationship Management
- Merchant's Local Data Management
- Revenue Management
- Online Payment Management

8.3.10 Stock Trading Solution

Analyzing millions of data points and their relationship and making predictions for the best trade at the optimal price are the objectives that are only achievable through AI-based tools in trading. The best part of AI-based tools is that these applications can run on simple low-end smartphones and PCs. In a study, the *Wall Street Journal* reported that because of AI and machine learning, trillions and trillions of data points can be analyzed easily in real-time scenarios, and in the future it is going to touch the market value of approximately $20 billion by 2028. Companies working in the field of stock trading at a global level are

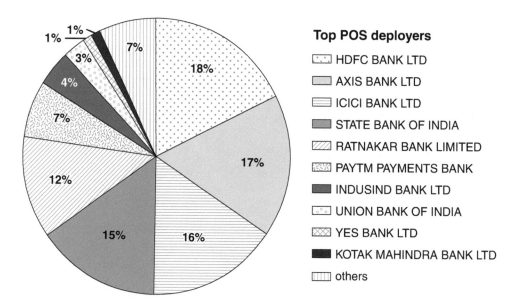

FIGURE 8.7
Distribution of PoS players in the digital economy of India.

Trading Technologies, Kavout Corporation, Numerai, Auquan, Intotheblock, Trade Ideas, Sentieo, Two Sigma, etc. [54].

8.3.11 Classifying and Redistributing the Risk among All Stakeholders

Being accountable means taking responsibility for the actions that were performed by you, and in this way, AI is a major key player that ensures that the right resource is accessible by the right user only. Identity and Access Management (IAM) ensures defining and managing the resources at individual standalone PCs as well as networked PCs. Three major acts HIPAA, GLBA, and SOX are implemented well as a policy in almost all AI-based IAM tools. Some important activities that are performed in banking applications include separation of custodian rights from owners, separation of user rights from custodian rights, merger of rights, acquisition of duties, review of manager's rights, deployment of rights, hiring of new employees, reimbursement of checks, user account lifecycle management, access governance and role-based access control, compliance violation, detection of discrepancy to take goods for themselves, etc. User-based multi-factor authentication are possible with AI [55]. The most common applications keeping pace with artificial intelligence in this field are Aviator, auth0, Curty, HID, IBM Tivoli, Manage Engine, Micro Focus, My1Login, Okata, Oracle IAM, Ping Identity, Radiant Logic, Sail Point, Secure Auth, SecZetta, etc. [56].

8.3.12 Deciding the Accountability in Case of Failure or Loss

This is possible only because of Identity and Access Management (IAM). IAM ensures certain algorithms of machine learning are achieved through artificial intelligence. In financial organizations, there may be a scenario where certain employees are granted superuser rights and in a typical case scenario if any mishappening occurs, then the rights-based classification of rights clarifies the accountability of each user. The following components are used in IAM:

a) Users
b) Roles
c) Groups
d) Policies

Overlapping of rights is easily distinguishable with the help of AI algorithms, i.e., Privileged Identity Management (PIM), Role-Based Access Control (RBAC), Mandatory Access Control (MAC), Discretionary Access Control (DAC), etc. [57].

8.3.13 Normalizing the Detection of Process of Inflation in Specialized Sector

When prices of commodities are unstable and policies framed by the government are quite flexible to track the defaulters, then forecasting inflation is important and has great significance for the stability of the economy. Many AI-based tools are being used for this purpose, and several research studies report that machine learning has shown its significant salient points to achieve this objective. From the last decade, many linear and nonlinear regression-based algorithms have been preferred for this; however, current research is moving around "Deep Learning"-based approaches these days [58]. Based on historical data availability, some research is also being reported supporting better prediction using Mean Square Error (MSE)-based models, Gated Recurrent Unit-Recurrent Neural Network (GRU-RNN), etc. [59].

8.3.14 Increasing the Number of Transactions

AI is also useful while providing the user with a smooth environment and in the long-term enhancing the revenue. Banking organizations are prioritizing operations in digital services and traditional services. Digitization of customers' online activity either analyzing cookies or temporary Internet files or using survey data is important, and here AI plays its trivial role [60]. According to the "Global Insight Report," there will be a 25% annual increase in digital transactions globally. Not only this but the historical data analysis of customers' activity in the digital world also improves the revenue. AI is also helping customers improve their trust in the digital world while protecting their privacy, user profile, log-in details, etc. [60]. Banking organizations are meeting the customers' expectations with the highest level of security and control, and this is one of the biggest reasons that drives online transactions not only in India but at a global level too. India is leading in digital transactions and as business organizations are expanding so is the need for AI [61] (Figure 8.8).

High use of digital transactions is also bringing new areas of development of FinTech, i.e., customized online natural language processing, customer-centric asset management, insurance e-based trading, access control, etc., emerging algorithms in the field of AI will be one key factor for growth driving to meet the demand of digital transactions in next 5 years. Many companies working in this domain are Dataminr, IBM Corp., Intel Corp., Microsoft Corp., Nuance Communications Inc., Onfido, Ripple, Salesforce.Com Inc., Sift, Tibco Software Inc., Upstart Network Inc., Verint Systems Inc., Wealthfront Corp., etc. [62]. A report by Boston Consulting Group states that India's digital transactions will cross the figure of $10 by the year 2026. Digital Payment Interface (DPI) touched 350.30 as of March 2022 compared to 305.06 in September 2021. In March 2020, it was at 153.47, and by

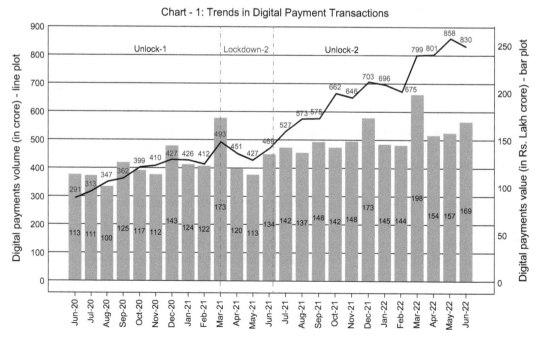

FIGURE 8.8
Digital payment trend analysis – the Reserve Bank of India in the last 2 years.

September 2019, it again rose to 174. Unified Payments Interface (UPI)-based mechanism rose to 6.28 billion transactions leading to nearly Rs 11 trillion in July, which is a tremendous record index for India's flagship digital payments platform since its starting and it is bound to increase [63].

8.3.15 Synthesizing Primary Data Using Machine Learning Algorithm

Because of the continuous change in the dynamics of the cybercrime being reported daily, every financial organization is bound to make its own policies to handle the different types of cybercrime and frauds. Each banking organization is different, each fraud type is different, and the modus operandi is unpredictable, so these challenges are forcing it to do research and to work on its own primary data generated by the bank itself. Search, strategy, synthesis, quick and on-time identification of normal and anomalous behavior, policy-making, and prevention include synthesis of the data in a unique manner so that pattern can be easily identified to prevent the crime in future [64]. The symbiosis of emerging cyberattacks and lack of enough security controls are leading financial organizations to come up with their own way of handling the attacks using their own generated data to minimize the losses. There is a need to develop new algorithms and new technologies to prevent further loss of the organizations, preserve the brand, keep the data intact, maintain privacy, etc., and these are possible by using deep learning and machine learning as recent reports suggest [65]. With enough well-structured, interrelated, relevant, unbiased data and well-established business logic well coupled with machine learning models, fraud detection is very likely to work well for your customers and your business, which is again represented in Figure 8.9 that depicts the most primary model of credit card fraud detection where user data is fetched while he is making the transaction. Based on his history the pattern is identified, and if the pattern is legitimate, the transaction details are shared with the user; the user approves the operation, and the transaction gets completed successfully [66].

Table 8.2 suggests and reviews the types of financial frauds and techniques used to handle those frauds.

8.3.16 24/7 Customer Interactions

Making reverse call, live chat facility, Bank of Things (BOT)-based chat, etc., have made banking organizations facilitate their services easily by covering a large number of customer bases with a backup of very small manpower [67]. Either be it agent assistance, robotic automation of documents (user uploads documents and after scanning the relevant fields are automatically filled), multi-lingual support, or IVR automation, AI is also able to handle if the same question is asked 100 times by 100 customers, and all this because of machine learning-based automation technologies. In a world of fading customer loyalty, AI is acting as a boon for small financial companies, which can have a big human resource at their end but are actively involved globally with their services [68]. The following services are possible with AI-based technologies in financial organizations:

- Round the clock BOT-based customer care services
- Cost reduction in product delivery
- Better interaction with customers
- Resource optimization

- Easy recovery and restore of services
- Event tracking
- Personalized user experience
- User data collection and further analysis
- Easy ticket generation and time-bound alarm generation
- Timely compliance of the services
- Assisting customers to make better decisions through live demos and chat
- Simplified task management

8.3.17 Claims Management

Automated claim processing and its timely management have become quite easy because of machine learning-assisted technologies in financial organizations. Be it life insurance or general insurance, insurance companies are using AI-based technologies to predict policy premiums, losses, risk ratios, future options of investment, etc. By identifying risks early in the process, insurers can make better use of their time and give insurers a significant competitive advantage [69].

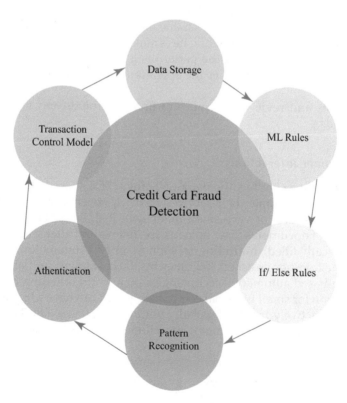

FIGURE 8.9
Credit card fraud detection model.

TABLE 8.2

Categorization of Digital Frauds and Algorithms Used

S. No.	Organization	Type of Fraud	Subcategory	Algorithm Used for Detection
1.	Bank	Credit card fraud	Authentication failure	• LUHN-10 Algorithm • Isolation Forest Algorithm • Local Outlier Factor Algorithm • One-Class Support Vector Machine (SVM) Algorithm • Autoencoders • Ensemble Models • K-Nearest Neighbor • Support Vector Model • Neural Network Model
2.	Bank	Card cloning fraud	• Authentication failure • Audit failure	• P-based Models • K-Nearest Neighbor • SVM-based Models • Random Forest • XG Boost Model • Neural Network Model
3.	Bank	Account theft and suspicious transactions	• Privacy failure • Storage policy failure • IAM failure	• Homomorphic encryption • Rivest–Shamir–Adleman (RSA) • Diffie–Hellman (DH) • Lock and key ecosystem Model • MD5 and SHA3 based Model
4.	Bank	Phishing	Authentication failure	• Heuristic Model • SVM-based Model • Naïve Bayes (NB) Model • Multiple ML Model • Deep Learning Model • Genetic Algorithm • CNN-based Model • Neural Network Model

(Continued)

TABLE 8.2 CONTINUED

Categorization of Digital Frauds and Algorithms Used

S. No.	Organization	Type of Fraud	Subcategory	Algorithm Used for Detection
5.	Bank	Shoulder-surfing	Authentication failure	• Drawmetrics-based Model • Locimetric Model • Searchmetrics systems • Visual identification protocol • Shoulder Guard Model
6.	Bank	Dumpster-diving	• Data storage policy failure • Audit failure	• R-CNN Algorithm • Hidden Markov Model • SVM Model • ANN Model
7.	Bank	Unauthorized transactions	• Authentication failure • Authorization failure • IAM policy failure	• Deep Learning-based Models • Naïve Bayes (NB) • Support Vector Machine (SVM) • K-Nearest Neighbor
8.	Bank	Odd credit reports Fraud	• Forgery • Data integrity attack	• Odd Rule-based Algorithm • Decision Tree (DT) • Random Forest (RF) • Artificial Neural Network (ANN) • Naïve Bayes (NB) • Logistic Regression
9.	Bank	False application fraud	• Forgery • Integrity attack	• Random Forest • CatBoost • Deep Neural Network (DNN) • Isolation Forest
10.	Bank	Credit card skimming	• Identity theft • Data theft • Storage policy failure	• Logistic RegressionNaïve Bayes • Random Forest • K-Nearest NeighborNeural Network • Light GBMModel

8.3.18 Credit Scoring and Churn Predictions

AI is taking a big leap in the field of credit scoring where a variety of machine learning algorithms are being used to improve the payment ecosystems, taxation system, and evaluation of customer profiles [70]. AI-based credit scoring is based on several parameters, i.e., customer risk profile, earning range, customer history, CIBIL score (Credit Information Bureau (India) Limited based index for keeping the credit records of users), income, credit history, loan history, transactional analysis, age, work experience, etc. Unlike the traditional credit-scoring method, AI-based method generates and keeps a chart to understand the dynamics of the credit history of the user and his previous record, and if historical records suggest, then the customer can be denied the loan. AI-based credit-scoring leverages in the following manner.

- Tracking all stakeholders
- Full access control of every data in a classified manner
- Access to credit data
- Fast analysis of operations and transactions
- Better customer focus

8.3.19 Robotic Recommender System

Starting from the journey in the year 2006, when Netflix announced the prize money of $1 million for designing a recommender system for its users, to date, Netflix recommendations for its customers are up to 80% accurate, and in a similar fashion, recommender systems-based applications are being used in banking organization too. With perfect use of reinforcement learning, recommenders systems are used by almost all tier 1 companies globally. With the use of statistical data analysis, the recommendation system allows the bank to evaluate whether it is about college loans or real estate investments [71]. This is a great advantage as it increases the bank's revenues given the personalized activities offered to customers. Based in Dubai, United Arab Emirates' famous bank, Emirates NBD is currently developing its own specialized product recommendation engine based on collaborative filtering. BBVA Corp., Spain, has been using its own recommendation engine for several years for providing customized services to its customers [72]. Citibanamex via Citi Wealth Builder also provided recommendations based on client needs and goals using a content filtering technique. This was very convenient for the client and very accurate too. HSBC bank has also developed a new financial product for providing services to its customers based on a recommendation system, MoneyWise App [73].

8.4 Challenges for AI in Financial Services

8.4.1 Use of Efficient Algorithms in Prediction and Its In-house Development

Considering the financial instability in many countries, i.e., Pakistan, Greece, Ghana, etc., concern about the exact prediction of depositors' money has raised several issues as well as trust in the banking system too. Machine learning has been viewed as an important tool to investigate and analyze this problem using parametric and nonparametric models and to predict the next phase of the economy. Studies have been done, and many algorithms have been promising for this, i.e., Data Envelopment Analysis (DEA), Decision Tree, C5.0, Synthetic Minority Oversampling Technique (SMOTE), CART method, etc. Bank's operation efficiency and leading to failure situation has been a topic of study in machine learning for a long time; however, optimization of all the processes and development of the best prediction model matching with constraints is still a challenge. After COVID-19, the use of online banking has made the situation more challenging where massive data is being generated digitally through many dimensions, and the adoption of AI/ML brings unique risks and challenges at the same for financial organizations [74]. AI/ML-based decisions taken by automated models in financial institutions are not easily explained and can be biased. Financial stability issues may also arise, related to the robustness of AI/ML algorithms in the face of structural changes, and interconnectedness due to widespread reliance on a small number of AI/ML service providers as well because of regular changes in dynamics [75]. In investment management industry, the penetration of AI/ML in banking is lesser in comparison to the advances in other fields. There are some inherent issues also lying with banking organizations, i.e., confidentiality and the proprietary nature of banking data have slowed AI/ML adoption where supervisory control is based on individual basis and its verification too. There are high chances that the methodology and model used to predict the scenario in one bank may not be fully adoptable for other banks, so banks need to develop their internal AI Research Lab to cater their own problem, with rapidly evolving capabilities such as natural language processing, image processing, big data issues, data storage in cloud, computer vision techniques, AI agents and bots, and augmented-based or virtual reality-based technologies in their core business processes. This will leverage their business in the best manner as well as free them up from the concern of data privacy and data leakage [76]. In developing countries, most of the banks lack the appetite to establish such labs and develop these technologies for them, instead these organizations are dependent on third parties, which poses a challenge in the long term [77].

8.4.2 Availability of Relevant and Quality Data

Data-driven analysis and prediction are only successful when quality data is available. For the best AI-based world, data transparency must be established, and for this, clear data management policies must be recognized. All the best data operations, such as the ability to manage, access, analyze, share, revoke, invoke, stop, append, create, delete, track, etc., are only possible when data-liquidity models are implemented in their best manner in that organization [78]. Decision-making layers must be seamless either at the internal level or at the external level so that the chances of generation of fuzzy data are minimum. Banks must design their own in-house data management system, which will ensure the quality of data, lack of redundant data, and regularity compliance while supporting open source mechanisms which will empower them in long-term business by reducing the cost spent on third-party software [79].

8.4.3 Availability of the Trained Staff

Due to lack of skills, initial adoption of AI is not enough. Skilled employees are needed, and they must be trained in a regular manner to understand the changing dynamics of the organization and challenges too. Better decisions can be expected only from a team working together to achieve a common goal, and this cohesiveness is only possible if they are enough trained and skilled in their respective field of work [80]. A labor shortage in banking was pre-expected after the pandemic but in the automation department, this issue is seriously an alarming situation. Lack of enough trained employees is increasing the workload on individuals, so the stress level is also increasing, which is again a big issue in financial organizations. In many reports in the last 5 years, independent agencies like JPMorgan, Goldman Sachs, UBS, and Citi have highlighted that there is a huge shortage of talented people in the banking sector [81]. Because of this critical situation, the majority of the core services are now being outsourced to other countries from the Western world to Eastern countries. Employees of major banks and other financial sectors and some of the world's largest financial technology companies are increasingly moving to FinTech start-ups [82].

8.4.4 Availability of Efficient Resources

After the pandemic, the migration from urban to rural has increased, and it has catalyzed the digital transfer of money; however, lack of digital infrastructure and mobile services is not enough matured in many developing to cater all the issues efficiently. Remittances are increasing in rural parts of every country all over the world; however, modes to transfer money are limited [83]. Digital transfers are cheaper and faster than cash transfers through banks; however, it is also true that all the banks are not providing this facility at a large level, and those which are providing are not fully functional and not enough loaded with features. Due to the high degree of specialization in AI/ML systems and network effects, AI/ML service providers have the potential to become systemically important participants in the financial market infrastructure, and therefore, the chances of the financial system's single point of failure increase as lack of good IT infrastructure makes the whole system vulnerable. These barriers of digital divide in developing countries must be resolved for better IT-based banking services [84].

8.4.5 Accountability and Authorization

There is no accountability when machines perform activities. Who would be responsible if a self-driving car crashed? It is like the same situation in a banking scenario where an algorithmic trading crashed the stock market, or an automated program grossly erred in credit analysis. This poses a serious obstacle to the adoption of new technologies [85]. Better research-based optimization techniques are needed to smoothen the process of governance where multiple players are involved.

8.4.6 Compliance of Regulation

Several studies by independent agencies have reported that regularity frameworks and compliance are not being followed by financial organizations leading to distrust in the banking domain, creating a panic situation among its shareholders, and finally leading to an unstable economy [86]. If we take India for example, then many banks have been slapped with massive fines for noncompliance of regulations. These banks are the Overseas Bank of India and the Union Bank of India (each fined Rs 1.5 crore), the Bank of Maharashtra and Allahabad Bank (each fined Rs 2 crore), and the Oriental Bank of Commerce [87]. The apex regulator bank, the Reserve Bank of India, is framing and implementing strict guidelines for others too for noncompliance. The major issues observed in noncompliance of the regulations are as follows:

- Noncompliance of Know Your Customer (KYC)
- Noncompliance of credit history of overseas customers
- Noncompliance of digital transaction record and its storage
- Noncompliance of digital signature and timely renewal
- Noncompliance of international banking acts and standards, i.e., ISO, COBIT, BASEL, etc.
- Noncompliance of PCIDSS regulation
- Deposit of balance sheet in a timely manner
- Lack of monitoring in product delivery and use
- Fraud classification and its reporting in a stipulated manner of time
- Development of reporting of cyber fraud and its handling
- Discounting/rediscounting of bills by banks
- Compliance is a factor that every company or business has to follow as per the given guidelines, which is missing most of the time

8.5 Case Studies on the Use of AI in Financial Services

8.5.1 Use of UPI in India in Digital Payment

The use of the Unified Payments Interface (UPI) has changed the digital payment system in India. It is a kind of revolution made by information technology-based application, which positioned India as a leader in digital transactions all over the world by having the highest number of transactions touching the figure of 49 billion in the year 2022 [88]. This figure is seven times greater than the combined real-time digital payments operations of the world's leading economies – the United States, Canada, the United Kingdom, France, and Germany. The most interesting scenario is that it is going to be available in most of the nearby countries, which proves that data synchronization and other technologies related to AI and machine learning are looped together. There are reports that several new use cases for UPI-based transactions have been made possible by technological innovations including different market players. QR code payments, multi-platform payment, cardless cash withdrawals using UPI, e-RUPI, UPI, SMS-based UPI services, etc., are going to be launched in the United Arab Emirates, Nepal, Bhutan, Thailand, Myanmar, and Singapore [89].

8.5.2 Amazon Book Sale Case

A book on Amazon's platform was auctioned off with the help of two booksellers who sold the books using AI, and an AI algorithmic pricing engine worked in such a manner that the price generated more revenue [90]. Profits came out to be higher than expected than its main competitor, which pushed the price of the book to a record price for "Peter Lawrence," an evolutionary biology book. Amazon sellers use algorithmic pricing to allow them to automatically change product prices based on competitors, for example. So, it is understandable why the company constantly tries to lower the prices of its competitors with the help of artificial intelligence-powered algorithms [91].

8.5.3 Loan Grant System Using AI-Based Weather Prediction Model

In a separate and independent research-based study, it has been reported that weather data can be used for the prediction of the production of crops in a particular region, and this prediction can be a base for granting the loan for the customer by matching the constraints and risk going to occur in that crop-year for a particular crop variety. A company named WorldCover is working on a smart contract that uses AI to evaluate satellite data, weather station data, and agricultural data to determine the risk of weather "events" and trigger automatic payments using AI and blockchain [92].

8.6 Conclusion

In the future, the amalgamation of AI and ML is going to rule, and it will drive the growth of "FinTech" (financial technology). The trend of inclusion of AI in financial services will accelerate the growth covering its related components' computing power, storage capacity, and big data, as well as significant advances in modeling and custom use cases. In developing economies like India, many financial service providers are wary of the time and cost required to implement AI in digital financial services; however, they soon realize the potential of these innovative technologies and the long-term return on investment they provide. A combination of sufficient funding, availability of technical expertise in specialized areas, core domain knowledge, and openness of senior management awareness will play a major role in a long-term AI strategy. The companies most likely to succeed will attract multidisciplinary teams with strong backgrounds in AI and financial services, which ultimately paves the path of long-term growth for financial companies.

References

1. CE Shannon and J McCarthy. 1956. *Automata Studies. (AM-34) (Annals of Mathematics Studies)*. Princeton University Press.
2. How a know-your-customer utility could increase access to financial services in emerging markets, 2017. Govt. of India, CGAP Survey.
3. Christoph Molnar. A guide for making black box models explainable. https://www.hindawi .com/journals/cin/2021/1071145/ accessed on 05/01/2023.
4. PM Kulkarni and C Domeniconi. Network-based anomaly detection for insider trading. arXiv 2017, arXiv:1702.05809.
5. Q Wang, W Xu, X Huang, and K Yang. 2019. Enhancing intraday stock price manipulation detection by leveraging recurrent neural networks with ensemble learning. *Neurocomputing* 347, 46–58.
6. SR Islam, SK Ghafoor, and W Eberle. 2018. Mining illegal insider trading of stocks: A proactive approach. In *Proceedings of the 2018 IEEE International Conference on Big Data (Big Data)* , Seattle, WA, 10–13 December 2018, pp. 1397–1406.

7. PM Kulkarni and C Domeniconi. Network-based anomaly detection for insider trading. arXiv 2017, arXiv:1702.05809.

8. M Mirtaheri, S Abu-El-Haija, F Morstatter, GV Steeg, and A Galstyan. 2021. Identifying and Analyzing Cryptocurrency Manipulations in social media. *IEEE Transactions on Computational Social Systems* 8(3), 607–617.

9. Deloitte SAS - Member of Deloitte Touche Tohmatsu Limited Link - deloitte_artificial-intelligence-credit-risk.pdf accessed on 05/01/2023.

10. Credit Risk Report 2022, by Deloitte, UK. deloitte_artificial-intelligence-credit-risk.pdf accessed on 05/01/2023.

11. M Purbay and D Kumar. 2021. Split behavior of supervised machine learning algorithms for phishing URL detection. *Lecture Notes in Electrical Engineering* 683.

12. E Gandotra and D Gupta. 2021. An efficient approach for phishing detection using machine learning. In *Algorithms for Intelligent Systems*, Springer, Singapore. https://doi.org/10.1007/978-981-15-8711-5_12.

13. Hung Le, Quang Pham, Doyen Sahoo, and Steven CH Hoi. 2017. URLNet: Learning a URL representation with deep learning for malicious URL detection. Conference'17, Washington, DC. arXiv:1802.03162.

14. J Hong, T Kim, J Liu, N Park, and SW Kim. 2020. Phishing URL detection with lexical features and blacklisted domains. In *Autonomous Secure Cyber Systems*. Springer. https://doi.org/10.1007/978-3-030-33432-1_12.

15. J Kumar, A Santhanavijayan, B Janet, B Rajendran, and BS Bindhumadhava. 2020. Phishing website classification and detection using machine learning. In *2020 International Conference on Computer Communication and Informatics (ICCCI)*, Coimbatore, India, pp. 1–6. https://doi.org/10.1109/ICCCI48352.2020.9104161.

16. YA Hassan and B Abdelfettah. 2017. Using case-based reasoning for phishing detection. *Procedia Computer Science* 109, 281–288.

17. RS Rao and AR Pais. 2019. Jail-Phish: An improved search engine-based phishing detection system. *Computers and Security* 83, 246–267.

18. A Aljofey, Q Jiang, Q Qu, M Huang, and JP Niyigena. 2020. An effective phishing detection model based on character level convolutional neural network from URL. *Electronics* 9(9), 1514.

19. A AlEroud and G Karabatis. 2020. Bypassing detection of URL-based phishing attacks using generative adversarial deep neural networks. In *Proceedings of the Sixth International Workshop on Security and Privacy Analytics*, pp. 53–60.

20. D Gupta and R Rani. 2020. Improving malware detection using big data and ensemble learning. *Computer Electronic Engineering* 86, no.106729.

21. J Anirudha and P Tanuja. 2019. Phishing attack detection using feature selection techniques. *Proceedings of the International Conference on Communication and Information Processing (ICCIP)*. http://doi.org/10.2139/ssrn.3418542.

22. CY Wu, CC Kuo, and CS Yang. 2019. A phishing detection system based on machine learning. In *2019 International Conference on Intelligent Computing and its Emerging Applications (ICEA)*, pp. 28–32.

23. KL Chiew, EH Chang, WK Tiong, WK Tiong. 2015. Utilisation of website logo for phishing detection. *Computers and Security*, 54, 16–26.

24. R Srinivasa Rao and AR Pais. 2017. Detecting phishing websites using automation of human behavior. In *Proceedings of the 3rd ACM Workshop on Cyber-Physical System Security Academic Medicine*, pp. 33–42.

25. OK Sahingoz, E Buber, O Demir, and B Diri. 2019. Machine learning based phishing detection from URLs. *Expert Systems with Applications* 117, 345–357.

26. A Zamir, HU Khan, T Iqbal, N Yousaf, F Aslam et al. 2019. Phishing web site detection using diverse machine learning algorithms. *The Electronic Library* 38(1), 65–80.

27. M Almseidin, AA Zuraiq, M Al-kasassbeh, N Alnidami. 2019. Phishing detection based on machine learning and feature selection methods. *International Journal of Interactive Mobile Technology* 13(12), 171–183.

28. CL Tan, KL Chiew, K Wong, SN Sze. 2016. PhishWHO: Phishing webpage detection via identity keywords extraction and target domain name finder. *Decision Support Systems* 88, 18–27.
29. S Gull and SA Parah. 2019. Color image authentication using dual watermarks. In *2019 Fifth International Conference on Image Information Processing (ICIIP)* , pp. 240–245.
30. KJ Giri, R Bashir, and JI Bhat. 2019. A discrete wavelet based watermarking scheme for authentication of medical images. *International Journal of E-Health and Medical Communications*, 10, 30–38.
31. E Gandotra, D Bansal, and S Sofat. 2016. Malware threat assessment using fuzzy logic paradigm. *Cybernetics and Systems*, 12, 29–48.
32. D Gupta and R Rani. 2019. A study of big data evolution and research challenges. *Journal of Information Science*, 45, 322–340.
33. https://spd.group/machine-learning/credit-card-fraud-detection/ accessed on 05/01/2023.
34. Ali, Abdulalem, Abd Razak Shukor, Othman, Siti Hajar, Eisa, Taiseer, Abdalla Elfadil, Al-Dhaqm, Arafat, Nasser, Maged, Elhassan, Tusneem, Elshafie, Hashim, Saif, Abdu. Financial fraud detection based on machine learning: A systematic literature review, *Applied Sciences*, 12, (19), p. 9637.
35. https://www.efinancialcareers-gulf.com/news/2022/04/macro-jobs-banks accessed on 05/01/2023.
36. Tariq Abbasi and Hans Weigand. 2017. The impact of digital financial services on Firm's performance: A literature review. *Clinical Orthopaedics and Related Research.* abs/1705.10294.
37. Rasha AbdelKawy, Walid M Abdelmoez, and Amin A Shoukry. 2021. A synchronous deep reinforcement learning model for automated multi-stock trading. *Progress in Artificial Intelligence* 10(1), 83–97.
38. Hussein A Abdou and John Pointon. 2011. Credit scoring, statistical techniques and evaluation criteria: A review of the literature. *Intelligent Systems in Accounting Finance & Management* 18(2–3), 59–88.
39. Masaya Abe and Hideki Nakayama. 2018. Deep learning for forecasting stock returns in the cross-section. In *PAKDD'2018*, 10937, pp. 273–284.
40. Jae Joon Ahn, Suk Jun Lee, Kyong Joo Oh, and Tae Yoon Kim. 2009. Intelligent forecasting for financial time series subject to structural changes. *Intelligent Data Analysis* 13(1), 151–163.
41. Ali Abdallah Alalwan, Nripendra P Rana, Yogesh Kumar Dwivedi, and Raed Salah Algharabat. 2017. Social media in marketing: A review and analysis of the existing literature. *Telematics and Informatics* 34(7), 1177–1190.
42. Mousa Albashrawi. 2016. Detecting financial fraud using data mining techniques: A decade review from 2004 to 2015. *Journal of Data Science* 14(3), 553–570.
43. Pamela P Alvarez, Alejandra Espinoza, Sergio Maturana, and Jorge R Vera. 2020. Improving consistency in hierarchical tactical and operational planning using Robust Optimization. *Computers and Industrial Engineering* 139, 106112.
44. Marian H Amin, Ehab KA Mohamed, and Ahmed Elragal. 2020. Corporate disclosure via social media: A data science approach. *Online Information Review* 44(1), 278–298.
45. Chainarong Amornbunchornvej, Elena Zheleva, and Tanya Y Berger-Wolf. 2019. Variable-lag granger causality for time series analysis. In *DSAA'2019*, pp. 21–30.
46. Torben Gustav Andersen, Richard A Davis, Jens-Peter Kreiß, and Thomas V Mikosch. 2009. *Handbook of Financial Time Series.* Springer.
47. Manoj Apte, Sushodhan Vaishampayan, and Girish Keshav Palshikar. 2021. Detection of causally anomalous time-series. *International Journal of Data Science and Analytics* 11(2), 141–153.
48. Douglas W Arner, Janos Nathan Barberis, and Ross P Buckley. 2015. The evolution of fintech: A new post-crisis paradigm? http://doi.org/10.2139/ssrn.2676553.
49. Henri Arslanian and Fabrice Fischer. 2019. *The Future of Finance: The Impact of FinTech, AI, and Crypto on Financial Services.* Palgrave Macmillan.
50. Susan Athey. 2018. The impact of machine learning on economics. In Ajay Agrawal, Joshua Gans, and Avi Goldfarb (Eds.), *The Economics of Artificial Intelligence: An Agenda.* University of Chicago Press, pp. 507–547.

51. Arash Bahrammirzaee. 2010. A comparative survey of artificial intelligence applications in finance: Artificial neural networks, expert system and hybrid intelligent systems. *Neural Computing and Applications* 19(8), 1165–1195.

52. Manoj Bahuguna and Ravindra Khattree. 2020. A generic all-purpose transformation for multivariate modeling through copulas. *International Journal of Data Science and Analytics* 10(1), 1–23.

53. Yoshua Bengio, Aaron Courville, and Pascal Vincent. 2013. Representation learning: A review and new perspectives. *IEEE Transactions on Pattern Analysis and Machine Intelligence* 35(8), 1798–1828.

54. Jonathan Berk and Peter DeMarzo. 2019. *Corporate Finance (Global Edition)*. P&C Business.

55. Ranjeeta Bisoi and Pradipta K Dash. 2014. A hybrid evolutionary dynamic neural network for stock market trend analysis and prediction using unscented Kalman filter. *Applied Soft Computing* 19, 41–56.

56. Zvi Bodie, Alex Kane, and Alan J Marcus. 2020. *ISE Investments* (12th ed.). McGraw-Hill Education.

57. Andrew Brim. 2020. Deep reinforcement learning pairs trading with a double deep Q-network. In *CCWC'2020*.

58. Lorán Chollete, Andréas Heinen, and Alfonso Valdesogo. 2009. Modeling international financial returns with a multivariate regime-switching copula. *Journal of Financial Econometrics*, 437–480.

59. Eunsuk Chong, Chulwoo Han, and Frank C Park. 2017. Deep learning networks for stock market analysis and prediction: Methodology, data representations, and case studies. *Expert Systems With Applications* 83, 187–205.

60. Junyoung Chung, Kyle Kastner, Laurent Dinh, Kratarth Goel, Aaron C Courville, and Yoshua Bengio. 2015. A recurrent latent variable model for sequential data. *Advances in Neural Information Processing Systems* 28, 2980–2988.

61. Gérard Cornuéjols, Javier Peña, and Reha Tütüncü. 2018. *Optimization Methods in Finance* (2nd ed.). Cambridge University Press.

62. Patricia Craja, Alisa Kim, and Stefan Lessmann. 2020. Deep learning for detecting financial statement fraud. *Decision Support Systems* 139, 113421.

63. Herbert Dawid and Domenico Delli Gatti. 2018. Agent-based macroeconomics. Bielefeld Working Papers in Economics and Management (No. 02-2018).

64. Min-Yuh Day and Chia-Chou Lee. 2016. Deep learning for financial sentiment analysis on finance news providers. In *ASONAM2016*, pp. 1127–1134.

65. Jan G De Gooijer and Rob Hyndman. 2006. 25 years of time series forecasting. *International Journal of Forecasting* 22(3), 443–473.

66. Alexander Denev. 2015. *Probabilistic Graphical Models: A New Way of Thinking in Financial Modelling*. Risk Books.

67. Yue Deng, Feng Bao, Youyong Kong, Zhiquan Ren, and Qionghai Dai. 2017. Deep direct reinforcement learning for financial signal representation and trading. *IEEE Transactions on Neural Networks and Learning Systems* 28(3), 653–664.

68. Vasant Dhar and Roger M Stein. 2017. FinTech platforms and strategy. *Communications of the ACM* 60(10), 32–35.

69. .Qianggang Ding, Sifan Wu, Hao Sun, Jiadong Guo, and Jian Guo. 2020. Hierarchical multiscale Gaussian transformer for stock movement prediction. In *IJCAI'2020*, pp. 4640–4646.

70. Cris Doloc. 2020. *Applications of Computational Intelligence in Data-Driven Trading*. John Wiley & Sons.

71. Renato P dos Santos. 2017. On the philosophy of Bitcoin/Blockchain technology: Is it a chaotic, complex system? *Clinical Orthopaedics and Related Research*. abs/1711.00509 (2017).

72. Peter Duchessi and Salvatore Belardo. 1987. Lending Analysis Support System (LASS): An application of a knowledge-based system to support commercial loan analysis. *IEEE Transactions on Systems, Man and Cybernetics* 17(4), 608–616.

73. Ila Dutta, Shantanu Dutta, and Bijan Raahemi. 2017. Detecting financial restatements using data mining techniques. *Expert Systems With Applications* 90, 374–393.

74. Chien-Cheng Lin, Chun-Sheng Chen, and An-Pin Chen. 2018. Using intelligent computing and data stream mining for behavioral finance associated with market profile and financial physics. *Applied Soft Computing* 68, 756–764.

75. Chen Liu, Weiyan Hou, and Deyin Liu. 2017. Foreign exchange rates forecasting with convolutional neural network. *Neural Processing Letters* 46(3), 1095–1119.

76. Rong Liu, Feng Mai, Zhe Shan, and Ying Wu. 2020. Predicting shareholder litigation on insider trading from financial text: An interpretable deep learning approach. *Information Management* 57(8), 103387.

77. Yang Liu, Qi Liu, Hongke Zhao, Zhen Pan, and Chuanren Liu. 2020. Adaptive quantitative trading: An imitative deep reinforcement learning approach. In *AAAI'2020*, pp. 2128–2135.

78. Wen Long, Linqiu Song, and Ying-jie Tian. 2019. A new graphic kernel method of stock price trend prediction based on financial news semantic and structural similarity. *Expert Systems With Applications* 118, 411–424.

79. Theo Lynn, John G Mooney, Pierangelo Rosati, and Mark Cummins. 2019. *Disrupting Finance: Fintech and Strategy in the 21st Century*. Palgrave Pivot.

80. Ye Ma, Lu Zong, and Peiwan Wang. 2020. A novel distributed representation of news (DRNews) for stock market predictions. *Clinical Orthopaedics and Related Research*. abs/2005.11706 (2020).

81. N Gregory Mankiw. 2016. *Principles of Economics* (8th ed.). Southwest College ISE.

82. Anna Maria and Gil Lafuente. 2005. *Fuzzy Logic in Financial Analysis*. Springer.

83. AI Marqués, Vicente García, and José Salvador Sánchez. 2013. A literature review on the application of evolutionary computing to credit scoring. *JORS* 64(9), 1384–1399.

84. Sidra Mehtab, Jaydip Sen, and Subhasis Dasgupta. 2020. Analysis and forecasting of financial time series using CNN and LSTM-based deep learning models. *Clinical Orthopaedics and Related Research*. abs/2011.08011 (2020).

85. Omer Berat Sezer and Ahmet Murat Özbayoglu. 2019. Financial trading model with stock bar chart image time series with deep convolutional neural networks. *Clinical Orthopaedics and Related Research*. abs/1903.04610 (2019).

86. Dev Shah, Wesley Campbell, and Farhana H Zulkernine. 2018. A comparative study of LSTM and DNN for stock market forecasting. In *IEEE International Conference on Big Data (Big Data)*. IEEE, pp. 4148–4155.

87. Delei Sheng and Peilong Shen. 2020. Portfolio optimization with asset-liability ratio regulation constraints. *Complexity* 2020, 1435356:1–1435356:13.

88. B Shravankumar and Vadlamani Ravi. 2016. A survey of the applications of text mining in financial domain. *Knowledge-Based Systems* 114, 128–147.

89. Yauheniya Shynkevich, T Martin McGinnity, Sonya A Coleman, and Ammar Belatreche. 2016. Forecasting movements of health-care stock prices based on different categories of news articles using multiple kernel learning. *Decision Support Systems* 85, 74–83.

90. Mieko Tanaka-Yamawaki and Seiji Tokuoka. 2006. Minority game as a model for the artificial financial markets. In *CEC2006*, pp. 2157–2162.

91. Jing Tang, Xueyan Tang, and Junsong Yuan. 2018. Profit maximization for viral marketing in online social networks: Algorithms and analysis. *IEEE Transactions on Knowledge and Data Engineering* 30(6), 1095–1108.

92. Mitchell M Waldrop. 1992. *Complexity: The Emerging Science at the Edge of Order and Chaos*. Simon & Schuster Paperbacks.

9

AI-Based Machine Learning and Deep Learning Smart Electricity Grids for Society 5.0

Prabhjot Kaur and Anand Muni Mishra

9.1 Introduction

Due to the introduction of dispersed and viable sources of energy, it has become progressively difficult to maintain stability amongst power supply and need, and also its quality in the electric system. Because the old power grid was not intended to accommodate two-way movement of power, electric systems are failing to control the backflow of energy from dispersed generating origins like air as well as sun [1]. Renewable energy sources are inherently intermittent, which makes it difficult to maintain a consistent power movement in the electric network. The conventional power grid of Society 5.0 can be converted into a smart, automatic, and receptive power system by merging information and communication technologies with machine intelligence. The term "smart grid society 5.0" is used to characterize this form of a grid. According to digital technology, "grid" refers to the electric grid, which is a bi-directional network communication line between consumers and utilities shown in Figure 9.1. Electricity outages are becoming more regular, resulting in a slew of failures in industries such as banking, communications, traffic, and security [2]. Smart grid technology is used for this goal, and it is based on a variety of artificial intelligence approaches. This method permits supervising, investigating, organizing, and communicating within the supply chain to improve efficiency, reduce energy consumption and costs, and maximize the energy supply chain's transparency and reliability. The smart grid system addresses the disadvantages of old electrical grids that used to use smart net meters [3]. The smart grid concept focuses not only on utilities and technologies but also on customer choices surrounding electricity and energy usage. The purpose of smart grid development is to provide long-term production, circulation, as well as consumption of traditional and viable energy that is stable, dependable, efficient, and cost-effective [4]. A smart grid can benefit producers, transport and circulation workers, and users alike.

Smart grid technology of Society 5.0 permits customers as well as network managers to monitor power usage and avoid network overloading [5]. The smart grid maintains dispense and needs balance and adjusts voltage by altering production as well as management needs. Smart grid technology permits network operators to remotely foresee and find errors and disruptions, perhaps leading to speedier power restoration [6]. The smart grid makes it simple to combine alternating viable power sources by creating immediate energy-transmitting decisions as well as controlling load. In

DOI: 10.1201/9781003397052-9

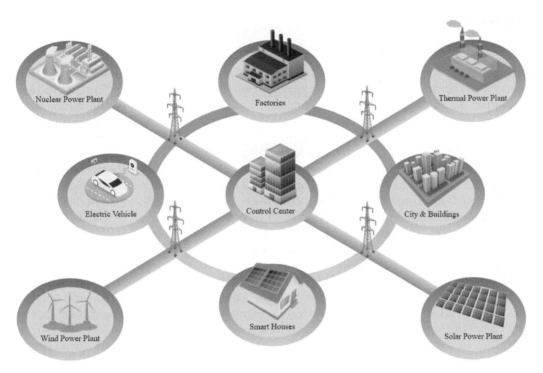

FIGURE 9.1
Smart grid power heads.

comparison to regular electrical grids, the smart grid is a completely new concept for all researchers. The smart grid is an upgrade to the power distribution infrastructure. As a result, this topic is important in the research community. A smart grid refers to a combination of information and all digital communication approaches used by power grid systems to promote two-way communication and power flow, which can improve the power scheme's safety, dependability, and efficacy [7]. Furthermore, the smart grid is an arrangement of tools, techniques, and procedures for creating an intelligent and computerized power grid. Due to the massive amount of data collected from various sources at all times, all power companies must take responsibility for all obtained data and gain a clear understanding of electricity consumption practices. As a result, artificial intelligence is necessary, in which machine learning learns autonomously from data without human intervention, and deep learning (DL) algorithms are employed for feature extraction and data analysis [8]. The majority of the investigations, such as load outlining, client classification, load forecasting, and anomaly detection, were conducted using smart meter data. Flexible demand management and meaningful energy control smart meter data analysis of Society 5.0 are required for a better understanding of electricity use [9]. Machine learning algorithms encapsulate the approaches for detecting designs and interrelationships in input as well as creating a structure to depict the designs and interrelationships. The machine can forecast upcoming actions on the basis of earlier instances thanks to the learning experience.

9.2 Machine Learning in Smart Grids Society 5.0

Unsupervised and supervised machine learning are both possible. The algorithm has been given training data having results in supervised machine learning. The data hidden inside the patterns created a model/function [10]. The algorithm infers outcomes from new data using the model/function it has already created. No such information related to labels is provided by unsupervised learning. Without knowing how to name or label the unknown patterns and structures inside the data, the algorithm finds them. Regression and Classification come under supervised learning algorithms. The categorization problem divides information into specified outcome labels [11]. The outcome variable in a classification problem consists of limited types (e.g., "male/female", "low/moderate/high"). The "regression problem" is concerned with forecasting an outcome's true value (such as age and price). The resulting variable in a "regression problem," unlike a classification problem, has continuous values. Clustering and association are the two main kinds of unsupervised learning methods. The algorithm in a clustering problem attempts to determine the inherent group of data according to data point resemblance (like the group of patients according to symptoms/syndrome). K-means clustering, hierarchical clustering, DBSCAN, OPTICS, and other clustering techniques are popular. The coincidence of actions having higher occurrence in a big dataset is identified as well as stated like association rules in the association problem. Semi-supervised learning algorithms are a type of machine learning algorithm that falls somewhere amongst supervised and unsupervised learning algorithms [3]. When the great majority of data is not labelled and just a tiny fraction of the data is labelled, this type of learning algorithm is used. This circumstance occurs when data labelling needs a high level of skill and/or is resource-intensive.

9.3 Deep Learning in Smart Grids Society 5.0

DL is a branch of machine learning that began with a multilayer Artificial Neural Network (ANN) in smart grid Society 5.0 [12]. Although DL technically has a broader connotation, when we think of it nowadays, we only think of massive deep neural networks or deep neural networks. Deep in this context usually refers to the number of layers. "Convolutional Neural Networks (CNN)," Feedforward Deep Networks (FDN), "Boltzmann Machine (BM)," "Recurrent Neural Networks (RNN)" [13], "Deep Belief Networks (DBN)," "Long-Short Term Memory (LSTM) Networks," and Generative Adversarial Networks are some of the numerous types of DL (GAN). The most widely used structures are CNN and RNN. RNN excels in managing time-series data, while CNN excels at spatial distribution data. Deep learning uses huge neural networks having multiple layers of processing components to grasp a variety of patterns from huge inputs with improved computational power and training methodologies. Image and speech recognition are two common uses. Neural networks are used to implement deep learning [14]. The biological neuron inspires neural networks. As shown in Figure 9.2, deep learning is a subset of machine learning, while machine learning is a subset of artificial intelligence. To acquire better results for calculating the exact electricity demand, companies employed modern approaches such as fuzzy logic, data mining, machine learning, support vector machines (SVM), artificial neural networks (ANN), and genetic algorithms, amongst others. Deep learning is one of the most important methods for smart grid applications.

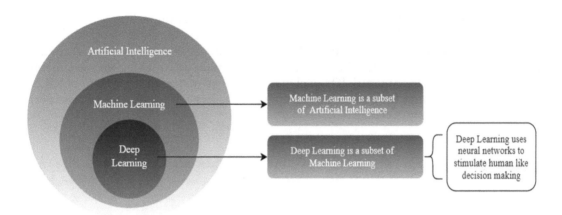

FIGURE 9.2
Depiction of AI, ML, and DL.

9.4 Reinforcement Learning in Smart Grids Society 5.0

Reinforcement learning is the process of learning how to execute the optimum action in a given situation to maximize the total reward [14]. This approach makes an agent grasp using trial and error as per the reward obtained by the outcome of activities. The labels reflect the answer in supervised learning, whereas the agent must decide the correct action in reinforcement learning by associating the late returns and actions. To describe reinforcement learning, "Markov Decision Process" (MDP) [15] has a limited series of states, a defined series of actions, as well as benefits that can be employed. In MDP, an agent takes a course of action to move from one state to another and gets rewards. To maximize their reward, MDP allows agents to select the finest action within every state. A policy is a set of actions made by an actor that are optimal. Q-learning is a reinforcement learning technique in which an action-value task is learned that predicts the predictable efficacy of a given task in a given condition.

9.5 Energy Dispatch Decisions in Smart Grids Society 5.0

Power grid operators depend upon energy demand projections to regulate energy production to satisfy needs as well as evade burden. With the rise of viable and dispersed energy sources, matching electricity supply to demand has become more difficult [16]. To establish how much power must be provided by traditional generators to satisfy requirements, it is now required to assess the power requirements as well as dispersed production. Battery storage serves to smooth out variations in power requirements and dispersed generation. Batteries could reserve energy at the time of high output and then supply afterwards to satisfy those gaps in low production periods. A consumer can pick from three power sources: grid, battery, or PV, as per grid energy pricing and battery or PV power availability [17]. During high feed-in tariff, the customer can sell extra PV or battery energy; during feed-in tariff, the customer may store or use excess PV energy.

A wide range of empirical algorithms (like particle swarm optimization and evolutionary algorithms) and approaches grounded on game theory were established to achieve ideal power transmit verdicts in smart grids [7]. Energy management algorithms grounded on reinforcement learning could help consumers save money by making the best energy dispatch decisions. Hossain et al. [6] developed an energy management system based on Q-learning that acquires to create improved energy transmission verdicts based on experience rather than past knowledge.

9.6 Challenges

Supervised learning techniques need training data that is labelled completely, but this input is sparse or hard to acquire [18]. Because power system breakdowns are rare, the lack and imbalance of event data makes predicting power outages difficult. Many sorts of failures occur in distribution feeders, for example, but training cases for each category are limited. After some time, a failing pattern might evolve; also the prediction prototype can become outdated. The efficacy of deep learning algorithms for simulating smart grid Society 5.0 [19] difficulties will be determined by the availability of a huge volume of high-quality data. To offer higher quality, artificial data for training, modelling, and sampling can be used. Effective classification/characterization of hazards and the origin of risk are crucial in the reliable identification of safety assaults in the smart grid. As fresh forms of attacks emerge eventually, frequent change in classification is needed. As a result, the problem is to provide a reliable classification technique that can effectively detect various forms of developing threats [20]. As previously stated, the lack of past labelled data makes utilizing supervised learning-based algorithms difficult, making anomaly identification in the smart grid a difficult task.

9.7 Benefits of Smart Grid

- The transfer of electricity is significantly more efficient.
- When electrical power problems occur, smart grids Society 5.0 provides a faster resolution.
- Consumers benefit from a smart grid approach since it reduces their power and operating costs.
- Decreased peak requirements, ensuring decreased electricity charges.
- Well-bonded systems to generate power, including viable power system, are owned by customers. The security feature has been improved.

9.8 Conclusion

The majority of the researchers focused their research on smart grids, with the use of artificial learning and machine learning techniques. It is still a difficult factor for everyone.

Deep learning is being utilized to solve more complicated smart grid Society 5.0 challenges that have not yet been solved using machine learning approaches. Deep neural networks are the primary direction in deep learning because they increase the number of layers in well-known artificial neural networks. Although this method has enormous application potential in the context of smart grids, researchers are currently grappling with deep learning approaches due to the system's many hidden layers. A few obstacles in applying machine learning approaches regarding smart grids Society 5.0 were also explored in this study. These include challenges in producing good quality artificial training input, discovering effective approaches for selecting attributes, and smart meters' limited memory and computing capability. The smart grid is growing more complex and sensitive as new energy sources and technologies are integrated. In the literature, even though many solutions grounded on machine learning were offered for smart grid, there is always room for development. Deep learning and Big Data have the potential to solve smart grid concerns in the future.

References

1. Gautam V, Parimala N. E-Metadata versioning system for data warehouse schema. *International Journal of Metadata, Semantics and Ontologies.* 2012 Jan 1;7(2):101–113.
2. Kotsiopoulos T, Sarigiannidis P, Ioannidis D, Tzovaras D. Machine learning and deep learning in smart manufacturing: The smart grid paradigm. *Computer Science Review.* 2021;40:100341.
3. Hellingrath B, Lechtenberg S. Applications of artificial intelligence in supply chain management and logistics: Focusing onto recognition for supply chain execution. In *The Art of Structuring.* Springer, 2019, pp. 283–296.
4. Suryateja PS. A comparative analysis of cloud simulators. *International Journal of Modern Education & Computer Science.* 2016 Apr 1;8(4).
5. Zhang D, Han X, Deng C. Review on the research and practice of deep learning and reinforcement learning in smart grids. *CSEE Journal of Power and Energy Systems.* 2018;4(3):362–370.
6. Hossain E, Khan I, Un-Noor F, Sikander SS, Sunny MSH. Application of big data and machine learning in smart grid, and associated security concerns: A review. *IEEE Access.* 2019;7:13960–13988.
7. Simaiya S, Gautam V, Lilhore UK, Garg A, Ghosh P, Trivedi NK, Anand A. EEPSA: Energy efficiency priority scheduling algorithm for cloud computing. In *2021 2nd international conference on smart electronics and communication (ICOSEC).* 2021 Oct 7, pp. 1064–1069. IEEE.
8. Azad S, Sabrina F, Wasimi S. Transformation of smart grid using machine learning. In *2019 29th Australasian Universities Power Engineering Conference (AUPEC).* 2019, pp. 1–6. IEEE.
9. Günel K, Ekti AR. Exploiting machine learning applications for smart grids. In *2019 16th International Multi-Conference on Systems, Signals & Devices (SSD).* 2019, pp. 679–685. IEEE.
10. Zoph B, Yuret D, May J, Knight K. Transfer learning for low-resource neural machine translation. arXiv preprint arXiv:1604.02201, 2016.
11. Lamnatou C, Chemisana D, Cristofari C. Smart grids and smart technologies in relation to photovoltaics, storage systems, buildings and the environment. *Renewable Energy.* 2022 Feb 1;185:1376–1391.
12. Judge MA, Khan A, Manzoor A, Khattak HA. Overview of smart grid implementation: Frameworks, impact, performance and challenges. *Journal of Energy Storage.* 2022 May 1;49:104056.
13. Li Y, Wei X, Li Y, Dong Z, Shahidehpour M. Detection of false data injection attacks in smart grid: A secure federated deep learning approach. *IEEE Transactions on Smart Grid.* 2022 Sep 6;13(6):4862–4872.

14. Nafees MN, Saxena N, Cardenas A, Grijalva S, Burnap P. Smart grid cyber-physical situational awareness of complex operational technology attacks: A review. *ACM Computing Surveys*. 2023 Feb 2;55(10):1–36.
15. Zidi S, Mihoub A, Qaisar SM, Krichen M, Al-Haija QA. Theft detection dataset for benchmarking and machine learning based classification in a smart grid environment. *Journal of King Saud University – Computer and Information Sciences*. 2023 Jan 1;35(1):13–25.
16. Conchas RF, Sanchez EN, Ricalde LJ, Alvarez JG, Alanis AY. Sensor fault-tolerant control for a doubly fed induction generator in a smart grid. *Engineering Applications of Artificial Intelligence*. 2023 Jan 1;117:105527.
17. Rouzbahani HM, Karimipour H, Lei L. Multi-layer defense algorithm against deep reinforcement learning-based intruders in smart grids. *International Journal of Electrical Power and Energy Systems*. 2023 Mar 1;146:108798.
18. Bitirgen K, Filik ÜB. A hybrid deep learning model for discrimination of physical disturbance and cyber-attack detection in smart grid. *International Journal of Critical Infrastructure Protection*. 2023 Mar 1;40:100582.
19. Zheng S, Shahzad M, Asif HM, Gao J, Muqeet HA. Advanced optimizer for maximum power point tracking of photovoltaic systems in smart grid: A roadmap towards clean energy technologies. *Renewable Energy*. 2023 Jan 17.
20. Haq EU, Pei C, Zhang R, Jianjun H, Ahmad F. Electricity-theft detection for smart grid security using smart meter data: A deep-CNN based approach. *Energy Reports*. 2023 Mar 1;9:634–643.

10

Securing Smart Grids Using Machine Learning Algorithms

**Moushumi Das, Vandana Mohindru Sood, Kamal
Deep Garg, and Sushil Kumar Narang**

10.1 Introduction

The acronym "grid" has typically been used to describe an energy system capable of performing all or any of the four power production, transmission, allocation, and tracking functions [1]. A smart grid (SG), additionally referred to as a smart electronic systems/power grid, is a twenty-first-century power infrastructure update. Traditional transmission lines are commonly used to convey energy from a few fixed producers to a large number of consumers or customers. Through two-way electrical and communication exchanges, the SG, on the other hand, creates highly automated and unsupervised intelligent power delivery networks [2].

Electricity generation, transmission, consumption, and cost are all changing. It is no longer a straightforward unidirectional flow of electrons at a fixed cost from a centralized power plant to end customers. Consumer power demand profiles are becoming more complex, intermittent renewables are rapidly rising, and off-grid decentralized power production is becoming more common. The power grid is already growing smarter [3], driven by cost-cutting initiatives as well as the need to manage the complexities of today's energy systems.

A "smart" grid is difficult to explain, but it is more than simply a phrase. It is essentially an electric grid that uses multi-directional connectivity and analytics to deliver energy as efficiently as possible. Grid technology, like the generation resources that fuel it, is becoming more decentralized [4]. Smart demand-side monitoring in the form of better metering infrastructure, sometimes known as smart meters, is required for a smart grid [5]. Figure 10.1 depicts the fundamental framework of a smart grid system. As the electrical power system continues to transition to next-generation smart grid (SG) technology, the challenge has piqued the scientific community's interest [6].

Smart grid systems establish the best generation–transmission–distribution pattern and preserve data from the power system. Distributed energy resources (DER) combined with intelligent microgrids may provide a feasible solution to mounting environmental issues while also ensuring effective generation and transmission [5]. Decentralized smart microgrids, some suggest, will be much more advantageous to global power planning. In other terms, smart grid technology (SG) is a collection of techniques and technologies that allow the electrical grid to become autonomous and automated [5]. According to analysts, the current electrical power grid has remained stable for the previous century. As

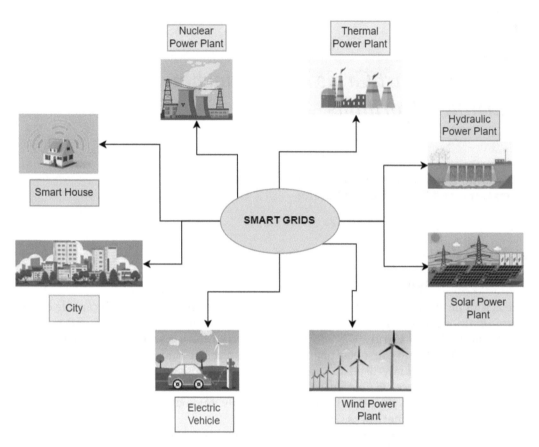

FIGURE 10.1
Fundamental framework of smart grid.

the population grows, so does the demand for electricity [7]. Figure 10.2 depicts a built-in framework for a conceptual model.

Climate change, energy consumption, component failure, population increase, a lack of energy storage, the usage of fossil fuels, a decrease in electric power output, asymmetric telecommunication, and a variety of other issues all contributed to the need for new grid technology. As a result, new grid infrastructure is needed to address these challenges. The next phase of power transmission architecture is developing as a critical technology for achieving such high-priority goals in order to improve modern human life [8].

Smart grid infrastructure is composed of a number of complex components that must be connected in order to work effectively, and it is divided into two parts: virtual and difficulties faced [9]. Power firms employ an advanced metering infrastructure (AMI) network to connect with the service providers. AMI uses a wireless network to automate power distribution/outage management metering, monitoring, and management [10].

Large numbers of utility companies connect to an energy service provider center through a unidirectional connection that can be mesh, multilayer, or hybrid in design. We can integrate though the Internet of Things into all essential aspects in a power grid, including energy production, communication, transmission, and demand [11]. The various infrastructure levels involved in smart grids are depicted in Figure 10.3.

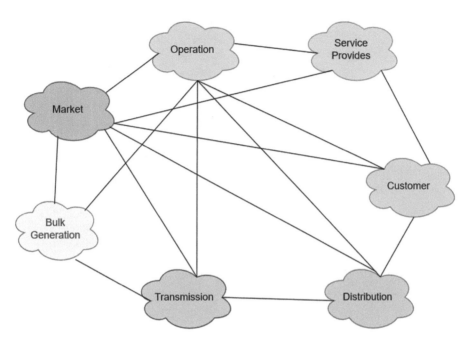

FIGURE 10.2
Conceptual model of smart grid system.

The latest technologies based on machine learning and deep learning will have a grow-ing and potentially global impact. The initial ML and DL applications may be found in the monitoring of electric machinery [12]. Such models developed for predicting problems in rotating motors and rolling bearings are improving, allowing for more exact assessments. There are applications in supply chains and logistics networks as well. An interconnected production process will adjust and accommodate new information as it is supplied [13].

If a delivery is delayed due to inclement weather, a data center can respond by adjust-ing manufacturing priorities. Transportation is another area that makes use of ML and DL algorithms [14]. When receiving cargo containers from ships, several transport yards use robotic cranes or vehicles to help with efficiency. Furthermore, secure IIoT (Industrial Internet of Things) infrastructures for storing and analyzing scalable sensor readings (big data) for medical purposes are being created. A different framework that makes use of machine learning (ML) and deep learning (DL) models is Smart Grids[15]. The various data sources of grids are given in Figure 10.4.

Traditional power infrastructure is obviously old and incapable of providing our cur-rent expanding demand for continuously consistent electricity delivery [16], owing to the increased use of technological gadgets and previously inconceivable patterns of electricity usage. Its centralized system, in particular, involved large-scale data interactions, result-ing in significant records latency, making it incapable of meeting the need for authentic control and oversight; its one-way electricity distribution channels aid in the shutdown of the grid from open and friendly customer-owned energy sources that are renewable to enhance the power utilization [17].

Many countries have increased their efforts in the last decade to build next-generation electricity networks, sometimes known as smart grids [18]. Smart grids are designed to integrate the current disconnected energy system and cloud resources, allowing a wide

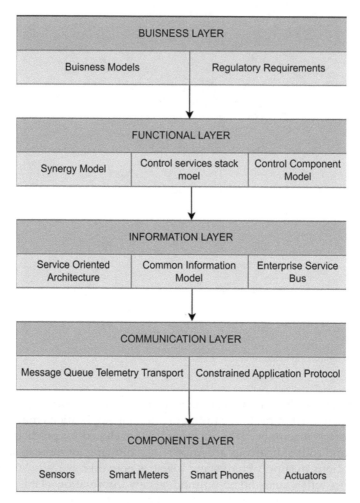

FIGURE10.3
Infrastructure layers of smart grids.

spectrum of people can have unauthorized connections in compliance with government-mandated open-access legislation. By integrating a command and interaction layer, smart grid will aid in local data management, decentralized regulation, two-way electricity transfer, and reliability-efficiency-driven reaction [18].

10.1.1 Contribution

This work identifies and addresses several concerns of security and privacy in relation to smart grids. The objectives of the work are:

a) Addressing the issue of security and the urge to work on it with the help of the latest technologies.

b) Comparing the various algorithms and models proposed in this area and identifying the limitations to overcome the research gap addressed.

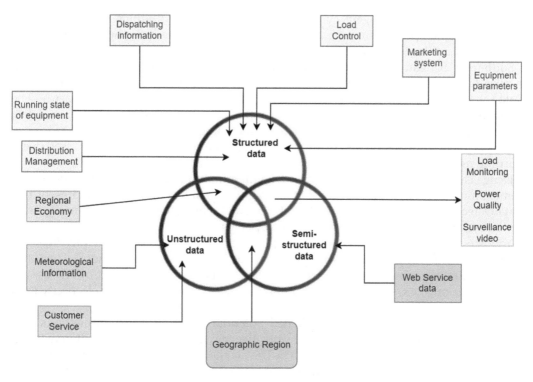

FIGURE 10.4
Data sources for grids.

c) Discussing the various AI, ML, and DL-based techniques being used in smart grids nowadays.

The novelty of this chapter is to use machine learning algorithms along with IoT-based systems that would help improve the smart grid system with much more accuracy and ease in work.

We just reviewed the power grid and smart grid system's introduction. Furthermore, the study chapter is separated into various sections, that is, Section 10.2 discusses the previous work and the research done in this field. Section 10.3 discusses the various attacks in smart grids. Section 10.4 discusses a variety of assault detection methods using machine learning, and in Sections 10.5 and 10.6 the results, discussion, conclusions, and future scope are discussed.

10.2 Related Work

Methods for reducing computing costs while finding causal linkages between subsystems were suggested using feature extraction via symbolic dynamic filtering (SDF) by Hadis Karimipour et al. [19]. With large-scale smart grids, the aim was to build an adaptable anomaly identification engine capable of distinguishing an actual malfunction from an interruption and an intelligent cyber-attack. The simulation findings validate the proposed technique's performance in a variety of operating conditions. The reliability of the test was 99%, with a 98% true positive rate and a 2% fake positive rate.

Sudharkar Sengan et al. [20] emphasized the significance of erroneous information cyber-attacks at smart grid physical levels. As an initial furthermore, the proposed Real Data Integrity approach uses an Agent-Based Model to show an attack risk measure. The study then shifts to the use of an agent-based approach to decentralize the integrity of data security in the system. Finally, the developed modeling methods' output and efficiency are experimentally assessed and compared to contemporary framework-supervised deep-learning models.

Deng et al. [21] constructed an FDIA model with minimum information on system states, demonstrating the potential of attacks that might stay undiscovered by the present Bad Data Detection (BDD) process. They then broadened their research from balanced distribution systems to asymmetrical distribution systems.

Youbiao He et al. [5] while maintaining high accuracy suggested that the detection approach successfully relaxes assumptions about diverse assault situations. They also developed an optimization model for analyzing the behavior of one sort of FDI assault that puts the power system's restricted number of state measurements for electricity theft in jeopardy.

Mitchell and Chen et al. [22] investigated potential intrusion detection methods over cyber-physical system (CPS), as well as the positive and negative aspects of different intrusion detection strategies when used in CPS. They contend that physical quality assurance, closed control loops, attack intensity, and legacy technology all contribute to the distinctiveness of intrusion prevention, along with emphasizing the importance of data types and shared IDS.

Varun Badrinath Krishna et al. [23] established a unique model for theft detection to detect meticulously planned energy theft attacks that outperform detectors proposed previously. Lastly, the detector is put to test by introducing bogus data into real smart meter data. In comparison to previous experiments, we demonstrate that our detection significantly reduces electricity theft for each assault class.

Ucar at al. [24] suggested a model for detecting energy instances was created using extreme learning (ELM). Weights between the layers of input and concealed were determined at random and never change throughout training, whereas the hidden and output layers' relative weights fluctuate. Because of its single layer, ELM has a modest level of complexity. As a result, it may be swiftly trained while still working properly.

Parvez et al. [25] created a smart meter security framework that uses a locally relevant important administration system for meter cryptography along with the K-nearest neighbors for meter certification. To find a meter, a probabilistic estimator (MLE) based on radio signal was used in this method. Based on signal intensity, this method produces an area chart, with each meter getting a unique coordinate. To prevent data hacking, each meter is linked to a secret key, which is used to encrypt data in conjunction with a random key index.

Kurt et al. [26] applied a model-free reinforcement learning approach to build an online attack/anomaly physical function for partially observable Markov Decision Processes (MDP). This method could be able to identify an unidentified attack type without any prior knowledge of attack models. The modeling results show that the workaround could identify cyber-attacks fast, but it could be further enhanced by integrating supervised learning, intelligent storage management methods, and linear/nonlinear modeling methods.

Zhang et al. [27] researched numerous ways for machine learning that may be used to detect and protect against DDoS attacks. To detect traffic irregularities, the total amount of packets, typical packet size, discontinuous temporal change, packet size dispersion, packet percentage, and information rates are commonly used. The researchers discovered that the performance in distinguishing between hazardous and ordinary traffic may be improved.

Table 10.1 summarizes the multiple studies done in the field of smart grids utilizing various algorithms. Despite the usage of these technologies, there are various research gaps, such as the use of tiny data sets, time-consuming procedures, privacy and security concerns, the need for much more precise algorithms and development, as well as some superior components.

TABLE 10.1

Summary of the Related Work

References	Year	Model	Accuracy	Advantage	Research Gap
[19]	2022	Feature extraction Methods	99%	Reduces computing load while identifying causal relationships across subsystems	Time consuming
[20]	2022	Agent-based model	98.19%	Integrity of misleading data cyber-attacks was highlighted	Small dataset
[21]	2022	FDIA model	80%	Demonstrates the viability of attacks	Low accuracy
[5]	2021	Optimization model	89.9%	Relaxes the assumptions on various assault situations, resulting in excellent accuracy	Can be improved using real-time data
[22]	2021	Intrusion detection approaches	92%	Effectiveness of CPS's vulnerability scanning	Time consuming
[23]	2020	Theft detector	96%	Detect ingeniously designed electricity theft attacks that avoid detection	Privacy and security concerns
[24]	2020	Method to detect power quality events	90%	Can be trained quickly while displaying adequate performance	Much more accurate algorithms needed
[25]	2020	Smart meter security method with two levels	88%	Based on the signal strength, it generates a local location map	Low accuracy
[36]	2019	A model-free reinforcement learning framework for online attack/ anomaly detection	95%	Detection of unknown attacks without the need for prior attack model knowledge	Better-performing components needed
[1]	2018	Investigated different machine learning algorithms	90%	Used for effective DDoS detection and defence	Performance and robustness cannot yet be guaranteed

10.3 Various Attacks in Smart Grids

We have explored in depth the origins of smart grids, their technology, and the technologies, models, or algorithms introduced thus far. Yet, because smart grids are networks, there is always the fear of security, which means that there might be a lot of attacks in this field. Several forms of attacks are covered in length in this section. Figure 10.5 is a visual illustration of several attacks, which are explained more below (Figure 10.6).

a) **Passive Attacks:** These types of attacks are intended to collect data about a country's capabilities and advanced support while avoiding disruption of links between authorized users. Due to the difficulty in detecting these attacks, the network must design countermeasures. Passive assaults can put network security at risk. Passive assaults include eavesdropping and data processing [6].

b) **Active Attacks:** This type of attack tries to interfere with network performance, user communications, and data transmission over the network. In contrast, active assaults are primarily concerned with network availability and integrity. These assaults have the potential to interrupt system functionality, perhaps resulting in major financial loss and brief or lengthy blackouts. Additionally, a significant percentage of contemporary attacks aim to modify network data (e.g., operating, control, watching, and billing information). Any security breach or alteration to this data could cause a slew of issues throughout the system [27].

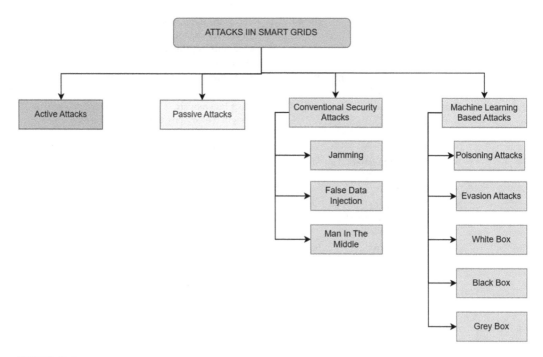

FIGURE 10.5
Different types of attacks in smart grids.

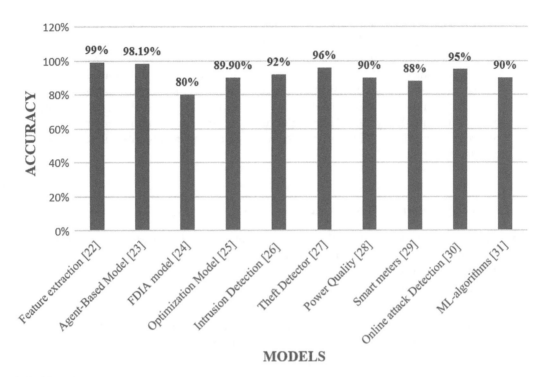

FIGURE 10.6
Accuracy comparison of various discussed models.

10.3.1 Conventional Security Attacks

a) **Jamming:** The jammer assault scenario seeks to limit the amount of spectrum available to legitimate network users. Jamming attacks significantly reduce the signal-to-noise ratio by injecting hostile electrical radiation into the system bandwidth. A jammer attack is a type of DoS attack that can impair software performance [26]. An attacker can jam the channel of communication if the monitoring follows a static, pre-set pattern. A simulation model jamming assault may weaken utility reliability and result in incorrect power pricing [24].

b) **False Data Injection:** The estimator of the state is an essential component of the SG energy monitoring system, and it is in charge of analyzing the grid's load, voltage intensity, angles, and state variables. The goal is to minimize errors and collaborate with the Bad Data Detection (BDD) system to identify any anomalous data measurement patterns. These operational components of the most essential state estimation are the primary targets of the dangerous assault known as Fsi. The main goal of this attack is to alter actual-world information in order to fool the system. Changed data is received by the SG for a variety of causes, including power theft, load reduction, delays, and data blockage. Data manipulation in energy use is one of the most common attacks on the power monitoring system [29].

$$z = h(x) + e$$

c) **Man in the Middle (MITM):** An MITM assault is the second most typical kind among the attacks. A cyber-attacker opens a conversation between two legitimate hosts, disrupting regular communication. The MITM attacker has two options: either he or she can impersonate both parties and change the data sent during the transaction, or they can listen in on the discussion and steal information [30]. As a result, when he invades the network, an MITM offender has the ability to enter bogus data into the system. Through eavesdropping, packet alteration or loss, and network disruption, MITM can put security requirements like integrity and confidentiality at risk [31].

10.3.2 Machine Learning-Based Attacks

a) **Poisoning Attacks:** By injecting wrong inputs or model parameters, poisoning, also known as pathogenic assault, seeks to deceive the Iterative approach even during the training phase.

b) **Evasion Attacks:** During the testing step, attackers attempt to fool the ML algorithm into reaching the incorrect conclusion.

c) **White Box:** The attacker is intimately aware of the detection approach, classification strategy, and modeling approach in a white-box assault.

d) **Black Box:** In black box, attackers in contrast hand would be only associated with the detection model's fundamental concepts but not its specific settings.

e) **Gray Box:** Gray-box attackers are typically uninformed of the condition of the system. Attackers are assumed to understand attributes and supervised learning but still not training datasets or categorization parameters [32].

10.4 Attack Detection Using Machine Learning Methods

a) **Supervised Learning Methods:** A network operator computes the computation of the classification function f in a supervised training approach using a training data set as described in the following. The class label, y(i), of a new observation, s(i), is predicted using Equation 10.2.

$$Y(i) = f[s(i)]$$

To detect attacks, four learning algorithms are utilized. To minimize the characteristic of vectors' dimension, feature selection approaches can be applied. The development of algorithms for selecting features could be a sensible approach for smart grid security, as well as a fascinating issue for additional investigation. SVMs and other kernel machines may be utilized to map a characteristic, maps in S to Hilbert spaces, with the feature vectors being simple processing in the maps and learning model calculation. Smaller samples, like one-dimensional samples, can be processed by using a particular measurement vector as a collection [33].

b) **Semi-Supervised Learning Methods:** In this type of technique, the information obtained from unlabeled test samples is used to generate the learning model. The S3VM semi-supervised SVM (S3VM) methodology is used to discover the logical relationship between supervised and semi-supervised learning methods. In this strategy, the unlabeled samples are included in the optimization issue's minimization problem [34].

The basic assumption of the S3VM is that observations in the same cluster have the same labels and that the number of subclusters is limited. To put it another way, attacked and secure measurement matrices should be pooled in separate feature space regions. To avoid the formation of subcultures, the difference between the number of attacks and the number of protected observations should be kept as small as possible.

c) **Decision and Feature-Level Methods:** The statistical learning theory's one objective is to discover a classification rule that outperforms a collection of distinct classifier rules, or a feature set that performs a set of individual features. To increase the performance of individual classifiers, one way is to combine a set of classifiers or a set of features. The former is referred to as decision-level synthesis or supervised learning, whereas the latter is referred to as feature-level fusion, Equation 10.3 is used to determine the accuracy mathematically. This section [35] discusses Adaboost engineering.

$$D_{t+1(i)} = \frac{D_{t(i)} exp^{-\alpha_t y_t f_i(s_i)}}{z_i}$$

d) **Online Learning Methods for Real-Time Attack Detection:** In a general online learning setting, a sequence of training samples (or a single sample) is given to the learning algorithm at each observation or algorithm processing time. Then, the algorithm computes the learning model using only the given samples and predicts the labels. The learning model is updated with respect to the error of the algorithm, which is computed using a loss function on the given samples. Therefore, the perceptron and Adaboost are convenient for online learning in this setting. For instance, an online perceptron (OP) is implemented by predicting the label (yi) of a single sample (si) at each time t, and updating the weight vector w using w for the misclassified samples with (yi) = sign(f (si)). This simple approach is applied to the development of online MKL and regression algorithms [36].

e) **State Estimation of Power System:** In smart grid power systems, state estimation is used to forecast the system's state, which determines optimal power generation. This technique displays a link between the system's status variables and actual power grid data.

f) **Data Mining-Based Algorithms:** Data mining is the practice of discovering patterns in enormous data collections. Data mining methods are widely used to process variable data observations acquired from a specific system in order to find underlying data features or trends. Data mining frequently intersects with analytics and machine learning approaches, making it a multidisciplinary area. According to some academics, data mining approaches are unsupervised machine learning methodologies. However, because these tactics differ from learning algorithms in the literature, they also differ from this study. Data mining-based FDIA detection algorithms are regarded premature due to their limited applicability in this field. Nonetheless, several approaches have been presented [37].

10.5 Results and Discussion

The purpose of this study was to investigate how various algorithms based on machine learning could be used to enhance smart grid stability, reliability, safety, effectiveness, and speed. The chapter's findings show how algorithms based on machine learning can be used to effectively estimate transformer life, detect power quality incidents and faults, optimize power dispatch decisions for lowering expenses for energy, effective electrical industry operational processes, safeguard information, and avoid assaults.

Figure 10.6 depicts the graphical representation of the accuracy given by various models and algorithms proposed by various authors using machine learning. It is clearly visible that the feature extraction methods proposed by Hadis Karimipour [19] give the highest accuracy of 99%, whereas the FDIA model proposed by Deng [21] results in the least accuracy as compared to the other models.

Table 10.2 is a comparison of the authors' suggested model up to this point, as explained above in the chapter on the basis of limitations discussed in Table 10.1. The tick (✓) marks represent that the given limitation was rectified in that particular model, whereas the cross (×) marks represent that the particular model has that limitation and was not rectified.

10.6 Conclusion and Future Scope

For training reasons, supervised learning systems require multi-label data; yet, correct data with labels is very uncommon. While power network disruptions are uncommon, a fundamental barrier to predicting power outages is the limited and uneven distribution of event data. In distribution feeders, for example, many different types of failures occur, but each kind has a limited number of training occurrences. Smart grids are one of the most promising areas for DL, RL, and DRL applications. Efforts have been made to research their application in smart grids. Many publications on this issue have been published, the vast majority of which were written in the prior three years.

The attacker identification issue has been rebuilt as a machine learning problem, and the effectiveness of monitored, electronic systems-supervised, encoder and encoding space fusion, and online learning approaches for different attack scenarios has been investigated. Initially, the fundamental components of the Industrial AI Ecosystem are investigated, and a novel Industrial AI application strategy is proposed.

Furthermore, these types of techniques and models used in the production are extensively explored and illustrated. Initially, the basic components of the Industrial AI Ecosystem are explored followed by the proposal of a novel Corporate artificial intelligence strategy. Furthermore, the ML and DL techniques and models used in manufacturing are extensively explored and depicted. A study of the ML and DL models and algorithms on the smart grid, a key subject of Industry 4.0, is additionally carried out in terms of efficiency and utility.

TABLE 10.2

Limitation-Based Comparison of Various Models

Research Gap → Models ↓	Time Consuming	Small Dataset	Low Accuracy	Real-Time Data	Privacy & Security Concerns	Better Components Needed	No Robustness and Performance
Feature extraction [19]	✗	✓	✓	✗	✓	✗	✗
Agent-based model [20]	✓	✗	✓	✗	✗	✓	✓
FDIA model [21]	✗	✓	✗	✓	✓	✓	✗
Optimization model [5]	✓	✗	✓	✗	✗	✗	✓
Intrusion detection [22]	✗	✓	✗	✓	✓	✗	✓
Theft detector [23]	✓	✗	✓	✗	✗	✓	✗
Power quality [24]	✓	✓	✗	✓	✓	✗	✗
Smart meters [25]	✗	✓	✗	✓	✗	✓	✓
Online attack detection [26]	✓	✗	✗	✗	✓	✗	✗
ML algorithms [1]	✗	✓	✓	✗	✓	✗	✗

As a future work proposal, an analogy is suggested to better emphasize the type of machine learning algorithm to be used for every sub-area of the intelligent grid. To accomplish this, a methodology for applying a wide range of algorithms in each of the parts must be developed, to choose those that yield the best possible outcomes.

References

Hossain, Eklas, Imtiaj Khan, Fuad Un-Noor, Sarder Shazali Sikander, and Md. Samiul Haque Sunny. "Application of big data and machine learning in smart grid, and associated security concerns: A review." *IEEE Access* 7 (2019): 13960–13988.

Karagiannopoulos, Stavros, Petros Aristidou, and Gabriela Hug. "Data-driven local control design for active distribution grids using off-line optimal power flow and machine learning techniques." *IEEE Transactions on Smart Grid* 10, no. 6 (2019): 6461–6471.

Bashir, Ali Kashif, Suleman Khan, B. Prabadevi, N. Deepa, Waleed S. Alnumay, Thippa Reddy Gadekallu, and Praveen Kumar Reddy Maddikunta. "Comparative analysis of machine learning algorithms for prediction of smart grid stability." *International Transactions on Electrical Energy Systems* 31, no. 9 (2021): e12706.

Azad, Salahuddin, Fariza Sabrina, and Saleh Wasimi. "Transformation of smart grid using machine learning." In *2019 29th Australasian Universities Power Engineering Conference (AUPEC)*, pp. 1–6. IEEE, 2019.

Kotsiopoulos, Thanasis, Sarigiannidis, Panagiotis , Ioannidis, Dimosthenis , and Tzovaras, Dimitrios. "Machine learning and deep learning in smart manufacturing: The smart grid paradigm." *Computer Science Review* 40 (2021): 100341.

Zhang, Dongxia, Xiaoqing Han, and Chunyu Deng. "Review on the research and practice of deep learning and reinforcement learning in smart grids." *CSEE Journal of Power and Energy Systems* 4, no. 3 (2018): 362–370.

Yao, Donghuan, Mi Wen, Xiaohui Liang, Zipeng Fu, Kai Zhang, and Yang Baojia. "Energy theft detection with energy privacy preservation in the smart grid." *IEEE Internet of Things Journal* 6, no. 5 (2019): 7659–7669.

Wang, Ning, Jie Li, Shen-Shyang Ho, and Chenxi Qiu. "Distributed machine learning for energy trading in electric distribution system of the future." *The Electricity Journal* 34, no. 1 (2021): 106883.

Haque, Nur Imtiazul, Md. Hasan Shahriar, Md. Golam Dastgir, Anjan Debnath, Imtiaz Parvez, Arif Sarwat, and Mohammad Ashiqur Rahman. "Machine learning in generation, detection, and mitigation of cyberattacks in smart grid: A survey." arXiv preprint arXiv:2010.00661, 2020.

Chehri, Abdellah, Issouf Fofana, and Xiaomin Yang. "Security risk modeling in smart grid critical infrastructures in the era of big data and artificial intelligence." *Sustainability* 13, no. 6 (2021): 3196.

Zhou, Liang, Xuan Ouyang, Huan Ying, Lifang Han, Yushi Cheng, and Tianchen Zhang. "Cyber-attack classification in smart grid via deep neural network." In *Proceedings of the 2nd International Conference on Computer Science and Application Engineering*, pp. 1–5, 2018.

Lu, Renzhi, Seung Ho Hong, and Mengmeng Yu. "Demand response for home energy management using reinforcement learning and artificial neural network." *IEEE Transactions on Smart Grid* 10, no. 6 (2019): 6629-6639.

Fekri, Mohammad Navid, Ananda Mohon Ghosh, and Katarina Grolinger. "Generating energy data for machine learning with recurrent generative adversarial networks." *Energies* 13, no. 1 (2019): 130.

Yin, Linfei, Qi Gao, Lulin Zhao, and Tao Wang. "Expandable deep learning for real-time economic generation dispatch and control of three-state energies based future smart grids." *Energy* 191 (2020): 116561.

Hong, Ye, Yingjie Zhou, Qibin Li, Wenzheng Xu, and Xiujuan Zheng. "A deep learning method for short-term residential load forecasting in smart grid." *IEEE Access* 8 (2020): 55785–55797.

Alrasheedi, Abdullah, and Abdulaziz Almalaq. "Hybrid deep learning applied on Saudi smart grids for short-term load forecasting." *Mathematics* 10, no. 15 (2022): 2666.

Singh, Upma, Mohammad Rizwan, Muhannad Alaraj, and Ibrahim Alsaidan. "A machine learning-based gradient boosting regression approach for wind power production forecasting: A step towards smart grid environments." *Energies* 14, no. 16 (2021): 5196.

Bhattarai, Bishnu P., Sumit Paudyal, Yusheng Luo, Manish Mohanpurkar, Kwok Cheung, Reinaldo Tonkoski, Rob Hovsapian et al. "Big data analytics in smart grids: State-of-the-art, challenges, opportunities, and future directions" *IET Smart Grid* 2, no. 2 (2019): 141–154.

Berghout, Tarek, Mohamed Benbouzid, and S. M. Muyeen. "Machine learning for cybersecurity in smart grids: A comprehensive review-based study on methods, solutions, and prospects." *International Journal of Critical Infrastructure Protection* (2022): 100547.

Rivas, Angel Esteban Labrador, and Taufik Abrao. "Faults in smart grid systems: Monitoring, detection and classification." *Electric Power Systems Research* 189 (2020): 106602.

Li, Yang, Xinhao Wei, Yuanzheng Li, Zhaoyang Dong, and Mohammad Shahidehpour. "Detection of false data injection attacks in smart grid: A secure federated deep learning approach." *IEEE Transactions on Smart Grid* 13, no. 6 (2022): 4862–4872.

Cebekhulu, Eric, Adeiza James Onumanyi, and Sherrin John Isaac. "Performance analysis of machine learning algorithms for energy demand–supply prediction in smart grids." *Sustainability* 14, no. 5 (2022): 2546.

Rangel-Martinez, Daniel, K. D. P. Nigam, and Luis A. Ricardez-Sandoval. "Machine learning on sustainable energy: A review and outlook on renewable energy systems, catalysis, smart grid and energy storage." *Chemical Engineering Research and Design* 174 (2021): 414–441.

Sengan, Sudhakar, V. Subramaniyaswamy, V. Indragandhi, Priya Velayutham, and Logesh Ravi. "Detection of false data cyber-attacks for the assessment of security in smart grid using deep learning." *Computers & Electrical Engineering* 93 (2021): 107211.

Jahangir, Hamidreza, Hanif Tayarani, Saleh Sadeghi Gougheri, Masoud Aliakbar Golkar, Ali Ahmadian, and Ali Elkamel. "Deep learning-based forecasting approach in smart grids with microclustering and bidirectional LSTM network." *IEEE Transactions on Industrial Electronics* 68, no. 9 (2020): 8298–8309.

Wang, Zhenhua, Haibo He, Zhiqiang Wan, and Yan Sun. "Coordinated topology attacks in smart grid using deep reinforcement learning." *IEEE Transactions on Industrial Informatics* 17, no. 2 (2020): 1407–1415.

Babar, Muhammad, Muhammad Usman Tariq, and Mian Ahmad Jan. "Secure and resilient demand side management engine using machine learning for IoT-enabled smart grid." *Sustainable Cities and Society* 62 (2020): 102370.

Zidi, Salah, Alaeddine Mihoub, Saeed Mian Qaisar, Moez Krichen, and Qasem Abu Al-Haija. "Theft detection dataset for benchmarking and machine learning based classification in a smart grid environment." *Journal of King Saud University – Computer and Information Sciences* 35, no. 1 (2023): 13–25.

Majidi, Seyed Hossein, Shahrzad Hadayeghparast, and Hadis Karimipour. "FDI attack detection using extra trees algorithm and deep learning algorithm-autoencoder in smart grid." *International Journal of Critical Infrastructure Protection* 37 (2022): 100508.

Singh, Richa, Arunendra Singh, and Pronaya Bhattacharya. "A machine learning approach for anomaly detection to secure smart grid systems." In *Research Anthology on Smart Grid and Microgrid Development*, pp. 911–923. IGI Global, 2022.

Bitirgen, Kübra, and Ümmühan Başaran Filik. "A hybrid deep learning model for discrimination of physical disturbance and cyber-attack detection in smart grid." *International Journal of Critical Infrastructure Protection* 40 (2023): 100582.

11

Energy Management in IoT-Enabled Smart Grid: A Review

Vrinda Vritti, Kamal Deep Garg, Vandana Mohindru Sood, and Sushil Kumar Narang

11.1 Introduction

Modern society is dependent on energy since it gives us the power we need to live our daily lives. It is used to run our factories, light our houses, power our cars, and the extensive network of electronic equipment we depend on daily. Yet, because of the huge environmental effects of how we generate and use energy, it is crucial to create new and inventive technologies to sustainably fulfil the world's expanding energy demands. Unfortunately, the energy systems we currently use cannot be sustained. The main cause of greenhouse gas emissions contributing to global climate change is the burning of fossil fuels for energy. The ongoing use of fossil fuels severely impacts human health, accelerates climate change, and raises the danger of environmental catastrophes like oil spills. The development of sustainable energy solutions that can supply energy to a growing global population while reducing greenhouse gas emissions and environmental impacts is the key to solving this issue. The capacity to provide sustainable, clean energy can be found in a variety of renewable energy sources, such as solar, wind, hydropower, and geothermal energy.

Moreover, the way we produce, distribute, and use energy is changing, thanks to new Internet of Things (IoT)-enabled smart grids [1]. The conventional energy system is ageing and failing as a result of increasing demand and complexity. Smart grids, which are fuelled by IoT and energy management, offer an innovative method for regulating and optimising energy use while cutting costs and having a reduced environmental impact. IoT technology makes it possible to monitor and manage energy production and consumption in real time, making it easier to manage energy supply and demand. With IoT-enabled sensors and devices, energy data can be captured, analysed, and shared in real time across the grid. Understanding energy consumption trends, grid performance, and equipment upkeep may all be improved with the help of this data stored in them.

11.2 Towards Smart Grids

A power system that enables two-way communication between the grid and almost all connected devices is referred to as a "smart grid". Smart grids [2], intended to increase the

DOI: 10.1201/9781003397052-11

effectiveness, dependability, and resilience of the power system, have also been made possible by digital technologies. A smart grid monitors and manages the flow of power in real time using digital technologies including sensors, automation, and artificial intelligence. This enables the integration of renewable energy sources, such as wind and solar power, and creates a more flexible and responsive grid to better handle peak demand. The question is of why smart grids now arise. Smart grids help prevent authorised power transfers and blackouts, monitor the loads, and shed load when stress levels rise or frequency drops quickly. Moreover, it increases cybersecurity [3] and hinders communication between different LDS and distributed generation systems. The generational is a crucial part of the smart grid concept, but distributed generation sources like wind, solar, and many other customer-owned generating resources are used to augment it. In addition to producing electricity for end consumers, the smart grid can sell electricity back to the utility. India has begun developing smart grids to transform its power sector into a safe, flexible, resilient, and adaptively enabled ecosystem. Figure 11.1 shows the use of the smart grid in our daily lives.

Smart grids not only increase efficiency but also provide several financial advantages. Smart grids can save money by minimising the demand for new power production facilities and transmission lines by reducing the load on the system. In turn, this lowers the grid's operating and maintenance expenses, which can then be passed along to both industrial and residential consumers in the form of decreased energy costs. Additionally, smart grids give users the chance to produce their electricity using decentralised energy sources like solar and wind energy. This not only lessens their reliance on the grid but also enables them to sell any unused energy back to it, opening up a new revenue stream. Smart grids provide numerous economic advantages, and they also significantly increase the supply's dependability and quality of electricity. Smart grids can immediately adapt to any disturbances or outages by continuously monitoring the electricity flow in real time, minimising the impact on users. As a result, the electrical supply becomes more dependable and steadier, which is crucial for businesses and important infrastructure.

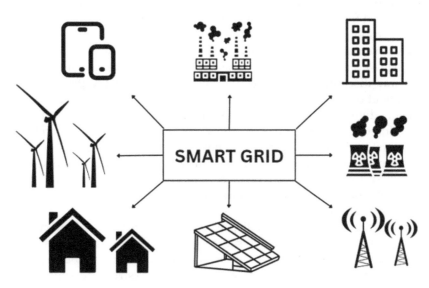

FIGURE 11.1
The use of the smart grid in our daily lives.

The technical and financial losses that happen during the transmission and distribution of electricity are significantly reduced, thanks to smart grids. These losses sometimes referred to as AT&C (aggregate technical and commercial) losses can be sizable and are frequently brought on by ineffective power transmission and electricity theft. Smart grids can lower these losses by using digital technology to monitor and control the electrical flow, leading to a more effective and economical power supply. Smart grids increase the security of the electricity supply while simultaneously increasing dependability and efficiency. Smart grids can protect the transmission and distribution of power from potential cyber risks like hacking and theft by utilising digital technologies like encryption.

Advanced capabilities for demand control and response are also provided by smart grids. Smart networks can better control peak demand and lessen the need for pricey peak power production units by continuously monitoring the electricity flow. This makes the grid more adaptable and responsive, enabling it to better balance the supply of electricity from power plants with the demand for it. India's economy is among the fastest growing in the world, and as a result, the country's demand for energy is rising quickly. As a result of its heavy reliance on fossil fuels, which are not only limited but also contribute to climate change, this poses a significant issue for the nation. The Indian government has set an ambitious goal to increase the proportion of renewable energy in its energy mix to solve this challenge. Several environmental factors, such as the need to decrease carbon dioxide (CO_2) emissions, decrease the effects of the greenhouse effect, increase the penetration of clean energy from renewable sources, and encourage consumer participation in energy conservation, are what motivate the development of a smart grid in India. By making it possible to include renewable energy sources in the system, smart grids can play a significant role in aiding India in achieving these goals. Smart grids can ensure the supply and demand of electricity from renewable energy sources, such as wind and solar power, by employing digital technologies to monitor and control the flow of electricity in real time. Decreasing the usage of fossil fuels lowers CO_2 emissions and lessens the consequences of the greenhouse effect. Consumers can take part in energy saving through smart grids as well. Smart grids can assist in lowering electricity demand by giving users real-time information on their energy use and enabling them to control their energy use, which eliminates the need for pricey peak power-producing facilities. This saves money on electricity bills in addition to saving energy.

Smart grids can enhance the integration of electric vehicles (EVs) into the grid in addition to the advantages already discussed [4]. Smart grids can be extremely useful in regulating the charging and discharging of EVs as their use grows, ensuring that they are charged effectively without overtaxing the grid. Smart charging, which optimises charging times and prices using digital technologies, can also lessen the demand on the grid during high usage times. Moreover, smart grids can enhance the entire management and operation of the electricity system, allowing utilities to identify issues earlier and take quick corrective action. Downtime must be minimised for key infrastructure like hospitals and data centres. By giving real-time information on their state, enabling preventive maintenance, and lowering the likelihood of equipment failure, smart grids can help utilities manage their assets, such as transformers and electrical lines, better.

Finally, smart grids can support resilience and energy independence. Smart grids can enable microgrids, which are compact, self-contained power systems that can function independently of the main grid in the case of a natural disaster or another emergency. By doing this, it may be possible to guarantee that vital infrastructure – like hospitals and emergency services – remains functional during a crisis. In conclusion, smart grids have the potential to revolutionise the power industry by enhancing efficiency, dependability, and resilience as well as fostering the use of renewable energy sources and facilitating increased consumer involvement in energy. Thus, smart grids will be essential in supplying the world's energy demands in the future because of the explosive growth in energy demand and the requirement to cut greenhouse gas emissions.

11.3 An Overview of IoT

The Internet of Things (IoT) is a network that connects physical objects to the internet. IoT monitors operations, offers services, tracks assets, and gathers data from these objects. IoT's beginnings may be traced back to the late 1990s when academics first looked into how to use low-tech protocols like Bluetooth or Wi-Fi to link physical objects with computers. An open protocol dubbed "Maverick" was created in 2003 by a Google team to connect devices over great distances without the use of wires or cables. Later, Maverick was renamed "Irma" in honour of a Firefly character. Nokia introduced its first product in 2005 that could be operated by an app on an iPhone or Android phone over Bluetooth Low Energy (BLE) [5]. Several manufacturers did the same after this and then released comparable products that could link cell phones directly with devices and sensors to remotely control them via BLE.

There are numerous types of IoT devices available today, including wearables like fitness trackers that track our daily movements, home appliances like thermostats and lighting systems that can be monitored from a distance, sensors installed throughout buildings to detect temperature changes, vehicles like cars and trucks that have IoT sensors to track performance and location, and industrial machineries like robots and machines. The Internet of Things is also changing how we communicate with our homes. Voice-activated technology is used by smart home devices like Google Home and Amazon Echo to control a variety of features in our homes, including entertainment, security, and lighting. With the development of smart houses, homeowners can now monitor and manage their properties from a distance, which makes it simpler to control energy usage and maintain contact with their properties even while they are away. With the emergence of intelligent workplaces and factories, the Internet of Things is also revolutionising how we work. To monitor equipment performance, maximise energy utilisation, and enhance workplace safety, IoT devices are deployed. IoT devices can also be used to monitor employee productivity, giving managers and employers useful information [6]. Figure 11.2 demonstrates how IoT is used in our daily lives.

The ability to gather and inspect substantial data sets from physical things in real time is one of the key advantages of IoT. This information can be used to boost customer satisfaction, cut expenses, and increase operational effectiveness. A manufacturer may track the functionality of their machinery in real time and receive notifications when maintenance is required, cutting down on downtime and repair expenses. However, the increased use of IoT devices also prompts worries about security and privacy. There is a higher risk of hacking and data breaches as more and more gadgets are online. Manufacturers must make sure that users have control over the data collected and exchanged and that their products are built with security in mind.

In addition to the advantages and risks highlighted, the IoT is also having a big impact on the creation of smart cities [7]. Smart cities use IoT technology to monitor and control different facets of urban life, including trash management, energy use, and traffic

FIGURE 11.2
How IoT is used in our daily lives.

flow. For instance, streetlight sensors can determine when a street is deserted and alter the brightness of the lights accordingly, saving electricity. IoT sensors that track garbage levels in trash cans and signal collection trucks when they need to be emptied can optimise waste management systems by preventing needless collection trips. These IoT-enabled solutions have the power to improve city efficiency, sustainability, and liveability for its citizens. However, putting such solutions into practice necessitates large infrastructure and technological investments, as well as careful consideration of privacy and security issues.

The IoT's potential to transform healthcare is yet another significant feature [8]. People can manage their health more effectively with the use of wearable devices that monitor vital signs and fitness levels, and hospital equipment equipped with sensors that can alert staff to possible problems before they develop into emergencies. With the ability to closely monitor patients' health and act immediately when necessary, remote monitoring of patients with chronic diseases is growing in popularity. The avoidance of hospital admissions and readmissions has the potential to enhance patient outcomes while lowering healthcare expenditures. In addition, IoT is accelerating digital transformation across a range of sectors, including industry and agriculture. IoT-enabled sensors, for instance, may track soil moisture levels and nutrient content, allowing farmers to increase crop yields and use less water. IoT sensors can monitor equipment performance in production and spot possible problems before they result in downtime, increasing productivity and lowering maintenance costs.

IoT is a rapidly developing industry and has the potential to drastically alter a variety of facets of our lives, including how we manage our houses and how we access healthcare. Like with any new technology, it is critical to address the privacy and security concerns that arise as it is used more frequently. With careful planning and implementation, IoT has the potential to greatly benefit individuals, organisations, and society at large [9].

11.4 IoT-Enabled Smart Grids

The potential of smart grids and IoT breakthroughs to revolutionise the distribution and use of energy is rapidly growing as technology develops and energy demand rises. Smart grids use real-time data and communication technology to create an intelligent energy distribution system that successfully regulates energy production and consumption. By integrating IoT devices like smart meters, sensors, and automated controls, the smart grid may collect and analyse data on energy consumption trends and adjust supply accordingly, resulting in more efficient use of energy resources [10].

Additionally, because it can track and regulate energy flows in real time and adjust to fluctuations in the supply of renewable energy to provide a consistent and reliable energy supply, the smart grid opens up the potential for incorporating renewable energy sources into the energy mix. Integration of the IoT and smart grid also opens up new possibilities for personal energy management. By employing linked appliances and thermostats to monitor and modify energy use depending on individual preferences and needs, homes and businesses can significantly reduce their energy and utility costs. IoT and smart grid adoption, however, are not without challenges. A sophisticated network of devices and systems needs to be guarded with efficient cybersecurity measures in order to protect important data and infrastructure. As more data is collected and sent across the network, privacy concerns increase. Together with major financial and technological investments, the deployment of the smart grid also requires the development of regulatory frameworks to oversee its implementation. The development of the smart grid and IoT generally offers several opportunities for more efficient and sustainable energy use. Careful planning and administration are still needed to overcome the challenges and ensure a successful implementation. The IoT and the smart grid have the potential to revolutionise how we produce, distribute, and utilise energy, paving the way for improved management and a more sustainable future.

11.5 Energy Management in IoT-Enabled Smart Grid

Energy management is a crucial part of IoT-enabled smart grids in order to maximise the use of energy resources, reduce waste, and increase the dependability and efficiency of the energy system. IoT-enabled smart grids use a variety of sensors and devices to continuously monitor energy use. This allows for more accurate energy demand forecasts and provides deep insights into consumption trends. The energy system might then be improved to be more economical, more environmentally friendly overall, and to use energy more effectively with the help of this knowledge. For instance, energy management systems can be used to automatically adjust energy usage based on real-time data such as the outside temperature, the weather, and the energy demand. This can lower peak demand times, prevent blackouts, and boost the effectiveness of the energy system as a whole. Additionally, IoT-enabled smart grids can aid in the integration of renewable energy sources, such as solar and wind power, by utilising advanced forecasting and monitoring technologies to anticipate energy generation and change energy use accordingly. As a result, it is possible to encourage the switch to a cleaner, more sustainable energy system while decreasing reliance on conventional energy sources. Increasing the overall security and safety of the energy system requires effective energy management in IoT-enabled smart grids. By detecting and responding to potential threats and weaknesses in real time, energy management systems can help prevent cyberattacks, physical security breaches, and other potential problems. Energy management is a key component of IoT-enabled smart grids in order to optimise energy resources, reduce waste, and enhance the stability and efficiency of the energy system. It provides the system with current energy usage information. As IoT technology continues to advance, we can expect to see even more cutting-edge energy management solutions in the years to come. These solutions will help with the transition to a more dependable and sustainable energy system. Energy management in IoT-enabled smart grids can improve the efficiency of energy systems while also reducing waste and maximising energy utilisation. By identifying locations with high energy use and waste, energy management systems can help utilities and consumers reduce their energy bills. Information regarding the state and functionality of the energy grid can also be provided through energy management systems. By keeping an eye on voltage, current, and other vital parameters, energy management systems can help utilities see potential problems before they lead to blackouts or other outages. Energy management with IoT-enabled smart grids allows prosumers, or individuals who both consume and produce energy, to participate in the energy market. By providing real-time data on energy usage and production, energy management systems can assist prosumers in optimising their energy production and consumption habits and participating in demand response programmes. Energy management in IoT-enabled smart grids can help the integration of EVs into the energy system. Energy management systems can help utilities by providing real-time data on EV charging habits and energy demand, which will help them manage the increasing electricity demand brought on by the widespread adoption of EVs. The following are a few briefly explained IoT-enabled smart grids' energy management methods.

11.5.1 Demand Response Management

Demand response management, a crucial element of energy management, can only be implemented with the help of IoT devices. Electricity supply and demand must be balanced as they fluctuate throughout the day in order to ensure a consistent and reliable energy supply. Utility companies may manage peak electricity demand while eliminating expensive and environmentally harmful power plants, thanks to IoT-enabled devices. Utilities can identify patterns in energy demand and modify supply by using IoT devices to monitor energy usage in real time. This information can be utilised to control the demand for energy during peak periods of energy use. Utilities can encourage customers to use less energy during peak hours by offering demand response management programmes [11]. For instance, smart thermostats may adjust the temperature automatically during peak hours to conserve energy without sacrificing comfort. It is possible to set connected lighting and appliances to consume less energy during peak hours, much like it is possible to regulate demand and save expenses. Demand response management has a favourable effect on the environment as well. By reducing the need for expensive and harmful power facilities, demand response management can help reduce carbon emissions and support a more sustainable energy system.

11.5.2 Energy Storage

The smart grid's energy storage system is essential for integrating renewable energy sources and optimising energy use. IoT gadgets can be crucial for managing energy storage since they can give energy storage systems real-time monitoring and management. Utilities can make sure that energy is stored and used effectively by monitoring energy storage systems with IoT devices. In order to ensure that energy is available when needed and to prevent waste, utilities are able to better regulate energy supply and demand. In order to detect possible problems before they become significant, utilities can employ IoT devices to perform predictive maintenance on energy storage systems. By doing this, maintenance expenses can be cut and the lifespan of energy storage devices can be increased.

11.5.3 Incorporating Renewable Energy

The utilisation of clean, sustainable energy sources like solar and wind power is made possible by the integration of renewable energy, which is a key element of the smart grid. Through monitoring and output optimisation, IoT devices can assist in integrating these renewable energy sources into the grid. Utilities may make sure that they are generating energy as efficiently as possible by deploying IoT devices to monitor the output of renewable energy sources. Because of this, utilities are better able to balance the supply and demand of energy, ensuring that there is always energy available and reducing waste. Moreover, utilities can employ IoT devices to perform predictive maintenance on renewable energy sources, identifying possible problems before they become serious. By doing so, maintenance expenses can be decreased and the lifespan of renewable energy sources can be increased. In order to provide a more sustainable and reliable energy system, it enables utilities to optimise energy usage and decrease waste. Figure 11.3 shows the energy management in IoT-enabled smart grids.

11.5.4 Efficiency in Energy

Energy efficiency is the capacity to utilise energy sources more effectively, hence minimising waste and bringing down energy prices. IoT gadgets can assist in increasing energy efficiency by giving utilities access to real-time data on energy consumption and allowing them to spot places where energy can be saved. Utilities may learn more about how energy

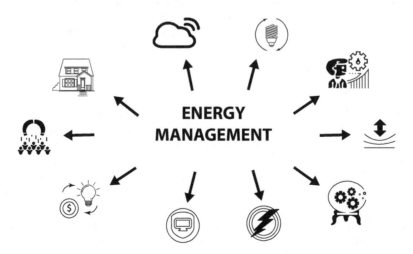

FIGURE 11.3
The energy management in IoT-enabled smart grids.

is being utilised throughout the grid by gathering and analysing data from IoT-enabled devices, such as smart meters and sensors. In order to prevent energy waste, this information can be used by utilities to pinpoint areas with excessive energy use. For instance, utilities can pinpoint places where energy efficiency can be increased, such as by updating insulation or switching to more energy-efficient lighting, by utilising IoT sensors to monitor building energy consumption. With IoT devices, energy consumption may also be managed in real time. For example, lights can be turned off or HVAC systems can be modified in response to occupancy patterns.

11.5.5 Grid Agility

The Internet of Things (IoT) can help improve grid resilience by utilising sensors and equipment to detect and respond to power outages. IoT technology enables utilities to immediately identify when and where outages occur, take steps to restore power, and stop further interruptions. IoT sensors can be mounted on transformers, power lines, and other equipment to monitor voltage and current levels and provide early warning of potential problems. Utility operators may swiftly identify and address problems before they worsen because of the real-time transmission of this data to a central control system. IoT gadgets can also automate the process of power restoration by remotely managing circuit breakers and switches. As a result, power may be restored to impacted areas more quickly, reducing downtime.

11.5.6 Predictive Maintenance

The Internet of Things (IoT) can help with the predictive maintenance of utility equipment in addition to enhancing grid resilience. Utility companies may keep an eye on the functionality and condition of the transformers, switchgear, and other vital pieces of equipment that make up their grid infrastructure. Changes in temperature, vibration, and other characteristics that could point to a potential equipment breakdown can be found by IoT sensors. In order to do preventive maintenance and avoid unplanned downtime, utilities can identify and diagnose problems early on by analysing this data.

Additionally, IoT devices can help schedule maintenance jobs, eliminating the need for pricey and time-consuming physical inspections. Predictive maintenance can help utilities increase the equipment's lifespan, lower maintenance costs, and boost the grid's overall dependability.

11.5.7 Power Quality Monitoring

By using sensors and devices to track the voltage, frequency, and harmonics of the energy supply, the Internet of Things (IoT) can assist in enhancing the quality of the current. Utilities can guarantee that customers receive high-quality electricity, which is necessary for the efficient operation of electrical appliances and equipment, by utilising IoT technology. The electrical distribution network can be equipped with IoT sensors that can be placed at various points to monitor the quality of the power supply. Real-time transmission of this data to a central control system makes it possible to identify problems as they develop and act swiftly to address them. IoT devices can inform utility operators, for instance, if the voltage or frequency of the energy supply is too low or high. The utility operators can then take the necessary steps to fix the issue. Similarly, to this, if harmonics are present in the energy supply, IoT devices may detect them and analyse the data, allowing utilities to locate the problem and fix it.

11.5.8 Cybersecurity

Smart grids frequently employ Internet of Things (IoT)-capable gadgets for data collection and network communication. Nevertheless, the introduction of IoT devices also introduces weaknesses that cybercriminals might take advantage of. For instance, if a hacker gains access to the smart grid, then they might be able to interfere with the electrical supply or even start a blackout. To safeguard IoT-enabled smart grids from potential dangers, it is essential to have strong cybersecurity safeguards in place. This entails taking precautions like encrypting data, updating software and firmware on a regular basis, keeping an eye on network traffic for odd behaviour, and educating staff on how to spot and handle cyber threats. By making sure that IoT-enabled smart grids are secure, we can contribute to the prevention of cyberattacks that might have catastrophic effects on our electricity infrastructure and our daily life.

11.5.9 Energy Trading

A decentralised energy market might be established using IoT (Internet of Things) technology, allowing consumers who generate excess energy, such as from solar panels, to exchange it with other consumers or the grid. As a result, energy can be shared and dispersed among many consumers, resulting in a system that is more efficient and sustainable. Customers can participate in energy trading and encourage the production of renewable energy by utilising IoT-enabled devices to monitor and manage energy production and consumption. This reduces dependency on centralised energy infrastructure and can also incentivise renewable energy production. This may also aid in lowering greenhouse gas emissions and advancing the usage of sustainable energy in the future.

Thus, the application of IoT technology to the energy trading industry can result in a more effective and sustainable energy market that benefits both small-scale consumers and the bigger community.

11.5.10 Customer Interaction

The Internet of Things (IoT) can help utilities interact with their consumers by giving them access to real-time data on their energy usage. Customers can monitor their energy usage in real time and gain a better understanding of their energy consumption trends by using smart meters and other IoT-enabled devices. Customers can use this information to find opportunities to minimise their energy use and save money, as well as to make informed decisions about how they use energy. Customers might, for instance, modify their energy consumption during times of high demand to lower total energy expenses. In addition, utilities can employ IoT technology to inform customers about programmes, incentives, and energy-saving advice. This could promote more sustainable energy practices and boost customer engagement.

11.6 Literature Review

Sarwat A (2018) summarised the local area sensor network (LASN), medium-area sensor network (MASN), and wide-area sensor network (WAN) components of the smart grid IoT

[12]. They used a well-known system as an example to further describe the architecture, significant uses, and potential difficulties for future research.

Li B (2018) presented a detailed study about the IoT and smart grid as the frontier of information and industry [13] and further told about the future of this technology including the knowledge about radio frequency identification, infrared induction, and neural networks used in these systems.

Ozger M (2017) reviewed information on IoT-enabled smart grids, their integration with cognitive radio (CR) techniques and energy harvesting (EH), as well as issues with SG like challenging channel conditions [14] and low battery power. Further explanations on the integration of these technologies were also provided.

Lombardi F (2018) talked about a system that uses smart contracts and blockchain technology to offer dependable and affordable transactive energy, with all capabilities implemented as fully decentralised apps [15]. Additionally, they discussed how energy transactions are recorded in the blockchain and how a high level of replication provides more robust anti-tampering assurances.

Barman B (2018) proposed a smart system that would allow consumers and producers to monitor and regulate energy use on a more immediate basis through the use of smart grids [16].

Tanwar S (2018) outlined the IoT's contribution to the development of a smart city, provided an architecture for such a city to make optimal use of its infrastructure, and discussed problems and potential solutions related to the development of IoT infrastructure [17]. They also provided a list of IoT applications according to the various fields in which they could be used.

Hidayatullah N (2018) illustrated the Internet of Things' (IoT) basic architecture before outlining its main technologies for the smart grid [18]. The concepts of applied communication and the IoT-based architecture for monitoring transmission and distribution for the smart grid were also explored.

Borgaonkar R (2019) detailed the security dangers to IoT-based smart grids resulting from compromised 5G network-related infrastructure and examined the security features of 5G security specifications provided by the 3GPP standards organisation from the perspective of IoT-based smart grids [19].

Saleem A (2020) presented a new fog-enabled privacy-preserving data aggregation approach (FESDA) that, by filtering out the inserted values from external attackers, is resistant to fake data injection assaults [20].

Chen S (2019) offered a data prediction method for IoT-enabled smart grids, together with an edge computing privacy protection approach [21] and hierarchical task grading (HDTG) pre-processing method.

Taghavinejad S (2020) suggested a clever approach for intrusion detection in these kinds of networks utilising a mixture of three decision trees [22] and the effectiveness of the proposed approach was compared with the K-Nearest Neighbours, Support Vector Machine (SVM), and other approaches (KNN).

Wang Z (2020) presented a lightweight privacy-preserving Q-learning framework (LiPSG) for the creation of smart grid energy management strategies and provided in-depth theoretical analysis [23] and experiments were also provided to demonstrate the security and effectiveness of LiPSG.

Zheng W (2020) showed the future cellular network in contrast to other wireless communication technologies [24] and new webs in an endeavour to effectively bring the energy of the internet into the future including the benefits and limitations of emerging cellular networks for the smart grid are also highlighted.

Guo H (2016) outlined the design of a dual failure-protected elastic optical network (EON) for varying protective light path-sharing capacities [25]. For such a network, routing and spectrum assignment (RSA) were also taken into account in order to reduce the use of the maximum number of frequency slots (FSs).

Revathi R (2021) provided an idealised description of how grid power [26] and renewable sources should be used with the goal of building and developing a smart grid system using IoT and renewable energy.

Avancini D (2021) suggested and demonstrated a new smart energy meter using an IoT approach [27] and the costs and advantages related to it. The offered solution is also evaluated and used in real-world settings.

Routray S (2021) offered research on Narrowband IoT (NBIoT) enabling features [28], which can assist in the smart grids.

Shahzad A (2021) provided a proof-of-concept blockchain-based system to manage all transactions in a smart grid system with IoT support. This approach produced an immutable transaction record [29] and was shared and transparent to all system participants.

Wang D (2021) proposed a hybrid blockchain architecture based on a 5G MEC smart grid [30], in which the MEC gateway/server serves as both a private blockchain and a public blockchain deployment.

11.7 Energy Problem in Smart Grids

The task of managing and distributing energy efficiently and dependably within a complicated network of linked devices, sensors, and systems is the smart grid's energy issue. Smart grids face unique technological and operational challenges when integrating renewable energy sources like wind and solar electricity into the existing energy infrastructure. The fluctuation of renewable energy sources is one of the major problems with smart grid energy management. Renewable energy sources can be impacted by weather patterns and other environmental conditions, unlike conventional power plants, which produce an energy output that is constant.

Energy output is difficult to estimate and control as a result of this variability, which can cause instabilities in grids. Another issue is that real-time energy distribution management necessitates sophisticated monitoring and control systems. Smart grids rely on a complex network of sensors and communication devices to monitor energy production and consumption as well as to make real-time adjustments to energy flow in order to maintain a reliable and stable system. Also, the increasing use of electric vehicles makes it more challenging to control energy in the smart grid (EVs). Smart grid solutions must be created to prioritise and optimise EV charging while also ensuring that energy is transported effectively throughout the grid in order to manage this challenge.

The integration of distributed energy resources presents another difficulty in controlling the energy in a smart grid (DERs). Battery storage units, microturbines, and rooftop solar panels are examples of small-scale power sources that generate electricity close to the point of consumption. The resilience and reliability of the grid may increase with the incorporation of DERs; however, there may be problems with interoperability, cybersecurity, and regulatory frameworks. Furthermore, managing energy in a smart grid requires striking a balance between conflicting priorities including cost, dependability, and environmental sustainability. Even if renewable energy sources like solar and wind are becoming more economical, they might not always be available or reliable enough to meet the energy needs of a particular place or time of day. The goal of boosting renewable energy sources and lowering greenhouse gas emissions might be difficult to reconcile with the requirement for a steady and stable energy supply. Stakeholders in the energy sector must collaborate and innovate to get past these challenges. This calls for the development of new energy regulation technologies, the adoption of legislation that permits the incorporation of renewable energy sources and distributed energy resources, and the dissemination of information to consumers about the benefits of smart grid technology. In general, overcoming these challenges would call for the use of cutting-edge technology, innovative laws, and collaborative efforts among actors in the energy sector.

11.8 Future Scope and Conclusion of IoT-Based Smart Grids

Smart grids powered by IoT can increase energy consumption flexibility by allowing consumers to manage their energy consumption in real time. Dynamic pricing models, in which energy prices are modified based on current supply and demand, can also be made possible by smart grids. Users may be encouraged to use energy off-peak when it is less expensive, resulting in the more effective use of energy resources and cost savings for customers. A variety of advantages that IoT-enabled smart grids provide are encouraging their development in the energy industry. These advantages include a rise in standardisation and new business models in the energy sector, as well as better efficiency, dependability, sustainability, and customer service. Smart grid adoption, however, also comes with difficulties, including the requirement for major infrastructure investment and cybersecurity hazards. Considering the aforementioned obstacles, IoT-enabled smart grids have a bright future as long as governments and energy companies continue to fund their creation and implementation. Smart grids have the power to revolutionise the energy industry by creating a more sustainable and effective energy system that benefits both energy providers and consumers.

In conclusion, by enhancing the effectiveness, dependability, and sustainability of energy systems, IoT-based smart grids are revolutionising the energy industry. Increased energy management capabilities, real-time monitoring and control, better customer service, and connectivity with smart cities are just a few advantages that come with IoT technology integration in smart grids [31, 32]. It is a promising technology for the future of energy, despite the fact that there are still issues to be solved, such as cybersecurity threats and the need for major infrastructure investment. Smart grids have the potential to change the energy industry with sustained investment and research, resulting in a more sustainable and effective energy system that benefits both consumers and energy providers.

References

1. Phuangpornpitak, Napaporn, and Suvit Tia. "Opportunities and challenges of integrating renewable energy in smart grid system." *Energy Procedia* 34 (2013): 282–290.
2. Fang, Xi, Satyajayant Misra, Guoliang Xue, and Dejun Yang. "Smart grid—The new and improved power grid: A survey." *IEEE Communications Surveys and Tutorials* 14, no. 4 (2011): 944–980.

3. D'Acunto, Lucia, Nitin Chiluka, Tamás Vinkó, and Henk Sips. "BitTorrent-like P2P approaches for VoD: A comparative study." *Computer Networks* 57, no. 5 (2013): 1253–1276.

4. Tan, Kang Miao, Vigna K. Ramachandaramurthy, and Jia Ying Yong. "Integration of electric vehicles in smart grid: A review on vehicle to grid technologies and optimization techniques." *Renewable and Sustainable Energy Reviews* 53 (2016): 720–732.

5. Khan, Jamil Y. "Introduction to IoT systems." In *Internet of Things (IoT)*, pp. 1–24. Jenny Stanford Publishing, 2019.

6. Khalid, Lawchak Fadhil, and Siddeeq Y. Ameen. "Secure Iot integration in daily lives: A review." *Journal of Information Technology and Informatics* 1, no. 1 (2021): 6–12.

7. Rajab, Husam, and Tibor Cinkelr. "IoT based smart cities." In *2018 International Symposium on Networks, Computers and Communications (ISNCC)*, pp. 1–4. IEEE, 2018.

8. Sharma, Aashima, Sanmeet Kaur, and Maninder Singh. "A comprehensive review on block-chain and Internet of Things in healthcare." *Transactions on Emerging Telecommunications Technologies* 32, no. 10 (2021): e4333.

9. Eeshwaroju, Sreenivas, Praveena Jakkula, and Subramanian Ganesan. "IoT based empow-erment by smart health monitoring, smart education and smart jobs." In *2020 International Conference on Computing and Information Technology (ICCIT-1441)*, pp. 1–5. IEEE, 2020.

10. Abir, S. M., Abu Adnan, Adnan Anwar, Jinho Choi, and A. S. M. Kayes. "Iot-enabled smart energy grid: Applications and challenges." *IEEE Access* 9 (2021): 50961–50981.

11. Haider, Haider Tarish, Ong Hang See, and Wilfried Elmenreich. "A review of residential demand response of smart grid." *Renewable and Sustainable Energy Reviews* 59 (2016): 166–178.

12. Sarwat, Arif I., Aditya Sundararajan, and Imtiaz Parvez. "Trends and future directions of research for smart grid IoT sensor networks." In *Proceedings of International Symposium on Sensor Networks, Systems and Security: Advances in Computing and Networking with Applications*, pp. 45–61. Springer International Publishing, 2018.

13. Li, Biao, Sen Lv, and Qing Pan. "The internet of things and smart grid." In *IOP Conference Series: Earth and Environmental Science* 113, no. 1, p. 012038. IOP Publishing, 2018.

14. Ozger, Mustafa, Oktay Cetinkaya, and Ozgur B. Akan. "Energy harvesting cognitive radio networking for IoT-enabled smart grid." *Mobile Networks and Applications* 23 (2018): 956–966.

15. Lombardi, Federico, Leonardo Aniello, Stefano De Angelis, Andrea Margheri, and Vladimiro Sassone. "A blockchain-based infrastructure for reliable and cost-effective IoT-aided smart grids." *Living in the Internet of Things: Cybersecurity of the IoT – 2018* (2018): 42–46.

16. Barman, Bibek Kanti, Shiv Nath Yadav, Shivam Kumar, and Sadhan Gope. "IOT based smart energy meter for efficient energy utilization in smart grid." In *2018 2nd International Conference on Power, Energy and Environment: Towards Smart Technology (ICEPE)*, pp. 1–5. IEEE, 2018.

17. Tanwar, Sudeep, Sudhanshu Tyagi, and Sachin Kumar. "The role of internet of things and smart grid for the development of a smart city." In *Intelligent Communication and Computational Technologies: Proceedings of Internet of Things for Technological Development, IoT4TD 2017*, pp. 23–33. Springer, 2018.

18. Hidayatullah, N. A., A. C. Kurniawan, and Akhtar Kalam. "Power transmission and distri-bution monitoring using Internet of Things (IoT) for smart grid." In *IOP Conference Series: Materials Science and Engineering*, vol. 384, no. 1, p. 012039. IOP Publishing, 2018.

19. Borgaonkar, Ravishankar, and Martin Gilje Jaatun. "5G as an enabler for secure IoT in the smart grid." In *2019 First International Conference on Societal Automation (SA)*, pp. 1–7. IEEE, 2019.

20. Saleem, Ahsan, Abid Khan, Malik Saif Ur Rehman, Haris Pervaiz, Hassan Malik, Masoom Alam, and Anish Jindal. "FESDA: Fog-enabled secure data aggregation in smart grid IoT net-work." *IEEE Internet of Things Journal* 7(7) (2019): 6132–6142.

21. Chen, Songlin, Hong Wen, Jinsong Wu, Wenxin Lei, Wenjing Hou, Wenjie Liu, Aidong Xu, and Yixin Jiang. "Internet of things based smart grids supported by intelligent edge computing." *IEEE Access* 7 (2019): 74089–74102.

22. Taghavinejad, Seyedeh Mahsan, Mehran Taghavinejad, Lida Shahmiri, Mohammad Zavvar, and Mohammad Hossein Zavvar. "Intrusion detection in IoT-based smart grid using hybrid decision tree." In *2020 6th International Conference on Web Research (ICWR)*, pp. 152–156. IEEE, 2020.

23. Wang, Zhuzhu, Yang Liu, Zhuo Ma, Ximeng Liu, and Jianfeng Ma. "LiPSG: Lightweight privacy-preserving Q-learning-based energy management for the IoT-enabled smart grid." *IEEE Internet of Things Journal* 7, no. 5 (2020): 3935–3947.

24. Zheng, Weiming, Ke Sun, Xiaodi Zhang, Quanming Zhang, Adil Israr, and Qiang Yang. "Cellular communication for ubiquitous internet of things in smart grids: Present and outlook." In *2020 Chinese Control And Decision Conference (CCDC)*, pp. 5592–5596. IEEE, 2020.

25. Guo, Hong, Gangxiang Shen, and Sanjay Kumar Bose. "Routing and spectrum assignment for dual failure path protected elastic optical networks." *IEEE Access* 4 (2016): 5143–5160.

26. Revathi, R., A. Nivedhitha, J. Priyadharshini, and K. M. Rashmithaa. "IoT based smart grid using node MCU." In *Journal of Physics: Conference Series*, vol. 1916, no. 1, p. 012156. IOP Publishing, 2021.

27. Avancini, Danielly B., Joel J. P. C. Rodrigues, Ricardo A. L. Rabêlo, Ashok Kumar Das, Sergey Kozlov, and Petar Solic. "A new IoT-based smart energy meter for smart grids." *International Journal of Energy Research* 45, no. 1 (2021): 189–202.

28. Routray, Sudhir K., Devarajan Gopal, Abhishek Javali, and Anindita Sahoo. "Narrowband IoT (NBIoT) assisted smart grids." In *2021 International Conference on Artificial Intelligence and Smart Systems (ICAIS)*, pp. 1454–1458. IEEE, 2021.

29. Shahzad, Aamir, Kaiwen Zhang, and Abdelouahed Gherbi. "Privacy-preserving smart grid traceability using blockchain over IoT connectivity." In *Proceedings of the 36th Annual ACM Symposium on Applied Computing*, pp. 699–706. 2021.

30. Wang, Dong, Huanjuan Wang, and Yuchen Fu. "Blockchain-based IoT device identification and management in 5G smart grid." *EURASIP Journal on Wireless Communications and Networking* 2021, no. 1 (2021): 125.

31. Al Shahrani, A. M., M. A. Alomar, K. N. Alqahtani, M. S. Basingab, B. Sharma, and A. Rizwan. "Machine learning-enabled smart industrial automation systems using Internet of things." *Sensors* 23, no. 1 (2023). doi: 10.3390/s23010324.

32. Uppal, M. et al. "A real-time data monitoring framework for predictive maintenance based on the Internet of things." *Complexity* 2023 (2023): 1–14. doi: 10.1155/2023/9991029.s.

12

E-Healthcare and Society 5.0

Rishu Chhabra and Saravjeet Singh

12.1 Introduction

Society 5.0 is based on the concept of a "Human-Centered Society," which aims to take advantage of the latest technologies such as artificial intelligence (AI), robotics, the Internet of Things (IoT), big data, and cloud computing to improve the quality of life and optimize social and economic systems (Fukuyama, 2018). Society 5.0 is the Japanese government's vision for a new economic and social model that combines traditional Japanese values with the latest digital technologies. It was first proposed in 2016 as part of the government's "Society of the Future" initiative. It also seeks to create a better balance between humanity and technology (Fukuda, 2020). According to the Japanese Cabinet Office, Society 5.0 is meant to create a "prosperous society in which people, the economy, and nature coexist harmoniously." The goal is to create a society that encourages collaboration between humans and machines and fosters an environment of innovation, creativity, and entrepreneurship. Society 5.0 also seeks to promote a greater sense of community, improve public safety and security, and reduce the environmental impact of urbanization. The different application areas that are part of Society 5.0 are: Robotic Process Automation, Autonomous Logistics, Predictive Analytics, Augmented Reality, Cyber Security, Smart Manufacturing, Digital Twin Technology, Natural Language Processing, Artificial Intelligence, Human-Machine Interaction, and Healthcare (Nair, Tyagi and Sreenath, 2021).

The healthcare and medicine sectors are poised to benefit significantly from the implementation of Society 5.0. In the healthcare sector, Society 5.0 will enable the use of AI and big data to improve the accuracy and speed of diagnosis, allowing for quicker and more accurate treatments. It will also enable remote monitoring of patients, allowing for quicker intervention in the event of a health emergency (De Felice, Travaglioni and Petrillo, 2021). The use of advanced analytics will enable a more personalized approach to medicine and healthcare, allowing doctors to gain a better understanding of a patient's individual needs and prescribe the right treatment. Finally, the implementation of Society 5.0 will enable the sharing of patient data between healthcare providers, allowing for a more efficient and reliable way of tracking patient information and medical history. This will reduce medical errors and allow for better coordination between doctors and healthcare providers. Overall, Society 5.0 has the potential to revolutionize the healthcare and medicine sector, leading to improved quality of care and more efficient treatments (Ioppolo et al., 2020).

The digital health market is a growing industry that involves the use of digital technology, such as mobile apps, wearables, and connected health devices, to improve healthcare outcomes. It includes products and services such as telemedicine, remote patient monitoring, digital health coaching, electronic medical records, and digital drug delivery systems. The

DOI: 10.1201/9781003397052-12

digital health market is predicted to reach a value of $392.3 billion by 2025, driven by rising demand for cost-effective and efficient healthcare solutions. The market is expected to experience strong growth, driven by the increasing implementation of digital health technologies by patients, healthcare providers, and insurers. The growing demand for digital health solutions is also being driven by the increasing prevalence of chronic diseases, aging populations, and the need to reduce healthcare costs (Klonoff, King and Kerr, 2019). Figure 12.1 shows the projected global growth of digital health market size by the year 2025 (Statista, 2022).

E-healthcare has been an influencing factor in driving the progress of the digital health market. By utilizing technologies such as telemedicine, remote health monitoring, and artificial intelligence, E-healthcare has the potential to make healthcare cost-effective, efficient, and accessible. Figure 12.2 shows the different domains of E-healthcare in Society 5.0 (Lwin, Punnakitikashem and Thananusak, 2023).

With E-healthcare, instead of having to wait for an appointment to see a doctor, patients can receive diagnoses and treatment virtually, saving both time and money. Additionally, E-healthcare can help bridge the gap between rural and urban areas, providing healthcare to those who may not have access to it otherwise. By making healthcare more accessible, E-healthcare can help to improve the overall health of society (Lwin, Punnakitikashem and Thananusak, 2023).

12.2 Need of E-healthcare

E-healthcare is needed nowadays to provide more accessible, efficient, and cost-effective healthcare services. With the advances in technology, E-healthcare allows people to access healthcare services such as seeking medical advice, scheduling appointments, and ordering medication from the comfort of their own home. E-healthcare also allows for better communication and collaboration between doctors, nurses, and other healthcare professionals, making it easier to provide more efficient and accurate care. Additionally, E-healthcare

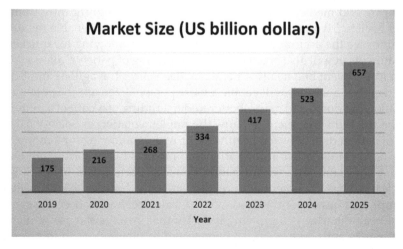

FIGURE 12.1
Projected growth of digital health market size.

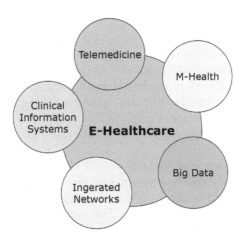

FIGURE 12.2
Domains of E-healthcare.

can help reduce healthcare costs by eliminating the need for office visits and other costly procedures (Walter and Tung, 2002). The benefits of E-healthcare are as follows:

1. **Improved Access to Care:** E-healthcare systems can help make healthcare more easily accessible to those living in isolated or rural areas, or have limited movement, or with busy lives having difficulty making it to the doctor during traditional office hours (Tanbeer and Sykes, 2021).

2. **Reduced Costs:** By eliminating the need to travel to a doctor's office, E-healthcare can help reduce the cost of healthcare delivery. Additionally, it can streamline the management of chronic conditions, reducing provider costs and potentially improving patient outcomes (Chaudhary and Chatterjee, 2020).

3. **Increased Patient Engagement:** E-healthcare systems can help increase patient engagement by providing access to health information, advice, and support. This can help motivate patients to take control of their health and make better lifestyle choices (Tanbeer and Sykes, 2021).

4. **Improved Quality of Care:** E-healthcare systems can provide providers with better data on their patients, enabling them to make better, more informed decisions about care. Additionally, E-healthcare systems can help providers to better coordinate care and reduce errors that can lead to costly medical treatments (Chaudhary and Chatterjee, 2020).

5. **Improved Data Security:** E-healthcare can help to protect patient data by using secure, encrypted technology. This can help to lower the risk of medical data infringements and ensure that patient information is kept safe and secure (Sahi et al., 2017).

12.3 Architecture of E-healthcare in Society 5.0

E-healthcare architecture in Society 5.0 is centered around an integrated platform that supports the connection of stakeholders, including patients, health professionals, and healthcare providers, in the healthcare delivery system. This platform will provide a single point of access to patient information, clinical data, and healthcare services, enabling personalized, data-driven healthcare. This will enable predictive health services, such as disease prevention and early detection, as well as personalized treatments. Additionally, the platform will support a variety of digital health applications and services, such as telemedicine, remote patient monitoring, and health tracking. The cloud-based service-oriented architecture of E-healthcare is given in Figure 12.3 (Sahi et al., 2017).

The description of the different layers of the E-healthcare architecture is as follows:

1. **Network Infrastructure and Data Storage:** This element of the E-healthcare architecture consists of the hardware, software, and telecommunications networks that enable data to be exchanged within and between healthcare providers, payers, patients, and other stakeholders. The network infrastructure may feature Machine Learning (ML), AI, and cloud-based analytics to better inform decisions and improve outcomes. This element of the E-healthcare architecture consists of the secure and reliable storage of patient data and other health-related documents. It is important for health information technology systems to be able to store and access patient data in an efficient and secure manner (Sahi et al., 2017).

2. **User Interfaces:** This element of the E-healthcare architecture consists of the user interfaces that enable healthcare providers and other stakeholders to interact with

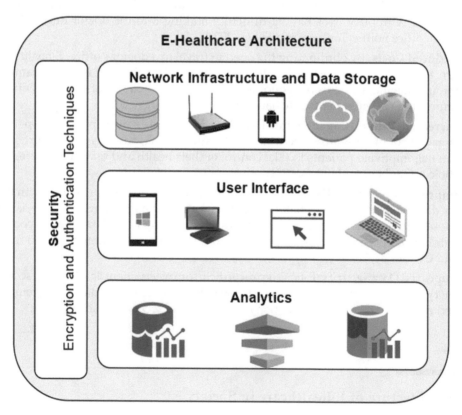

FIGURE 12.3
Architecture of E-healthcare in Society 5.0.

the system. These user interfaces should be designed to be intuitive and easy to use, as well as secure and reliable (Hameed et al., 2015).

3. **Analytics:** This element of the E-healthcare architecture consists of the analytics tools that can be used to analyze data in order to gain insights and make better decisions. Analytics tools can be used to identify trends, detect anomalies, and measure performance (Hameed et al., 2015).

4. **Security:** This element of the E-healthcare architecture consists of the security measures that are in place to protect patient data and other health-related documents. This includes authentication and encryption techniques. The underlying security and privacy of the platform will be ensured by the use of robust encryption techniques, secure authentication protocols, and data anonymization methods. Furthermore, the platform will adhere to relevant privacy regulations, such as the GDPR, to ensure the safety and security of patients' medical information (Sahi et al., 2017).

12.4 Technologies in E-healthcare in Society 5.0

E-healthcare leverages various innovative technologies to improve healthcare outcomes and enhance the patient experience. The different technologies that play a significant role in E-healthcare are shown in Figure 12.4.

The detailed description of these technologies is as follows (Razdan and Sharma, 2022) (Krishnamoorthy, Dua and Gupta, 2023):

1. **Telehealth:** It refers to the use of communication technologies and digital information through various devices like smartphones, computers, and the internet, which enable remote access to healthcare services. Telehealth services include virtual visits, remote patient monitoring, and electronic consultations. One of the main benefits of telehealth is that it can increase patient access to medical treatment, especially in isolated or underdeveloped locations. Without having to travel far to see a doctor, patients can get consultations, medications, and follow-up care in the convenience of their own homes (Andrews et al., 2020).

2. **Internet of Things (IoT):** IoT-enabled devices like wearables and sensors can collect real-time data on patients' vital signs and other health metrics. This data can be utilized for monitoring the patients and providing personalized suggestions to improve their health. Wearable devices are electronic devices that can be worn on

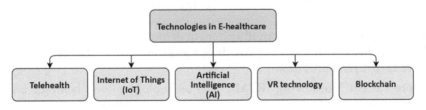

FIGURE 12.4
Technologies in E-healthcare in Society 5.0.

the body, such as wristbands, smartwatches, or other sensors. They can be used to track physical activity, monitor vital signs, and provide reminders to take medications (Huarng, Yu and fang Lee, 2022; Bhatia, Panda and Nagpal, 2020).

3. **Artificial Intelligence (AI):** AI is being used in healthcare to diagnose and treat diseases, as well as to help make predictions about a patient's future health. AI can also be used to analyze large datasets to help healthcare providers identify trends and patterns in patient care. AI-powered chatbots and virtual assistants are also becoming increasingly common in E-healthcare. It is also being used to develop predictive models that can help healthcare providers to detect patients that have greater risk of developing certain medical conditions (Krishnamoorthy, Dua and Gupta, 2023).

4. **VR Technology:** Virtual reality (VR) is a rapidly advancing technology that has the potential to transform E-healthcare in Society 5.0. VR refers to a computer-generated environment that can simulate a real-world experience and allow users to interact with it in a highly immersive way. In healthcare, VR is being used in a variety of applications, including training, therapy, and patient education. One of the main benefits of VR in E-healthcare is its ability to provide immersive and realistic training simulations for healthcare professionals (Kute, Tyagi and Aswathy, 2022).

5. **Blockchain:** Blockchain technology is being used in E-healthcare to securely store and share patient health data. This technology can help to improve data privacy and security and enable patients to have more control over their health data (Ray et al., 2020) (Agarwal et al., 2021).

12.5 Application Areas of E-healthcare in Society 5.0

E-healthcare has numerous applications across the healthcare industry, and its usage is increasing with advancements in technology. Here are some of the key applications of E-healthcare:

1. **Electronic Health Records (EHRs):** These refer to a patient's medical history in digital form. They allow healthcare providers to quickly access a patient's health information, such as medications, allergies, and immunization records (Loan et al., 2017).

2. **Mobile Health Apps:** Mobile health apps are software applications that can be used on mobile devices, such as smartphones or tablets, and are a key component of the shift toward E-healthcare, as they provide patients with greater access to healthcare services and allow for more personalized care. These apps can be used for a variety of purposes, including tracking and monitoring health conditions, scheduling appointments, accessing medical records, and receiving health-related notifications and reminders. Another benefit of mobile health apps is that they can help reduce healthcare costs by providing a more efficient and streamlined way to deliver care (Chauhan, 2023).

3. **Remote Patient Monitoring (RPM):** This technology allows healthcare providers to monitor patients' health status and vital signs from a remote location using various types of devices, such as wearable sensors, mobile apps, and other internet-connected devices. This technology has gained popularity in recent years,

especially in the context of the COVID-19 pandemic, as it allows patients to receive care without the need for in-person visits, reducing the risk of transmission of infectious diseases. One of the major challenges is training healthcare providers on how to use RPM technologies effectively, and regulatory frameworks that must be established to ensure the quality and safety of RPM devices and services (Andrews et al., 2020).

4. **Telemedicine:** Telemedicine involves the use of video conferencing, mobile apps, remote monitoring, and other communication technologies to connect patients with healthcare professionals. Telemedicine has become increasingly important in the context of E-healthcare in Society 5.0, which emphasizes the integration of technology into healthcare to improve patient outcomes and quality of life. In Society 5.0, telemedicine plays a crucial role in achieving the goal of providing personalized healthcare services to individuals based on their unique needs and preferences (Raj, Jain and Arif, 2017).

5. **Online Appointments Scheduling:** Online appointment scheduling can improve accessibility and convenience for patients, allowing them to schedule appointments from the comfort of their own homes, at any time of the day or night. This is particularly important for patients with mobility or transportation issues, those who live in remote areas, or those with busy schedules. Online appointment scheduling platforms can incorporate AI-powered chatbots that can answer patients' questions and provide them with relevant information, reducing the burden on healthcare providers and improving patient satisfaction (Nadarzynski et al., 2019).

6. **Health Education:** In Society 5.0, health education can be delivered through various technological platforms, such as mobile apps, online portals, social media, and virtual reality. These platforms can provide a range of health education materials, including articles, videos, infographics, and interactive tutorials. By leveraging technology to deliver health education materials, individuals can be empowered to take charge of their own health and improve their overall well-being (Tichon, 2002).

7. **Mental Health Services:** Mental health services in E-healthcare can take different forms, including online counseling, self-help programs, and digital therapeutic interventions. These services have the potential to increase access to mental healthcare, reduce stigma, and improve the quality of care. Moreover, e-mental health services can provide personalized and adaptive interventions based on individual needs and preferences. ML algorithms can analyze data from user interactions with the platform to provide tailored recommendations and support. One of the benefits of e-mental health services is that they can reach people who might not otherwise seek help due to geographical, financial, or social barriers (Kaoura, Kovas and Boutsinas, 2020).

12.6 Challenges of E-healthcare in Society 5.0

E-healthcare, which refers to the delivery of healthcare services through electronic means, is one of the key areas where Society 5.0 could make a significant affect. However, there are various challenges that must be addressed to achieve the full potential of E-healthcare in Society 5.0. Some of these challenges are (Shamila, Vinuthna and Tyagi, 2019):

1. **Privacy and Security Concerns:** E-healthcare involves the use of personal health information that is sensitive and confidential. The unauthorized access, use, or disclosure of this information can result in significant harm to individuals. Thus, to protect the security and privacy of electronic health records and other health-related data, it is imperative to put the proper safeguards in place.

2. **Access and Equity:** E-healthcare could enhance access to healthcare services for people living in remote or underserved areas. However, there are still many people who lack access to the necessary technology or infrastructure to benefit from E-healthcare. Therefore, it is important to ensure that E-healthcare is accessible and equitable, especially for vulnerable populations.

3. **Digital Divide:** The term "digital divide" describes the discrepancy between those who can access and use digital technologies efficiently and those who cannot. This gap is a major challenge for E-healthcare, as it can lead to unfair access to healthcare services and information. Therefore, efforts must be made to bridge the digital divide and ensure that everyone has the necessary skills and resources to participate in E-healthcare.

4. **Interoperability:** E-healthcare involves the use of various electronic health records systems, health monitoring devices, and other health-related technologies. However, these systems are often not interoperable, meaning that they cannot communicate with each other. This can result in fragmented care and a lack of continuity in healthcare services. Therefore, efforts must be made to ensure that different E-healthcare systems can communicate with each other seamlessly.

5. **Data Quality and Standardization:** E-healthcare involves data collection, data storage, and data analysis of vast amounts of health-related data. However, the quality and standardization of this data are often inconsistent, making it difficult to compare and analyze data across different systems. Therefore, efforts must be made to ensure that E-healthcare data is accurate, complete, and standardized.

12.7 Conclusion and Future Research Directions

The objective of Society 5.0 is to build a society that is based on sustainability, safety, and inclusiveness. It also seeks to create a better balance between humanity and technology. E-healthcare in Society 5.0 is focused on using innovative technologies to improve patient outcomes, enhance the patient experience, and encourage patients to be functional in managing their health. In this chapter, we have discussed the architecture, technologies, and application areas of E-healthcare in Society 5.0. As E-healthcare is a rapidly growing field, there are several future research directions that could help to advance the field and improve patient outcomes. The development of advanced AI and ML algorithms to analyze larger datasets with greater accuracy, advancement in wearable technology for more personalized care, personalized treatment plans, and blockchain-based health management systems are some of the potential future research areas in E-healthcare.

References

Agarwal, A. K. et al. (2021) 'A systematic analysis of applications of blockchain in healthcare', in *2021 6th International Conference on Signal Processing, Computing and Control (ISPCC)*, pp. 413–417.

Andrews, E. et al. (2020) 'Satisfaction with the use of telehealth during COVID-19: An integrative review', *International Journal of Nursing Studies Advances*. Elsevier, 2, p. 100008.

Bhatia, H., Panda, S. N. and Nagpal, D. (2020) 'Internet of things and its applications in healthcare-A survey', in *2020 8th International Conference on Reliability, Infocom Technologies and Optimization (Trends and Future Directions) (ICRITO)*, pp. 305–310.

Chaudhary, R. R. K. and Chatterjee, K. (2020) 'An efficient lightweight cryptographic technique for IoT based E-healthcare system', in *2020 7th International Conference on Signal Processing and Integrated Networks (SPIN)*, pp. 991–995.

Chauhan, M. (2023) 'Smart healthcare solutions for smart cities', in *AI-Centric Smart City Ecosystems*. CRC Press, pp. 247–260.

De Felice, F., Travaglioni, M. and Petrillo, A. (2021) 'Innovation trajectories for a Society 5.0', *Data*. MDPI, 6(11), p. 115.

Fukuda, K. (2020) 'Science, technology and innovation ecosystem transformation toward society 5.0', *International Journal of Production Economics*. Elsevier, 220, p. 107460.

Fukuyama, M. (2018) 'Society 5.0: Aiming for a new human-centered society', *Japan Spotlight*, 27(5), pp. 47–50.

Hameed, R. T. et al. (2015) 'Design of e-Healthcare management system based on cloud and service oriented architecture', in *2015 E-Health and Bioengineering Conference (EHB)*, pp. 1–4.

Huarng, K.-H., Yu, T. H. and Lee, Cf. (2022) 'Adoption model of healthcare wearable devices', *Technological Forecasting and Social Change*. Elsevier, 174, p. 121286.

Ioppolo, G. et al. (2020) 'Medicine 4.0: New technologies as tools for a society 5.0', *Journal of Clinical Medicine*. MDPI, p. 2198.

Kaoura, G., Kovas, K. and Boutsinas, B. (2020) 'Ontology-based case retrieval in an E-mental health intelligent information system', *Ontology-Based Information Retrieval for Healthcare Systems*. Wiley Online Library, pp. 167–191.

Klonoff, D. C., King, F. and Kerr, D. (2019) 'New opportunities for digital health to thrive', *Journal of Diabetes Science and Technology*, pp. 159–163.

Krishnamoorthy, S., Dua, A. and Gupta, S. (2023) 'Role of emerging technologies in future IoT-driven Healthcare 4.0 technologies: A survey, current challenges and future directions', *Journal of Ambient Intelligence and Humanized Computing*. Springer, 14(1), pp. 361–407.

Kute, S. S., Tyagi, A. K. and Aswathy, S. U. (2022) 'Industry 4.0 challenges in e-healthcare applications and emerging technologies', *Intelligent Interactive Multimedia Systems for e-Healthcare Applications*. Springer, pp. 265–290.

Loan, N. A. et al. (2017) 'Hiding electronic patient record (EPR) in medical images: A high capacity and computationally efficient technique for e-healthcare applications', *Journal of Biomedical Informatics*. Elsevier, 73, pp. 125–136.

Lwin, H. N. N., Punnakitikashem, P. and Thananusak, T. (2023) 'E-health research in Southeast Asia: A bibliometric review', *Sustainability*. MDPI, 15(3), p. 2559.

Nadarzynski, T. et al. (2019) 'Acceptability of artificial intelligence (AI)-led chatbot services in healthcare: A mixed-methods study', *Digital Health*. SAGE Publications, 5, p. 2055207619871808.

Nair, M. M., Tyagi, A. K. and Sreenath, N. (2021) 'The future with industry 4.0 at the core of society 5.0: Open issues, future opportunities and challenges', in *2021 International Conference on Computer Communication and Informatics (ICCCI)*, pp. 1–7.

Raj, C., Jain, C. and Arif, W. (2017) 'HEMAN: health monitoring and nous: An IoT based e-health care system for remote telemedicine', in *2017 International Conference on Wireless Communications, Signal Processing and Networking (WiSPNET)*, pp. 2115–2119.

Ray, P. P. et al. (2020) 'Blockchain for IoT-based healthcare: Background, consensus, platforms, and use cases', *IEEE Systems Journal*. IEEE, 15(1), pp. 85–94.

Razdan, S. and Sharma, S. (2022) 'Internet of medical things (IoMT): Overview, emerging technologies, and case studies', *IETE Technical Review*. Taylor & Francis, 39(4), pp. 775–788.

Sahi, M. A. et al. (2017) 'Privacy preservation in e-healthcare environments: State of the art and future directions', *IEEE Access*. IEEE, 6, pp. 464–478.

Shamila, M., Vinuthna, K. and Tyagi, A. K. (2019) 'A review on several critical issues and challenges in IoT based e-healthcare system', in *2019 International Conference on Intelligent Computing and Control Systems (ICCS)*, pp. 1036–1043.

Statista. (2022) 'Global digital health market size 2019–2025 forecast'. Available at: https://www.statista.com/statistics/1092869/global-digital-health-market-size-forecast/.

Tanbeer, S. K. and Sykes, E. R. (2021) 'MyHealthPortal--A web-based e-Healthcare web portal for out-of-hospital patient care', *Digital Health*. SAGE Publications, 7, p. 2055207621989194.

Tichon, J. G. (2002) 'Problem-based learning: A case study in providing e-health education using the Internet', *Journal of Telemedicine and Telecare*. SAGE Publications, 8(3_suppl), pp. 66–68.

Walter, Z. and Tung, Y. A. (2002) 'E-healthcare system design: A consumer preference approach', *International Journal of Healthcare Technology and Management*. Inderscience Publishers, 4(1–2), pp. 53–70.

13

Role of Disruptive Technologies in the Smart Healthcare Sector of Society 5.0

Prerna, Prabhdeep Singh, and Devesh Pratap Singh

13.1 Introduction

Good health is not just the absence of illness but a state of complete physical, mental, and social well-being. It is a precious asset that requires conscious effort and care. We can achieve optimal health and a fulfilling life by adopting healthy habits, such as eating well, exercising regularly, and seeking medical advice when needed. Smart health is an essential aspect of Society 5.0, which is a concept that emphasizes the integration of technology and society for the betterment of people's lives. Smart health uses advanced technologies, such as Artificial Intelligence (AI), the Internet of Things (IoT), and Big Data analytics, to improve healthcare delivery, management, and outcomes. In Society 5.0, smart health aims to empower individuals to take control of their health through wearable devices, mobile apps, and other digital tools that provide personalized health monitoring and support. These technologies enable healthcare providers to deliver more efficient and effective care, such as remote consultations, telemedicine, and predictive analytics for early disease detection and prevention. Smart health in Society 5.0 also emphasizes the importance of ethical and inclusive healthcare practices prioritizing patient privacy, data security, and equitable access to healthcare services. By leveraging technology to enhance healthcare delivery and promote healthy living, Smart health in Society 5.0 can help improve health outcomes and overall well-being for individuals and society.

Society 5.0 is a proposed future society that aims to balance economic development with social progress and environmental sustainability by utilizing advanced technologies like AI, IoT, Big Data, Robotics, and other emerging technologies. It is a concept that originated in Japan and is currently being promoted by the Japanese government to address various challenges society faces. Society 5.0 builds upon previous stages of human development, including hunter-gatherer societies (Society 1.0), agricultural societies (Society 2.0), industrial societies (Society 3.0), and information societies (Society 4.0). The key feature of Society 5.0 is the integration of physical space and cyberspace, creating a seamless and connected world where information, goods, and services can be exchanged efficiently and effectively. Society 5.0 uses technology to increase economic growth and efficiency and address social issues such as aging populations, healthcare, education, and environmental problems. For instance, advanced robotics and AI can be used to assist the elderly and disabled, while Big Data analytics can be used to improve healthcare outcomes and reduce environmental impacts. Society 5.0 envisions a future where advanced technologies are harnessed to create a more sustainable and prosperous society. One of the key features of this society is the integration of physical space and cyberspace, which enables seamless communication and interaction between humans and machines. Society 5.0 aims to enhance human capabilities and address pressing societal challenges such as climate change, aging populations, and urbanization by leveraging Artificial Intelligence, Robotics, and the Internet of Things. For example, advanced robotics can improve healthcare outcomes by assisting doctors and nurses in surgery or elderly care. The Internet of Things can help to optimize energy consumption in buildings, reducing carbon emissions and contributing to a more sustainable environment. AI-powered traffic management systems can help to alleviate traffic congestion in cities, improving the quality of life for residents. Society 5.0 also seeks to create a symbiotic relationship between humans and machines, combining the strengths to achieve common goals. For instance, AI algorithms can process vast amounts of data and provide insights that inform human decision-making. Robots can perform repetitive and dangerous tasks, allowing humans to focus on more creative and fulfilling work [1].

However, the success of Society 5.0 depends on ensuring that the benefits of advanced technologies are shared equitably across society. There are concerns that such technologies may exacerbate social inequalities, as those who do not have access to them may be left behind. Therefore, it is essential to ensure that the benefits of Society 5.0 are accessible to all, regardless of socioeconomic status or geographic location. Society 5.0 represents a vision for a future society that leverages advanced technologies to enhance human capabilities and address pressing societal challenges. Society 5.0 seeks to achieve a more sustainable and prosperous future for all by creating a symbiotic relationship between humans and machines [2].

13.2 Technologies Involved in the Development of the Smart Healthcare Sector in Society 5.0

Society 5.0 is a concept that envisions the integration of advanced technologies such as Artificial Intelligence, robotics, and the Internet of Things to create a more sustainable and

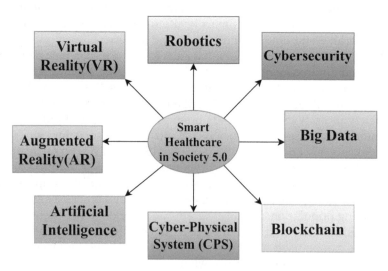

FIGURE 13.1
Smart healthcare in Society 5.0.

prosperous society. The development of smart healthcare in Society 5.0 involves the use of various advanced technologies that enable healthcare providers to offer personalized, efficient, and effective care (Figure 13.1). The following are some of the key technologies involved in the development of smart healthcare in Society 5.0.

13.2.1 Big Data in Smart Healthcare Sector of Society 5.0

Big Data plays a crucial role in developing smart healthcare in Society 5.0. With the massive amount of daily healthcare data, Big Data analytics enables healthcare providers to gain valuable insights, improve diagnoses, and personalize treatments. In smart healthcare, Big Data can track and manage chronic conditions, predict and prevent diseases, and optimize healthcare delivery. Healthcare providers can identify patterns and trends by analyzing patient data, including medical records, biometric data, and social determinants of health, leading to earlier diagnoses and better treatments. Furthermore, Big Data analytics can help healthcare providers make more informed decisions about resource allocation, such as predicting patient demand and managing staff schedules. This can lead to a more efficient and cost-effective healthcare system [3].

While Big Data has numerous potential applications in Society 5.0, several challenges and limitations must be addressed. Some of these challenges and limitations include the following:

1. Privacy Concerns: Big Data raises significant privacy concerns, as collecting and analyzing large amounts of personal data can compromise individuals' privacy rights. This can lead to data ownership, protection, and sharing issues.

2. Data Quality Issues: The quality of Big Data can vary widely, and there can be issues around data accuracy, completeness, and consistency. This can lead to issues around the reliability and validity of Big Data analytics and decision-making.

3. Data Security Concerns: Big Data raises significant security concerns, as the data being analyzed can be sensitive and valuable. This can lead to issues around data breaches, cyber-attacks, and other security threats.

4. Technical Limitations: There are technical limitations to using Big Data, including issues around data storage, data processing, and data visualization. These limitations can impact Big Data analytics' speed, accuracy, and scalability.

5. Resource Requirements: Big Data can require significant resources, including computing power, storage capacity, and skilled personnel. This can lead to cost and resource access issues, particularly for smaller organizations.

6. Ethical Considerations: Using Big Data raises ethical considerations around bias, discrimination, and the responsible use of data. There are concerns that Big Data analytics may reinforce existing inequalities and biases in society.

Using Big Data in Society 5.0 requires careful consideration of these challenges and limitations to ensure that the potential benefits of Big Data are realized while mitigating potential risks and negative impacts. It is essential to develop appropriate governance frameworks, regulations, and ethical guidelines to guide the use of Big Data in Society 5.0 [4].

13.2.2 Blockchain Technology in Smart Healthcare Sector of Society 5.0

Blockchain technology has significant potential to transform the healthcare industry and advance the development of smart healthcare in Society 5.0. In healthcare, Blockchain is a distributed ledger technology that can securely and transparently store and share patient data, streamline administrative processes, and enable secure and efficient data exchange between healthcare providers. One of the key benefits of Blockchain technology in smart healthcare is its ability to protect patient privacy and data security. Blockchain enables secure data sharing without compromising the patient's privacy by ensuring that only authorized parties can access the data. It also provides a tamper-proof and auditable record of all data transactions, reducing the risk of data breaches and fraud. Another advantage of Blockchain technology in smart healthcare is that it can streamline administrative processes, such as claims processing and payments, reducing costs, and improving efficiency. Blockchain-based platforms can enable automatic insurance coverage verification and processing of claims, reducing administrative overhead and increasing transparency. Furthermore, Blockchain technology can facilitate the development of new healthcare models and systems, such as decentralized healthcare platforms and peer-to-peer healthcare networks. These models can empower patients to take control of their health and facilitate more effective collaboration between healthcare providers [5].

While Blockchain has numerous potential applications in Society 5.0, several challenges and limitations are associated with its use. Some of these include the following:

1. Scalability: One of the biggest challenges of Blockchain is scalability. As the number of transactions on a Blockchain network grows, the network can become slower and more costly. This can limit its use in large-scale applications.

2. Interoperability: Different Blockchain networks may use different protocols and standards, making working together difficult. This can limit the ability to share data and resources across different Blockchain networks.

3. Regulation: As Blockchain becomes more widely used in various industries, regulation is needed to ensure its safe and responsible use. However, a lack of consistent regulation across different countries and industries makes it challenging for businesses to comply with the regulations.

4. Security: While Blockchain is often touted for its security features, it is not completely immune to cyber threats. Several high-profile hacks of Blockchain networks have highlighted the need for ongoing cybersecurity measures.

5. Energy consumption: The process of mining and validating transactions on a Blockchain network can be energy-intensive, which can be a concern for its environmental impact and long-term sustainability.

6. Cost: Implementing and maintaining Blockchain technology can be expensive, limiting its adoption by smaller businesses or organizations.

While Blockchain has the potential to revolutionize various industries in Society 5.0, these challenges and limitations must be carefully considered and addressed to ensure its effective and responsible use.

13.2.3 Cyber-Physical Systems (CPSs) in Smart Healthcare Sector of Society 5.0

Cyber-physical systems (CPSs) are important in developing smart healthcare in Society 5.0. CPSs are systems that integrate physical processes with computational algorithms, enabling real-time monitoring, analysis, and control of physical processes. In smart healthcare, CPSs can monitor and analyze patient health data in real time, enabling earlier diagnoses, personalized treatments, and improved patient outcomes. For example, wearable sensors and remote monitoring devices can collect biometric data such as heart rate, blood pressure, and blood glucose levels, which can be analyzed in real time to detect abnormalities and trigger appropriate interventions. CPSs can also be used to optimize healthcare delivery, such as managing patient flow in hospitals and reducing wait times. For example, real-time data on patient flow can be used to allocate resources more efficiently and reduce bottlenecks in the healthcare system.

Additionally, CPSs can facilitate the development of new healthcare models and systems, such as telemedicine and home-based care. Remote monitoring and telemedicine technologies can enable patients to receive care from the comfort of their own homes, reducing hospital readmissions and improving patient satisfaction. However, using CPS in smart healthcare also concerns data privacy and security. Healthcare providers must ensure that patient data is securely stored, accessed, and shared and that patients are informed and in control of their data [6].

While cyber-physical systems (CPSs) have significant potential in developing smart healthcare in Society 5.0, several challenges and limitations must be addressed to realize their full potential. One of the key challenges is data privacy and security. As CPS involves collecting, storing, and analyzing sensitive patient data, there is a risk of data breaches and unauthorized access. Healthcare providers must ensure that patient data is securely stored, accessed, and shared and that patients are informed and in control of their data. Another challenge is the interoperability of different systems and technologies. As CPS involves integrating multiple physical and digital systems, ensuring they are all compatible and work together seamlessly can be challenging. This can lead to data silos and inefficiencies in healthcare delivery. CPS also raises ethical and regulatory concerns. As CPS involves collecting and analyzing large amounts of data, there is a risk of bias and discrimination in healthcare delivery. Healthcare providers must ensure that CPS is designed and implemented fairly and equitably for all patients. Finally, there are concerns about the cost and scalability of CPS in healthcare. As CPS involves the integration of multiple technologies, they can be expensive to implement and maintain. Healthcare providers must ensure that CPS is cost-effective and scalable to ensure widespread adoption and accessibility [7].

To address these challenges and limitations, healthcare providers and policymakers must prioritize data privacy and security, ensure interoperability between different systems and technologies, promote ethical and regulatory frameworks for CPS, and prioritize cost-effectiveness and scalability.

13.2.4 Robotics Technology in the Smart Healthcare Sector of Society 5.0

Robotic technology has significant potential to transform the healthcare industry and advance the development of smart healthcare in Society 5.0. Robotics technology refers to the development and use of robots in healthcare settings, aiming to improve patient outcomes, increase efficiency, and reduce costs. One of the key benefits of robotics technology in smart healthcare is its ability to perform repetitive and time-consuming tasks, freeing healthcare providers to focus on more complex and specialized tasks. For example, robots can perform routine procedures such as medication delivery, sample collection, and patient monitoring, enabling healthcare providers to spend more time on diagnosis and treatment. Additionally, robotics technology can improve the accuracy and precision of healthcare procedures, reducing the risk of human error and improving patient safety. For example, robotic surgery systems can enable minimally invasive procedures with improved precision and control, leading to faster recovery and reduced hospital stays [8].

Moreover, robotics technology can facilitate remote healthcare delivery and telemedicine, enabling patients in remote or underserved areas to access healthcare services. For example, robots can remotely monitor and interact with patients, enabling healthcare providers to diagnose and treat patients from a distance. However, the use of robotics technology in smart healthcare also raises concerns about the safety and efficacy of these technologies. Healthcare providers must ensure that robotics technology is safe and effective for patients and that they are properly trained to use it. While robotics technology holds significant potential in developing smart healthcare in Society 5.0, several challenges and limitations must be addressed to realize their full potential. One of the key challenges of robotics technology in smart healthcare is cost. Developing, purchasing, and maintaining robots can be expensive, making it difficult for healthcare providers to invest in these technologies. However, as technology advances and the cost of robotics technology decreases, it is becoming more accessible and affordable for healthcare providers [9].

Another challenge is the need for specialized training and expertise to operate and maintain these technologies. Healthcare providers must ensure that their staff is properly trained to use and maintain these technologies, which can be time consuming and expensive. Additionally, as robotics technology is still relatively new in healthcare, there is a shortage of trained personnel with the necessary expertise. Moreover, integrating robotics technology with existing healthcare systems can be challenging. Robots must be compatible with electronic health record (EHR) systems and other healthcare technologies to ensure seamless integration and efficient workflows. However, achieving this level of interoperability can be challenging and may require significant investment and coordination among different stakeholders.

Additionally, the safety and efficacy of robotics technology in healthcare must be carefully considered. Robots must be designed and operated to minimize the risk of harm to patients, and their efficacy must be carefully evaluated to ensure that they are achieving their intended outcomes. Regulatory frameworks must be developed to ensure the safety and efficacy of these technologies, and healthcare providers must adhere to these frameworks to ensure patient safety. Another challenge of robotics technology in healthcare is the potential for job displacement. As robots are increasingly used to perform routine tasks in healthcare, there is a risk that healthcare jobs may become automated, leading to job displacement and loss of employment for healthcare workers. This highlights the importance of investing in retraining and upskilling programs to ensure healthcare workers have the skills and knowledge to work alongside robots and other advanced technologies [10].

Finally, ethical and societal concerns surround using robotics technology in healthcare. Some argue that using robots in healthcare may dehumanize the patient experience, leading to a loss of empathy and compassion in healthcare delivery.

To address these challenges and limitations, healthcare providers and policymakers must prioritize investment in robotics technology research and development, ensure that personnel is properly trained and equipped to operate and maintain these technologies, develop regulatory frameworks to ensure safety and efficacy, invest in retraining and upskilling programs for healthcare workers, and address ethical and societal concerns surrounding the use of these technologies in healthcare. Additionally, healthcare providers must consider the specific applications of robotics technology in different healthcare settings. For example, robotics technology may be well-suited for use in remote and rural areas with limited healthcare services. In these settings, robots can provide remote healthcare services and support healthcare workers in delivering care to patients. Moreover, healthcare providers can leverage robotics technology to enhance the patient experience and improve patient outcomes. For example, robots can provide social and emotional support to patients, improving their overall well-being and quality of life.

13.2.5 Augmented Reality (AR) and Virtual Reality (VR) in the Smart Healthcare Sector of Society 5.0

Augmented reality (AR) and Virtual reality (VR) are two emerging technologies that have the potential to revolutionize the way healthcare is delivered in Society 5.0. AR and VR can provide immersive and interactive experiences that enhance patient engagement, improve diagnosis, and aid medical education and training. AR overlays digital information in the real-world environment, while VR creates a completely artificial environment that users can interact with. In healthcare, AR and VR technologies can enhance the patient experience by providing visual aids to explain medical conditions, procedures, and treatments. These technologies can also train healthcare professionals in a safe and controlled environment, reducing the risk of error and improving patient outcomes. One potential application of AR and VR in healthcare is medical education and training. Medical students can use AR and VR technologies to practice surgical procedures in a simulated environment, improving their skills and confidence before performing the procedure on a real patient. This can improve patient outcomes by reducing the risk of error and complications during surgery. AR and VR can also improve patient outcomes by aiding in diagnosing medical conditions. AR and VR can provide 3D visualizations of the patient's anatomy, allowing healthcare professionals to understand the patient's condition better and plan their treatment accordingly. This can improve the accuracy of diagnoses and reduce the risk of misdiagnosis.

Moreover, AR and VR can enhance patient engagement and satisfaction by providing interactive and immersive experiences. For example, patients can use AR and VR technologies to visualize their medical condition and treatment plan, improving their understanding and involvement in their care. Additionally, AR and VR technologies can create virtual support groups and provide mental health support to patients. However, several challenges and limitations are associated with using AR and VR technologies in healthcare. One challenge is the need for specialized hardware and software to operate these technologies, which can be expensive and difficult to acquire [11].

Additionally, developing AR and VR applications in healthcare requires collaboration between healthcare providers and technology developers, which can be challenging due to differences in culture and language. Another challenge is the need for regulatory frameworks to ensure the safety and efficacy of these technologies. AR and VR technologies must be designed and operated to minimize the risk of patient harm. Their efficacy must be carefully evaluated to ensure they achieve their intended outcomes. Regulatory frameworks must be developed to ensure the safety and efficacy of these technologies, and healthcare providers must adhere to these frameworks to ensure patient safety. Moreover, there are concerns about the potential for AR and VR technologies to be used in unethical ways, such as in the creation of addictive gaming experiences or the development of surveillance systems. Healthcare providers and policymakers must address these concerns to ensure that these technologies are used ethically and for the benefit of patients.

To address these challenges and limitations, healthcare providers and policymakers must prioritize investment in AR and VR technology research and development, ensure that personnel is properly trained and equipped to operate and maintain these technologies, develop regulatory frameworks to ensure safety and efficacy, and address ethical and societal concerns surrounding the use of these technologies in healthcare.

13.2.6 Cybersecurity in the Smart Healthcare Sector of Society 5.0

Cybersecurity is a critical aspect of the smart healthcare sector in Society 5.0. With the increasing use of digital technologies and the growing amount of sensitive patient data being stored and transmitted electronically, healthcare providers must prioritize cybersecurity to protect patient privacy and prevent data breaches. One of the primary concerns with cybersecurity in healthcare is the risk of data breaches. Hackers can target healthcare organizations to steal patient data, which can be sold on the dark web for profit. This puts patient privacy at risk and can harm the healthcare organization's reputation and erode patient trust. Cyber threats can also affect the functionality of medical devices, such as pacemakers and insulin pumps, which can have life-threatening consequences for patients. These devices are often connected to the internet, making them vulnerable to cyber-attacks. Ensuring the security of these devices is crucial to protecting patient safety. To mitigate these risks, healthcare providers must implement robust cybersecurity measures to protect patient data and ensure medical devices' safe and effective operation. This includes implementing firewalls, encrypting sensitive data, and regularly monitoring and updating security protocols to stay ahead of evolving cyber threats [12].

Moreover, healthcare providers must also prioritize cybersecurity training and employee awareness. Employees must be trained to identify and respond to cyber threats, such as phishing emails and malware, to prevent data breaches and ensure patient safety. However, implementing effective cybersecurity measures in the healthcare sector can be challenging. Healthcare providers must balance the need for security with the accessibility and usability of digital technologies. Additionally, cybersecurity measures can be expensive, and many healthcare organizations may lack the resources to implement comprehensive cybersecurity protocols. Furthermore, the healthcare sector must also navigate a complex regulatory environment regarding cybersecurity. Healthcare providers must comply with regulations such as the Health Insurance Portability and Accountability Act (HIPAA), which requires healthcare organizations to protect patient privacy and safeguard electronic patient health information [13].

To address these challenges, healthcare providers must prioritize investment in cybersecurity research and development, allocate resources to implement comprehensive cybersecurity protocols, and collaborate with technology providers to develop innovative cybersecurity solutions that balance security and accessibility.

13.3 Integration of Different Technologies in Various Sectors of Society 5.0

Integrating various digital technologies in the smart healthcare sector of Society 5.0 can revolutionize the healthcare industry by increasing efficiency, improving patient outcomes, and reducing costs. The integration of Big Data analytics, Blockchain technology, Cyber-physical systems (CPSs), Augmented reality (AR), Virtual reality (VR), Robotics, and Cybersecurity can create a comprehensive and interconnected digital ecosystem that enhances the delivery of healthcare services. For example, by utilizing Big Data analytics, healthcare providers can identify patterns and trends in patient data, which can help to inform treatment decisions and improve patient outcomes. Blockchain technology can facilitate the secure and transparent sharing of patient data among healthcare providers, improving care coordination and reducing errors. CPS can improve the efficiency of healthcare delivery by automating routine tasks, such as inventory management and patient monitoring. Robotic technology can assist in performing complex surgeries by reducing the risk of human error, greater precision and improving patient outcomes. AR and VR can enhance medical training and education by providing immersive and interactive experiences for medical professionals and students. However, the integration of these technologies also presents several challenges. Healthcare providers must ensure that these technologies are user-friendly and accessible to all patients, regardless of their level of digital literacy. Additionally, healthcare providers must ensure these technologies are secure and protect patient privacy, complying with regulatory requirements such as HIPAA [14].

Moreover, integrating these technologies also requires significant investment in healthcare providers' research and development, infrastructure, and training. The lack of resources and funding for healthcare providers can hinder the adoption and integration of these technologies, limiting their potential to improve patient outcomes and reduce costs. To address these challenges, healthcare providers must collaborate with technology providers to develop innovative and accessible digital solutions that prioritize patient safety, privacy, and regulatory compliance. Additionally, healthcare providers must prioritize investment in research and development, infrastructure, and training for healthcare professionals to ensure they can effectively utilize these technologies [15].

13.4 Conclusion

The integration of disruptive technologies in the smart healthcare sector of Society 5.0 has transformed how healthcare is delivered, making it more efficient, effective, and personalized. The technologies discussed here, including Big Data, Blockchain, Cyber-physical systems, Robotics, Augmented–virtual reality, and Cybersecurity, have immense potential to improve patient outcomes, enhance medical education and training, and revolutionize healthcare research.

Big Data analytics and Machine learning algorithms enable healthcare professionals to diagnose diseases more accurately. Blockchain is revolutionizing medical data sharing, providing a secure and transparent system that gives patients greater control over their medical information. Cyber-physical systems and Robotics enhance patient care by enabling remote monitoring and improving surgical precision. Augmented–virtual reality enhances medical education and training and provides virtual reality therapy for patients, reducing pain and anxiety. Finally, Cybersecurity is essential to protect patient data and ensure that the healthcare industry operates safely and effectively.

The future scope of these disruptive technologies in the smart healthcare sector of Society 5.0 is vast. These technologies' continued development and integration will likely lead to improved patient outcomes, reduced healthcare costs, and more effective healthcare research. Artificial Intelligence and Big Data analytics will enable healthcare professionals to develop more personalized treatment plans and make more accurate diagnoses. Blockchain technology will become more widespread in the healthcare sector, ensuring the security and privacy of medical data. Cyber-physical systems and Robotics will become more sophisticated, enabling more precise diagnosis and treatment. Augmented–virtual reality technologies will continue to enhance medical education and training, providing a safe and effective way to train medical professionals.

In conclusion, the role of disruptive technologies in the smart healthcare sector of Society 5.0 is transforming the healthcare industry. Their continued integration holds immense potential for improving patient outcomes, enhancing medical education and research, and reducing healthcare costs. However, addressing the challenges associated with these technologies, including privacy concerns, regulatory issues, and ethical considerations, is essential to ensure they are used safely and effectively. Overall, the future of healthcare looks bright with the continued development and integration of these disruptive technologies.

References

1. Angurala, Mohit, Manju Bala, Sukhvinder Singh Bamber, Rajbir Kaur, and Prabhdeep Singh. "An internet of things assisted drone based approach to reduce rapid spread of COVID-19." *Journal of Safety Science and Resilience* 1, no. 1 (2020): 31–35.

2. Khullar, Vikas, Harjit Pal Singh, Yini Miro, Divya Anand, Heba G. Mohamed, Deepali Gupta, Navdeep Kumar, and Nitin Goyal. "IoT fog-enabled multi-node centralized ecosystem for real time screening and monitoring of health information." *Applied Sciences* 12, no. 19 (2022): 9845.

3. Potočan, Vojko, Matjaž Mulej, and Zlatko Nedelko. "Society 5.0: Balancing of Industry 4.0, economic advancement and social problems." *Kybernetes* 50, no. 3 (2020): 794–811.

4. Fukuda, Kayano. "Science, technology and innovation ecosystem transformation toward society 5.0." *International Journal of Production Economics* 220 (2020): 107460.

5. Salgues, Bruno. *Society 5.0: Industry of the Future, Technologies, Methods and Tools.* John Wiley & Sons, 2018.

6. Narvaez Rojas, Carolina, Gustavo Adolfo Alomia Peñafiel, Diego Fernando Loaiza Buitrago, and Carlos Andrés Tavera Romero. "Society 5.0: A Japanese concept for a superintelligent society." *Sustainability* 13, no. 12 (2021): 6567.

7. Aquilani, Barbara, Michela Piccarozzi, Tindara Abbate, and Anna Codini. "The role of open innovation and value co-creation in the challenging transition from industry 4.0 to society 5.0: Toward a theoretical framework." *Sustainability* 12, no. 21 (2020): 8943.

8. Ellitan, Lena. "Competing in the era of Industrial Revolution 4.0 and society 5.0." *Jurnal Maksipreneur: Manajemen, Koperasi, dan Entrepreneurship* 10, no. 1 (2020): 1–12.

9. Alimohammadlou, Moslem, and Zahra Khoshsepehr. "The role of Society 5.0 in achieving sustainable development: A spherical fuzzy set approach." *Environmental Science and Pollution Research* 30, (2023): 1–25.

10. Gross-Gołacka, Elwira, Teresa Kupczyk, Agnieszka Rzepka, Małgorzata Smolarek, and Katarzyna Szczepańska-Woszczyna. " The concept of inclusion and diversity as an accelerator for building Society 5.0 and creating a managed organization in the 5.0 era." *Innovation in the Digital Economy: New Approaches to Management for Industry 5.0* (2023): 62.

11. Eni, Desak Ketut Angraeni, Tri Aspiyana, and Susi Susi. "The role of women in education to face the era of Society 5.0: English language." *International Proceeding on Religion, Culture, Law, Education, and Hindu Studies* (2022): 54–66.

12. Acioli, Carina, Annibal Scavarda, and Augusto Reis. "Applying Industry 4.0 technologies in the COVID–19 sustainable chains." *International Journal of Productivity and Performance Management* 70, no. 5 (2021): 988–1016.

13. Piest, Jean Paul Sebastian, Yoshimasa Masuda, and Maria Eugenia Iacob. "Digital architectures under Society 5.0: An enterprise architecture perspective." In *International Conference on Enterprise Design, Operations, and Computing*, pp. 5–24. Springer, 2023.

14. Grover, Amit, R. Mohan Kumar, Mohit Angurala, Mehtab Singh, Anu Sheetal, and R. Maheswar. "Rate aware congestion control mechanism for wireless sensor networks." *Alexandria Engineering Journal* 61, no. 6 (2022): 4765–4777.
15. Tiwari, Raj Gaurang, Alok Misra, Ambuj Kumar Agarwal, and Vikas Khullar. "Communication jamming in body sensor network: A review." In *2021 10th International Conference on System Modeling & Advancement in Research Trends (SMART)*, pp. 135–139. IEEE, 2021.

14

Agriculture in Society 5.0

Meenakshi Aggarwal, Vikas Khullar, and Nitin Goyal

14.1 Introduction

Society 5.0 describes humanity's fifth stage. The Japanese government of 2016 invented it. It envisions a high-tech, eco-friendly civilisation that improves people's lives (Yuji Nagasaki, 2019). Digital technology is fully interwoven with healthcare, transportation, agriculture, and industry in Society 5.0. To create a civilisation that functions better, lasts longer, and can solve 21st-century issues, Society 5.0 builds on hunter-gatherer, agricultural, industrial, and information cultures. New technology and social systems transformed life and work at each stage (Deguchi A.C. Hirai, 2020). Society 5.0 uses digital technology to address climate change, resource depletion, and an ageing population. Technology and a shift in thinking about sustainability, inclusivity, and well-being are needed. Artificial intelligence (AI), the Internet of Things (IoT), robots, and blockchain will power Society 5.0 (Fukuyama, 2018). These technologies aim to improve, sustain, and equalise society 5.0. Society 5.0 claims digital technology is becoming increasingly pervasive. Agriculture is essential for food security, sustainability, and digital technologies in this circumstance.

Agriculture is the foundation of all production and essential to existence. Farming practices affect everyone. According to the FAO, the world's population might exceed 10 billion by 2050 (Friha et al., 2021), requiring additional food production. Work increases the quality of life. Agricultural output and quality are declining. Weather, water, animal assaults, and other factors affect crop output (Srivastava & Das, 2022). "Smart agriculture" is a novel management concept that uses modern technology and methods at different phases of food production to improve food quality and productivity (Walter et al., 2017). Smart farming uses sensors to detect temperature, light, pressure, humidity, wetness, and more, as well as communication protocols and data processing tools. Smart agriculture aims to protect the environment, make it lucrative, and last. Farming practices have changed. Farmers now use precision agriculture, smart farming, site-specific crop management, and satellite farming (Khanna & Kaur, 2019). AI, machine learning, deep learning, federated learning, and the IoT may make agriculture more productive, efficient, and sustainable, which is vital to human existence.

In Society 5.0, precision agriculture, sustainable agriculture, smart logistics, and rural revitalisation will be explored. These places can teach us how digital technology can tackle agriculture's biggest issues.

14.1.1 Precision Agriculture

Society 5.0's sustainable agricultural plan relies on precision agriculture. IoT sensors and AI technology allow farmers to track and adjust their farming methods in real time to

DOI: 10.1201/9781003397052-14

maximise resources and yield (Akhter & Sofi, 2022). Precision agriculture's advantages and current applications will be discussed in this section.

14.1.2 Sustainable Agriculture

Society 5.0 stresses sustainability in all areas, including agriculture. Digital technology can help farmers utilise renewable energy and less chemical fertilisers and pesticides. Sustainable agriculture improves soil health, environmental impact, and climate change adaptation (Walter et al., 2017).

14.1.3 Smart Logistics

Society 5.0 envisions digital technology improving food supply chain operations. Digital technology can track food from farm to table, assuring food safety and decreasing waste (Ramirez-Asis et al., 2022). We will also discuss smart logistics issues in agriculture.

14.1.4 Rural Renewal

Rural locations may lack education, health care, and other amenities. Society 5.0 emphasises the need of employing digital technology to improve rural living (Van Der Ploeg, 2000). This section will discuss how digital technology may enable rural residents to work from home and access education and health care and other benefits. These technologies' agricultural applications are here.

14.2 Agriculture-Related Search

Society 5.0, often known as the fifth industrial revolution, emphasises how digital technology and human intelligence may create a sustainable, people-centred society. Society 5.0 may enhance food production, minimise environmental harm, and ensure future generations have food. Society 5.0 agriculture literature reviews.

Society 5.0 might utilise robots and self-driving systems in agriculture (Marinoudi et al., 2019). Drones and self-driving tractors can assist in monitoring, sowing, and harvesting crops, according to the authors. They also investigate how robotic devices may reduce labour expenses and improve agriculture. In Society 5.0, robots and self-driving systems might boost agricultural output and sustainability, but safety and regulations must be considered. Data management and smart farming practices are needed to boost crop yields, cut costs, and make agriculture sustainable (Saiz-Rubio & Rovira-Más, 2020). The writers then discuss the progress of agriculture from Agriculture 1.0, which employed manual labour and rudimentary instruments, to Agriculture 5.0, which employs AI, IoT, and blockchain to better crop management. The authors also stress the need of collecting, processing, analysing, and understanding agricultural data to improve choices and yields.

Khanna and Kaur (2019) explain how farmers employ IoT devices and data to maximise agricultural yields. IoT technology affects precision agriculture's crop monitoring, animal breeding, and equipment maintenance. Farm sensors monitor soil moisture, temperature, and other environmental conditions in real time, according to the report. The results demonstrate the importance of real-time data collection and analysis for crop yields, disease prevention, and equipment efficiency. Farmers and other agricultural professionals looking to better their jobs with IoT technology can benefit from the article. Torky and Hassanein (2020) use blockchain and IoT to make precision agriculture's supply chain more transparent, secure, and resource-efficient. The authors discuss how blockchain and IoT can track livestock and manage agricultural supply chains in precision agriculture.

Decision trees, random forests, support vector machines, and neural networks are examined in Wireless Sensor Network (WSN)-based precision agriculture (Mekonnen et al., 2020). The authors stress the need for effective data collection, analysis, and modelling. Temperature, humidity, and wind influence machine learning algorithms, too. Segarra et al. (2020) discuss precision agriculture and remote sensing, focusing on Sentinel-2. The authors discuss Sentinel-2's high-resolution and multispectral cameras. Sentinel-2 data may be utilised in precision agriculture for crop monitoring, yield calculation, and vegetation mapping.

These literature studies explain how new technology and methods might affect agriculture in Society 5.0. They emphasise the importance of using these technologies and practices ethically, morally, environmentally, and economically.

14.3 IoT in Agriculture 5.0

Smart farming uses IoT. IoT technology can help farmers and producers generate more money (Sekaran et al., 2020). IoT's top smart agriculture applications are addressed.

14.3.1 Precision Farming

IoT technology like soil moisture sensors, weather stations, and drones can offer farmers real-time data on crop health, soil quality, and weather (Maduranga & Abeysekera, 2020). This information can assist farmers in choosing when to sow, irrigate, and select their crops for greater yields and reduced costs. Gaikwad et al. (2021) describe their real-time agro-field monitoring system for soil moisture, temperature, air humidity, and temperature. Arduino-based IoT devices measured metrics and immediately transferred them to a cloud server for web-based analysis.

14.3.2 Animal Monitoring

IoT sensors can monitor animal health and behaviour so farmers can immediately identify and address issues. Wearable sensors can watch cows' activity and alert farmers when they're unwell or angry (Shah et al., 2008) by measuring temperature, humidity, and heartbeat and sending data to an Arduino Uno. The Arduino Uno sends the correct data from the sensor. The technology monitors animal health and whereabouts using GPS.

14.3.3 Supply Chain Management

IoT can track food from farm to table. This can assist in delivering items on schedule and in good shape, reduce waste, and improve efficiency. IoT devices (Android applications on mobile phones) update product quality and transport time in farmers in real time (Borah et al., 2020). An integrated system was suggested to track and use supply chain items. They created a web platform where farmers utilise blockchain technology to construct an honest value chain from farm to fork.

14.3.4 Environmental Monitoring

IoT sensors can monitor air and water quality, helping farmers identify and address environmental issues that might harm crop health and yield. Ullo and Sinha (2020) discuss how sensor technologies, the Internet of Things (IoT), and deep learning make environmental monitoring a smart system. Strong machine learning, demonising, and WSN requirements are also recommended. IoT helps farmers make better decisions and operate their farms more effectively by providing real-time data. Farmers can boost productivity, save expenses, and sustain their enterprises with IoT.

14.4 Agriculture and Machine Learning

Agriculture is increasingly using machine learning and deep learning to boost agricultural yields, reduce resource usage, and reduce environmental impact. These technologies are employed in the following ways.

14.4.1 Predictive Analytics

Machine learning algorithms can analyse historical data and weather trends to anticipate agricultural yields and harvests. This helps them pick the correct crops, plant at the proper time, and squander less. Araby et al. (2019) propose a smart system that leverages IoT and machine learning to anticipate potato and tomato late blight before it occurs. This preserves yield during infection seasons and reduces pesticide consumption by alerting farmers when to apply protective chemicals.

14.4.2 Agricultural Monitoring and Recommendation Systems

Deep learning models can analyse drone, satellite, or sensor photos of crops to discover illnesses, pests, and other concerns that might lower agricultural output. This can help farmers spot issues early and address them. Machine learning algorithms may also analyse soil and meteorological data to determine which crops would flourish best. This can assist farmers in choosing crops based on weather, soil, and water availability. Jia et al. (2019) discuss large-scale agricultural landscape monitoring using automated, remote sensing, and machine learning technologies. It requires adequate data and the danger of algorithm bias.

14.4.3 Harvest Optimisation

Based on weather, crop readiness, and crew availability, machine learning algorithms can optimise harvesting. This helps farmers squander less and maximise agricultural yields. Lu (2010) examines how a novel harvest aid might improve North China Plain machine-picked cotton. Field experiments will determine when and how much harvest assistance to apply and how it impacts cotton productivity and quality characteristics like fibre length and strength. Harvest assistance improves cotton quality, depending on the variety and growth circumstances.

Machine learning algorithms can detect and track crop-damaging pests and illnesses. These models can detect early infestation indicators and offer ways to cure or avoid them using sensors and other data. The red palm weevil and smaller date moth, which consume date palms, can be controlled by the biocontrol fungus *Beauveria bassiana* (Latifian et al., 2014). The *B. bassiana* spores on date palms using a liquid-to-solid-to-liquid agricultural product. Results show *B. bassiana* treatment greatly reduced insect populations without harming date palm growth or output. This biological pest management strategy might replace chemical pesticides in date palms, according to the study.

Deep learning and machine learning can make farming more efficient, feasible, and lucrative. These technologies will be employed in agriculture more creatively as data and algorithms get more complicated.

14.5 Agriculture 5.0 Blockchain

Blockchain technology is being investigated and applied in agriculture to make supply chains more transparent, trackable, and efficient. These farming applications use blockchain.

14.5.1 Food Safety

Blockchain can verify food authenticity and origin. This makes it easy to recall tainted or unsafe food. This reduces foodborne illness and boosts food system trust. Blockchain technology may impact agriculture and the food supply chain (Kamilaris et al., 2019). The paper describes blockchain technology's transparency, immutability, and decentralisation, which improve supply chain traceability and efficiency. Blockchain technology might alter the agriculture and food industries, but interoperability and scalability difficulties remain.

14.5.2 Payment and Financing

Blockchain can simplify and secure payments and loans for farmers, wholesalers, and others in the agriculture value chain. This can reduce transaction costs, increase financial inclusion, and improve market access for smallholder farmers. AgriDigital, a blockchain-based platform for agricultural commerce and financing, was studied by Xu et al. (2019). The paper describes how AgriDigital's blockchain platform simplifies and secures farm-to-consumer interactions. AgriDigital's platform might transform the agriculture business, but more study is needed to determine how.

14.5.3 Land Registration

Farmers may utilise blockchain to create safe, unambiguous land records to confirm legal ownership. This can help farmers acquire loans and other financial services and lessen land conflicts. Blockchain technology can create a decentralised land-lending system (Shaji et al., 2019). The technology allows lenders and borrowers to communicate directly without middlemen, lowering transaction costs. Consider the security, immutability, and transparency of blockchain technology for land lending, which can reduce fraud and increase accountability. This article discusses regulatory issues and data privacy concerns while implementing such a system. The authors conclude that a blockchain-based decentralised land-lending system might help small farmers acquire loans and enhance land management. More research is needed to determine its efficacy in different situations.

14.5.4 Carbon Credits

Carbon credits from conservation tillage and agroforestry can be traded on a blockchain-based market. This can promote sustainability and slow climate change. Kim and Huh (2020) advocate employing blockchain technology for carbon trading to achieve the UN SDGs. Blockchain can provide a transparent and secure carbon trading market. This reduces greenhouse gas emissions and fights climate change. Blockchain for carbon trading reduces transaction costs, simplifies tracking, and improves trust, according to the authors. The report also discusses issues like regulation and carbon offset fraud that may arise when implementing such a system. Blockchain technology can help achieve climate action and environmental sustainability SDGs, but more study and collaboration are needed to overcome its difficulties and maximise its potential.

Blockchain has several agricultural applications. As blockchain technology develops and more individuals in the agriculture value chain adopt it, these uses will proliferate (Xu et al., 2019).

14.6 Agriculture 5.0 with Federated Learning

Federated learning lets devices collaborate on a machine learning model without exchanging data (Vimalajeewa et al., 2022). In agriculture, data security is crucial. Agriculture uses federated learning in these ways.

14.6.1 Crop Disease Detection

Federated learning may train machine learning models on data from several farms without needing them to exchange data with each other or a central server (Kumar et al., 2021). This can help farmers rapidly and correctly identify crop diseases and pests to prevent further damage.

14.6.2 Weather Forecasting

Federated learning may train machine learning models on weather station data without requiring the stations to provide their data. This can improve localised weather predictions and assist farmers in making planting, harvesting, and other agricultural choices.

14.6.3 Irrigation Management

Federated learning can train machine learning models on data from different farms about soil moisture levels, weather conditions, and other factors that affect irrigation needs without requiring the farms to share their data with each other or a central server. This can improve water efficiency, agricultural yields, and water waste.

14.6.4 Insect Management

Federated learning may train machine learning models on data from multiple farms on insect populations and environmental variables without needing the farms to share their data with each other or a central server. This makes pest management more focused and effective, lowering pesticide use and making the environment more sustainable.

14.6.5 Livestock Breeding

Federated learning can train machine learning models using data regarding the genetics, health, and productivity of animals from various livestock farms without the farms needing to share their data with each other or a central server. This can enhance breeding plans, animal welfare and production, and antibiotic and medication use.

14.6.6 Soil Analysis

Federated learning may train machine learning models on data from multiple farms on soil features and nutrient levels without needing the farms to exchange their data with each other or a central server. This can improve soil health and reduce nutrient runoff by targeting fertilisation and crop rotation. Federated learning in agriculture can improve production, distribution, and consumption across the value chain (Manoj et al., 2022). Federated learning may help farmers and other agriculture stakeholders make better decisions, decrease waste, enhance sustainability, and raise profitability by using dispersed data.

14.7 Conclusion

Society 5.0 relies on agriculture for food security. Digital technology helps farmers reduce waste, enhance farming, and live better. This chapter included precision agriculture, sustainable agriculture, smart logistics, and rural revitalisation in Society 5.0. AI and ML can analyse soil quality, weather, and crop health data to assist farmers in making data-driven decisions. IoT lets farmers remotely monitor soil moisture, temperature, humidity, and other environmental factors. This can help them choose irrigation, fertilisation, and insect management, saving resources. Federated learning and blockchain technology might revolutionise agriculture. Federated learning and blockchain can boost agriculture. Farmers may train machine learning models to anticipate weather, agricultural yields, and pests using federated learning. Shared knowledge from these models on a blockchain platform can help farmers make better decisions and increase yields. These new technologies can boost agriculture's efficiency, production, and sustainability, improving food security and the environment.

References

Akhter, R., & Sofi, S. A. (2022). Precision agriculture using IoT data analytics and machine learning. *Journal of King Saud University - Computer and Information Sciences*, 34(8), 5602–5618. https://doi.org/10.1016/j.jksuci.2021.05.013

Araby, A. A., Elhameed, M. M. A., Magdy, N. M., Said, L. A., Abdelaa, N., Tarek Abd Allah, Y., Darweesh, M. S., Fahim, M. A., & Mostafa, H. (2019). Smart IoT monitoring system for agriculture with predictive analysis. *8th International Conference on Modern Circuits and Systems Technologies (MOCAST)*, 3–6.

Borah, M. D., Naik, V. B., Patgiri, R., Bhargav, A., Phukan, B., & Basani, S. G. M. (2020). Supply chain management in agriculture using blockchain and IoT. In *Studies in Big Data* (Vol. 60). Springer. https://doi.org/10.1007/978-981-13-8775-3_11

Friha, O., Ferrag, M. A., Shu, L., Maglaras, L. A., & Wang, X. (2021). Internet of things for the future of smart agriculture a comprehensive survey of emerging technologies. *IEEE/CAA Journal of Automatica Sinica*, 8(4), 718–752.

Fukuyama, M. (2018). Society 5.0: Aiming for a new human-centered society. Japan spotlight. August, 8–13. https://www.academia.edu/download/62213365/soc_5.020200227-84216-1291i85.pdf

Gaikwad, S. V., Vibhute, A. D., Kale, K. V., & Mehrotra, S. C. (2021). An innovative IoT based system for precision farming. *Computers and Electronics in Agriculture*, 187(September 2020), 106291. https://doi.org/10.1016/j.compag.2021.106291

Hakak, S., Ray, S., Khan, W. Z., & Scheme, E. (2020). A framework for edge-assisted healthcare data analytics using federated learning. *Proceedings - 2020 IEEE International Conference on Big Data, Big Data 2020*, 3423–3427. https://doi.org/10.1109/BigData50022.2020.9377873

Hitachi-UTokyo Laboratory(H-UTokyo Lab.). (2020). Society 5.0 a people-centric super-smart society. Springer Open 2020.

Jia, X., Khandelwal, A., Mulla, D. J., Pardey, P. G., & Kumar, V. (2019). Bringing automated, remote-sensed, machine learning methods to monitoring crop landscapes at scale. *Agricultural Economics (United Kingdom)*, 50(S1), 41–50. https://doi.org/10.1111/agec.12531

Kamilaris, A., Fonts, A., & Prenafeta-Boldú, F. X. (2019). The rise of blockchain technology in agriculture and food supply chains. *Trends in Food Science and Technology*, 91, 640–652. https://doi.org/10.1016/j.tifs.2019.07.034

Khanna, A., & Kaur, S. (2019). Evolution of Internet of Things (IoT) and its significant impact in the field of Precision Agriculture. *Computers and Electronics in Agriculture*, 157(November 2018), 218–231. https://doi.org/10.1016/j.compag.2018.12.039

Kim, S. K., & Huh, J. H. (2020). Blockchain of carbon trading for UN sustainable development goals. *Sustainability (Switzerland)*, 12(10). https://doi.org/10.3390/SU12104021

Kumar, P., Gupta, G. P., & Tripathi, R. (2021). PEFL: Deep privacy-encoding-based federated learning framework for smart agriculture. *IEEE Micro*, 42(1), 33–40.

Latifian, M., Rad, B., & Amani, M. (2014). Mass production of entomopathogenic fungi *Metarhizium anisopliae* by using agricultural products based on liquid-solid diphasic method for date palm pest control. *International Journal of Farming and Allied Sciences*, 3(4), 368–372. http://ijfas.com/wp-content/uploads/2014/04/368-372.pdf

Lu, Q. Zhang, Y., & Harvey, J. T. (2009). Estimation of Truck Traffic Inputs for Mechanistic–Empirical Pavement Design in California. *Transportation Research Record*, 2095(1), 62–72. https://doi.org/10.3141/2095-07

Maduranga, M. W., & Abeysekera, R. (2020). Machine learning applications in IoT based agriculture and smart farming: A review. *International Journal of Engineering Applied Sciences and Technology*, 4(12), 24–27. https://doi.org/10.33564/ijeast.2020.v04i12.004

Manoj, T., Makkithaya, K., & Narendra, V. G. (2022, February). A federated learning-based crop yield prediction for agricultural production risk management. In *2022 IEEE Delhi Section Conference (DELCON)* (pp. 1–7). IEEE.

Marinoudi, V., Sørensen, C. G., Pearson, S., & Bochtis, D. (2019). Robotics and labour in agriculture. A context consideration. *Biosystems Engineering*, 184, 111–121. https://doi.org/10.1016/j.biosystemseng.2019.06.013

Mekonnen, Y., Namuduri, S., Burton, L., Sarwat, A., & Bhansali, S. (2020). Review—Machine learning techniques in wireless sensor network based precision agriculture. *Journal of the Electrochemical Society*, 167(3), 037522. https://doi.org/10.1149/2.0222003jes

Nagasaki, Y. (2019). *Realization of Society 5.0 by Utilizing Precision Agriculture into Smart Agriculture in NARO Japan*. Food and Fertilizer Technology Center in Asia and Pacific Region. https://ap.fftc.org.tw/article/1414

Ramirez-Asis, E., Bhanot, A., Jagota, V., Chandra, B., Hossain, M. S., Pant, K., & Almashaqbeh, H. A. (2022). Smart logistic system for enhancing the farmer-customer corridor in smart agriculture sector using artificial intelligence. *Journal of Food Quality*, 2022. https://doi.org/10.1155/2022/7486974

Saiz-Rubio, V., & Rovira-Más, F. (2020). From smart farming towards agriculture 5.0: A review on crop data management. *Agronomy*, 10(2). https://doi.org/10.3390/agronomy10020207

Segarra, J., Buchaillot, M. L., Araus, J. L., & Kefauver, S. C. (2020). Remote sensing for precision agriculture: Sentinel-2 improved features and applications. *Agronomy*, 10(5), 1–18. https://doi.org/10.3390/agronomy10050641

Sekaran, K., Meqdad, M. N., Kumar, P., Rajan, S., & Kadry, S. (2020). Smart agriculture management system using internet of things. Telkomnika (telecommunication computing electronics and control), 18(3), 1275–1284. https://doi.org/10.12928/TELKOMNIKA.v18i3.14029

Shah, K., Shah, K., Thakkar, B., & Hetal Amrutia, M. (2008). Livestock monitoring in agriculture using IoT. *International Research Journal of Engineering and Technology*, 2414. www.irjet.net

Srivastava, A., & Das, D. K. (2022). A comprehensive review on the application of Internet of Thing (IoT) in smart agriculture. In: *Wireless Personal Communications* (Vol. 122, Issue 2). Springer US. https://doi.org/10.1007/s11277-021-08970-7

Torky, M., & Hassanein, A. E. (2020). Integrating blockchain and the internet of things in precision agriculture: Analysis, opportunities, and challenges. *Computers and Electronics in Agriculture*, 178(November 2019), 105476. https://doi.org/10.1016/j.compag.2020.105476

Ullo, S. L., & Sinha, G. R. (2020). Advances in smart environment monitoring systems using IoT and sensors. *Sensors (Switzerland)*, 20(11), 1–18. https://doi.org/10.3390/s20113113

Van Der Ploeg, J. D. (2000). Revitalizing agriculture: Farming economically as starting ground for rural development. *Sociologia Ruralis*, 40(4), 497–511. https://doi.org/10.1111/1467-9523.00163

Vimalajeewa, D., Kulatunga, C., Berry, D. P., & Balasubramaniam, S. (2022). A service-based joint model used for distributed learning: Application for smart agriculture. *IEEE Transactions on Emerging Topics in Computing*, 10(2), 838–854. https://doi.org/10.1109/TETC.2020.3048671

Walter, A., Finger, R., Huber, R., & Buchmann, N. (2017). Smart farming is key to developing sustainable agriculture. *Proceedings of the National Academy of Sciences of the United States of America*, 114(24), 6148–6150. https://doi.org/10.1073/pnas.1707462114

Xu, X., Weber, I., & Staples, M. (2019). Case study: AgriDigital: Blockchain technology in the trade and finance of agriculture supply chains. *Architecture for Blockchain Applications*, 239–255. http://link.springer.com/10.1007/978-3-030-03035-3_12

15

Personalized Navigation System in Society 5.0

Saravjeet Singh and Rishu Chhabra

15.1 Introduction

Society 5.0 is a concept that envisions the fifth stage of human society, following the hunting society, agricultural society, industrial society, and information society. Society 5.0 is characterized by the integration of digital technology, such as artificial intelligence, the Internet of Things, and big data, into all aspects of our lives. The goal is to create a human-centring society that is sustainable, inclusive, and provides a high quality of life for all its members (Deguchi et al. 2018). The 5th Science and Technology Basic Plan outlined Society 5.0 as the ideal society for Japan to strive for in the future. It comes after the agrarian society (Society 1.0), the industrial society (Society 3.0), the information society (Society 3.0), and the hunting society (Society 4.0). Trans learning and information dissemination were insufficient in the information society (Society 4.0), and collaboration was challenging (Rojas et al. 2021). Figure 15.1 shows the generation-wise evolution of Society 5.0. The difficulty of extracting the essential information from the abundance of information and analysing it was a burden, and the range of work and activity was constrained by age and varied levels of skill because there is a limit to what people can do. However, it was challenging to respond appropriately due to a number of constraints on problems like a declining birth rate, an elderly population, and local depopulation. With social reform, Society 5.0 will become a progressive society that overcomes the current sense of stagnation, a society where people respect one another across generations, and a society where everyone may live an active and fulfilling life (Pereira, Lima, and Charrua-Santos 2020).

In Society 5.0, virtual space and physical space collide to a great extent. In the past, members of the information society (Society 4.0) would use the internet to search for, obtain, and analyse information or data from cloud services (databases) in cyberspace (Rojas et al. 2021).

In Society 5.0, a vast amount of data collected by sensors in physical space is stored online. Artificial intelligence (AI) analyses this huge data in cyberspace, and the analysis' findings are relayed back to people in physical space in a variety of ways. In the past, collecting information through some kind of network and having it examined by humans was standard procedure in an information society. But, in Society 5.0, everything is interconnected in virtual space, and the best outcomes produced by AI that are more advanced than humans are fed back into the actual world. Industry and society both benefit from this process in ways that were not before feasible (Aquilani et al. 2020; "RIETI – Blockchain and Society 5.0 – The Creation of a New Marketplace Based on Distributed Consensus" n.d.).

DOI: 10.1201/9781003397052-15

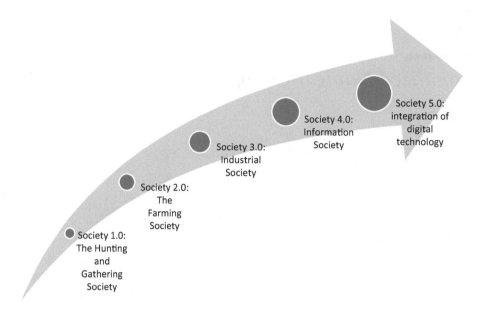

FIGURE 15.1
Evolution of Society 5.0.

In Society 5.0, technology is used to solve social problems, such as ageing populations, environmental issues, and resource depletion. For example, smart cities with sensors and automation can reduce waste and energy consumption, while robots and AI can help with caregiving and medical support for the elderly. The concept of Society 5.0 emphasizes the importance of collaboration between different sectors, including government, industry, academia, and citizens, to achieve a better future for humanity (Deguchi et al. 2018; Lavalle et al. 2020).

15.1.1 Society 5.0 and 4.0

Society 5.0 and Society 4.0 represent two different stages of human society, each with its own set of characteristics and goals. Society 4.0, also known as the Fourth Industrial Revolution, is characterized by the integration of digital technology into all aspects of our lives. It emphasizes the use of advanced technologies such as artificial intelligence, robotics, and the Internet of Things to drive productivity, efficiency, and innovation (Huang et al. 2022).

Society 5.0 takes a more holistic approach to technology and society. It aims to create a human-centred society that is sustainable, inclusive, and provides a high quality of life for all its members. Society 5.0 emphasizes the use of technology to solve social problems, such as ageing populations, environmental issues, and resource depletion (Skobelev and Borovik 2017).

While Society 4.0 is focused on improving productivity and efficiency through technology, Society 5.0 aims to use technology to create a better future for humanity. Society 5.0 emphasizes collaboration between different sectors, including government, industry, academia, and citizens, to achieve a better future for all (Martynov, Shavaleeva, and Zaytseva 2019).

Figure 15.2 shows the transition from Society 4.0 to Society 5.0. Society 4.0 was information based and more focus was on cloud computing. Information processing and analysis were more dependent on human intervention and less focus was on automation. Whereas in Society 5.0, the focus is on the Internet of Things and sensors. Automation is applicable in every field of society. More dependence is on automation, robotics, and artificial intelligence. According to Figure 15.2, the basic terms associated with Society 5.0 are the following:

- Artificial Intelligence (AI): The simulation of human intelligence processes by computer systems, including learning, reasoning, and self-correction.
- Internet of Things (IoT): The interconnection of everyday devices, vehicles, buildings, and other objects, with embedded electronics, software, sensors, and network connectivity, allowing them to collect and exchange data.
- Big Data: Large, complex data sets that can be analysed to reveal patterns, trends, and associations, especially relating to human behaviour and interactions.
- Robotics: The design, construction, and operation of robots, which are automated machines that can perform tasks autonomously or under human control.
- Smart Cities: Cities that use digital technology and data to improve urban planning, reduce waste, enhance public services, and increase efficiency.

15.1.2 Components of Society 5.0

Society 5.0 is a concept that envisions a human-centred society that is sustainable, inclusive, and provides a high quality of life for all its members. It is characterized by the integration of digital technology into all aspects of our lives, with the aim of using technology

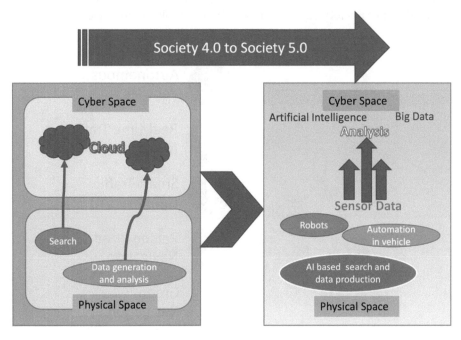

FIGURE 15.2
Transition from Society 4.0 to 5.0.

to solve social problems and create a better future for humanity. The following are some of the key components of Society 5.0 (Ritzer 2008):

- Digital Technology: Society 5.0 emphasizes the use of advanced digital technologies such as artificial intelligence, robotics, big data, and the Internet of Things (IoT) to drive innovation and improve quality of life.
- Human-Centred Society: Society 5.0 puts human beings at the centre of society, with a focus on meeting human needs and improving quality of life.
- Sustainability: Society 5.0 aims to create a sustainable society that balances economic development with environmental protection and social well-being.
- Collaboration: Society 5.0 emphasizes collaboration between different sectors, including government, industry, academia, and citizens, to achieve common goals.
- Inclusivity: Society 5.0 strives to create an inclusive society that ensures equal access to opportunities and resources for all its members.
- Social Problem-Solving: Society 5.0 aims to use technology to solve social problems, such as ageing populations, environmental issues, and resource depletion.
- Smart Cities: Society 5.0 promotes the development of smart cities that use digital technologies to improve urban planning, reduce waste, and enhance public services.

15.1.3 Road Navigation and Society 5.0

Road navigation in Society 5.0 involves the use of digital technology, such as artificial intelligence (AI), big data, and the Internet of Things (IoT), to create a safer, more efficient, and sustainable transportation system. Figure 15.3 shows the areas of road navigation that can be evolved as per Society 5.0. Road navigation is evolving in Society 5.0 using the following ways:

FIGURE 15.3
According to Society 5.0, areas of road navigation.

- Autonomous Vehicles: Autonomous vehicles, or self-driving cars, are becoming increasingly common, thanks to advances in AI, sensors, and mapping technology. These vehicles can navigate roads and highways without human intervention, reducing the risk of accidents and improving traffic flow.

- Real-Time Traffic Management: Digital technology is being used to monitor traffic in real time, using sensors and data analysis to identify congestion, accidents, and other traffic issues. This information can be used to optimize traffic flow, reduce delays, and improve safety.

- Smart Traffic Lights: Traffic lights are being connected to digital networks, allowing them to communicate with other traffic lights and adjust their timing based on traffic conditions. This can reduce congestion and improve safety by preventing accidents at intersections.

- Personalized Navigation: Navigation systems are becoming more personalized, using data on a driver's preferences, behaviour, and traffic patterns to optimize routes and provide real-time traffic information. This can reduce travel time and improve safety.

- Green Navigation: Navigation systems are being designed to help drivers choose the most environmentally friendly routes, based on factors such as traffic congestion, air quality, and emissions. This can help reduce the carbon footprint of transportation and contribute to a more sustainable society.

This chapter provides information about Society 5.0 and its application in road navigation. After the introduction section, this chapter describes personalized navigation system, the architecture of personalized navigation system, the routing algorithm used in personalized navigation, and the challenges associated with personalized navigation.

15.2 Personalized Navigation

A major element of Society 5.0's concept of a more effective and adaptable transportation system is personalized navigation. Navigation systems are becoming increasingly personalized in Society 5.0 by incorporating information about a driver's preferences, behaviour, and traffic patterns to optimize routes and give real traffic statistics.

Big data, artificial intelligence, and the Internet of Things can all be used in personalized navigation to help drivers save time, reduce stress, and drive more safely. In Society 5.0, personalized navigation is changing in the following ways:

- Dynamic Routing: Dynamic routing provides more effective routing to drivers by considering real-time traffic conditions. Since traffic situations change in real time, navigation systems are becoming more dynamic, providing drivers with the most effective route depending on their present location, traffic patterns, and selected method of transportation.

- Personalized Recommendations: Based on a driver's preferences and prior actions, navigation systems are being developed to offer personalized recommendations. For instance, a navigation system might suggest a certain route in the context of a driver's recent driving patterns, such as preferred speed and driving technique.

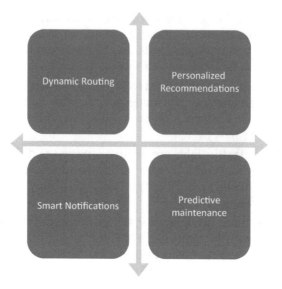

FIGURE 15.4
Components of personalized navigation.

- Smart Notifications: Navigation systems are becoming more proactive, notifying drivers regarding traffic conditions, accidents, and other potential risks on the road. Drivers may stay vigilant while driving and avoid potential risks by following many measures.

- Predictive Maintenance: By using data to forecast when a vehicle may need maintenance or repairs, navigation systems can assist drivers in staying ahead of potential maintenance concerns. Drivers can save money and lower their risk of unforeseen breakdowns through this approach.

- Personalized navigation in Society 5.0 can be achieved by integrating all components (as shown in Figure 15.4) of navigation systems like driver, vehicle, road network, and other stakeholders.

15.3 Personalized Navigation Architecture

Navigation system plays a very important role in daily life. For road transportation, these systems are used for route finding, location identification, and geo-referencing activities. The main goal of modern outdoor navigation systems is to increase localization performance and provide a better user experience. Traditional navigation system was based on the compass-based tool, and with the advancement of positioning technologies, Global Positioning System (GPS) was being used as part of the navigation system. These navigation systems use electronic devices and satellite signals to determine the location of a user or vehicle. The system can then use this information to provide turn-by-turn directions to a desired location. Navigation systems typically consist of a GPS receiver, which receives signals from satellites, and a display screen that shows the user's current location and the route to the destination. A GPS navigation system that is specifically intended for use on roads and highways is known as a road-based navigation system. These systems locate the vehicle using GPS technology, and then they employ digital mapping information to give turn-by-turn directions to a specific area. According to Society 5.0, the navigation system has evolved to personalized navigation system. These systems use sensors and electronic devices to fetch location/ spatial information, traffic conditions, and driver information. This collected information is processed and analysed using machine learning and cloud-based techniques to provide a personalized driving solution. These navigation systems can be carried while walking or travelling or they can be put in automobiles as handheld tools. Many smartphones also come with GPS, and with the support of a navigation app, they can serve as navigational aids. Voice prompts are another feature of personalized navigation systems that provide the user with spoken directions. Personalized road-based navigation systems can give directions as well as details on the flow of traffic, alternate routes, and nearby attractions like restaurants, motels, and petrol stations. In general, Society 5.0's architecture for a personalized navigation system is built to gather and analyse huge amounts of data and utilize that data to customize individual user's driving experience. Drivers can save time, feel less stressed, and drive more safely with the aid of customized navigation systems, which take advantage of data analysis and new technologies.

The basic architecture of a personalized navigation system in Society 5.0 is shown in Figure 15.5, and the following are the details of the key components of these systems.

- Data Collection: Data collection is the first step of personalized navigation systems. GPS sensors, traffic details, spatial data information, road conditions, and weather conditions are a few of the information sources that are used in personalized navigation systems to gather data. These devices used sensors and devices to capture real-time information on traffic patterns, road hazards, and driver's behaviour to make the decision. This collected data acts as part of physical space and is used in data analysis and processing component.

- Data Analysis: In a personalized navigation system, the data analysis component is the transition process between physical space and virtual space. This process uses an internet connection to process the data. In most scenarios, a cloud environment acts as a data analysis system. Machine learning algorithms are used to analyse the collected data in order to find patterns and trends in driving. These trends are further used for the actual processing. Weather conditions and other factors that may affect driving conditions and these factors are also considered in the processing unit and the analysis unit.

- Processing unit: It is the core of the navigation system and is also known as the personalization engine. This unit uses the analysed data to create a personalized driving experience for each user. This unit provides route and location information by using GPS data, road data, analysed data, driver's preferences, driving habits, preferred routes, driver's personal data, and traffic patterns. Localization and routing algorithms are used for the data processing. This component is part of virtual space.

- Output unit: This component is responsible for the output. The user can interact with the system using this component. This component is part of physical space. It typically includes a dashboard that displays real-time traffic information,

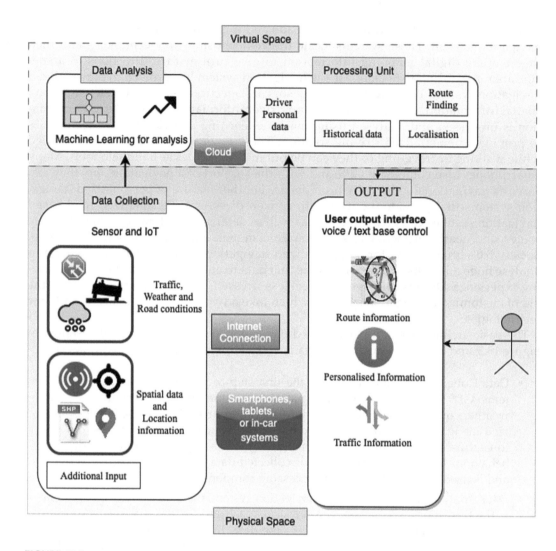

FIGURE 15.5
General architecture of personalized road navigation system in Society 5.0 environment.

recommended routes, and other personalized recommendations. The user interface may also include voice-activated controls, allowing drivers to operate the system hands-free.

Apart from the above-mentioned components, the personalized navigation systems rely
on cloud infrastructure to store and process the large amounts of data generated by the
system. The cloud infrastructure may also be used for data analysis, machine learning,
data processing, and actual algorithm execution. To enable personalized navigation, the
connectivity is backbone. For connectivity, personalized navigation systems rely on a network of connected devices, such as smartphones, tablets, and in-car systems, to provide
real-time traffic information and other personalized recommendations. The strong connectivity combines physical and virtual space in a single unit. Figure 15.6 shows the role of
connectivity in personal navigation.

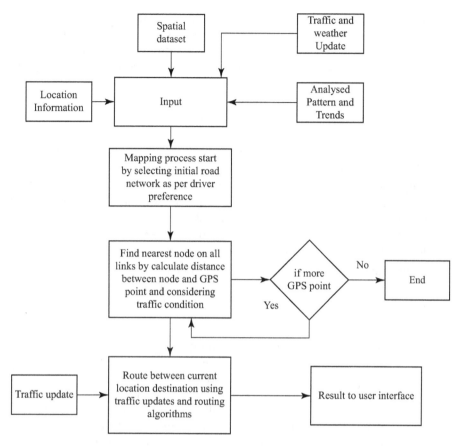

FIGURE 15.6
General working of localization and routing algorithm.

15.4 Personalized Navigation Algorithms

Navigation algorithm is a key component of a navigation system, but in personalized navigation system in Society 5.0, some additional algorithms are used to provide the customized user services. These algorithms include machine learning techniques to analyse data on driving behaviour, traffic patterns, and other factors to create a personalized driving experience and algorithms used to provide localization and routing services. Details of these algorithms are provided in the following.

15.4.1 Algorithms for Data Analysis

Personalized navigation systems gather data about a user's driving patterns, preferences, and behaviour in order to offer recommendations and directions that are specific to that user. For data analysis, pattern identification, and behaviour trend prediction, these systems use machine learning algorithms (Sethi Monika, Ahuja Sachin, and Bawa Puneet 2021). The following are the commonly used algorithms:

- Decision trees: Decision trees are a form of machine learning method that models decisions and potential outcomes using a tree-like structure. Decision trees can be used in personalized navigation systems to examine data on a user's previous routes, preferences, and behaviours in order to forecast their future behaviour and suggest customized routes and destinations.

- Random forests: Random forests are an ensemble learning technique that mixes various decision trees to increase prediction accuracy. Random forests can be used in personalized navigation systems to assess a range of data sources, including traffic statistics, weather data, and user's preferences, to generate recommendations for routes and destinations.

- Gradient boosting: This is another machine learning technique that combines a number of models to get a more accurate predictive model. Gradient boosting is a technique that can be used in personalized navigation systems to study user's driving patterns, preferences, and behaviour in order to generate recommendations for routes and destinations.

- Clustering: Clustering can be used to deliver personalized recommendations for routes and destinations that are suited to the driver. Clustering can be used in personalized navigation systems to group users with similar driving behaviours and preferences.

Apart from the above-mentioned algorithms, many other machine learning algorithms can be used to generate the user's preferences, trends, and patterns. These algorithms use a vast amount of data to produce effective solutions.

Personalized navigation algorithm in Society 5.0 is designed to use data analysis and machine learning techniques to create a personalized driving experience for each user. By analysing data on driving behaviour, traffic patterns, and other factors, the algorithm can help drivers save time, reduce stress, and improve safety on the road.

Machine learning techniques for data analysis used in personalized navigation systems follow the following general steps:

- Data Collection: Data collection is the first step in machine learning algorithms. In personalized navigation collected include driving behaviour, traffic patterns, road information, location details, and other factors that may affect the user's driving experience. This data may come from a variety of sources, such as GPS sensors, traffic cameras, spatial data sources, and weather reports.

- Data Pre-processing: Pre-processing is performed to remove the noise and impurities from the collected data. This step includes the removal of null values, errors, duplicate values, out-of-range data, and other types of anomalies.

- Feature Selection: The next common step in machine learning algorithm is the extraction of relevant features from the pre-processed data.

- Machine Learning Model: The algorithm uses a machine learning model to analyse the selected features and to create a personalized driving experience for each user. The machine learning model may use techniques such as decision trees, neural networks, or support vector machines.

- Data classification and visualization: For the opted data, the machine learning algorithm provides classification, and based on the classification, data patterns and trends are generated to be used for the processing unit, recommendation system, and real-time updates.

15.4.2 Location and Route Processing algorithms

In personalized navigation system, the analysed data is further used for localization and route identification. Localization and routing are based on map-matching algorithms. These algorithms use the output of a machine learning model, location information, spatial data, and driver personal data to generate routes and create personalized recommendations for each user. Based on the analysed data and updated information, the personalized navigation system updates recommendations in real time. These updates are based on traffic conditions and other factors. This allows the system to provide the user with the most up-to-date information on traffic congestion, accidents, and other road hazards.

15.5 Challenges of Personalized Navigation in Society 5.0

While personalized navigation systems offer many benefits, there are also several challenges associated with implementing these systems in Society 5.0. Here are some of the key challenges:

- Network Connectivity: Network connectivity is the core of the personalized navigation system, but in many areas (mostly in under-development areas) network connection is not stable. Due to lack of network, the navigation system does not work effectively. In such situations, some alternate procedures are required for the location identification. Similarly, analysis and trend generation in virtual space also get affected by poor internet connection (Singh and Singh 2022; 2020c) (Fukuda 2020).

- Data Privacy: Personalized navigation systems rely on collecting and analysing large amounts of data about users. This data may include sensitive information such as location data, driver's personal data, and driving behaviour. Ensuring the privacy and security of this data is a major challenge for personalized navigation systems (Sharma and Kaushik 2019; Gupta, Wadhwa, and Rani 2021; Arora, Ramkumar, and Kaur 2022).

- Quality of Spatial Data: Spatial data acts as reference data for navigation systems. Errors in reference data lead to poor performance of localization and routing techniques (Singh and Singh 2020b; 2020a).

- Data Quality: The accuracy and reliability of the data collected by personalized navigation systems are crucial to their success. However, data quality can be affected by factors such as weather conditions, road construction, and sensor malfunction. Maintaining high-quality data is a challenge for personalized navigation systems (Jiang 2020; Fan et al. 2019).

- Processing Error: Algorithms used in personalized navigation systems may be subject to processing errors and bias, which can result in inaccurate or unfair recommendations for certain users (Fukuda 2020).

- User Consent: For customized recommendations, personalized navigation systems require users' information and location. Sometimes, users hesitate to share personal information and so driving behaviour was tracked. So every time ensuring user's acceptance of these systems can be a challenge (Fan et al. 2019).

- Infrastructure: Personalized navigation systems rely on a robust and reliable infrastructure, including connectivity, cloud storage, and computational resources. Ensuring that the necessary infrastructure is in place to support personalized navigation systems is a challenge (A. Almusaylim and Jhanjhi 2020).

15.6 Conclusion

With the notion of "Society 5.0," highly developed and interconnected technologies like artificial intelligence, the Internet of Things, and robotics are combined to address societal issues. Personalized navigation systems that use cutting-edge algorithms and data analytics to offer tailored recommendations to individuals are one of the fundamental elements of Society 5.0.

Personalized navigation systems have the potential to completely change how we live. They can direct us to the fastest path to our destination, assist us in avoiding traffic, and even give us personalized recommendations for things like restaurants, shops, and entertainment. These systems can learn about our preferences, interests, and behaviour patterns with the use of machine learning algorithms and big data analytics, and then offer highly customized recommendations. Until now, there are also security and privacy issues with regard to customized navigation systems. There is a concern that the huge amounts of personal data that these systems collect will indeed be misused or even stolen. Therefore, it is crucial that companies and governments implement strict regulations and security measures to protect users' privacy and data.

In conclusion, personalized navigation systems are a significant technological advancement that has the potential to enhance our lives and make them more convenient. However, we must be aware of the potential risks and work together to ensure that these systems are developed and implemented responsibly. When combined with the concepts of Society 5.0, personalized navigation systems can help us create a more efficient, sustainable, and integrated society.

References

Almusaylim, Zahrah A., and Nz Jhanjhi. 2020. "Comprehensive Review: Privacy Protection of User in Location-Aware Services of Mobile Cloud Computing." *Wireless Personal Communications* 111(1): 541–64. https://doi.org/10.1007/S11277-019-06872-3/METRICS.

Aquilani, Barbara, Michela Piccarozzi, Tindara Abbate, and Anna Codini. 2020. "The Role of Open Innovation and Value Co-Creation in the Challenging Transition from Industry 4.0 to Society 5.0: Toward a Theoretical Framework." *Sustainability* 12(21): 8943. https://doi.org/10.3390/SU12218943.

Arora, Jatin, Ketti Ramchandran Ramkumar, and Pavneet Kaur. 2022. "A Survey of Multi-Signature Schemes for XML Documents." *International Journal of Cloud Computing* 11(2): 171–86. https://doi.org/10.1504/IJCC.2022.122035.

Deguchi, Atsushi, Chiaki Hirai, Hideyuki Matsuoka, Taku Nakano, Kohei Oshima, Mitsuharu Tai, and Shigeyuki Tani. 2018. "What Is Society 5.0?." In *Society 5.0 a People-Centric Super-Smart Society* 1: 1–24. Springer.

Fan, Wenqi, Yao Ma, Qing Li, Yuan He, Eric Zhao, Jiliang Tang, and Dawei Yin. 2019. "Graph Neural Networks for Social Recommendation." *The Web Conference 2019 - Proceedings of the World Wide Web Conference*, WWW 2019, May, 417–26. https://doi.org/10.1145/3308558.3313488.

Fukuda, Kayano. 2020. "Science, Technology and Innovation Ecosystem Transformation toward Society 5.0." *International Journal of Production Economics* 220(February): 107460. https://doi.org/10.1016/J.IJPE.2019.07.033.

Gupta, Divya, Shivani Wadhwa, and Shalli Rani. 2021. "On the Role of Named Data Networking for IoT Content Distribution." In *International Conference on Communication and Electronics Systems, ICCES 2021*, 544–49. Institute of Electrical and Electronics Engineers Inc. https://doi.org/10.1109/ICCES51350.2021.9488946.

Huang, Sihan, Baicun Wang, Xingyu Li, Pai Zheng, Dimitris Mourtzis, and Lihui Wang. 2022. "Industry 5.0 and Society 5.0—Comparison, Complementation and Co-Evolution." *Journal of Manufacturing Systems* 64(July): 424–28. https://doi.org/10.1016/J.JMSY.2022.07.010.

Jiang, Dingfu. 2020. "The Construction of Smart City Information System Based on the Internet of Things and Cloud Computing." *Computer Communications* 150(January): 158–66. https://doi.org/10.1016/J.COMCOM.2019.10.035.

Lavalle, Ana, Miguel A. Teruel, Alejandro Maté, and Juan Trujillo. 2020. "Improving Sustainability of Smart Cities through Visualization Techniques for Big Data from IoT Devices." *Sustainability* 12(14): 5595. https://doi.org/10.3390/SU12145595.

Martynov, Vitaly V., Diana N. Shavaleeva, and Alena A. Zaytseva. 2019. "Information Technology as the Basis for Transformation into a Digital Society and Industry 5.0." In *IEEE International Conference Quality Management, Transport and Information Security, Information Technologies IT and QM and IS 2019*, 539–43. Sochi: IEEE. https://doi.org/10.1109/ITQMIS.2019.8928305.

Monika, Sethi, Ahuja Sachin, and Bawa Puneet. 2021. "Classification of Alzheimer's Disease Using Neuroimaging Data by Convolution Neural Network | IEEE Conference Publication | IEEE Xplore." In *6th International Conference on Signal Processing, Computing and Control (ISPCC)*, 7–9. Solan: IEEE. https://ieeexplore.ieee.org/abstract/document/9609431.

Pereira, Andreia G., Tânia M. Lima, and Fernando Charrua-Santos. 2020. "Society 5.0 as a Result of the Technological Evolution: Historical Approach." In *Advances in Intelligent Systems and Computing* 1018: 700–5. Springer Verlag. https://doi.org/10.1007/978-3-030-25629-6_109/COVER.

"RIETI - Blockchain and Society 5.0-The Creation of a New Marketplace Based on Distributed Consensus." n.d. Accessed March 10, 2023. https://www.rieti.go.jp/en/rieti_report/222.html.

Ritzer, George. 2008. *The McDonaldization of Society 5*. Vol. 1. Pine Forge Press. https://books.google.com/books/about/The_McDonaldization_of_Society_5.html?id=v86NK7SGoPkC.

Rojas, Carolina Narvaez, Gustavo Adolfo, Alomia Peñafiel, Diego Fernando, Loaiza Buitrago, Carlos Andrés, Tavera Romero, Pedro Verga Matos, Tania Pereira Christopoulos, and G A A P Co. 2021. "Society 5.0: A Japanese Concept for a Superintelligent Society." *Sustainability* 13(12): 6567. https://doi.org/10.3390/SU13126567.

Sharma, Surbhi, and Baijnath Kaushik. 2019. "A Survey on Internet of Vehicles: Applications, Security Issues & Solutions." *Vehicular Communications* 20(December): 100182. https://doi.org/10.1016/J.VEHCOM.2019.100182.

Singh, Saravjeet, and Jaiteg Singh. 2020a. "Analysis of GPS Trajectories Mapping on Shape Files Using Spatial Computing Approaches." In *International Conference on Big Data Analytics*, 91–100.

———. 2020b. "Intrinsic Parameters Based Quality Assessment of Indian OpenStreetMap Dataset Using Supervised Learning Technique." In *2020 Indo--Taiwan 2nd International Conference on Computing, Analytics and Networks (Indo-Taiwan ICAN)*, 52–7.

———. 2020c. "Location Driven Edge Assisted Device and Solutions for Intelligent Transportation." *Fog, Edge, and Pervasive Computing in Intelligent IoT Driven Applications*, December, 123–47. https://doi.org/10.1002/9781119670087.CH7.

———. 2022. "Map Matching Algorithm: Empirical Review Based on Indian OpenStreetMap Road Network Data." *International Arab Journal of Information Technology* 19(2): 143–49.

Skobelev, P. O., and S. Yu. Borovik. 2017. "On the Way from Industry 4.0 to Industry 5.0: From Digital Manufacturing to Digital Society – STUME Journals." *Industry 4.0* 2(6): 307–11. https://stume-journals.com/journals/i4/2017/6/307.

16

Role of Geospatial Technology in the Development of Society 5.0

Sangeetha Annam

16.1 Introduction

Industry 4.0 (I4.0) has lately gained popularity and is one of the most significant global issues in both business and academia right now. The term "I4.0" refers to the fusion of physical and automated technologies, including artificial intelligence (AI), cloud computing, Big Data, adaptive robotics, augmented reality (AR) and virtual reality (VR), and the Internet of Things (IoT).

I4.0 is viewed as an all-encompassing tool for transforming the information society and addressing the actual demands of people, viz. the exchange of learning and information. I4.0 can spread the professional initiatives examined in the social sphere's producing environment. Applying the findings from agile manufacturing lays the groundwork for an advanced social composition exemplary, extending the benefits of the digital (cyber) realm to non-productive parts. To accomplish this instance, here we have the booming technology named Society 5.0. In this information era, people use the Internet to search, retrieve, and analyse data or information by using a cloud service in cyberspace.

In Society 5.0, a large collection of data is obtained from the sensors in physical mode and they are stored online. AI analyses Big Data and returns the findings in physical space to the people. In this way, Society 5.0 conveys to humanity, the next phase of civilisation's growth.

16.1.1 Factors Responsible for the Transition to Society 5.0

The socio-debate, technology usage, and engagement of the people at all societal levels are crucial steps in the development of Society 5.0. A live society is one that is both socially and environmentally conscious. Products and services with stakeholder and governance support that adhere to sustainability standards have more importance and are acknowledged by society. Additionally, it offers a favourable setting for cross-disciplinary communication. Greater participation in the procedures required for sustainable innovation is made possible by this form of communication. The execution of sustainable development initiatives is dependent on technological potential and the exchange of data and proficiency with stakeholders. As a result, creating an incentive programme is vital to inspire all parties. In this setting, technology is crucial to the business. Figure 16.1 portrays the pictorial representation of the transition of Society from 1.0 to 5.0.

Social discourse, technological exploitation, and engagement at all levels of society are crucial steps towards achieving Society 5.0. The effects of technology can also be seen in

DOI: 10.1201/9781003397052-16

FIGURE 16.1
Transition from Society 1.0 to 5.0.

how well citizens are able to live their lives. The analysis in the areas of intelligent manufacturing (IM), intelligent transportation (IT), and intelligent healthcare (IH) all focus on various aspects of the digital world. One of Society 5.0's goals is healthcare, which is heavily reliant on the other goals. The methods that people can use technology to communicate with one another and with one another represent the potential role that people may play in society in the future.

16.1.2 Framework for Relationships between the Components That Determine the Boom of Society 5.0

Primarily, it is possible to bridge the difference between I4.0 and Society 5.0, but this is done through collaborative efforts between government and technology, using smart solutions. The foundation of this society is the demand for effective engagement in socio-concerns, with more opportunities, and the fusion of cutting-edge technology and society with an eye towards sustainable development. Industries and governance are concerned with how the social ecosystem integrates digital and physical space. The significance of technology in the industry is crucial. Robots and data analysis leverage I4.0 technologies to establish an environment and provide the chance to increase stakeholders' abilities.

Information required for real-time analysis and its processing has grown as a result of I4.0's development and inventive innovations. Stakeholder participation has allowed for the improvement of all activities undertaken to meet the goals of sustainable development thanks to the advancement of data processing technologies. These technologies, which enable real-time activity monitoring with the interaction of humans and computers, include data analytics, mobile Internet apps, and the sensor-based information industry. With communication and connection technologies, I4.0 combines smart data processing with manufacturing.

A growing environment for the improvement in knowledge management methods uses data processing technologies created by Industry 4.0's sustainable development. The institutions that make up the governance ecosystem are crucial in advancing technology. The results show that governance and technology both have a similar amount of driving force. Figure 16.2 explains the factors governing Society 5.0.

16.2 Geospatial Technologies

The term "geospatial technology" is used to describe a wide range of modern tools that help to locate and analyse the Earth's geography and human cultures that are booming and evolving very fast. Since the prehistoric era, these technologies have been growing in

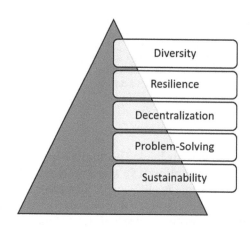

FIGURE 16.2
Factors responsible for Society 5.0.

some way. This technology is nothing but the acquiring, storing, and organising of geographical information. This is possible with the help of satellite technology that maps and analyses Earth's geography. The field of geospatial technology is expanding and evolving quickly. These cutting-edge technologies help users gather, analyse, and interpret spatial information. It discusses how natural and artificial objects interact and behave in space, whether they are located on this planet or beyond. Table 16.1 briefly summarises the various geospatial technologies.

In India, geospatial technology has gained attraction in several fields: agriculture, telecommunications, oil and gas, environmental management, public safety, infrastructure, logistics, and various industries. Figure 16.3 represents the various applications of geospatial techniques.

Some of the research works to support this are briefly explained in this section. In particular research work, the author discusses the patterns in Ghana country and forecasts the future trends of the virus to emphasise the application of geospatial technology during COVID-19. It was clear that Ghana has used geospatial technologies in a similar way to other areas and that it was still forging new ground with its solutions. The pattern in Ghana is consistent with a population concentration and tends to indicate higher populations in the southern parts [1]. In an article [2], the author speaks about how geospatial technology, including geographic information systems (GIS), is becoming more important in the field of public health, notably for techniques for modelling and surveillance of infectious diseases. The task of mapping diseases has historically been fraught with difficulties, and the authors rarely provided proof that was helpful in map creation. In addition to this, prior to the development of GIS, various errors were discovered in aligning tasks that are

TABLE 16.1

Applications of Geospatial Technologies

GIS/Spatial Analytics	Earth Observation	Global Navigation Satellite System	Scanning
Software	Satellite-based upstream	Navigation	LiDAR
Services and Solutions	Downstream of commercial data	Indoor positioning	Laser scanning
Contents	Aerial mapping	Surveying	Radar

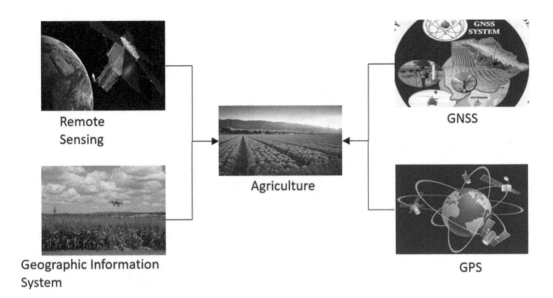

Remote Sensing

Agriculture

GNSS

Geographic Information System

GPS

FIGURE 16.3
Applications of geospatial techniques.

greatly expanded at global levels; and finally, there was no map assessment, leading to inaccurateness.

Many technologies have aided in the current landscape ecology growth, but these technological advancements in particular have revolutionised the field. The requirement for such research in this area is suggested by the widespread applications of these technologies, such as geographic information systems (GIS), remote sensing (RS), global positioning system (GPS), and many more. The authors studied with a brief overview of fractal theory, GIS, and RS and their usage in landscape ecology. The state of the art at the time was then compiled and evaluated as a guide for advancing the study of landscape ecology research and its applications [3]. The innovation of this technology software, maps, and datasets on environmental phenomena are nothing but geographic information systems [4]. The creation of tree spectral signatures and spatial mapping are among the agroforestry applications of optical remote sensing, according to the review. Based on the above literature, it is clear that geospatial technology has a wide range of applications.

During the past 10 years, these technologies have developed dramatically into a network of business, research, and security satellites that are backed by powerful GIS. Additionally, non-military applications for aerial RS platforms, such as unmanned aerial vehicles (UAVs) like the Global Hawk surveillance drone, are emerging. High-quality equipment and information are now accessible to newer groups of people, including academic institutions, businesses, and non-governmental organisations. Informing judgers on subjects including control of forest fire, monitoring of agricultural activities, humanitarian comfort, and many other topics, these fields and industries are currently expanding at a rapid rate.

16.2.1 How Geospatial Technology Is Vital to Earth's Observation

Earth observation is currently a pressing global concern. It is used to map out the future, keep an eye on the environment, manage our limited resources, and anticipate, document, and react to major world changes and crises. To achieve these goals, Earth observation is a significant component of all global space missions. Geospatial technology is essential and vital to the data collection, processing, interpretation, and information extraction processes for such scientific investigations. This quick development has put geospatial technology in a transitional stage. On the one hand, sensing technology offers a wealth of data with ever-higher radiometric, spatial, spectral, and temporal resolutions. The workflow of the geospatial technology in Earth's observation is depicted in Figure 16.4.

16.2.2 Geospatial Applications

The use of geospatial data affects enterprises, industries, and the general public significantly. Geospatial technology has various applications in many fields such as risk and resources management, environmental change, agriculture, telecommunication, community development, and estimation due to floods. Geospatial data focuses on the details of an event or an object, or other features that are close to the surface of the Earth. Location, attribute, and temporal information are generally referred to in geospatial data. This type of data is categorised into two forms: (i) vector data, and (ii) raster data where the former represents the features aligned with points, lines, and polygons and the latter represents the features in the form of grid cells. Some of the typical geospatial applications are mentioned in Figure 16.5.

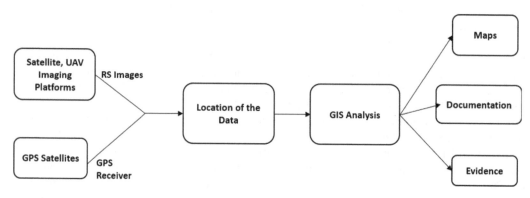

FIGURE 16.4
Workflow of the geospatial data.

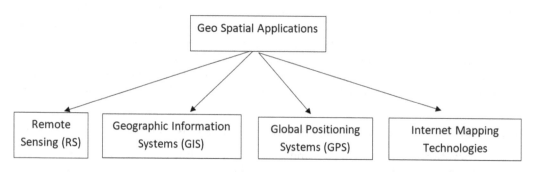

FIGURE 16.5
Geospatial applications.

16.2.2.1 Remote Sensing (RS)

Images and information over the Earth's surface are gathered using RS. This means that the information is acquired from a distance. This technology developed in 1972 with the information gathered from LANDSAT1 satellite. Remote sensors are available in active or passive form. The most preferred form is passive as it uses reflected sunlight. RS is used in various applications such as coastal and ocean applications, hazard and resource management, and many more. Some of the literature that proves RS in different fields are discussed here.

In a paper, the authors offer a thorough analysis of the creation and use of SSCM for crops using RS. This review article offers comprehensive information on the technology that is available for the SSCM fruit and nut crop. They can be duplicated exactly as stated or altered to suit regional needs and requirements. The authors also offer a thorough analysis of different factors that influence the production of blueberry and explain, with the help of references, how to create geographic models based on those factors to make management plans. To manage the crop, similar models can be created utilising relevant crop characteristics [5]. Different remote sensors for crop practices were studied by one of the researchers [6]. Remote sensing techniques are very effective, cheaper, and valuable tools to assess different parameters for agricultural soil, water quality parameters [7], and many more.

16.2.2.2 Geographic Information Systems (GIS)

GIS's prime task is to physically transform the information visually. Many software tools are used to map and analyse georeferenced data. The component of the GIS includes hardware, software, data, people, procedure, and network. They are used to identify geographic trends in different types of data, such as disease clusters and inadequate water supply. The benefits of using GIS are reduction in operational costs, improved communication, improved way of acquiring geographical data, ease of decision-making, and many more. With these advantages, this has major applications in the areas of mobile maps, maintaining work order history, maintaining customer information systems, etc. The workflow of the GIS is shown in Figure 16.6.

Some of the literature studies which focused on GIS are discussed in this section. In a paper, the author discussed the representation and spatial analysis of GIS in the development of frontiers that include gaps [8]. Many reviews were studied by authors on statistical spatial analysis using GIS [9]. Analysis of policy disputes in a geographical context is made possible by integrating GIS and multi-criteria analysis [10].

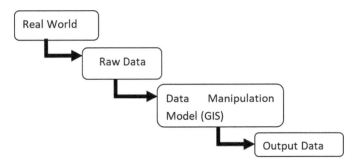

FIGURE 16.6
Workflow of the GIS using real-world data.

16.2.2.3 Global Positioning System (GPS)

GPS is used to locate objects on the Earth, through a network of satellites with the receiving equipment. Some receivers are more accurate, as they establish a connection less than 1 cm. These systems not only locate the objects but also locate humans. The main functions of GPS include location, navigation, tracking, mapping, and timings. An antenna, a receiver-processor unit, and a control/display are the major components of GPS. The major applications include public safety, aviation, military, local planning, recreation, business, surveying, and environmental resource agents. This service is provided and operated by the Defense Department in the United States that provides coordinate locations to users on the ground and in the air who have the receiving equipment. There are various procedures to process the data acquired through GPS studied in the paper [11].

16.2.2.4 Internet Mapping Technologies (IMTs)

IMTs are used to visualise the geospatial data in the map form. The technology used for this are satellites having high resolution with multispectral and hyperspectral data; the satellites majorly differentiate digital images, etc. Static and interactive are the two major kinds of web mapping. General reference, thematic, navigation charts, plans, and topographical are some of the different types of maps used in IMT. Some literature based on IMT are discussed here. Given that the Internet is currently the main medium for the transmission and distribution of maps, Internet maps represent the principal method of spatial information delivery. The author studied the various trends in vector-based Internet mapping technologies [12] with emerging technologies [13–15] also studied by researchers in this field.

16.3 Conclusion

This review has covered the basic introduction about Industry 4.0 on Society 5.0. In the first section, we studied the factors influencing the transition to Society 5.0, and the relation between the components was studied. In the second section, geospatial technologies were discussed in detail along with the applications in remote sensing, global information systems, global positioning systems, and Internet mapping technologies. This review also discussed the transformation of current uses of geospatial technology, along with their restrictions and limits with some state-of-the-art literature.

References

1. A. K. Sarfo and S. Karuppannan, "Application of geospatial technologies in the COVID-19 fight of Ghana," *Trans. Indian Natl. Acad. Eng.*, vol. 5, no. 2, pp. 193–204, 2020.
2. S. Saran, P. Singh, V. Kumar, and P. Chauhan, "Review of geospatial technology for infectious disease surveillance: Use case on COVID-19," *J. Indian Soc. Remote Sens.*, vol. 48, pp. 1121–1138, 2020.

3. H. Yu, X. Liu, B. Kong, R. Li, and G. Wang, "Landscape ecology development supported by geospatial technologies: A review," *Ecol. Inform.*, vol. 51, pp. 185–192, 2019.
4. P. Sharma *et al.*, "Geospatial technology in agroforestry: Status, prospects, and constraints," *Environ. Sci. Pollut. Res. Int.*, pp. 1–29, 2022.
5. S. S. Panda, G. Hoogenboom, and J. O. Paz, "Remote sensing and geospatial technological applications for site-specific management of fruit and nut crops: A review," *Remote Sens.*, vol. 2, no. 8, pp. 1973–1997, 2010.
6. A. Bégué *et al.*, "Remote sensing and cropping practices: A review," *Remote Sens.*, vol. 10, no. 1, p. 99, 2018.
7. N. Usali and M. H. Ismail, "Use of remote sensing and GIS in monitoring water quality," *J. Sustain. Dev.*, vol. 3, no. 3, p. 228, 2010.
8. H. J. Miller and E. A. Wentz, "Representation and spatial analysis in geographic information systems," *Ann. Assoc. Am. Geogr.*, vol. 93, no. 3, pp. 574–594, 2003.
9. T. C. Bailey, S. Fotheringham, and P. Rogerson, "A review of statistical spatial analysis in geographical information systems," *Spat. Anal. GIS*, vol. 26, pp. 13–44, 1994.
10. R. Janssen and P. Rietveld, "Multicriteria analysis and geographical information systems: an application to agricultural land use in the Netherlands," *Geogr. Inf. Syst. Urban Reg. Plan*, vol. 17, pp. 129–139, 1990.
11. L. Shen and P. R. Stopher, "Review of GPS travel survey and GPS data-processing methods," *Transp. Rev.*, vol. 34, no. 3, pp. 316–334, 2014.
12. C. Lienert, B. Jenny, O. Schnabel, and L. Hurni, "Current trends in vector-based Internet mapping: A technical review," *Online Maps with APIs WebServices*, pp. 23–36, 2012.
13. M. Haklay, A. Singleton, and C. Parker, "Web mapping 2.0: The neogeography of the GeoWeb," *Geogr. Compass*, vol. 2, no. 6, pp. 2011–2039, 2008.
14. M. Angurala and V. Khullar, "Federated learning based privacy preserved English accent training ecosystem for people with Indian language accent," in *Entertainment Computing.* Elsevier, p. 100572, 2023.
15. V. Khullar and H. P. Singh, "Privacy protected internet of unmanned aerial vehicles for disastrous site identification," in *Concurrency and Computation: Practice and Experience.* John Wiley & Sons, Inc., p. e7040, 2022.

17

Application of Machine Learning for IoT Security: A Step Toward Society 5.0

Swapnil Morande, Veena Tewari, Mohit Kukreti, Aarti Dangwal, Tahseen Arshi, and Amitabh Mishra

17.1 Introduction

We are in the early stages of the evolution of the Internet of Things along with integrated applications that can provide a glimpse into future networked intelligence (Ibarra-Esquer et al., 2017). While the use of such technologies encompasses fields such as government, education, finance, and transportation; on the consumer side, there are nearly endless combinations of services and applications that are making a direct impact on their lives. As of today, technology has been domesticated, where it combines the ability to feed on sensor-based data, and the Internet allows it an ideal ground to experiment with our digital lives. According to Farrokhi et al. (2021) with the help of computing devices and the right applications, users can make use of several utilities and derive great value.

The Internet of Things (IoT) refers to the growing network of physical devices, vehicles, home appliances, and other objects that are connected to the Internet and can collect and exchange data (Kiran, 2019). IoT is rapidly changing the way we live and work, and its growth can be attributed to several key factors. The applications of the Internet of Things (IoT) are diverse and growing rapidly, as more and more devices become connected to the internet. The Internet of Things (IoT) has found applications in various sectors, including healthcare, manufacturing, agriculture, transportation, and smart homes (Kumar et al., 2019). In consonance with Rojas et al. (2021), the rise of IoT envisions the fifth stage of human society known as "Society 5.0," which aims to create a super-smart community, where all aspects of life are highly interconnected and powered by advanced technology, while also promoting sustainability and human well-being. Society 5.0 initiatives include the development of smart cities, where IoT devices, sensors, and data are used to optimize traffic flow, reduce energy consumption, and improve public safety, which places human well-being at the center of its development (Deguchi et al., 2018; Mishra et al., 2022).

The security of these devices is crucial for protecting personal information, preventing cyberattacks, ensuring safety, protecting intellectual property, and maintaining the trust of users (Borky & Bradley, 2018). Personal information such as financial data and location data are vulnerable to theft or misuse without proper security measures in place. Cybercriminals often target IoT devices, either to gain unauthorized access to sensitive information or to launch attacks on other systems. Ensuring the security of critical applications such as healthcare, transportation, and industrial control systems is essential to maintaining public safety. IoT devices are often used to collect and transmit sensitive

DOI: 10.1201/9781003397052-17

business information, so protecting the security of these devices is crucial to protecting a company's intellectual property (Tawalbeh et al., 2020). Finally, the trust of users is essential to promote further adoption of IoT technology.

Machine learning can be used for IoT security by enabling automated threat detection and response. Machine learning algorithms can analyze large volumes of data from IoT devices and networks, detecting patterns and anomalies that may indicate potential security breaches (Hasan et al., 2019). Machine learning is a powerful tool for enhancing the security of IoT devices and networks, enabling organizations to stay ahead of emerging threats and protect their systems and data from cyber-attacks. This research identifies technological challenges that are involved in the process of IoT data transfer and related security issues. The proposed research looks forward to ubiquitous computing with amazing possibilities emerging via the Internet of Things. In consideration of the same research explores the application of machine learning for maintaining IoT security.

17.2 Review of Literature

As stated by Kumar et al. (2019), the Internet of Things can be considered a driving and thriving technological marvel that is capable of reshaping our lives. IoT has the potential to unlock new avenues with its variety of applications in research and industrial domains (Perwej et al., 2019).

Pursuant to Osei and Kwao-Boateng (2023), the Internet of Things (IoT) combines a growing network of physical objects, such as devices, vehicles, and buildings, that are embedded with sensors, software, and connectivity, allowing them to collect and exchange data over the internet. This data can then be analyzed to provide insights and automate various tasks, making our lives more convenient and efficient. The evolution of IoT can be traced back to the early 2000s, when the first Internet-connected devices, such as RFID tags, began to emerge. Since then, technology has evolved rapidly, with advances in wireless connectivity, sensors, and cloud computing enabling the proliferation of connected devices (Ibarra-Esquer et al., 2017). IoT has the potential to revolutionize various sectors, from healthcare to manufacturing, by providing real-time monitoring and control, improving decision-making, and enhancing overall efficiency. As technology continues to evolve and become more widespread, we can expect to see even more innovative use cases and benefits emerge (Brous et al., 2020).

The Internet of Things (IoT) has numerous applications across various industries and domains. One of the key application areas of IoT is in the field of smart homes and buildings, where it is used for home automation, energy management, and security systems (Alaa et al., 2017). IoT is also extensively used in the healthcare industry for remote patient monitoring, health tracking, and drug management (Javaid & Khan, 2021). In the industrial sector, IoT is used for predictive maintenance, supply chain optimization, and process automation (Rejeb et al., 2020). In the transportation industry, IoT is used for vehicle tracking, fleet management, and traffic management (Argha Ghosh, 2018). Other application areas of IoT include agriculture, retail, logistics, and smart cities. IoT has the potential to improve the quality of life for individuals and businesses by providing personalized experiences, optimizing processes, and reducing costs (Sestino et al., 2020). Additionally, advances in wireless connectivity, sensors, and cloud computing have made it easier and more affordable to develop and deploy IoT devices and systems, making the technology more accessible to a wider range of users. As confirmed by Syafrudin et al. (2018) data transferred using IoT enables real-time monitoring and control and provides insights that can be used to improve efficiency and optimize processes.

As noted by Hassan et al. (2020) although IoT applications sound quite futuristic and enable greater possibilities, they may not always be effective as a system. There are limitations in terms of communication standards, computing operations, and data security (Hussein, 2019). One of the major threats is the potential for data breaches or hacking. IoT devices are often connected to the Internet and may not have adequate security measures in place, making them vulnerable to cyber-attacks. Additionally, the use of multiple devices and networks can increase the risk of data interception and unauthorized access. Malware and viruses can also be introduced into IoT devices, causing them to malfunction or transmit incorrect data (Nižetić et al., 2020). The lack of standardization in IoT devices and networks can make it challenging to implement security measures consistently, leading to potential vulnerabilities. Also, the vast amounts of data generated by IoT devices can be difficult to manage and secure, making it more challenging to protect against security threats. Hence, the IoT mechanism should encompass people, processes, and technologies as its application shall help improve the overall digital ecosystem (Morande & Tewari, 2017).

On these lines, machine learning can be used to enhance the security of data transfer in IoT by detecting anomalies and potential threats in the data (Abed & Anupam, 2022). One way to use machine learning for this purpose is to train models on historical data to learn normal patterns of data transfer and identify any deviations from these patterns in real time. Another way to use machine learning for security in IoT is to apply predictive modeling techniques to identify potential security risks before they occur. In addition, machine learning can be used to identify vulnerabilities in IoT devices and systems and develop effective countermeasures (Tahsien et al., 2020). By analyzing data from various sources, machine learning algorithms can identify potential weaknesses in the system and recommend strategies to improve security.

Machine learning is a type of artificial intelligence (AI) that enables computer systems to automatically learn and improve from experience, without being explicitly programmed (Arshi et al., 2022). Machine learning algorithms are designed to analyze large amounts of data, identify patterns, and use these patterns to make predictions or decisions. Machine learning has become increasingly popular in recent years, as the availability of big data and advances in computing power have enabled more sophisticated machine learning models to be developed and deployed (Krishna et al., 2019; Najafabadi et al., 2015; Panch et al., 2018).

Machine learning can play a crucial role in addressing security threats associated with IoT data transfer; hence, this paper explores how this can be achieved using ML models. It would enable digital devices with IoT to act as context-aware entities and leverage state-of-the-art technologies to provide a glimpse of consumer electronics in the future.

17.3 Research Methodology

As the given study was a culmination of insights driven by the data, its nature was Quantitative.

The collection of data was carried out with wearable health-monitoring devices (also termed Healthcare IoT). Using the collected data, machine learning algorithms offered the ability to simulate real-world problems (Morande et al., 2022) related to data security explicitly using statistical techniques.

17.3.1 Data Modeling

With IoT devices, it is possible to generate an incredible amount of digital information and such a wealth of data presents an exciting opportunity to utilize it in real-world scenarios (Morande, 2022). For the represented research the data generated by IoT devices were made to lose their integrity to portray information security issues. To check outliers in the data received from such IoT device machine learning was used as a part of the research design.

Machine learning is categorized as a supervised (i.e., consists of output variables that are predicted from input variables) or unsupervised (i.e., deals with clustering of different groups for an intervention) learning process that simulates complex real-life scenarios (Battineni et al., 2020). In consonance with Arbet et al. (2020) to accomplish the research outcome, a machine learning model was trained to identify several conditions that represented the manipulation of data. For the given study, a machine learning model was created in an "Anomaly detection," as shown in Figure 17.1.

Anomaly detection refers to the process of identifying data points that deviate significantly from the norm or expected behavior in a dataset (Foorthuis, 2021). It is a common technique used in various domains and Anomaly detection in machine learning involves identifying unusual data points or patterns that do not conform to the expected behavior of a system (Calikus, 2022).

It is a type of unsupervised learning problem that involves detecting rare events, outliers, or anomalies in a dataset. In the given study the data from IoT devices were utilized to predict specific outcomes. During model building, an unsupervised machine learning algorithm requires a dataset that is split into a "training" data set and a "validation" data set (Harrison & Sidey-Gibbons, 2021). Training and validation data are two subsets of data used in machine learning to develop and evaluate predictive models. The training data is used to train the model by optimizing its parameters or weights using supervised or unsupervised learning techniques. The validation data is then used to evaluate the performance of the trained model on new, unseen data. The goal of using validation data is to assess the generalization ability of the model and prevent overfitting (Nijjer et al., 2023), which occurs when a model becomes too complex and fits the training data too closely. Splitting the data into training and validation sets is a common practice in machine learning to ensure that

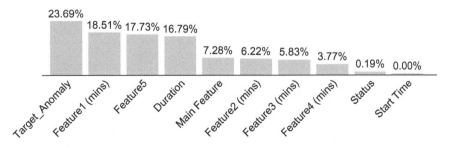

FIGURE 17.1
Field importance in the ML model.

the model is both accurate and robust to new data (Maleki et al., 2020). The ratio of training to validation data was maintained as 80% to 20% in the given study.

Based on the dataset of a sample size of 95 transmitted by IoT devices, 10 anomalies were detected using the specified Anomaly score. The forest size was maintained at 128, which refers to the number of decision trees in a random forest model used to detect anomalies in a dataset. Tokovarov and Karczmarek (2022) believe that the optimal forest size depends on the complexity of the dataset and the performance requirements of the anomaly detection system.

17.3.2 Data Analysis

As per Diro et al. (2021), anomaly detection in machine learning can help make IoT data trustworthy by identifying unusual patterns or outliers in the data that may indicate potential errors or security breaches. By analyzing the streaming data from IoT sensors or devices, machine learning algorithms can learn to recognize the normal behavior patterns of the system and detect deviations from them. This can help prevent false alarms or missed events and improve the overall reliability and security of the IoT system (Chatterjee & Ahmed, 2022). As can be seen from Table 17.1, the anomalies in the transmitted data were captured by the machine learning algorithms and highlighted in real time. By detecting and responding to anomalies in real-time, anomaly detection in machine learning (marked in red highlights) can help ensure that the IoT data is accurate, reliable, and trustworthy (Asharf et al., 2020).

17.3.3 Validity and Reliability

According to Noble and Smith (2015), such quantitative research calls for scientific rigor as well as transparency in the analytical procedures and avoidance of researcher bias. Validity and reliability are two important metrics used to evaluate the performance of machine learning models (O'Driscoll et al., 2021). Validity refers to the degree to which a model accurately represents the underlying real-world phenomenon that it is intended to predict. A valid model is one that makes accurate predictions on new, unseen data and is not affected by biases or errors in the training data (Montesinos López et al., 2022). Reliability, on the other hand, refers to the degree to which a model produces consistent results over time or across different datasets. A reliable model is stable and consistent in its predictions and is not overly sensitive to small changes in the input data (Nicora et al., 2022). Validity establishes the soundness of the methodology, sampling process, and data analysis process while reliability focuses on the process and the results that have replicable outcomes (Golafshani, 2015; Mohamad et al., 2015).

17.3.4 Findings

Aligned with the findings of Saarikko et al. (2017) with the evolution of the Internet, technology has been introduced to the "Internet of Things" where it is no more simply a web-based interface and possesses the computational ability and smart connections as one of the inherent functionalities (Gusmeroli et al. (2009). It works with smart devices equipped with sensors, RFID, NFC, sensors, and compatible communication technologies (wired or wireless) to build a context-aware system. By leveraging autonomous computing power

TABLE 17.1

Representation of Anomaly Score for the Data Received from IoT Device

Duration	Status	Main Feature	Feature1 (mins)	Feature2 (mins)	Feature3 (mins)	Feature4 (mins)	Feature5	Target_ Anomaly	Anomaly Score
27	Yes	75	5	5	10	7	0	Undefined	0.64417
298	No	70	18	50	120	110	0	Undefined	0.33468
74	No	30	24	0	50	0	0	Undefined	0.49985
412	No	74	62	90	140	120	0	Undefined	0.34403
435	No	68	45	70	200	120	0	Undefined	0.3203
284	No	60	44	40	120	80	0	Undefined	0.37144
291	No	72	41	50	110	90	0	Good	0.54753
129	No	48	39	1	40	50	0	Undefined	0.43959
445	No	74	35	80	190	140	0	Undefined	0.31551
369	No	72	49	70	120	130	0	Undefined	0.33866
228	No	68	48	50	60	70	0	Undefined	0.39144
212	No	56	62	20	60	70	0	Undefined	0.40105
244	No	56	64	30	5	80	0	Undefined	0.45573
447	No	72	67	110	150	120	0	Undefined	0.359
346	No	76	0	127	119	100	0	Undefined	0.34403
566	No	80	10	180	229	146	0	Undefined	0.48089
376	No	76	0	90	159	127	0	Undefined	0.29802
516	No	80	0	140	235	140	0	Undefined	0.43959
467	No	70	1	1	1	119	0	Excellent	0.67441
384	No	72	0	60	214	110	0	Undefined	0.33163
416	No	78	10	130	136	140	0	Undefined	0.36018
489	No	82	10	110	219	150	0	Undefined	0.38685
274	No	76	0	50	138	86	0	Undefined	0.36089
356	No	74	0	80	166	110	0	Undefined	0.29222
425	No	80	20	126	139	140	0	Undefined	0.35247
383	No	76	10	60	133	180	0	Undefined	0.38357
336	No	70	0	40	146	149	0	Undefined	0.32989
356	No	74	0	70	176	110	0	Undefined	0.29241
322	No	72	0	80	142	100	0	Undefined	0.31926
286	No	56	0	20	137	129	0	Undefined	0.36685
376	No	66	10	50	178	138	0	Undefined	0.32009
506	No	81	20	90	237	159	0	Undefined	0.39376
326	No	67	10	70	127	120	0	Undefined	0.32009
284	No	52	0	45	129	110	0	Undefined	0.35572
370	No	60	10	50	174	135	0	Undefined	0.33033
354	No	76	0	100	124	130	0	Undefined	0.31161
366	No	78	0	80	159	127	0	Undefined	0.30156
425	No	91	0	120	179	125	0	Undefined	0.36445

and communication technologies IoT can fulfill the promise of Society 5.0 (Morande & Pietronudo, 2020).

As presented in the given study, IoT devices face a range of security issues, including lack of encryption, outdated software, lack of authentication, insecure communication, physical security, and data privacy. IoT devices also lack proper authentication mechanisms, making it easy for hackers to impersonate legitimate users and gain access to the device or network (El-Hajj et al., 2019). IoT devices often collect and transmit sensitive data, such as personal and financial information, without adequate safeguards to protect the privacy of this data. To mitigate these security issues, machine learning can be deployed (Ashish Ghosh et al., 2018).

Machine learning is a subset of artificial intelligence that enables computer systems to learn and improve from experience without being explicitly programmed. It has transformed the way organizations make decisions, improving efficiency, accuracy, and profitability. Machine learning also plays a crucial role in the development of autonomous systems to learn and adapt to new environments (Bathla et al., 2022). As demonstrated in the study, machine learning algorithms can be used to identify anomalous behavior that may indicate a potential security breach, such as unusual traffic patterns or data requests (Alshammari & Aldribi, 2021; Martín et al., 2021). Anomaly detection using machine learning involves identifying abnormal patterns or outliers in data that may indicate potential security breaches or system failures. The process typically involves training a machine learning model on a dataset of normal behavior and then using the model to detect deviations from this baseline (Liu & Lang, 2019). The model may use a range of techniques to identify anomalies in real time. As demonstrated by Foorthuis (2021), once an anomaly is detected, the system can trigger an alert or take automated actions to mitigate the threat.

Anomaly detection using machine learning can be applied to a range of IoT applications, from monitoring network traffic to detecting unusual behavior in individual devices (Achiluzzi et al., 2022; Pathak et al., 2021). The process can help to improve the security and reliability of IoT systems, enabling organizations to detect and respond to potential threats before they can cause significant harm.

The advantage of machine learning for IoT security is that it enhances the effectiveness and efficiency of security measures, helping organizations stay ahead of emerging threats and protect their systems and data from cyber-attacks (Hussain et al., 2020). Overall, machine learning can help secure data transfer using IoT by providing intelligent and adaptive security solutions that can identify and mitigate potential threats in real time. With the continued development of machine learning techniques and algorithms, we can expect to see even more innovative solutions emerge in the future.

17.4 Discussions

The utilization of the Internet of Things (IoT) in sensitive fields, such as national security and defense, presents both opportunities and challenges. IoT devices can be used to monitor and track activities in real time, providing valuable insights and situational awareness. However, the use of IoT in sensitive fields also raises concerns about data security and privacy. The vast amounts of data generated by IoT devices can be sensitive and confidential, making it essential to ensure that appropriate security measures are in place to protect against unauthorized access. Additionally, the interconnected nature of IoT devices can increase the risk of cyber-attacks and hacking, potentially compromising critical infrastructure and operations. Overall, the utilization of IoT in sensitive fields requires careful consideration of both the potential benefits and risks, as well as robust security measures to mitigate any potential threats.

The Internet of Things (IoT) devices rely on accurate data to perform their intended functions effectively. Accurate data is essential to ensure reliable performance, as it enables

IoT devices to make informed decisions and take appropriate actions. Inaccurate data can result in suboptimal performance, leading to inefficient energy usage, false alarms, and other undesirable outcomes. Therefore, ensuring the accuracy of data is crucial for the reliable performance of IoT devices and the overall success of the Digital ecosystem.

If IoT devices are hacked, it can have severe consequences both for the device owner and society as a whole. Hackers can take control of the devices and use them for malicious purposes, such as launching cyber-attacks or stealing sensitive data. In some cases, hackers may use compromised IoT devices to create botnets, which can be used to carry out Distributed Denial of Service (DDoS) attacks that can bring down entire networks. In addition to the security risks, hacked IoT devices can also compromise the privacy of individuals, as they may be used to monitor personal data or record audio and video without consent. Furthermore, IoT devices are often connected to critical infrastructure, such as power grids and transportation systems, and a successful hack could lead to widespread disruption and chaos. Therefore, securing IoT devices is critical to safeguarding personal privacy and the security and stability of society.

Machine learning techniques, specifically Anomaly detection, can be applied to detect anomalies in equipment behavior and prevent potential failures when using IoT devices. Effective anomaly detection in machine learning can help organizations detect and respond to unusual events, minimize losses, and improve system performance.

17.5 Implications and Future Research

The implications of applying machine learning for IoT security are both positive and negative. On the positive side, machine learning can enhance the effectiveness and efficiency of security measures, improving the accuracy of threat detection and response. This can help to reduce the risk of cyber-attacks and data breaches, safeguarding sensitive data and protecting the integrity of connected systems. Furthermore, machine learning can enable predictive maintenance, identifying potential vulnerabilities before they can be exploited, and optimizing security measures for pervasive computing (Hussain et al., 2020). On the negative side, there are also implications associated with the use of machine learning for IoT security (Ahmad et al., 2022). One concern is the potential for false positives or false negatives, where the system may incorrectly identify a threat or overlook a genuine risk. This can result in unnecessary alerts or, worse, missed threats that can cause significant damage. Also, the use of machine learning for IoT security may require significant investments in infrastructure and resources, which may be a barrier for some organizations (ALAmri et al., 2022)

Future research for using machine learning for IoT security shall focus on addressing the challenges and limitations of current approaches (Khullar et al., 2022). This includes developing more accurate and robust machine-learning models that can learn from diverse and dynamic data sources (Linardatos et al., 2021). Future research will also explore new techniques for securing IoT devices and networks, including the use of blockchain and other emerging technologies (Morande & Vacchio, 2022). Additionally, future research shall focus on developing more transparent and explainable machine learning algorithms to mitigate the risk of bias and improve accountability (Felzmann et al., 2020). Future research in machine learning for IoT security should aim to enhance the effectiveness, efficiency, and reliability of security measures, enabling organizations to protect their systems and data from emerging threats.

17.6 Inference

The evolution of ubiquitous information and communication networks is apparent with the increasing adoption of the Internet of Things (IoT). Keeping the core of Society 5.0 in mind, the suggested study investigates the use of machine learning for the security of IoT devices. The suggested study offers a glimpse of machine learning-driven possibilities for securing over-the-air data transfer carried out by IoT devices. The proposed study, which employs an anomaly detection mechanism, goes beyond traditional mobile computing scenarios and delves into embedding intelligence to solve current technology management problems. The study not only addresses the state-of-the-art Internet technology relevant to Society 5.0 but also contributes to the exploration of emerging technology reflecting the new era of connected services. It demonstrates the potential of enabling technologies such as machine learning and applies it to meaningful applications for the Internet of Things. It discusses recent developments in the technological landscape for an increased convergence between computing devices and the Internet.

References

Abed, A. K., & Anupam, A. (2022). Review of security issues in Internet of Things and artificial intelligence-driven solutions. *Security and Privacy*, e285. https://doi.org/10.1002/spy2.285

Achiluzzi, E., Li, M., Al Georgy, F., & Kashef, R. (2022). *Exploring the Use of Data-Driven Approaches for Anomaly Detection in the Internet of Things (IoT) Environment*.

Ahmad, W., Rasool, A., Javed, A. R., Baker, T., & Jalil, Z. (2022). Cyber security in IoT-based cloud computing: A comprehensive survey. In *Electronics* (Vol. 11, Issue 1). https://doi.org/10.3390/electronics11010016

Alaa, M., Zaidan, A. A., Zaidan, B. B., Talal, M., & Kiah, M. L. M. (2017). A review of smart home applications based on Internet of Things. *Journal of Network and Computer Applications, 97*, 48–65. https://doi.org/10.1016/j.jnca.2017.08.017

ALAmri, S., ALAbri, F., & Sharma, T. (2022). *Artificial Intelligence Deployment to Secure IoT in Industrial Environment* (L. D. Kounis (ed.); p. Ch. 13). IntechOpen. https://doi.org/10.5772/intechopen.104469

Alshammari, A., & Aldribi, A. (2021). Apply machine learning techniques to detect malicious network traffic in cloud computing. *Journal of Big Data, 8*(1), 1–24. https://doi.org/10.1186/s40537-021-00475-1

Arbet, J., Brokamp, C., Meinzen-Derr, J., Trinkley, K. E., & Spratt, H. M. (2020). Lessons and tips for designing a machine learning study using EHR data. *Journal of Clinical and Translational Science, 5*(1), e21. https://doi.org/10.1017/cts.2020.513

Arshi, T. A., Ambrin, A., Rao, V., Morande, S., & Gul, K. (2022). A machine learning assisted study exploring hormonal influences on entrepreneurial opportunity behaviour. *The Journal of Entrepreneurship, 31*(3), 575–602. https://doi.org/10.1177/09713557221136273

Asharf, J., Moustafa, N., Khurshid, H., Debie, E., Haider, W., & Wahab, A. (2020). A review of intrusion detection systems using machine and deep learning in Internet of things: Challenges, solutions and future directions. In *Electronics* (Vol. 9, Issue 7). https://doi.org/10.3390/electronics9071177

Bathla, G., Bhadane, K., Singh, R. K., Kumar, R., Aluvalu, R., Krishnamurthi, R., Kumar, A., Thakur, R. N., & Basheer, S. (2022). Autonomous vehicles and intelligent automation: Applications, challenges, and opportunities. *Mobile Information Systems, 2022*, 7632892. https://doi.org/10.1155/2022/7632892

Battineni, G., Sagaro, G. G., Chinatalapudi, N., & Amenta, F. (2020). Applications of machine learning predictive models in the chronic disease diagnosis. *Journal of Personalized Medicine, 10*(2). https://doi.org/10.3390/jpm10020021

Borky, J. M., & Bradley, T. H. (2018). Protecting information with cybersecurity. In *Effective Model-Based Systems Engineering* (pp. 345–404). https://doi.org/10.1007/978-3-319-95669-5_10

Brous, P., Janssen, M., & Herder, P. (2020). The dual effects of the Internet of Things (IoT): A systematic review of the benefits and risks of IoT adoption by organizations. *International Journal of Information Management, 51*, 101952. https://doi.org/10.1016/j.ijinfomgt.2019.05.008

Calikus, E. (2022). Together We Learn More: Algorithms and Applications for User-Centric Anomaly Detection. Doctoral Thesis, Halmstad University Dissertations No. 89

Chatterjee, A., & Ahmed, B. S. (2022). IoT anomaly detection methods and applications: A survey. *Internet of Things, 19*, 100568. https://doi.org/10.1016/j.iot.2022.100568

Deguchi, A., Hirai, C., Matsuoka, H., Nakano, T., Oshima, K., Tai, M., & Tani, S. (2018). *Society 5.0 A People-Centric Super-Smart Society*. Springer.

Diro, A., Chilamkurti, N., Nguyen, V.-D., & Heyne, W. (2021). A comprehensive study of anomaly detection schemes in IoT networks using machine learning algorithms. In *Sensors* (Vol. 21, Issue 24). https://doi.org/10.3390/s21248320

El-Hajj, M., Fadlallah, A., Chamoun, M., & Serhrouchni, A. (2019). A survey of Internet of Things (IoT) authentication schemes. *Sensors (Basel, Switzerland), 19*(5). https://doi.org/10.3390/s19051141

Farrokhi, A., Farahbakhsh, R., Rezazadeh, J., & Minerva, R. (2021). Application of Internet of Things and artificial intelligence for smart fitness: A survey. *Computer Networks, 189*. https://doi.org/10.1016/j.comnet.2021.107859

Felzmann, H., Fosch-Villaronga, E., Lutz, C., & Tamò-Larrieux, A. (2020). Towards transparency by design for artificial intelligence. *Science and Engineering Ethics, 26*(6), 3333–3361. https://doi.org/10.1007/s11948-020-00276-4

Foorthuis, R. (2021). On the nature and types of anomalies: A review of deviations in data. *International Journal of Data Science and Analytics, 12*(4), 297–331. https://doi.org/10.1007/s41060-021-00265-1

Ghosh, A. (2018). *Vehicle Tracking System Using Internet of Things*. https://doi.org/10.13140/RG.2.2.12437.96482

Ghosh, A., Chakraborty, D., & Law, A. (2018). Artificial intelligence in Internet of things. *CAAI Transactions on Intelligence Technology, 3*(4), 208–218. https://doi.org/10.1049/trit.2018.1008

Golafshani, N. (2015). Understanding reliability and validity in qualitative research. *The Qualitative Report, 8*(4), 597–606. https://doi.org/10.46743/2160-3715/2003.1870

Gusmeroli, S., Haller, S., Harrison, M., Kalaboukas, K., Tomasella, M., Vermesan, O., & Wouters, K. (2009). Vision and challenges for realizing the internet of things. In *Proceedings of the 3rd STI Roadmapping Workshop* (Vol. 1, Issue April).

Harrison, C. J., & Sidey-Gibbons, C. J. (2021). Machine learning in medicine: A practical introduction to natural language processing. *BMC Medical Research Methodology, 21*(1), 1–18. https://doi.org/10.1186/s12874-021-01347-1

Hasan, M., Islam, M. M., Zarif, M. I. I., & Hashem, M. M. A. (2019). Attack and anomaly detection in IoT sensors in IoT sites using machine learning approaches. *Internet of Things, 7*, 100059. https://doi.org/10.1016/j.iot.2019.100059

Hassan, R., Qamar, F., Hasan, M. K., Aman, A. H. M., & Ahmed, A. S. (2020). Internet of things and its applications: A comprehensive survey. *Symmetry, 12*(10), 1–29. https://doi.org/10.3390/sym12101674

Hussain, F., Hussain, R., Hassan, S., & Hossain, E. (2020). Machine learning in IoT security: Current solutions and future challenges. *IEEE Communications Surveys and Tutorials*. https://doi.org/10.1109/COMST.2020.2986444

Hussein, A. R. H. (2019). Internet of Things (IOT): Research challenges and future applications. *International Journal of Advanced Computer Science and Applications, 10*(6), 77–82. https://doi.org/10.14569/ijacsa.2019.0100611

Ibarra-Esquer, J. E., González-Navarro, F. F., Flores-Rios, B. L., Burtseva, L., & Astorga-Vargas, M. A. (2017). Tracking the evolution of the Internet of things concept across different application domains. *Sensors (Basel, Switzerland), 17*(6). https://doi.org/10.3390/s17061379

Javaid, M., & Khan, I. H. (2021). Internet of Things (IoT) enabled healthcare helps to take the challenges of COVID-19 Pandemic. *Journal of Oral Biology and Craniofacial Research, 11*(2), 209–214. https://doi.org/10.1016/j.jobcr.2021.01.015

Khullar, V., Tiwari, R. G., Agarwal, A. K., & Dutta, S. (2022). Physiological signals based anxiety detection using ensemble machine learning. In *Lecture Notes in Networks and Systems* (Vol. 291, pp. 597–608). https://doi.org/10.1007/978-981-16-4284-5_53/COVER

Kiran, D. R. (2019). *Chapter 35 - Internet of Things* (D. R. B. T.-P. P. and C. Kiran (ed.); pp. 495–513). Butterworth-Heinemann. https://doi.org/10.1016/B978-0-12-818364-9.00035-4

Krishna, C. V., Rohit, H. R., & Mohana. (2019). A review of artificial intelligence methods for data science and data analytics: Applications and research challenges. *Proceedings of the International Conference on I-SMAC (IoT in Social, Mobile, Analytics and Cloud), I-SMAC 2018, March 2021,* 591–594. https://doi.org/10.1109/I-SMAC.2018.8653670

Kumar, S., Tiwari, P., & Zymbler, M. (2019). Internet of Things is a revolutionary approach for future technology enhancement: A review. *Journal of Big Data, 6*(1). https://doi.org/10.1186/s40537-019-0268-2

Linardatos, P., Papastefanopoulos, V., & Kotsiantis, S. (2021). Explainable AI: A review of machine learning interpretability methods. In *Entropy* (Vol. 23, Issue 1). https://doi.org/10.3390/e23010018

Liu, H., & Lang, B. (2019). Machine learning and deep learning methods for intrusion detection systems: A survey. In *Applied Sciences* (Vol. 9, Issue 20). https://doi.org/10.3390/app9204396

Maleki, F., Muthukrishnan, N., Ovens, K., Reinhold, C., & Forghani, R. (2020). Machine learning algorithm validation: From essentials to advanced applications and implications for regulatory certification and deployment. *Neuroimaging Clinics of North America, 30*(4), 433–445. https://doi.org/10.1016/j.nic.2020.08.004

Martín, A. G., Beltrán, M., Fernández-Isabel, A., & Martín de Diego, I. (2021). An approach to detect user behaviour anomalies within identity federations. *Computers and Security, 108,* 102356. https://doi.org/10.1016/j.cose.2021.102356

Mishra, P., Thakur, P., & Singh, G. (2022). Sustainable smart city to Society 5.0: State-of-the-art and research challenges. *SAIEE Africa Research Journal, 113*(4), 152–164. https://doi.org/10.23919/SAIEE.2022.9945865

Mohamad, M. M., Sulaiman, N. L., Sern, L. C., & Salleh, K. M. (2015). Measuring the validity and reliability of research instruments. *Procedia - Social and Behavioral Sciences, 204,* 164–171. https://doi.org/10.1016/j.sbspro.2015.08.129

Montesinos López, O. A., Montesinos López, A., & Crossa, J. (2022). Multivariate statistical machine learning methods for genomic prediction. In *Multivariate Statistical Machine Learning Methods for Genomic Prediction.* https://doi.org/10.1007/978-3-030-89010-0

Morande, S. (2022). Enhancing psychosomatic health using artificial intelligence-based treatment protocol: A data science-driven approach. *International Journal of Information Management Data Insights, 2*(2). https://doi.org/10.1016/j.jjimei.2022.100124

Morande, S., & Pietronudo, M. C. (2020). Pervasive health systems: Convergence through artificial intelligence and blockchain technologies. *Journal of Commerce and Management Thought, 11*(2), 155. https://doi.org/10.5958/0976-478x.2020.00010.5

Morande, S., & Tewari, V. (2017). Impact of digital ecosystem on business environment. In R. Rajesh & B. Mathivanan (Eds.), *De Grutyer* (pp. 233–241). De Gruyter. https://doi.org/10.1515/9783110469608-023

Morande, S., Tewari, V., & Gul, K. (2022). *Reinforcing Positive Cognitive States with Machine Learning: An Experimental Modeling for Preventive Healthcare* (P. A. E. Onal (ed.); p. Ch. 24). IntechOpen. https://doi.org/10.5772/intechopen.108272

Morande, S., & Vacchio E., Del. (2022). Digital strategy with blockchain in healthcare ecosystem using service-dominant architecture. *International Journal of Management and Decision Making, 21*(2), 161–177. https://doi.org/10.1504/IJMDM.2022.121906

Najafabadi, M. M., Villanustre, F., Khoshgoftaar, T. M., Seliya, N., Wald, R., & Muharemagic, E. (2015). Deep learning applications and challenges in big data analytics. *Journal of Big Data, 2*(1), 1. https://doi.org/10.1186/s40537-014-0007-7

Narvaez Rojas, C., Alomia Peñafiel, G. A., Loaiza Buitrago, D. F., & Tavera Romero, C. A. (2021). Society 5.0: A Japanese concept for a superintelligent society. *Sustainability (Switzerland), 13*(12). https://doi.org/10.3390/su13126567

Nicora, G., Rios, M., Abu-Hanna, A., & Bellazzi, R. (2022). Evaluating pointwise reliability of machine learning prediction. *Journal of Biomedical Informatics, 127*, 103996. https://doi.org/10.1016/j.jbi.2022.103996

Nijjer, S., Bathla, D., Sharma, S., & Raj, S. (2023). Customer analytics: Deep dive into customer data. In J. Wang (Ed.), *Encyclopedia of Data Science and Machine Learning* (pp. 1092–1107). IGI Global. https://doi.org/10.4018/978-1-7998-9220-5.CH063

Nižetić, S., Šolić, P., López-de-Ipiña González-de-Artaza, D., & Patrono, L. (2020). Internet of Things (IoT): Opportunities, issues and challenges towards a smart and sustainable future. *Journal of Cleaner Production, 274*, 122877. https://doi.org/10.1016/j.jclepro.2020.122877

Noble, H., & Smith, J. (2015). Issues of validity and reliability in qualitative research. *Evidence-Based Nursing, 18*(2), 34–35. https://doi.org/10.1136/eb-2015-102054

O'Driscoll, R., Turicchi, J., Hopkins, M., Duarte, C., Horgan, G. W., Finlayson, G., & Stubbs, R. J. (2021). Comparison of the validity and generalizability of machine learning algorithms for the prediction of energy expenditure: Validation study. *JMIR mHealth and uHealth, 9*(8), e23938. https://doi.org/10.2196/23938

Osei, B. A., & Kwao-Boateng, E. (2023). *Critical Review on Internet of Things (IoT): Evolution and Components Perspectives* (M. Gordan, K. Ghaedi, & V. Saleh (eds.); p. Ch. 3). IntechOpen. https://doi.org/10.5772/intechopen.109283

Panch, T., Szolovits, P., & Atun, R. (2018). Artificial intelligence, machine learning and health systems. *Journal of Global Health, 8*(2), 20303. https://doi.org/10.7189/jogh.08.020303

Pathak, A. K., Saguna, S., Mitra, K., & Ahlund, C. (2021). Anomaly detection using machine learning to discover sensor tampering in IoT systems. *IEEE International Conference on Communications.* https://doi.org/10.1109/ICC42927.2021.9500825

Perwej, Y., Haq, K., Parwej, F., & M., M. (2019). The Internet of Things (IoT) and its application domains. *International Journal of Computer and Applications, 182*(49), 36–49. https://doi.org/10.5120/ijca2019918763

Rejeb, A., Simske, S., Rejeb, K., Treiblmaier, H., & Zailani, S. (2020). Internet of Things research in supply chain management and logistics: A bibliometric analysis. *Internet of Things, 12*, 100318. https://doi.org/10.1016/j.iot.2020.100318

Saarikko, T., Westergren, U. H., & Blomquist, T. (2017). The Internet of Things: Are you ready for what's coming? *Business Horizons, 60*(5), 667–676. https://doi.org/10.1016/j.bushor.2017.05.010

Sestino, A., Prete, M. I., Piper, L., & Guido, G. (2020). Internet of Things and Big Data as enablers for business digitalization strategies. In *Technovation* (Vol. 98, p. 102173). https://doi.org/10.1016/j.technovation.2020.102173

Syafrudin, M., Alfian, G., Fitriyani, N. L., & Rhee, J. (2018). Performance analysis of IoT-based sensor, big data processing, and machine learning model for real-time monitoring system in automotive manufacturing. In *Sensors* (Vol. 18, Issue 9). https://doi.org/10.3390/s18092946

Tahsien, S. M., Karimipour, H., & Spachos, P. (2020). Machine learning based solutions for security of Internet of Things (IoT): A survey. *Journal of Network and Computer Applications, 161*(April). https://doi.org/10.1016/j.jnca.2020.102630

Tawalbeh, L., Muheidat, F., Tawalbeh, M., & Quwaider, M. (2020). IoT privacy and security: Challenges and solutions. In *Applied Sciences* (Vol. 10, Issue 12). https://doi.org/10.3390/app10124102

Tokovarov, M., & Karczmarek, P. (2022). A probabilistic generalization of isolation forest. *Information Sciences, 584*, 433–449. https://doi.org/10.1016/j.ins.2021.10.075

18

Emerging Trends in Cybersecurity Challenges with Reference to Pen Testing Tools in Society 5.0

Gaganpreet Kaur, Bharathiraja N., Kiran Deep Singh, Veeramanickam M.R.M., Ciro Rodriguez Rodriguez, and Pradeepa K.

18.1 Introduction

These days, the internet plays a significant part in our lives. The rising use of the Internet is mostly due to recent developments and inexpensive costs [1]. All operations in the modern world, including those of people, nongovernmental organizations, governments, and governmental institutions, take place online [2]. Cyberspace has important and delicate systems and structures [3]. Governments face a variety of security issues in cyberspace, including low entry barriers, privacy concerns, and a lack of public transparency. These factors have encouraged both powerful and weak players, such as governments, terrorist organizations, and even individuals, to operate there. Cyber-terrorism, cyber-crime, cyber-warfare, and cyber-espionage are all common risks today [4]. Threats can be categorized as either a national threat or an organizational threat. National insecurity threats from conventional meaning have been a challenging task and rendered ineffective in this domain since dangers are obvious in form and have agents that can be identified as governments and nations in a certain geographic area [5].

For a long time, security experts have been considering the potential dangers of cyber threats [6]. Thus, it is necessary to develop a precise definition of cyberattacks that can be acknowledged by all [7]. A legal path will be provided with a precise and clear definition, which will ultimately aid in the application and the achievement of results [8]. Therefore, the primary goal should be to raise public knowledge of cyberattacks and to understand their features and the effects they have on the system when exploitable vulnerabilities emerge [9]. In its truest sense, cybersecurity is a science that deals with all cyberattacks and crimes. Hence, cyber science can be used to describe cybersecurity. Key ideas, problems, and technology related to cybersecurity are discussed in this chapter. The classification of cyberattacks is researched in cyber science together with security analysis, and then web server fingerprinting and penetration testing techniques in connection to reconnaissance are discussed in reference to Society 5.0. Finally, the conclusion is delivered.

18.2 Cyber-Physical Systems and Security Challenges in Society 5.0

The challenges in Society 5.0 element are viewed as a cyber-physical system (CPS) which is built on the integration of heterogeneous data and knowledge. In order to manage

DOI: 10.1201/9781003397052-18

interconnected among different working nodes between its physical systems and computing systems, CPS is defined as a collection of transformative working models. It develops a service-oriented, adaptive, and scalable manufacturing process. With real-time communication between machines, it enables an intelligent flow of manufactured components across a factory. These systems depend on new technologies.

18.3 Cybersecurity Fundamentals

Cybersecurity is evaluated in terms of access, data integration, security, storage, and data transit via electronic or other channels [10, 11]. There are a number of definitions received from various specialists in the field of cybersecurity.

- The term "cybersecurity" refers to the process of preventing unauthorized access to, use of, interruption of, modification of, or destruction of information held on computers, equipment, various devices, computers, and their resources [12].
- "Cybersecurity" strives to lower the danger of cyberattacks and protect against unauthorized access to technologies, systems, and networks.

18.3.1 Cybersecurity Principles

There are prevailing five principles in which the design of cybersecure systems can be considered.

- To create the environment formerly designing a secure system: Before creating a secure system design, one must have a good understanding of the fundamentals and then take action to address any identified limitations.
- To create a compromise for a system is challenging: Designing with security in observance entails adopting fundamental principles and, as a result, strategies that make it difficult for hackers to breach systems or data.
- To create interruptions hard: It is imperative that the technology be available when vital services depend on it for delivery, but the interruptions must be severe.
- To create compromise detection easier: Even with every defense against attacks in place, there is a potential that the system will still be vulnerable to another, unidentified attack. One should be in a situation where they can easily spot compromise.
- To lessen the influence of compromise: The system is designed to lessen the impact of any compromise.

18.3.2 Pillars in Cybersecurity Science

The CIA triad is one of the most significant security models and is known as a pillar of cybersecurity. It provides policies for securing information within an organization. It includes three parameters:

- Integrity: Meaning data should be integral to an organization or in the network and unauthorized modification of assets should not be allowed.
- Availability: Meaning data should be available at all times.
- Confidentiality: Meaning confidentiality of data should be preserved.

Figure 18.1 depicts the CIA triad model for securing a system.

18.3.3 Domains in Cybersecurity Science

Cybersecurity does not work individually but has different domains. Good cybersecurity always needs coordinated efforts across an organization's systems as its assets are made up of a sort of diverse platforms. As a result, cybersecurity has the following sub-domain areas:

- User Education and Security Engineering
- Security Operations and Threat Intelligence
- Risk Assessment, Framework, and Standards

Figure 18.2 represents different domains available in cybersecurity. Table 18.1 represents basic definitions prevalent in cybersecurity science.

18.3.4 Cybersecurity Science Threats and Cyberattacks

In the present age, each nation and its organizations are almost reliant on cyberspace for all kinds of communications and are inseparable [13]. Since software and hardware products are globally produced. Cyberspace has no doubt opened various avenues in the field

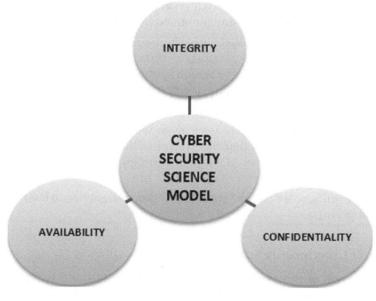

FIGURE 18.1
CIA triad for cybersecurity.

FIGURE 18.2
Various domain areas in cybersecurity.

of global business, but on the other hand, has led to cyber threats and attacks that pose a threat to valuable information [14].

Talking about cyberspace, it is relatively controlled by a small group of people that efficiently manage cyber-warfare [15]. Because of the increase in computing and communication knowledge, cyber science is expanding quickly. This rate of cyber cohesiveness has accelerated. Every new transition brings along a fresh vulnerability and response. Cyber-attacks can be defined as:

> "Cyber-attacks or cyber threats" are activities done by various countries to penetrate into the computers or networks of a country or various other countries so as to cause disruption. Cybersecurity, on the other hand, helps to protect our vulnerable information [16].

The main threats in cyberspace science include foreign or antagonistic nation threats and internal threats due to organizational spies [17]. Intelligence services apply cyber tools for reconnaissance activities. There have been numerous reports of information setups in countries being harmed, including the network systems and processors integrated into crucial sectors. Another source of attacks is teams of individuals that target computer systems in an effort to get financial gain [18].

TABLE 18.1

Basic Concepts of Cyber Science

Terminology	Description
Cyberspace	It is a complex environment that involves communications between people, software, and services.
Assets	An asset is any data or other component of the environment that supports information-related actions.
Attacks	It aims to disable, interrupt, destroy, or control computer systems or steal the data held within these systems.
Vulnerabilities	It is a weakness in a security system that can be exploited.
Cyber defense	It is a concern for large companies and government agencies.
Cyber weapon	Cyber weapon is a malware agent engaged for military or intelligence with the main objective as part of a cyberattack.
Cyber-crime	It is an unlawful activity that involves a computer, devices, and network.
Cyber threat level	Cyber threats affect national cyber assets at the national, institutional, and critical levels of organization.
Hackers	People who hack devices and systems with good intentions.
Crackers	They are the ones who hack a system by breaking into it and further disrupting it with bad intentions.
Crypto-jacking	It is a type of attack that uses scripts to mine cryptocurrencies inside browsers without the user's permission.
Cyberattack Vector	It is a way a rival can breach or penetrate an entire system. Attack vectors allow hackers to exploit system vulnerabilities, which may include the human element too.
Cyber law	It is the branch of law that deals with legal matters related to the usage of the internet through information technology.

Hackers are people who enter the network to misuse and harm the system. Nowadays, it is possible to penetrate systems in a network with basic knowledge and skill set. Sometimes, discontented insiders in an organization also pose a serious threat. Next are hacktivists, who are considered to be politically motivated people that attack common web pages. These groups levy amplified loads on email host systems, by penetrating the different websites and announcing their politically motivated messages [19]. Figure 18.3 depicts cyber threat sources.

It is important to know about major vulnerable areas which lead to cyber threats or cyberattacks on systems. It includes the following:

- Configuration Mistakes: It may occur if some configuration update has been updated from a website that may not be authentic.
- Second, due to bad cyber hygiene measures. Cyber hygiene includes the best practices for protecting the data and information from being compromised.
- Third, includes social engineering, which uses psychological influence to hoax users into making security mistakes and hence giving away sensitive information.

Figure 18.4 presents vulnerable areas for cyber threats in cybersecurity science. Cybersecurity experts are now working to curb extensive supply chain attacks. The most significant cyberattacks methods are scareware, DDOS, zero-day exploits, logical bomb, Trojan horse, virus, Man-in-Middle, worm, malvertising, phishing, and vishing. Some new cybercrimes are also added to the existing list. Figure 18.5 presents various cyberattacks

FIGURE 18.3
Cyber threat sources in cybersecurity.

existing in cybersecurity science, which are discussed in Table 18.2. In these attacks, computers can be used in two ways. One computer is a weapon and the other, the computer itself, is a target.

18.4 Ethical Hacking and Security Auditing Process in Cyber Science

Security test or analysis's foremost goal is to evaluate the existing status of any system or network. It is also popularly known as penetration or pen test or ethical hacking. Ethical hacking is an influential module for risk assessment, inspecting fraud, and information systems security best practices. It is used to identify risks and emphasize remedial actions. It also reduces information and communications technology costs by solving the vulnerabilities or weaknesses present in a system. Ethical hacking focuses on protecting our systems, and ethical hackers are cybersecurity experts who support the government and organizations by performing penetration testing and detecting security flaws. It is

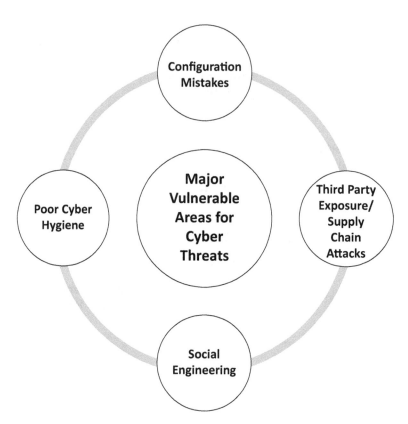

FIGURE 18.4
Major vulnerable areas in cybersecurity for cyber threat.

important to know about ethical hacking or penetration testing phases. The phases for the pen test are:

- Footprinting or Reconnaissance: It includes gathering information about the system or network which needs to be accessed.
- Scanning the System Thoroughly: There is a thorough need to scan a system on which security analysis is to be performed so as to know about the privilege rights etc.
- Obtaining Access to the System: It is required to get proper access to the system for performing any testing.
- Preserving Access to the System: Finally, access should be maintained for the period needed to perform testing.
- Clearing Tracks or Log Files: Lastly, after performing vulnerability tests, it is required to clear all log files and any kind of applications installed on the network.

Proper documentation is required to be prepared in each phase so that all the steps necessary to reproduce the attack are available readily. The documentation also assists as the basis for preparing a detailed report at the end of a penetration test.

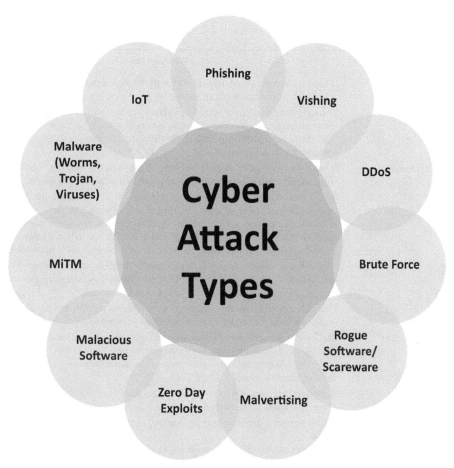

FIGURE 18.5
Categorical analysis of cyberattacks in cybersecurity.

18.5 Penetration Testing and Vulnerability Analytics

After estimating vulnerabilities, penetration testing comes next [20]. Different browsers are compatible with penetration testing tools. The Mozilla Firefox browser is considered to be the most promising browser by nearly every Ethical Hacker and Security Scientist when undertaking pen testing for any web-based application. Comparing Mozilla Firefox to other browsers like Chrome, Opera, etc., it has been shown to be more feature-rich.

The More Tools features, which embrace Task Manager, Extension for developers, and Web Developer Tools, are the primary factors in its acceptability. For ethical hackers and safety investigators, a variety of extensions are available to automate and simplify their testing. Not all penetration tests are performed in a similar manner or may not have the same purpose [21].

TABLE 18.2

Available Cyberattacks Cyber Science

Cyberattacks	Description
IoT	It aims to overtax a system's resources to the extent that it becomes unable to react to legitimate service requests.
Phishing	Phishing attacks occur when an adversary sends emails that seem to come from trustworthy, reputable sources in an effort to dupe the victim into disclosing sensitive information. Phishing attacks mix social engineering and different technologies.
VoIP phishing/vishing	It is a type of cyberattack that deceives targets into disclosing confidential information to unauthorized parties using voice and telephony technologies.
DDoS	By overloading a system's resources, a denial-of-service (DoS) attack tries to prevent it from responding to legitimate service requests. A DDoS attack seeks to exhaust a system's resources, just like a denial-of-service (DoS) assault does. A DDoS attack is launched when a large number of host computers controlled by the attacker and infected with malware do so.
Brute force	"Brute-force assault" is an attack that uses a "brutish" methodology. The attacker tries to figure out a user's login credentials so they can access the target system. Once they get it right, they are admitted.
Scareware	Users are tricked into downloading or purchasing potentially dangerous software using a malware tactic known as scareware.
Malvertising/malicious advertising	Malicious malware is being inserted into web adverts as a new cyberattack technique. It is challenging for both internet users and publishers to find these infected ads because they are often sent to clients through trustworthy advertising networks.
Zero-day exploits	A zero-day exploit is an attack that targets a software vulnerability that hasn't been disclosed to the software manufacturer or to antivirus providers.
Drive by attacks	A hacker uses a drive by assault to infect an unsecured website with malicious code. The script automatically runs on a user's computer after they view the website, corrupting it.
MiTM	Man-in-the-middle (MiTM) attacks are a subset of cyberattacks that give the attacker the ability to eavesdrop on information being exchanged between two parties across networks or computers.
Malware/malicious software	Malware degrades a computer's performance, destroys data, or eavesdrops on online activities or network traffic. Malware can either spread from one device to another or persist and just impact its host device.
Domain fronting	By hiding user traffic behind a distinct domain, domain fronting is used to mask user traffic.
Ransomware	In this attack, the target downloads the malevolent software, from any website or any email attachment. The virus is built to exploit bugs that neither the system's developer nor the IT team have addressed.
XSS attack	Cross-site scripting, also known as XSS, is the action of an attacker sending injurious scripts to a target's computer. When the victim touches on the content, the script starts.
URL poisoning/interpretation	By manipulating and fabricating specific URL addresses, attackers can use URL interpretation to access the target's personal and business data. It refers to the fact that the attacker is aware of the correct sequence in which to input the URL components for a web page. The attacker then interprets this syntax, utilizing it to determine how to gain entry to restricted areas.

(Continued)

TABLE 18.2 CONTINUED

Available Cyberattacks Cyber Science

Cyberattacks	Description
Crypto-jacking	When hackers gain entry to other person's workstation to pit cryptocurrencies, is known as crypto-jacking. Access is obtained, by corrupting a website or deceiving the victim into clicking on a malevolent link.
IoT-based attacks	Security flaws are exploited in Internet of Things (IoT) devices like smart thermostats and surveillance cams to steal information.
Social engineering	It is a trick used by cyber-criminals to get users to reveal confidential information.
Cloud-based, targeted personal attacks	In order to launch highly targeted phishing attacks or try direct password resets on high-value accounts, targeted cloud-based personal attacks take advantage of all the information users divulge on social media and other websites.
Keylogger	It is malware made to record keystrokes that a target types into their computer. Passwords, credit card details, and other private information fall under this category.
Embedded hardware attacks	These transient execution attacks, which make use of recently released CPUs' shoddy performance improvement methods (like speculative execution, out-of-order execution, and pipeline), allow attackers to basically capture all memory contents.

18.5.1 VAPT Life Cycle

The VAPT (vulnerability assessment and penetration testing) life cycle consists of eight stages in total. Figure 18.6 shows all these stages. The size of the job must first be established by the tester. The tester conducts studies to discover more network information, operating system, and its IP address after establishing the test's parameters [22–25]. The tester then conducts a range of vulnerability evaluation procedures on the testing object.

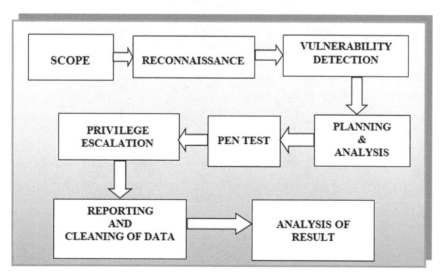

FIGURE 18.6
VAPT life cycle in cybersecurity.

The tester then conducts a vulnerability assessment and creates a plan for penetration testing. This method is used by the evaluator to access the victim's system. The tester elevates his standing after hacking the system. The tester examines all findings and formulates recommendations to address the system vulnerability during the result analysis stage.

These actions are all recorded and reported to management for any additional action that may be required. The victim's system and program are affected by and altered by these activities. During the clean-up phase, we returned the system to the condition it was in before the VAPT procedure.

All of these steps are documented and reported to management in case any further action is needed. The victim's system and program are affected by and altered by these activities. During the clean-up phase, the system is returned to the condition it was in before the VAPT procedure began.

18.5.2 Techniques for Vulnerability Assessment and Penetration Testing

Global businesses' key infrastructure continues to be impacted by the constantly evolving threat landscape. With over 25,000 published, 2022 marked a record-breaking growth year for Common Vulnerabilities and Exposures (CVE) data. Every day, on average, 69 CVEs were published. For the year 2023, approximately 7800 CVEs have been reported till April [22]. Figure 18.7 shows CVE data for the last five years.

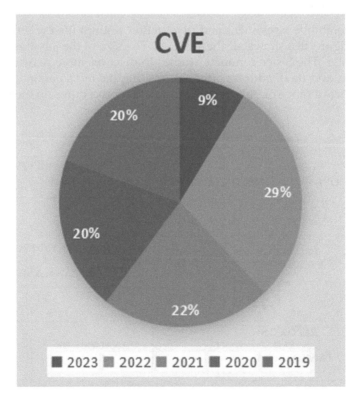

FIGURE 18.7
CVEs in recent years.

This section discusses penetration testing and vulnerability assessment techniques. The vulnerability assessment techniques are as follows:

- Static Evaluation

There are no test cases done using this technique. We look at the parts of the system and the code structure. We can find a variety of flaws using this strategy [26–28]. Because we do not do any manipulation in the system, so there would be no consequences of this testing on it. It takes a lot of time and labor to perform this procedure, which is just one of its many important negatives.

- Manual Analysis/Evaluation

In this method, finding flaws does not require any tool or software. In this test, the tester observes vulnerabilities in the system using his proficiency and knowledge [29]. This technique costs less than others because it does not call for the purchase of a vulnerability assessment instrument.

- Fuzz Analysis/Evaluation

This is also referred to as fuzzing. In this, the system is fed with erroneous or random data, and system faults and breakdowns are then investigated. Very minimal interaction with other individuals is necessary for this strategy. This approach can be used to find zero-day vulnerabilities [30–32].

- Automated Evaluation

The automated vulnerability testing tools in automated testing methods to find system vulnerabilities. These tools run through each test situation in search of flaws. As a consequence, less labor and time are required to finish testing. The tool makes it very easy to perform repeated testing [33].

Automated testing is more accurate than other techniques. For subsequent tasks, the same test cases can be used, and it takes very little time [34, 35].

Some additional penetration testing methods that are used are as follows:

- Black Box Analysis/Testing

The tester does not need to have any prior knowledge of the systems or network architecture of the testing network to use this method [36]. Typically, black box testing is done from an external network to an inside network. To carry out this check, the tester must use his knowledge and abilities.

- Grey Area Evaluation/Testing

The tester gains a general overview of the testing network using this technique. Even so, the tester is not aware of the complete network architecture. The foundations of testing network and system configuration are some things that rather is familiar with. Actually, this testing approach includes the previous two techniques. Both internal and exterior networks are capable of performing this.

- White Box Testing/Evaluation

The testing network's network setup and its system configuration are completely understood by the tester. Usually, internal networks are used for this research. White box testing demands in-depth knowledge of the testing network.

18.5.3 Web Server Fingerprinting

Web server fingerprinting is an important task for the penetration tester. To know the version and type of a web server that is running. It allows pen testers to determine common vulnerabilities and the suitable exploits to be used during testing.

18.5.4 Pen Testing Tools

If Security 4.0 is to succeed, it must ensure that security is incorporated into the system from the beginning of its life cycle through a process [34, 37]. Penetration testing allows one to view an organization from the viewpoint of the enemy. This approach can lead to a lot of unexpected discoveries and give you ample time to patch up your systems before an actual attacker launches an assault. The overall security strategy for any organization needs to include penetration testing as a critical element [35]. Penetration testing needs to be included in your overall security plan, just as policies, risk assessments, business continuity planning, and disaster recovery have evolved into crucial elements in keeping an organization safe and secure [38]. Various pen tools are discussed in this chapter.

- Nmap

It is an open-source tool known as a network mapper that scans the computer network and system for security flaws. It can run on all operating systems and is generally suitable for all small and large networks. This program is primarily used for a variety of activities, such as network attack area modeling and host or service up-time monitoring [37, 39, 40]. The program makes it simpler to comprehend the many characteristics of every target system, host on network, operating system type, and firewalls.

- Metasploit

It is a collection of several penetration tools. It is used to carry out a number of tasks, such as locating vulnerabilities and organizing security evaluations and other defense strategies. This technology can be applied to servers, networks, and software applications. It is primarily employed to evaluate the infrastructure's security against identified weaknesses.

- Wireshark

It is the tool used to monitor even the minute details of network activity. It performs tasks like those of a network tester, sniffer, or protocol analyzer to assess network vulnerabilities. The device is used for intercepting data packets and learning more about their source, target, and other details.

- NetSparker

It is a scanner used to examine the safety of web-based applications and can automatically find flaws like injection of SQL and XSS. The scanner's simple settings allow it to automatically recognize URL rules. It is eternally extendable.

- OWASP

It is referred to as the Open Web Application Security Project. Its main objective is to improve software security. To test the setting and protocol penetration, many tools are available. Zed Attack Proxy, OWASP dependence check, and OWASP web testing environment project are among the many tools that may be utilized to inspect the project's dependency and test against the vulnerabilities.

- Accunetix

It is a completely automated penetration testing tool. It meticulously examines JavaScript, HTML5, and single-page applications. It examines sophisticated and authorized web applications and generates a report on network and system vulnerabilities. It is rapid and scalable and discovers a significant number of vulnerabilities.

- Nessus

Nessus, a common firewall testing tool, is renowned for its vulnerability analyses and continuous upgrades, which guarantee comprehensive protection and vulnerability detection. A free version is offered.

- W3af

Due to its standards, W3af is a framework for online penetration testing that improves any penetration testing tool. It is able to spot approximately 200 different types of faults in web apps.

- Zed Attack Proxy

The greatest open-source, free pen test tool is ZAP, which is offered by OWASP. Run penetration tests on online programmers to find a variety of problems on Linux, Microsoft, and Mac systems.

- Kali Linux

Kali Linux, a Debian-based environment designed for penetration testing, is available from Offensive Security. With Kali Linux, a variety of tools for penetration testing are available.

- Burp Suite

The Port Swigger company offers the Burp Suite penetration testing tool, which offers a number of features that are crucial for any penetration tester. Spider, Proxy, Repeater Intruder, and other tools are some of the available ones.

18.6 Conclusion

Everywhere, IoT infrastructure is being used to advance the development of smart systems, from smart home products to smart cities. When this kind of adoption is carried out, a smart environment will be developed where a significant amount of personal and public data will be handled. Data security and user identity privacy must be protected against hackers. The fundamental infrastructure, however, is unable to meet this demand in order to find vulnerabilities. The penetration testing technology is the greatest option for achieving this goal because one of its primary components is the discovery of vulnerabilities. This chapter is well-versed in the stages that make up a normal penetration test as well as the tools needed to perform each phase. More significantly, it comprehends the flow of the penetration testing process and how to incorporate the data and output from each phase into the following phase. Many people are eager to learn about penetration testing and hacking, yet most newbies only know how to use one tool or carry out one action. They are unaware of the mechanics of the entire process and how to utilize the capacity of each phase to make the phases that follow it stronger. So, a better understanding of the processes and terminology of attacks and pen testing will enhance the knowledge therefore. Penetration testing should be a key component of your organization's overall security plan. Penetration testing must be included in your overall security plan, just as policies, risk assessments, and disaster recovery have evolved into crucial elements in keeping your organization safe and secure for Society 5.0.

References

1. Tan, S., Xie, P., Guerrero, J. M., Vasquez, J. C., Li, Y., & Guo, X. (2021). Attack detection design for dc microgrid using eigenvalue assignment approach. *Energy Reports, 7*, 469–476.
2. Aghajani, G., & Ghadimi, N. (2018). Multi-objective energy management in a micro-grid. *Energy Reports, 4*, 218–225.
3. Akhavan-Hejazi, H., & Mohsenian-Rad, H. (2018). Power systems big data analytics: An assessment of paradigm shift barriers and prospects. *Energy Reports, 4*, 91–100.
4. Niraja, K. S., & Rao, S. S. (2021). A hybrid algorithm design for near real time detection cyber attacks from compromised devices to enhance IoT security. *Materials Today: Proceedings.*
5. Sarker, I. H. (2021). Cyberlearning: Effectiveness analysis of machine learning security modeling to detect cyber-anomalies and multi-attacks. *Internet Things, 14*, 100393.
6. Shin, J., Choi, J. G., Lee, J. W., Lee, C. K., Song, J. G., & Son, J. Y. (2021). Application of STPA-SafeSec for a cyber-attack impact analysis of NPPs with a condensate water system test-bed. *Nuclear Engineering & Technology, 53*(10), 3319–3326.
7. Cao, J., Ding, D., Liu, J., Tian, E., Hu, S., & Xie, X. (2021). Hybrid-triggered-based security controller design for networked control system under multiple cyber attacks. *Information Sciences, 548*, 69–84.
8. Alhayani, B., Abbas, S. T., Khutar, D. Z., & Mohammed, H. J. (2021). Best ways computation intelligent of face cyber attacks. *Materials Today: Proceedings*, 26–31.
9. Bhol, S. G., Mohanty, J. R., & Pattnaik, P. K. (2021). Taxonomy of cyber security metrics to measure strength of cyber security. *Materials Today: Proceedings.*
10. Waters, G., & Blackburn, J. (2011). Optimising Australia's response to the cyber challenge. . Available at https://api.semanticscholar.org/CorpusID:155468922
11. Bennett, L. (2012). Cyber security strategy. *ITNow, 54*(1), 10–11.

12. Under Section act: Sec.2(1)(nb) of IT Act, 2000.

13. Zhao, J., Yan, Q., Li, J., Shao, M., He, Z., & Li, B. (2020). TIMiner: Automatically extracting and analyzing categorized cyber threat intelligence from social data. *Computers & Security, 95,* 101867.

14. Shah, S., & Mehtre, B. M. (2013). A modern approach to cyber security analysis using vulnerability assessment and penetration testing. *International Journal of Electronics and Communication Engineering, 4*(6), 47–52.

15. Zhang, X., Xu, M., Da, G., & Zhao, P. (2021). Ensuring confidentiality and availability of sensitive data over a network system under cyber threats. *Reliability Engineering & System Safety, 214,* 107697.

16. Motsch, W., David, A., Sivalingam, K., Wagner, A., & Ruskowski, M. (2020). Approach for dynamic price-based demand side management in cyber-physical production systems. *Procedia Manufacturing, 51,* 1748–1754.

17. Al-Ghamdi, M. I. (2021). Effects of knowledge of cyber security on prevention of attacks. *Materials Today: Proceedings, 10.*

18. Beechey, M., Kyriakopoulos, K. G., & Lambotharan, S. (2021). Evidential classification and feature selection for cyber-threat hunting. *Knowledge-Based Systems, 226,* 107120.

19. Solomon, R. (2017). Electronic protests: Hacktivism as a form of protest in Uganda. *Computer Law & Security Review, 33*(5), 718–728.

20. Goel, J. N., & Mehtre, B. M. (2015). Vulnerability assessment & penetration testing as a cyber defence technology. *Procedia Computer Science, 57,* 710–715.

21. Engebretson, P. (2013). *The Basics of Hacking and Penetration Testing: Ethical Hacking and Penetration Testing Made Easy.* Elsevier.

22. https://www.cvedetails.com/index.php.

23. Thakur, K., Qiu, M., Gai, K., & Ali, M. L. (2015, November). An investigation on cyber security threats and security models. In *2015 2nd International Conference on Cyber Security and Cloud Computing* (pp. 307–311). IEEE.

24. Chivukula, R., Lakshmi, T. J., Kandula, L. R. R., & Alla, K. (2021, November). A study of cyber security issues and challenges. In *2021 IEEE Bombay Section Signature Conference (IBSSC)* (pp. 1–5). IEEE.

25. Gallaher, M. P., Link, A. N., & Rowe, B. (2008). *Cyber Security: Economic Strategies and Public Policy Alternatives.* Edward Elgar Publishing.

26. Pasqualetti, F., Dörfler, F., & Bullo, F. (2013). Attack detection and identification in cyber-physical systems. *IEEE Transactions on Automatic Control, 58*(11), 2715–2729.

27. Kaur, S., & Kaur, G. (2021, March). Threat and vulnerability analysis of cloud platform: A user perspective. In *2021 8th International Conference on Computing for Sustainable Global Development (INDIACom)* (pp. 533–539). IEEE.

28. Thiruneelakandan, A., Kaur, G., Vadnala, G., Bharathiraja, N., Pradeepa, K., & Retnadhas, M. (2022). Measurement of oxygen content in water with purity through soft sensor model. *Measurement: Sensors, 24,* 100589.

29. Shabaz, M. (2022). A secure two-factor Authentication framework in cloud computing. *Security & Communication Networks, 2022.*

30. Kaur, H., Kaur, G., & Pannu, H. S. (2020). Novel similarity measure-based random forest for fingerprint recognition using dual-tree complex wavelet transform and ring projection. *Modern Physics Letters. Part B, 34*(2), 2050022.

31. UmaMaheswaran, S. K., Kaur, G., Pankajam, A., Firos, A., Vashistha, P., Tripathi, V., & Mohammed, H. S. (2022). Empirical analysis for improving food quality using artificial intelligence technology for enhancing healthcare sector. *Journal of Food Quality, 2022.*

32. Kaur, G., Braveen, M., Krishnapriya, S., Wawale, S. G., Castillo-Picon, J., Malhotra, D., & Osei-Owusu, J. (2023). Machine learning integrated multivariate water quality control framework for prawn harvesting from fresh water ponds. *Journal of Food Quality, 2023.*

33. Pasqualetti, F., Dörfler, F., & Bullo, F. (2012). Attack detection and identification in cyber-physical systems--part I: models and fundamental limitations. *arXiv Preprint ArXiv:1202.6144.*

34. Bharathiraja, N., Pradeepa, K., Murugesan, S., Hariharan, S., Vinoth Kumar, M., & Veeramanickam, M. R. M. (2022). A novel framework for cyber security attacks on cloud-based services. In *2022 Fourth International Conference on Cognitive Computing and Information Processing (CCIP)* (pp. 1–4). IEEE. https://doi.org/10.1109/CCIP57447.2022.10058673.

35. Veeramanickam, M. R. M., Khullar, V., Bhosle, A. A., Salunke, M. D., Bangare, J. L., & Ingavale, A. (2022). Streamed incremental learning for cyber attack classification using machine learning. In *2022 2nd International Conference on Innovative Sustainable Computational Technologies (CISCT)* (pp. 1–5). IEEE. https://doi.org/10.1109/CISCT55310.2022.10046651.

36. Gill, S. K., Kaur, G., Shankar, G., & Murugappan, V. (2023). Solving the element detecting problem in graphs via quantum walk search algorithm (QWSA). In *Mobile Radio Communications and 5G Networks: Proceedings of Third MRCN 2022* (pp. 433–442). Springer Nature Singapore.

37. .Hajda, J., Jakuszewski, R., & Ogonowski, S. (2021). Security challenges in Industry 4.0 PLC systems. *Applied Sciences, 11*(21), 9785.

38. Jayanthi, E., Ramesh, T., Kharat, R. S., Veeramanickam, M. R. M., Bharathiraja, N., Venkatesan, R., & Marappan, R. (2023). Cybersecurity enhancement to detect credit card frauds in health care using new machine learning strategies. *Soft Computing*. https://doi.org/10.1007/s00500-023-07954-y.

39. Gautam, V., Tiwari, R. G., Jain, A. K., & Agarwal, A. (2022, December). Research pattern of Internet of things and its impact on cyber security. In *2022 11th International Conference on System Modeling & Advancement in Research Trends (SMART)* (pp. 260–263). IEEE.

40. Datta, P., Panda, S. N., Tanwar, S., & Kaushal, R. K. (2020, March). A technical review report on cyber crimes in India. In *2020 International Conference on Emerging Smart Computing and Informatics (ESCI)* (pp. 269–275). IEEE.

19

Role of Delay-Sensitive Smart Health Framework Using Nature-Inspired Load Balancer in Society 5.0

Navneet Kumar Rajpoot, Prabhdeep Singh, and Bhaskar Pant

19.1 Introduction

19.1.1 Smart Healthcare in Society 5.0

Society 5.0 is all about creating a sustainable and efficient society. Smart healthcare is a critical component of Society 5.0 as it aims to improve individuals' health and well-being while reducing healthcare costs. Smart healthcare in Society 5.0 leverages artificial intelligence (AI), the Internet of Things (IoT), and other advanced technologies to create a healthcare system that is more efficient, accurate, and responsive.

Smart healthcare in Society 5.0 is designed to be patient-centric, focusing on providing personalized care that meets the specific requirements of each patient. This is achieved through the use of cutting-edge technologies, for example, wearables, mobile devices, as well as IoT-enabled sensors that collect and transmit data about a patient's health in real time [1]. This data is then analyzed using AI algorithms to provide insights into a patient's health status, enabling healthcare professionals to provide personalized care that is tailored to the specific needs of the patient.

19.1.2 Role of Delay-Sensitive Smart Health Framework Using Nature-Inspired Load Balancer in Society 5.0

Delay-Sensitive Smart Health Framework Using Nature-Inspired Load Balancer is an advanced technology that can be vital in realizing smart healthcare in Society 5.0. The framework leverages AI and nature-inspired load-balancing algorithms to optimize the delivery of healthcare services, ensuring that patients receive the care they need in a timely and efficient manner [2].

The framework is designed to address the issue of delay in healthcare delivery, which is a critical challenge that affects the quality of care provided to patients. Delays can occur due to various factors, including the workload of healthcare professionals, the availability of resources, and the complexity of healthcare delivery systems. Delay-Sensitive Smart Health Framework Using Nature-Inspired Load Balancer aims to address these challenges by optimizing the allocation of healthcare resources and reducing the workload of healthcare professionals [3].

The framework is based on a nature-inspired load-balancing algorithm that mimics the behavior of natural systems such as ant colonies and immune systems. The algorithm is designed to optimize the allocation of healthcare resources by dynamically adjusting the

DOI: 10.1201/9781003397052-19

load on each resource based on the current workload and the urgency of patient needs. The algorithm uses real-time data about the workload of healthcare professionals, the availability of resources, and the urgency of patient needs to make intelligent decisions about allocating healthcare resources.

The framework also leverages AI to predict the workload of healthcare professionals and the demand for healthcare services, enabling healthcare organizations to plan and allocate resources more effectively. By optimizing the allocation of healthcare resources, Delay-Sensitive Smart Health Framework Using Nature-Inspired Load Balancer can reduce the workload of healthcare professionals as well as make sure that patients receive the care they need in a quick as well as efficient manner [4].

Delay-Sensitive Smart Health Framework Using Nature-Inspired Load Balancer is an advanced technology with several healthcare benefits in Society 5.0. The framework leverages AI and nature-inspired load-balancing algorithms to optimize the delivery of healthcare services, ensuring that patients receive the care they need in a timely and efficient manner. Some of the benefits of this framework are discussed below.

19.1.2.1 Improved Patient Outcomes

One of the significant benefits of the Delay-Sensitive Smart Health Framework Using Nature-Inspired Load Balancer is that it can improve patient treatment results [5]. By ensuring that patients receive the care they need in a timely and efficient manner, the framework can moderate the risk of complications as well as improve the quality of care provided to patients. In a patient-centric healthcare system, this is of utmost importance as it can enhance individuals' overall health and well-being.

The framework can achieve this by optimizing the allocation of healthcare resources and reducing the workload of healthcare professionals [6]. By dynamically adjusting the load on each resource based on the current workload and the urgency of patient needs, the framework ensures that patients receive the care they need when needed. This can significantly reduce the risk of complications and improve patient outcomes.

19.1.2.2 Reduced Healthcare Costs

Another significant benefit of Delay-Sensitive Smart Health Framework Using Nature-Inspired Load Balancer is that it can reduce healthcare costs. In Society 5.0, where efficiency and sustainability are critical, this is of utmost importance. The framework achieves this by optimizing the allocation of healthcare resources, reducing healthcare professionals' workload, and minimizing resource wastage [7].

By dynamically adjusting the load on each resource based on the current workload and the urgency of patient needs, the framework ensures that healthcare resources are utilized optimally. This can significantly reduce the overall cost of healthcare delivery, making healthcare more affordable and accessible to everyone.

19.1.2.3 Increased Efficiency

Delay-Sensitive Smart Health Framework Using Nature-Inspired Load Balancer can also increase the efficiency of healthcare delivery. By leveraging AI and nature-inspired load-balancing algorithms, the framework can optimize the allocation of healthcare resources, reducing healthcare professionals' workload and minimizing resource wastage [8]. This can significantly improve the efficiency of healthcare delivery, enabling healthcare organizations to provide more healthcare services to a larger number of patients.

The framework achieves this by using real-time data about the workload of healthcare professionals, the availability of resources, and the urgency of patient needs to make intelligent decisions about allocating healthcare resources. This can significantly improve the overall efficiency of healthcare delivery, making it more effective and responsive to the needs of patients [9].

19.1.2.4 Personalized Care

Delay-Sensitive Smart Health Framework Using Nature-Inspired Load Balancer can also provide personalized care to patients. In Society 5.0, where the focus is on creating a patient-centric healthcare system, this is of utmost importance. The framework achieves this by collecting and analyzing real-time data about a patient's health status and using AI algorithms to provide insights into their health needs.

By providing personalized care, the framework can improve the overall quality of care provided to patients. This can significantly enhance the health and well-being of individuals, making healthcare more effective and responsive to the needs of patients [10].

19.2 Overview of Healthcare Technologies and Their Limitations in Society 5.0

- In Society 5.0, healthcare is being transformed by innovative technologies such as artificial intelligence (AI), machine learning, and the Internet of Things (IoT). These technologies are used to collect and analyze patient data, provide personalized care, and optimize healthcare delivery [11]. However, despite the potential benefits, there are also limitations to these technologies in the context of Society 5.0.

- One of the key limitations of these technologies is the lack of real-time data. In healthcare, real-time data is critical as it enables healthcare professionals to respond quickly to patient condition changes. However, collecting and analyzing real-time data requires significant computational power and advanced data analytics, which can be costly and complex [12].

- Another limitation of healthcare technologies in Society 5.0 is the lack of interoperability. Healthcare organizations use a variety of systems and technologies, which can make it difficult to share and analyze patient data across different platforms [13]. This lack of interoperability can lead to duplication of efforts, errors in diagnosis, and delays in treatment.

- Privacy and security are also major concerns regarding healthcare technologies in Society 5.0. Collecting and storing patient data can create significant risks for data breaches and identity theft. Medical care providers may ease patients' minds by taking extra precautions to secure sensitive patient information [14].

- Finally, there is a need for healthcare professionals to be trained in the use of these technologies. Adopting advanced technologies in healthcare requires significant

changes in workflow and processes, which can be challenging for healthcare professionals who are already under significant time and resource constraints [15].
Therefore, it is important to provide adequate training and support to healthcare
professionals to ensure that they can effectively use these technologies from the
perspective of Society 5.0.

19.3 Background on Society 5.0 and the Need for Advanced Healthcare Technologies

Society 5.0 is a vision of the future that seeks to integrate advanced technologies with society to benefit both people and the environment. This concept was first introduced in Japan
and is characterized by integrating physical and cyber systems to create a more sustainable and efficient society [16] (Figure 19.1).

One of the key areas where Society 5.0 is being applied is healthcare. The healthcare
sector is undergoing a major transformation due to advances in technology, demograph-
ics, and changing patient expectations. To meet these challenges, healthcare providers are
adopting cutting-edge technologies such as artificial intelligence (AI), machine learning,
and the Internet of Things (IoT) [17].

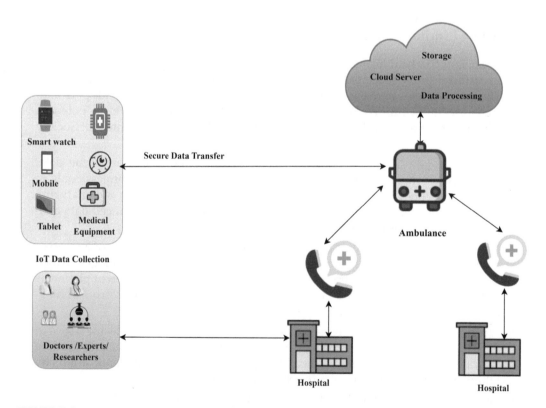

FIGURE 19.1
Society 5.0 and healthcare framework.

These technologies are used to collect and analyze patient data, provide personalized care, and optimize healthcare delivery. For example, IoT devices such as wearables can monitor a patient's vital signs in real time and alert healthcare professionals to changes in their condition. AI and machine learning can analyze large amounts of patient data to identify trends and patterns, which can help in the early diagnosis and treatment of diseases.

The need for advanced healthcare technologies in Society 5.0 is driven by several factors. First, there is a growing demand for healthcare services due to an aging population and the increase in chronic diseases. Advanced technologies can help healthcare providers meet this demand by enabling more efficient and effective healthcare delivery.

Second, there is a need to improve the quality of healthcare services. Healthcare technologies can help providers deliver more accurate diagnoses, better treatment plans, and improved patient outcomes.

Finally, there is a need to contain healthcare costs. Advanced technologies can help reduce healthcare costs by improving the efficiency of healthcare delivery, reducing the need for hospitalization, and preventing the progression of diseases [18].

19.4 Overview of Delay-Sensitive Smart Health Framework Using Nature-Inspired Load Balancer

- The Delay-Sensitive Smart Health Framework Using Nature-Inspired Load Balancer is an innovative method for delivering medical care that prioritizes better patient results. Artificial intelligence (AI), machine learning, and nature-inspired load-balancing algorithms to create a responsive and efficient healthcare system are just some of the cutting-edge technologies that may be used within this paradigm.

- The framework is designed to address one of the key challenges facing healthcare delivery in Society 5.0 – the need for real-time data. Real-time data is critical in healthcare as it enables healthcare professionals to respond quickly to changes in a patient's condition. However, collecting and analyzing real-time data can be challenging and costly [19].

- The Delay-Sensitive Smart Health Framework seeks to address this challenge using AI and machine learning algorithms to collect and analyze patient data in real time [20]. The framework also uses nature-inspired load-balancing algorithms to optimize healthcare delivery by balancing the workload across healthcare providers and facilities.

- The nature-inspired load-balancing algorithms used in the framework are inspired by the behavior of natural systems such as ant colonies and immune systems [21]. These algorithms are designed to adapt to changing conditions and optimize the allocation of resources based on patient needs.

- The framework also incorporates patient feedback and preferences to provide personalized care. Patients can provide feedback on their treatment and care experience, which can be used to optimize their treatment plans and improve their outcomes [22].

- Overall, the Delay-Sensitive Smart Health Framework Using Nature-Inspired Load Balancer has the potential to revolutionize healthcare delivery in Society 5.0. By enabling real-time data collection and analysis and optimizing healthcare delivery through nature-inspired load-balancing algorithms, this framework can improve patient outcomes, reduce healthcare costs, and enhance the overall quality of healthcare delivery.

19.5 Conclusion

The Delay-Sensitive Smart Health Framework Using Nature-Inspired Load Balancer is a powerful tool for optimizing healthcare delivery in Society 5.0. By integrating cutting-edge technologies, for example, AI, machine learning, and nature-inspired load-balancing algorithms, this framework enables real-time data collection and analysis, personalized care, and optimized healthcare delivery.

The healthcare sector is facing significant challenges in Society 5.0, including an aging population, rising healthcare costs, and increasing demand for high-quality care. In response, healthcare providers must embrace advanced technologies to improve patient outcomes, optimize healthcare delivery, and reduce costs.

The Delay-Sensitive Smart Health Framework offers several benefits, including the ability to collect and analyze real-time patient data, provide personalized care based on patient preferences, and optimize healthcare delivery by balancing the workload across healthcare providers and facilities.

As the healthcare sector evolves, healthcare providers must embrace these advanced technologies and develop new strategies for integrating them into their workflow. This will require collaboration between healthcare providers, technology companies, and policymakers to ensure that the benefits of these technologies are realized.

References

1. Khanam, Shaheen, and Muzammil Hasan. "Nature inspired load balancing algorithms-A review." In *2019 2nd International Conference on Power Energy, Environment and Intelligent Control (PEEIC)*, pp. 94–99. IEEE, 2019.
2. Alatawi, Hind Salem, and Sanaa Abdullah Sharaf. "Toward efficient cloud services: An energy-aware hybrid load balancing approach." In *2020 International Conference on Computing and Information Technology (ICCIT-1441)*, pp. 1–5. IEEE, 2020.
3. Rani, Shalu, Dharminder Kumar, and Sakshi Dhingra. "A review on dynamic load balancing algorithms." In *2022 International Conference on Computing, Communication, and Intelligent Systems (ICCCIS)*, pp. 515–520. IEEE, 2022.
4. Prasad, Ch Rajendra, Sandeep Kumar, P. Ramchandar Rao, Sreedhar Kollem, Srikanth Yalabaka, and Srinivas Samala. "Optimization of task offloading for smart cities using IoT with fog computing-a survey." In *2022 International Conference on Signal and Information Processing (IConSIP)*, pp. 1–5. IEEE, 2022.

5. Irfan, Shaik Muhammad, Hemanth Rathore, Harsh Bisen, Dheeraj Kumar, Suresh Kumar, and Kamlesh Sharma. "Comparative analysis of various load balancing techniques in cloud environment." In *2022 International Conference on Machine Learning, Big Data, Cloud and Parallel Computing (COM-IT-CON)*, vol. 1, pp. 859–866. IEEE, 2022.

6. Patel, Karan D., and Tosal M. Bhalodia. "An efficient dynamic load balancing algorithm for virtual machine in cloud computing." In *2019 International Conference on Intelligent Computing and Control Systems (ICCS)*, pp. 145–150. IEEE, 2019.

7. Paul, Souvik, and Mainak Adhikari. "Dynamic load balancing strategy based on resource classification technique in IaaS cloud." In *2018 International Conference on Advances in Computing, Communications and Informatics (ICACCI)*, pp. 2059–2065. IEEE, 2018.

8. Tyagi, Unnati, Vinay Bansal, Shefali Singhal, and Tanvi Gupta. "Challenges and issues in energy efficient load balancing in the cloud computing environment." In *2022 International Conference on Machine Learning, Big Data, Cloud and Parallel Computing (COM-IT-CON)*, vol. 1, pp. 634–638. IEEE, 2022.

9. Swarnakar, Soumen, Neeraj Kumar, Amit Kumar, and Chandan Banerjee. "Modified genetic based algorithm for load balancing in cloud computing." In *2020 IEEE 1st International Conference for Convergence in Engineering (ICCE)*, pp. 255–259. IEEE, 2020.

10. Sudhakar, Chapram, Rajul Jain, and T. Ramesh. "Cloud load balancing-honey bees inspired effective request balancing strategy." In *2018 International Conference on Computing, Power and Communication Technologies (GUCON)*, pp. 605–610. IEEE, 2018.

11. Srivastava, Ankita, and Narander Kumar. "An energy efficient robust resource provisioning based on improved PSO-ANN." *International Journal of Information Technology* 15, (2022): 1–11.

12. Sumathi, Muruganandam, Natarajan Vijayaraj, Soosaimarian Peter Raja, and Murugesan Rajkamal. "HHO-ACO hybridized load balancing technique in cloud computing." *International Journal of Information Technology* 15, (2023): 1–9.

13. Chaudhary, Ravi Raushan Kumar, and Kakali Chatterjee. "A lightweight security framework for electronic healthcare system." *International Journal of Information Technology* 14, no. 6 (2022): 3109–3121.

14. Yugank, Hanumant Kumar, Richa Sharma, and Sindhu Hak Gupta. "An approach to analyse energy consumption of an IoT system." *International Journal of Information Technology* 14, no. 5 (2022): 2549–2558.

15. Pawar, Renuka Sahebrao, and Dhananjay Ramrao Kalbande. "Optimization of quality of service using ECEBA protocol in wireless body area network." *International Journal of Information Technology* 15, (2023): 1–16.

16. Garg, Neha, Mohammad S. Obaidat, Mohammad Wazid, Ashok Kumar Das, and Devesh Pratap Singh. "Spcs-ioteh: Secure privacy-preserving communication scheme for iot-enabled e-health applications." In *ICC 2021-IEEE International Conference on Communications*, pp. 1–6. IEEE, 2021.

17. Garg, Neha, Mohammad Wazid, Ashok Kumar Das, Devesh Pratap Singh, Joel J.P.C. Rodrigues, and Youngho Park. "BAKMP-IoMT: Design of blockchain enabled authenticated key management protocol for internet of medical things deployment." *IEEE Access* 8 (2020): 95956–95977.

18. Pundir, Sumit, Mohammad Wazid, Devesh Pratap Singh, Ashok Kumar Das, Joel J.P.C. Rodrigues, and Youngho Park. "Intrusion detection protocols in wireless sensor networks integrated to Internet of Things deployment: Survey and future challenges." *IEEE Access* 8 (2019): 3343–3363.

19. Singh, Neelam, Devesh Pratap Singh, and Bhasker Pant. "ACOCA: Ant colony optimization based clustering algorithm for big data preprocessing." *International Journal of Mathematical, Engineering and Management Sciences* 4, no. 5 (2019): 1239.

20. Grover, Amit, R. Mohan Kumar, Mohit Angurala, Mehtab Singh, Anu Sheetal, and R. Maheswar. "Rate aware congestion control mechanism for wireless sensor networks." *Alexandria Engineering Journal* 61, no. 6 (2022): 4765–4777.

21. Singh, Kiran Deep, Prabhdeep Singh, Vikas Tripathi, and Vikas Khullar. "A novel and secure framework to detect unauthorized access to an optical fog-cloud computing network." In *2022 Seventh International Conference on Parallel, Distributed and Grid Computing (PDGC)*, pp. 618–622. IEEE, 2022.
22. Angurala, Mohit, Manju Bala, Sukhvinder Singh Bamber, Rajbir Kaur, and Prabhdeep Singh. "An internet of things assisted drone based approach to reduce rapid spread of COVID-19." *Journal of Safety Science and Resilience* 1, no. 1 (2020): 31–35.

20

Performance Comparison of AODV, DSDV, and DSR Routing Protocols in Wireless Sensor Networks

Shiva Mehta, Mankaj Mehta, Devesh Bathla, Prashant
Chauhan, Ruhi Sarangal, and Aarti Dangwal

20.1 Introduction

The wireless sensor networks (WSNs) are made up of unique sensor hubs dispersed throughout connected areas to monitor various variables via radio transmissions. The development of the WSN in research has proven valuable for defense objectives and has expanded to other regions like observing businesses, traffic signals, and well-being. The advancements in WSN deployment at a massive scale are considered for the disclosure cycle based on the explicit sending of sensor hubs. However, the sensors' various requirements, such as power depletion, memory limitations, poor data transmission, and a lack of handling power, reduce the organization's lifespan. This is due to the rationale that organizations that have been dispatched are left unattended in remote areas, even though energy requirement steering should be planned to extend the organization's lifespan.

Numerous scholars have proposed various steering conventions that may be considered the network's optimum solution to alleviate the energy necessity. Indeed, even the current steering methods were conveyed for the end goal of testing and tracking down the gaps in the research. Consequently, researchers altered the existing plans to diminish or nearly eliminate the limitations connected with WSN. To communicate steering, directing, source, and destination are anticipated to be in a fixed mode, although this is quite unrealistic in a real-world setting. Routing is therefore considered a way to extend the lifetime because the sensor will use less power while not in use. In advanced routing, different researchers have attempted to send information to the destination simply; however, because of countless sensors sent, scattered information is omnidirectional and impeded because the other sensors solicited affirmations and are close enough. Hence, to eliminate this limitation, as the gap between the source and destination widens, it is anticipated that a few hubs will be added to the network. This exploration demonstrated upgraded and gives a decent routing method for sending information to the destination, yet it isn't taken at a far level. The steering conventions like AODV, DSDV, and DSR appeared for distributing information. Every one of these conventions enjoys its benefits and limitations whenever taken autonomously and is made for tiny networks. AODV has been utilized for steering on-request protocol. It helps create a course provided that the association by the organization is mentioned. At each level, it stores the steering data to track down the specific way of the system by thinking about routing tables. Objective Sequenced Distance Vector is a circle-free routing convention in which the most limited way of estimation depends on the Bellman–Portage calculation. Information parcels are sent between the hubs utilizing routing tables put away at every intersection.

The remaining chapter is coordinated as follows. Section 20.2 discussed the connected task. The different WSN routing conventions are talked about in Section 20.3. The re-enactment apparatus and execution measurements are introduced in Section 20.4. Section 20.5 has involved Re-enactment results obtained. At last, the top end is attracted to Section 20.6.

20.2 Literature Review

The recent surge in academic interest in marine research has revolutionized the examination process and led to several WSN disclosure processes. Because Dynamic Source-based Directing (DSR) maintains all directing data, the analyst's idea of DSR made it possible to gather routing information from traffic (Kukreja & Sakshi, 2022). Consequently, DSR assisted in creating and examining steering by sending numerous steering affirmations with course demands called RREQs. It was likewise introduced that DSR supported the above-controlled parcels for a more extended time frame during the routing. Some dealt with DSDV as a protocol for tracking down the briefest distance among sensor hubs using a multi-jump disclosure process. DSDV ends up without circle routing when contrasted with conventional directing, yet it neglected to refresh its directing data in light of the high overhead. AODV is experienced in combining the practical applications based on DSDV and DSR while considering the information from sensor hubs and taking a single path to the destination. By avoiding sending other signals to corners that are really out of range and not storing the data from such hubs in the steering table, it aids in reducing energy consumption. This also aids with memory preservation. AODV distributes the data breaking of connections from surrounding hubs and features a circle-free direction. The transitional corners among source and objective give an answer provided that they are in the course of directing data connected with RREQs. AODV ends up being preferable, steering over existing conventions. Hence, it is stretched further to AODV-I by removing data for handled blockage. This helps decrease bundle misfortune rate and start-to-finish idleness by upgrading the use pace of assets accessible.

The authors have attempted to limit delay and work on the proportion of bundle conveyance by consolidating multi-jump gathering with AODV steering. It helps in lessening the recurrence of disclosure. A superior protocol is presented in light of AODV for looking at the hub's ability to hold data, battery status, and connection state with various choice methods. This has become a superior methodology for the high conveyance of parcels and bringing hub down-to-hub delay. AODV-ES is an augmentation to AODV, which utilizes the outsider model for answering the affirmations sent through halfway corners by the source to the objective. The central hubs, which store the equivalent routing data, need not advance messages to a destination. The scholars even attempt to consolidate different alterations on AODV to work on the adaptability of the organizations. It has been completed to take advantage of every nearby hub's data, and it appears to lessen above, yet the seats are restricted in this situation. Hence, neighborhood ring-based n-jump steering is finished involving AODV-ES to know which hubs are close to the focal corner. The outsider answer of AODV-ES ends up being a decent technique for the n-jump count; however, the seats here are restricted, and the focus is filled on the focal hub, as it were. A few researchers attempted to consolidate different directing conventions with TTL-based recuperation techniques to decrease the utilization of pointless data transmission. That's what here the creator introduced on the off chance that the connection breakage is close to the source or objective, go after a nearby fix. The AODV's versatility is checked at various boundaries like PDR, postponement, and throughput to read up on its reproduction situation for an arbitrary arrangement of portable hubs. An effort has been made to develop protocols like AODV that adhere to the states of a threatening climate to extend the sensor lifetime by introducing forwarder hubs. In general, the different boundaries are shown to work proficiently but are unrealistic for more considerable conditions where sensors are conveyed colossally. Right now, without progressive directing, the data can't be sent to long distances considering the different energy imperatives of the sensors organization. Consequently, by improving the parcel conveyance proportion in another tiered steering with the AODV protocol, we tried to control the start-to-finish defer in this study.

20.3 WSN Routing Protocols

There are different routing protocols for WSNs. The AODV, DSDV, and DSR are receptive directing protocols. These protocols fundamentally beat the everyday impediments of the networks, like lower data transmission, higher power utilization, or a high rate of errors.

20.3.1 An Ad-hoc On-Demand Distance Vector (AODV)

AODV is a receptive steering protocol that doesn't find or keep up a course until or unless requested by hubs. AODV uses objective game plan numbers to ensure the circle obviously has a potential open door and newness. AODV is suitable for both unicast and multicast directing. Then the activity of protocols is separated into two capabilities: route revelation and route upkeep. At the point when a hub requests to speak with another hub, it begins the route revelation component. A route request message. When RREQ sends a letter from a sourcing hub to one of its neighbors if any of those neighbors know the objective hubs, they will also transmit the message to their neighbors, and so on, until the real hub is located. The hub with information about the target hub sends the RREQ initiator a route answer message (RREP). The way is kept in the middle of the road hubs in the routing table, and this way recognizes the route. When the initiator gets the route answer message, the course is prepared, and the initiator can begin sending the bundles. The course mistake RRER is accounted for when the connection with the following bounce breaks.

20.3.2 Destination Sequenced Distance Vector (DSDV)

Destination Sequenced Distance Vector is a circle-free steering convention in which the most limited way of computation depends on the Bellman–Passage calculation (Sakshi & Kukreja, 2023). DSDV directing table development begins with the condition that each hub in the network occasionally exchanges control messages with its neighbors to set up multi-bounce ways to some other hub in the network. Information bundles are sent between the hubs utilizing directing tables put away at every hub. Each routing table contains every one of the potential destinations from a hub to some other hub in the network and the number of jumps to every destination. The protocol has three principal ascribes: staying away from circles, determining the count-to-infinity problem, and decreasing high directing above. Every hub gives a succession number connected to each new routing table update message. It uses two unique routing table updates to limit the number of control messages scattered in the organization.

20.3.3 Dynamic Source Routing (DSR)

DSR also serves as a source-routing-based receptive directing mechanism. When using standardized methodology, the sender knows the complete path to the target. All of the routes have been kept in the route repository. The plan for protocols like AODV should be to stick to the states of a threatening climate to extend the sensor lifetime by introducing forwarder hubs. The most significant point of preference for DSR is that no intermittent steering parcels are needed. DSR can likewise deal with unidirectional connections. DSR does not require infrequent boxes of any nature at every tier inside the network, unlike other protocols. The source of the packages decides and controls the route taken for its own packages, supporting features like load adjustment.

20.4 Simulation Tool and Performance Metrics

The test system apparatus used for compatibility examination of AODV, DSDV, and DSR conventions in NS-2. In light of the network, the test systems are proficient devices for breaking down different imperatives like directing, and protocols in a network, whether wired or remote. Table 20.1 shows the simulation boundaries.

Various execution measurements investigate the performance of the recreated results. Such quantitative estimation is valuable as an essential for surveying or assessing the exhibition of a network or even looking at the performance utilizing different routing protocols. The accompanying performance measurements are used in this review.

Energy Consumption – The energy model addresses the energy level of hubs in the framework. The energy model portrayed in a hub has an early worth, which is the degree of energy the hub has toward the recreation's beginning. The energy level of a network is still up by adding the whole hub's energy level to the network.

A. Packet Delivery Ratio: The packet delivery ratio is the total percentage of total packets sent in unit time.

B. Throughput: Throughput is the all-out parcels effectively conveyed to individual destinations throughout absolute time separated by all-out time.

TABLE 20.1

Simulation Results

Attributes	Value
Simulator	NETWORK SIMULATOR
Simulation time	100 ms
No. of nodes	30, 35, 40, 50, 100
Routing protocols	AODV, DSDV, DSR
Traffic type	UDP

C. Routing Overhead: Directing overhead is the total number of guiding groups sent over the framework and is imparted in bits or bundles consistently.

20.5 Simulation Results

In this part, we analyze the steering conventions presentation in light of the findings from simulated tests on directing protocols. The primary purpose of this study is to assess the expression and conduct of each routing convention regarding the impact of fluctuating the number of hubs for two different applications, for example, video conferencing and email. The outcomes depend on assessment measurements of deferral, load, media access postponement, throughput, and retransmission attempts. We have isolated our review into five arrangements of examinations: The first set examines the performance of three protocols over 30 nodes, whereas the following groups have 35, 40, 50, and 100 nodes. The main results are discussed at the end of the results metrics.

20.5.1 Energy Consumption

Figures 20.1–20.5 show the results for five different sets. These results provide the simulation scenarios for 30, 35, 40, 50, and 100 nodes, thus generating energy consumption by adding nodes at different techniques.

20.5.2 Packet Delivery

Figures 20.6–20.10 show the results for five different sets. These results provide the simulation scenarios for 30, 35, 40, 50, and 100 nodes and thus give the results of packet delivery by adding nodes at different systems.

20.5.3 Throughput

Figures 20.11–20.15 show the results for five different sets. These results provide the simulation scenarios for 30, 35, 40, 50, and 100 nodes, thus giving the results of throughput by adding nodes at different systems.

20.5.4 Overhead

Figures 20.16–20.20 show the results for five different sets. These results provide the simulation scenarios for 30, 35, 40, 50, and 100 nodes and thus give the results of throughput by adding nodes at different methods.

Thus, the comparative analysis of AODV, DSDV, and DSR from the above results is discussed in Table 20.2.

In scenario 1, AODV with 30 nodes showed a high energy consumed, average packet delivery ratio, average throughput, and high routing overhead. In contrast, DSDV with 30 nodes showed a high energy consumed, average packet delivery ratio, average throughput, and high routing overhead. DSR with 30 nodes showed a high energy consumed, average packet delivery ratio, average throughput, and high routing overhead.

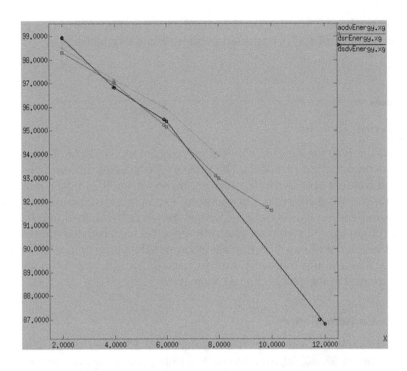

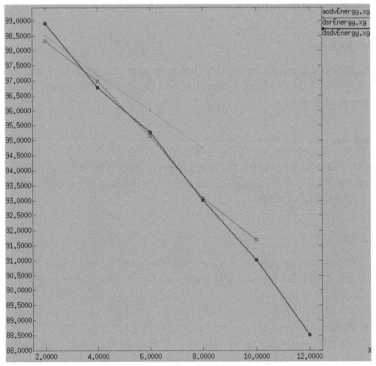

FIGURE 20.1
Energy consumption in five different experimental sets: (20.1) 30 nodes, (20.2) 35 nodes, (20.3) 40 nodes, (20.4) 50 nodes, and (20.5) 100 nodes.

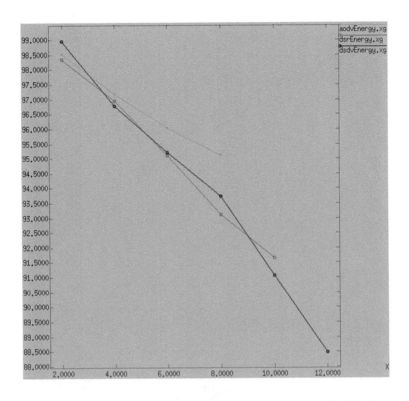

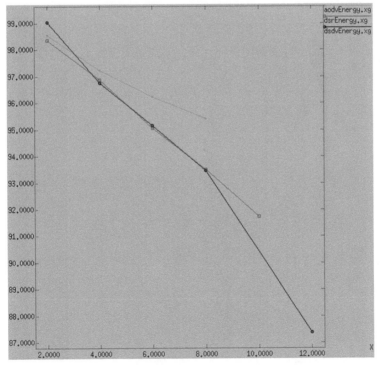

FIGURE 20.1
Continued

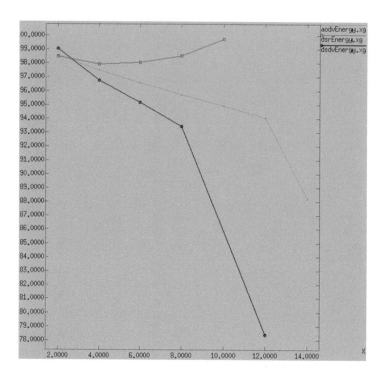

FIGURE 20.1
Continued

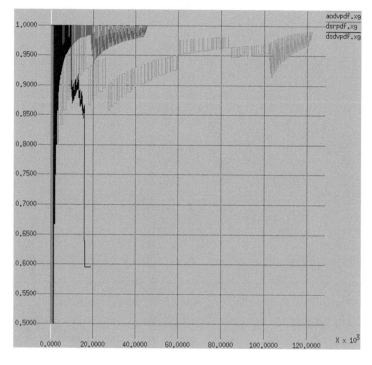

FIGURE 20.2
Packet delivery in five different experimental sets: (20.6) 30 nodes, (20.7) 35 nodes, (20.8) 40 nodes, (20.9) 50 nodes, and (20.10) 100 nodes.

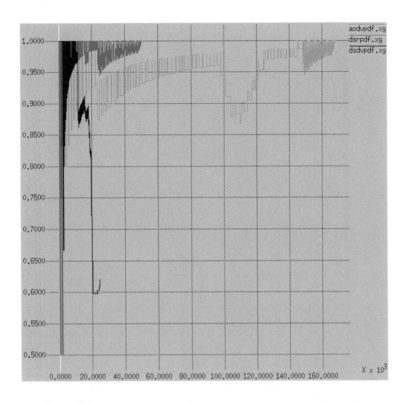

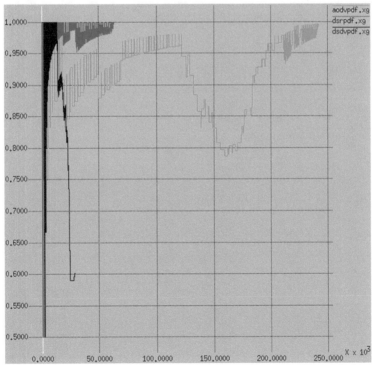

FIGURE 20.2
Continued

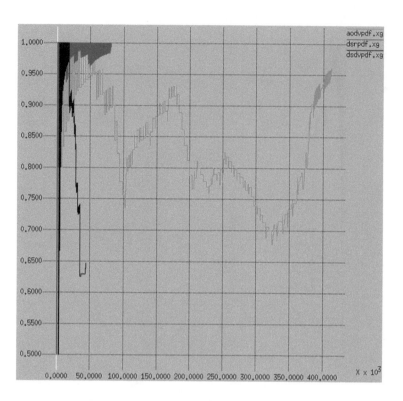

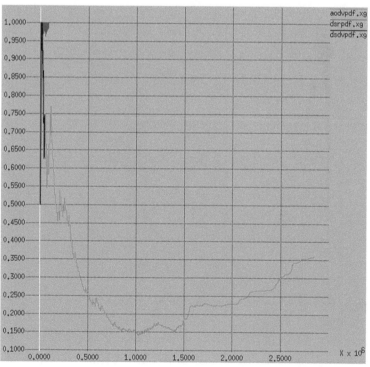

FIGURE 20.2
Continued

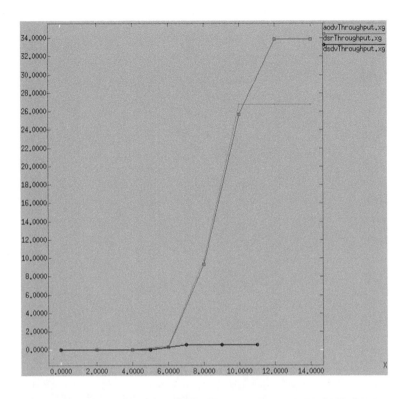

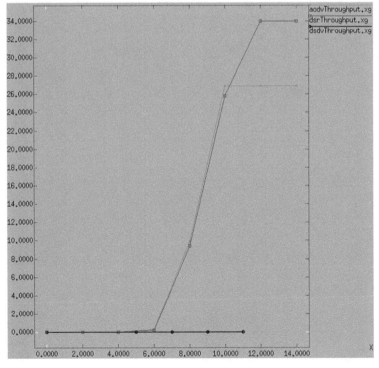

FIGURE 20.3
Throughput in five different experimental sets: (20.11) 30 nodes, (20.12) 35 nodes, (20.13) 40 nodes, (20.14) 50 nodes, and (20.15) 100 nodes.

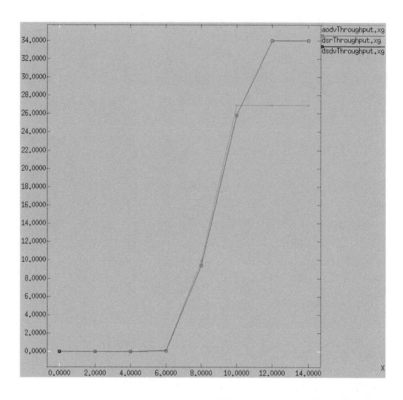

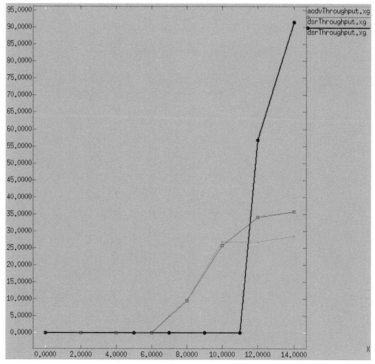

FIGURE 20.3
Continued

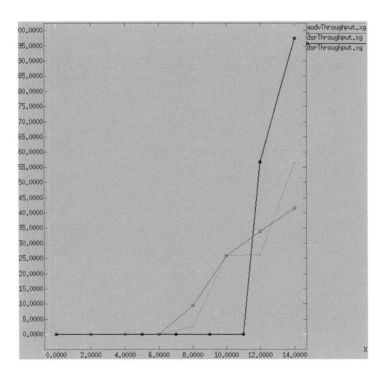

FIGURE 20.3
Continued

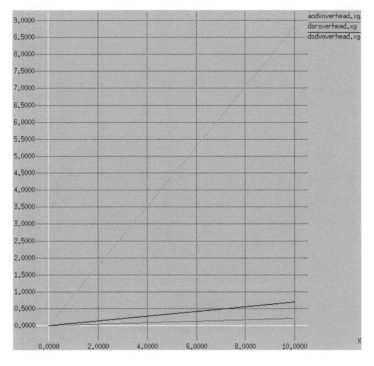

FIGURE 20.4
Overhead in five different experimental sets: (20.16) 30 nodes, (20.17) 35 nodes, (20.18) 40 nodes, (20.19) 50 nodes, and (20.20) 100 nodes.

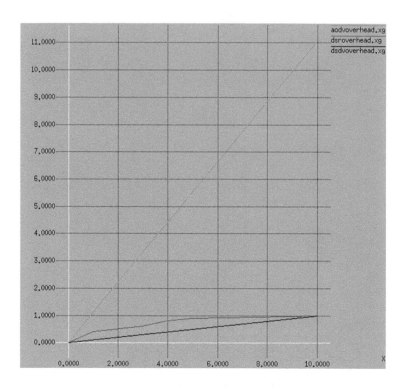

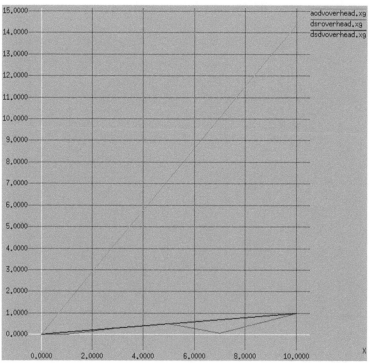

FIGURE 20.4
Continued

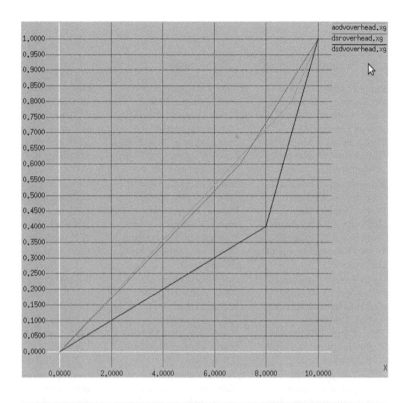

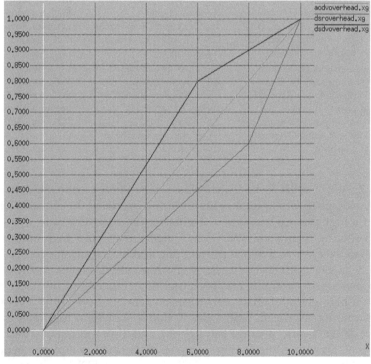

FIGURE 20.4
Continued

TABLE 20.2

Simulation Result

Scenario	AODV	DSDV	DSR
Scenario 1 (30 nodes)	Higher Energy Consumed (93% approx.), Average Packet Delivery Ratio (99% approx.), Average Throughput (26% approx.), Higher Routing Overhead (9% approx.)	Lower Energy Consumed (86% approx.), Lower Packet Delivery Ratio (59% approx.), Lower Throughput (0.7% approx.), Lower Routing Overhead (0.6 % approx.)	Average Energy Consumed (91% approx.), Higher Packet Delivery Ratio (100% approx.), Higher Throughput (33% approx.), Lower Routing Overhead (0.2 % approx.)
Scenario 2 (35 nodes)	Higher Energy Consumed (94% approx.), Higher Packet Delivery Ratio (100% approx.), Average Throughput (27% approx.), Higher Routing Overhead (12% approx.)	Lower Energy Consumed (88% approx.), Lower Packet Delivery Ratio (62% approx.), Lower Throughput (0.8% approx.), Lower Routing Overhead (1% approx.)	Average Energy Consumed (91% approx.), Higher Packet Delivery Ratio (100% approx.), Higher Throughput (34% approx.), Lower Routing Overhead (1% approx.)
Scenario 3 (40 nodes)	Higher Energy Consumed (95% approx.), Average Packet Delivery Ratio (99% approx.), Average Throughput (27% approx.), Higher Routing Overhead (15% approx.)	Lower Energy Consumed (88% approx.), Lower Packet Delivery Ratio (60% approx.), Lower Throughput (0.9% approx.), Lower Routing Overhead (1% approx.)	Average Energy Consumed (91% approx.), Higher Packet Delivery Ratio (100% approx.), Higher Throughput (34% approx.), Lower Routing Overhead (1% approx.)
Scenario 4 (50 nodes)	Higher Energy Consumed (95% approx.), Lower packet delivery Ratio (96% approx.), Average Throughput (28% approx.), Higher Routing Overhead (1% approx.)	Lower Energy Consumed (87% approx.), Average packet delivery Ratio (64% approx.), Higher Throughput (91% approx.), Lower Routing Overhead (1% approx.)	Average Energy Consumed (91% approx.), Higher packet delivery Ratio (100% approx.), Higher Throughput (35% approx.), Lower Routing Overhead (1% approx.)
Scenario 5 (100 nodes)	Average Energy Consumed (88% approx.), Lower Packet Delivery Ratio (35% approx.), Average Throughput (56% approx.), Lower Routing Overhead (1% approx.)	Lower Energy Consumed (78% approx.), Average Packet Delivery Ratio (74% approx.), Higher Throughput (97% approx.), Lower Routing Overhead (1% approx.)	Higher Energy Consumed (99% approx.), Higher Packet Delivery Ratio (100% approx.), Higher Throughput (41% approx.), Lower Routing Overhead (1% approx.)

In scenario 2, AODV with 35 nodes showed a high energy consumed, average packet delivery ratio, average throughput, and high routing overhead. In contrast, DSDV with 35 nodes showed a high energy consumed, average packet delivery ratio, average throughput, and high routing overhead. DSR with 35 nodes showed a high energy consumed, average packet delivery ratio, average throughput, and high routing overhead.

In scenario 3, AODV with 40 nodes showed a high energy consumed, average packet delivery ratio, average throughput, and high routing overhead. In contrast, DSDV with 40 nodes showed a high energy consumed, average packet delivery ratio, average throughput, and high routing overhead. DSR with 40 nodes showed a high energy consumed, average packet delivery ratio, average throughput, and high routing overhead.

In scenario 4, AODV with 50 nodes performs the higher energy and packet delivery ratio. In contrast, DSR has average compared to AODV whereas DSDV has average energy and higher throughput, and DSDV has average energy consumed and packet delivery ratio.

In scenario 5, AODV with 100 nodes performs the average energy and lower packet delivery ratio. In contrast, DSR has moderate compared to AODV, whereas DSDV has average energy and higher throughput, and DSDV has average energy consumed and packet delivery ratio.

20.6 Conclusion

This chapter presented a pursuance investigation of three routing protocols described concerning their energy utilization, bundle conveyance proportion, and throughput and steering above. All these metrics address the reliability of protocols.

Reactive routing protocol DSR execution is the optimum considering its capacity to keep up association by occasional trade of information, which is needed for DSDV-based movement. Regarding packet delivery fraction and routing overhead, DSR performs better than DSDV and AODV with a varied number of nodes. Hence for real-time traffic, DSR is preferred over DSDV. Also, AODV works on the principle of choosing the shortest and fastest path. The packet delivery fraction AODV and DSR can work well in specific scenarios where routing Overhead is not a priority criterion. DSR is the best protocol for low-capacity links. DSR is the opposite of AODV because its performance is best when DSDV does not perform well. One similarity in both protocols is that both had the same performance in routing overhead. DSR outperforms DSDV at high-speed mobility under medium and heavy network conditions. In terms of metrics like routing overhead and packet delivery ratio, DSDV performs poorly.

Bibliography

Downard I., "Simulating sensor networks in ns-2". In *Proceedings of International Conference on Wireless Communications, Networking and Mobile Computing*, pp. 2918–2921, 2009.

Flyd S., Jacobon V., Li C.G., McCane S., Zhag L., "A reliable multicast framework for light-weight sessions and application level framing". *IEEE Transactions on Networking*, 1997.

Johnson D.B., Maltz D.A., "Dynamic source routing in Ad Hoc wireless networks". *International Journal on Mobile Computing*, Vol. 353, Kluwer Academic, 1996.

Johnson D.B., Maltz D.A., Hu Y.-C., "The dynamic source routing protocol for mobile Ad Hoc networks (DSR)". Internet Draft, Draft-Ietf-Manet-Dsr-09.Txt, 2003.

Jutao H., Jingjing Z., Minglu L., "Energy level and link state aware AODV route request forwarding mechanism research". *Transactions on Communications*, pp. 292–299, 2009.

Kukreja V., Sakshi, "Machine learning models for mathematical symbol recognition: A stem to stern literature analysis". *Multimedia Tools and Applications*, 81, pp. 28651–28687, 2022. https://doi.org/10.1007/s11042-022-12644-2.

Le S.J., Royr E.M., Perkns C.E., "Scalability study of the Ad Hoc on-demand distance vector routing protocol". *ACM Wiley International Journal of Network Management*, Vol. 13, Issue 2, pp. 97–114, 2003.

Li Z., Gupta B., "A modified shared-tree multicast routing protocol in Ad Hoc network". *Journal of Computing and Information Technology*, Vol. 13, Issue 3, pp. 177–193, 2005.

Manjla S.H., Abhilsh C.N., Shila K., Vengopal K.R., Patnak L.M., "Performance of AODV routing protocol using group and entity mobility models in wireless sensor networks". In *Proceedings of International Multiconference of Engineers and Computer Scientists*, Vol. 2, Hong Kong, 2008.

Meng L., Fu W., Xu Z., Zhang J., Hua J., "A novel Ad Hoc routing protocol based on mobility prediction". *International Conference on Information Technology*, Vol. 7, Issue 3, pp. 537–540, 2008.

Naito K., Mori K., Kobayashi H., *Evaluation of Power-Aware Routing for Sensor Networks with Forwarder Nodes*.

Sakshi, Kukreja V., "Image segmentation techniques: Statistical, comprehensive, semi-automated analysis and an application perspective analysis of mathematical expressions". *Archives of Computational Methods in Engineering*, 30(1), pp. 457–495, 2023. https://doi.org/10.1007/s11831 -022-09805-9.

Yang Y., Chen H., "An improved AODV routing protocol for MANETs". In *Proceedings of International Conference on Wireless Communications, Networking and Mobile Computing*, pp. 2918–2921, 2009.

21

Enhancing Rating and Learning through Clustering in Artificial Intelligence

Ekta and Varsha

21.1 Introduction

AI Society 5.0 is a vision for the future of society in which AI and other advanced technologies are fully integrated into all aspects of life, from work and education to healthcare and transportation. It is the next stage in the evolution of human civilization, building on the previous four societal stages. Societal development and artificial intelligence (AI) are interrelated in many ways. AI has the potential to transform our societies by enabling the development of intelligent machines that can perform tasks that are beyond human capabilities. This can lead to new opportunities and innovations that can significantly impact our daily lives. However, AI also raises concerns about how it will affect society, such as job displacement and privacy concerns. Artificial intelligence has the potential to significantly contribute to societal development in various areas such as healthcare, education, transportation, and environmental sustainability. For instance, AI-powered healthcare tools can assist doctors in diagnosing illnesses and providing personalized treatments.

A decision tree is a machine learning and data mining model to predict outcomes by mapping decisions and their possible consequences. It is a tree-like graph or model of decisions and their possible consequences, including chance event outcomes, resource costs, and utility. They work by recursively partitioning the data into smaller and smaller subsets based on a series of binary decisions, ultimately arriving at a prediction for the target variable.

Clustering is a technique used in machine learning and data analysis to group similar data points together based on their characteristics or features. The goal of clustering is to find meaningful patterns or structures in the data, without being told what those patterns or structures should be in advance. In clustering, a set of data points are divided into groups or clusters based on their similarity. The similarity between data points is determined by comparing their features or attributes. There are many algorithms used in clustering, such as K-means, hierarchical clustering, and density-based clustering (Table 21.1).

The ratings and success rate of a film can be predicted using the models and procedures. This approach substantially aids in the growth of enterprises. These forecasts can be used by a variety of stakeholders, including actors, producers, directors, etc., to help them make better choices. The goal of the proposed work is to create a model using AI methods that could analyze and visualize the movie's rating while lowering the degree of content ambiguity. For commercial development, the technology aids in the analysis and visualization of movie ratings. Hollywood has a significant influence because over 100

DOI: 10.1201/9781003397052-21

TABLE 21.1

A Literature Review of the Papers

S. No.	Title of Paper	Year of Publication	Authors	Brief Understanding of the Paper
1	Data mining for analyzing and predicting the movie	2021	Kai Yan	This project provides the potential method that can be used to extract information to help analyze the movies and help make decisions.
2	A predictor for movie success	2020	Jeffrey Ericson and Jesse Grodman	Predict five different measures of success, based solely on what we know about a movie before its debut.
3	A data mining approach to the analysis and prediction of movie ratings	2019	M. Saraee, S. White, and J. Eccleston	Found that the IMDb is difficult to perform data mining upon, due to the format of the source data.
4	Principles of data mining	2020	Bramer	The supervised learning method is adopted, which is based on the notion of being able to predict an unknown attribute.
5	Pre-release prediction of crowd opinion on movies by label distribution learning	2016	Xin Geng and Peng Hou	The basic idea of LDSVR is to fit a sigmoid function to each component of the label distribution simultaneously by a multi-output support vector machine.
6	Prediction of movies popularity using machine learning techniques	2022	Muhammad Hassan Latif and Hammad Afzal	This paper created a dataset and then transformed it and applied machine learning approaches to build efficient models that can predict the popularity of the movie.
7	The saga of Kashmiri Pandit genocide	2021	Council, A. and Say, W. E.	This paper is all about the aspects of the movie Kashmiri Pandits by telling how genocide is done.
8	A massive 7T fMRI dataset to bridge cognitive neuroscience and artificial intelligence	2022	Allen, E. J., St-Yves, G., Wu, Y., Breedlove, J. L., Prince, J. S., Dowdle, L. T., …, and Kay, K.	This project provides the potential method that can be used to extract information to help analyze the movies, predict their success, and help make decisions.
9	Machine learning methods for predicting the popularity of movies	2022	Oyewola, D. O., and Dada, E. G	This project provides the potential method that can be used to extract information to help analyze the movies, predict their success, and help make decisions.
10	Suryani's struggles to prove harassment in the Mata Hari theatre group on movie copier light	2022	Damayanti, K., Ningrum, A. H., Barus, I. R. G., and Bernadtua, M.	This paper adopts the supervised learning method, used for predicting either discrete attributes with a finite number of distinct values or categories through classification or continuous numerical attributes through what is known as regression

countries import Hollywood dramas, plays, movies, and animations (of any type). This study employs analytical approaches like Classification (Decision tree), Clustering, and Regression (K-means). The Extraction, Transformation, Loading (ETL) method is used for transformation, and graphs and charts are used for visualization. The goal is to provide a precise model that can be used for model analysis and visualization.

21.2 Straightforward Approach

The approach to viewer rating prediction is very straightforward and can be easily applied by anyone. Movie prediction requires more experience, because of its dependency on the user to be able to interpret the different visualizations of the data in the right way and infer the right conclusions from it. Visual analytics will become more and more integrated into our lives for the great possibilities it enables. The human mind is very intelligent for extracting information from visualizations and thus can analyze data quicker and more complexly.

21.3 Proposed Implementation

The methodology for the implementation consists of five major components:

1. Data Collection
2. Data Cleaning
3. Data Transformation
4. Data Analysis
5. Data Visualization

By cleaning the dataset and discarding irrelevant data from the MovieLens dataset as well as through a detailed study of the dataset, we get the attributes that can affect the analysis and visualization of the rating of a movie. The textual data is transferred to numeric data and converted into a CSV format. Different decision tree algorithms are then studied so that the best-suited algorithm according to our problem could be determined. The best-suited algorithm should be the one that gives the most accuracy and the least error. The test data when tested according to the algorithm should give as accurate results as possible.

21.3.1 Data Collection

The raw MovieLens dataset is collected from the GroupLens website in a zipped form. This zipped file consists of the CSV files and one text file. This dataset describes five-star rating and free-text tagging activity from [MovieLens] (http://movielens.org), a movie recommendation service. It contains 100,836 ratings and 3683 tag applications across 9742 movies. The data are contained in the files "links.csv," "movies.csv," "ratings.csv," and "tags.csv." The text file consists of further information about the dataset. The collected data is further organized into the proper format for cleaning, transformation purpose, analysis, and visualization. The data is organized as movie id, title, genre, tag, and ratings in a tabular format of about 10,000+ rows.

21.3.2 Data Cleaning

The collected data was imported in the RapidMiner and is cleaned here using TurboPrep to reduce the size. Here several techniques were applied to the data set to make it more efficient and effective for analysis and visualization. Some of the Data Cleaning Techniques in RapidMiner include Replace Missings, Auto Cleansing, PCA, Remove Duplicates, Normalization, Discretization, and removing low quality.

21.3.3 Data Transformation

The transformation was applied to the cleansed data for further clarification. The types of transformation that we applied to the data are Rename, Change type, Remove, Copy, Filter, Range, Sample, Sort, Replace, and Split. These were applied to data for better understanding, analysis, and visualization of the ratings for movies.

21.3.4 Data Analysis

The transformed data is then used for Analysis. There are different ways of Analyzing the data like Classification like K-NN, Naive Bayes, Linear regression, and Decision tree; Clustering like K-means, Agglomerative, DBSCAN, etc. This chapter represents the Analysis based on the Decision tree and K-means clustering. A Decision tree is a helpful analysis technique. In this, the hierarchical tree is formed to decide if this will be the result. In K-means clustering, the dataset is given to the cluster model and after this, the clusters are formed.

This image shows the decision tree for predicting the rating of the movies. It follows the IF-THEN RULE. If Movie Rating>3,500->if Movie Rating>4,500||<=4,500->Drama||Comedy. Similarly, if Movie rating<=3,500->Movieid>15||<=15->Action, Crime, Thriller. If Movie Id>105,500->||<=105,500->Movie Rating || movieid, and so on. This is a tree-like structure having parent and child nodes. The parent node is also called the root node, and the child nodes are leaves. In the end, if Movieid >99 || <=99, then the movie can be comedy || comedy, drama, or romance. All these depend upon the data we are passing and should be cleaned and in the proper format. This is the correct way of analyzing the data using the decision tree. The final results are stored in the leaf nodes or the child and are the accurate ones.

Clustering is an unsupervised learning technique. A technique for arranging the data points into various clusters made up of related data points. The items with potential similarity continue to be in a group that shares little to no similarity with another group. K-mean clustering is one of the clustering methods. Unsupervised learning algorithm K-means clustering divides the unlabeled dataset into various clusters. Here, K specifies how many pre-defined clusters must be produced as part of the process; for example, if K=2, there will be two clusters, if K=3, there will be three clusters, and so on. It is an iterative technique that separates the unlabeled dataset into k distinct clusters so that each dataset only belongs to one group with a similar set of characteristics. This image shows the clustering process or K-means clustering process analysis. There are five clusters, namely Cluster 0, Cluster 1, Cluster 2, Cluster 3, and Cluster 4. For Cluster 0 Movie Id is average, i.e., 81.65%, and hence Movie rating is 7.57%. For Cluster 1 Movie Id is average, i.e., 82.21%, and hence Movie rating is 7.03%. Similarly, for Cluster 2 Movie rating is 5.68% and the Movie Id is 3.95% and is the average one.

21.3.5 Data Visualization

The last step is to visualize the analyzed data. This can be done using graphs and charts. Different graphs and charts are used in this chapter to visualize the analysis like scatter/bubble plots, 3D plots, sunbursts, and cluster model visualizers. The main visualization is between Movie Id and Movie rating. The other visualization is between the Movie title and Movie rating. The graphs for the same are shown below.

Vertical bar graphs represent the data vertically. It is a graph whose bars are drawn vertically. There are two colors shown in the graph, which helps visualize the graph. The x-axis represents the Movie Id and the y-axis represents the Movie rating of the movies. For Movie Id 2, 3, 6, 8, 12, 15, 17, 18, 20, 24, 28, 36, 41, 43, 45, 47, 52, 54, 60, and 64 the color is light blue; for the rest of the Id, the color is dark blue. The different ratings are also there for these colors. For the light blue color, the rating lies between 2.7 and 4.0, and for the dark blue the color rating is high, which is 5.0.

21.4 Conclusion and Future Work

In the real world, models and mechanisms are used to predict the rating of any movie. This chapter proposes a model using artificial intelligence and machine learning techniques to analyze and visualize the movie's rating. An attempt is made to check the certainty by using the decision tree and analyzing the data using clustering (K-means) and transforming using the ETL process, and data visualization is done using graphs or charts.

From the Experiment results, we found that it is difficult to apply AI techniques to the data in the MovieLens dataset. It requires proper cleaning and integration, which consumed a large proportion of the time for this analysis. The source data could not be integrated easily. By using natural language processing techniques, the data can be integrated properly. For overcoming these problems, we performed some useful data mining techniques on the MovieLens data. Other interesting patterns can be identified by the same technique if the additional dataset is available. Further on, it might also be relevant to evaluate whether or not the prediction performance and results are generalizable over multiple datasets as well as over larger and smaller datasets to be able to draw more general conclusions, as the current experimental setup only incorporated a single but well-established dataset. Another possibility would naturally also be to include a wider range of algorithms and algorithm configurations, as the methods included in the current study were narrowed down to fit the given time frame.

This chapter gives the proposed model for movie's rating by using AI and ML techniques. RapidMiner is one of the tools used in this chapter to use AI and ML techniques at their best. The focus is on the methods, implementations, and utility with the basic conclusion that the movie rating depends upon the Movie Id, which is associated with a particular movie, and Movie Id further depends upon the budget, performance, and the concept of the movie. The better the performance, the better the rating of the movie.

Bibliography

1. Saraee, M. H., White, S., & Eccleston, J. (2004). A data mining approach to analysis and prediction of movie ratings. *Transactions of the Wessex Institute*, 343–352.
2. Meenakshi, K., Maragatham, G., Agarwal, N., & Ghosh, I. (2018). A data mining technique for analyzing and predicting the success of movie. In *Journal of Physics: Conference Series* (Vol. 1000, No. 1, p. 012100). IOP Publishing.
3. Yan, K. (2021). Data mining for analyzing and predicting the success of movies. https://doi.org/10.17615/jf46-j653.
4. Joshi, M., Das, D., Gimpel, K., & Smith, N. A. (2010). Movie reviews and revenues: An experiment in text regression. In *Human Language Technologies* (pp. 293–296).
5. Kumar, S., Mehta, A., & Pal, J. (2019). *Movie Success Prediction Using Data Mining*. Vellore Institute of Technology.
6. Jain, V. (2013). Prediction of movie success using sentiment analysis of tweets. *The International Journal of Soft Computing and Software Engineering*, 3(3), 308–313.
7. Litman, B. R. (1998). *Predicting Financial Success of Motion Pictures*. The Motion Picture Mega-Industry.
8. Latif, M. H., & Afzal, H. (2016). Prediction of movies popularity using machine learning techniques. *International Journal of Computer Science and Network Security (IJCSNS)*, 16(8), 127.
9. Sahni, V., Bala, M., & Kumar, M. (2021). Enhanced MSEEC routing protocol involving TABU search with static and mobile nodes in WSNS. *Recent Advances in Computer Science and Communications*, 14(4), 1321–1335.
10. Sahni, V., Srivastava, S., & Khan, R. (2021). Modelling techniques to improve the quality of food using artificial intelligence. *Journal of Food Quality*, 1–10.
11. Oyewola, D. O., & Dada, E. G. (2022). Machine learning methods for predicting the popularity of movies. *Journal of Artificial Intelligence and Systems*, 65–82.
12. Verganti, R., Vendraminelli, L., & Iansiti, M. (2020). Innovation and design in the age of artificial intelligence. *Journal of Product Innovation Management*, 37(3), 212–227.
13. Zhang, Z., Wang, M., & Geng, X. (2015). Crowd counting in public video surveillance by label distribution learning. *Neurocomputing*, 166, 151–163.
14. Kaur, G., Pooja, P., & Sahni, V. (2016). Improving differently-illuminant images with fuzzy membership based saturation weighting. *International Journal of Advanced Engineering, Management and Science*, 2(6), 239504.
15. Kshirsagar, P. R. (2022). Accrual and dismemberment of brain tumours using fuzzy interface and grey textures for image disproportion. *Computational Intelligence and Neuroscience*. doi: 10.1155/2022/2609387.
16. Ericson, J., & Goodman, J. (2013). *A Predictor for Movie Success*. CS229, Stanford University.
17. Lee, K., Park, J., Kim, I., & Choi, Y. (2018). Predicting movie success with machine learning techniques: Ways to improve accuracy. *Information Systems Frontiers*, 20(3), 577–588.
18. Shinde, S. V., Shastri, R., Dwivedi, A. K., Haldorai, A., Sahni, V., & Adusumalli, B. (2021). Multi sensor data and temporal image fusion cross validation technique for agri yield monitoring system. https://doi.org/10.21203/rs.3.rs-943821/v1
19. Kudagamage, U. P., Kumara, B. T., & Baduraliya, C. H. (2018). Data mining approach to analysis and prediction of movie success. In *1st International Conference on Business Innovation* (p. 55).
20. Ahmad, I. S., Bakar, A. A., Yaakub, M. R., & Muhammad, S. H. (2020). A survey on machine learning techniques in movie revenue prediction. *SN Computer Science*, 1(4), 1–14.
21. Amin Shahraki, Amir Taherkordi, Øystein Haugen, & Frank Eliassen (2020) Clustering objectives in wireless sensor networks: A survey and research direction analysis. *Computer Networks*, 180, p. 107376.ISSN 1389-1286, https://doi.org/10.1016/j.comnet.2020.107376
22. Allen, E. J., & Kay, K. (2022). A massive 7T fMRI dataset to bridge cognitive neuroscience and artificial intelligence. *Nature Neuroscience*, 25(1), 116–126.

23. Damayanti, K., Ningrum, A. H., Barus, I. R. G., & Bernadtua, M. (2022). *Suryani's Struggles to Prove Harassment in the Mata Hari Theatre Group on Movie Copier Light* (p. 110).

24. Gracia, A., Dara, C., Noviana, D. A., & Simanjuntak, M. B. (2022). Analysis of Implied Messages in the Film Sing 2, Directed By Garth Jennings. In: Undergraduate Students' National Seminar. (p. 1).

25. Wang, Z., Zhang, J., Ji, S., Meng, C., Li, T., & Zheng, Y. (2020). Predicting and ranking box office revenue of movies based on big data. *Information Fusion*, 60, 25–40.

26. Khan, A., Gul, M. A., Uddin, M. I., Ali Shah, S. A., Ahmad, S., Al Firdausi, M. D., & Zaindin, M. (2020). Summarizing online movie reviews: A machine learning approach to big data analytics. *Scientific Programming*, 2020, 1–14.

22

Aquatic Weed Mining Using Artificial Intelligence

Aviraj Datta, Lubhan Cherwoo, Htet Ne Oo, Nagendra Prabhu,
Saurav Kumar, Anupma Sharma, and Amol P. Bhondekar

22.1 Introduction

Artificial intelligence (AI) is much more than a scientific buzz, where data acquisition, efficient storage-retrieval mechanism, and analysis play a critical role in developing solutions. Artificial Intelligence (AI) is an enabling technology that can help to make abatement strategies for various contemporary environmental problems more efficiently. Particularly, in the area of real-time monitoring, the application of AI tools can facilitate scientific and data-driven decision-making. As a result of climate change, local weather patterns are becoming increasingly unpredictable and hence empirical model-based decision support systems are fast becoming redundant. Artificial intelligence-based tools enable faster and often real-time detection of a change in any given system. For example, early detection of the emergence of a new pest in an agro-climatic zone using AI-based surveillance can faster responses with suitable abatement strategies. Such early detections can greatly enhance our ability to contain its spread as well as help to optimize abatement strategies by suggesting effective pest-specific pesticide formulations while going through historical data archives of past precedents and considering local site-specific realities. Globally, sustainable utilization of resources has become the central theme of development goals in our strive toward a circular economy. Weed mining in this regard is an emerging area of research where the changing perspectives now increasingly see them as an untapped natural resource. In this chapter, the use of AI-enabled techniques has been presented, which can augment the capabilities as well as efficiency of the emerging weed mining techniques. The global scenario of aquatic weeds includes a vast array of floating, submerged, or semi-submerged aquatic macrophytes living in different aquatic ecosystems. These aquatic ecosystems based on their eco-environment can be broadly divided into lakes, dams, ponds, tanks, and canals of various categories. All these surface water bodies experience infestation of various aquatic weeds (e.g., *Hydrilla*, *Pistia*, *Salvinia*, *Vossia cuspidata*, etc.) seasonally or perennially, particularly in stretches or sections suffering from anthropogenic water pollution. Among the common aquatic weeds, water hyacinth infestation in particular has been a major contemporary environmental challenge. This invasive weed whose scientific name is *Pontederia crassipes* is regarded as one of the worst weeds. It has infested numerous water bodies across the globe with widespread adverse environmental and economic consequences. This native species of Amazonia forms dense, rapidly growing, and free-floating mats in stagnant or slow-moving nutrient-rich water bodies. These mats adversely impact the water quality, life forms, and livelihood dependent on these

DOI: 10.1201/9781003397052-22

infested water bodies. Physical removal attempts of the water hyacinth mat only provide temporary relief. Moreover, such removal methods are labor-intensive and expensive, particularly at large scale. Biological and chemical control of water hyacinth infestation has received only limited success in real time and at large scale. This chapter gives a brief overview of how AI (artificial intelligence) aided techniques can greatly increase the efficiency of the physical removal of water hyacinth mat as well as its valorization. Also, it includes a brief description of the concept of weed mining using the AI and machine learning approach.

22.2 Water Hyacinth Weed Infestation

Water hyacinth came to India as an ornamental plant from its native Amazonia and was introduced in the Calcutta Botanical Garden in the 1890s. Its weed potential was unknown. However, its rapid spread across the then undivided Bengal made people aware of its nuisance potential, and by 1914, the government gazettes of the then Narayanganj Chamber of Commerce mentioned the menace as of "sufficient importance" to bring it to the notice of the government's formally. As per a conservative estimate, in 1936 the hyacinth covered about 10,000 square kilometers in the Bengal Delta region. Water hyacinth infestation adversely impacted crop production in Bengal. Particularly the low-lying paddy cultivation in the Mymensingh, Khulna, Nasirnagar, Munshiganj, and Comilla districts suffered due to encroachment of the marshy low-lands by water hyacinth. The water hyacinth infestation also impacted inland navigation critical for the transport to low-lying paddy and jute fields. The damage estimated was about 15–20% for the Aman paddy in the year 1926. Ultimately, such wide-scale adverse impacts led to the Bengal Water Hyacinth Bill (1933) as it was reported that annual damage done by the water hyacinth in Bengal was about 60,000,000 pre-independence Indian rupees (1 Indian rupee was equivalent to about $4 then). The damage was of course more than the crop loss alone; the damage to fisheries has also been reported. A field-level public health official in the Malaria Research Unit in Bengal described how a water hyacinth mat covered with stagnant water provides an ideal habitat for the growth of mosquito larvae. The mats lower water temperature as well as give shelter from their natural enemies. Around the world particularly in the frost-free zones widespread infestation of this aquatic weed, which used to be considered as an ornamental plant once, in surface water bodies has become a contemporary reality. Particularly, in tropical and subtropical regions, the weed exhibits a rapid growth rate and resurgence potential (Villamagna & Murphy, 2010). Rapidly growing water hyacinth mats cover the entire surfaces of eutrophicated water bodies and limit sunlight penetration as well as natural aeration. The rapid uptake of nutrients by water hyacinth limits the nutrient availability for other native aquatic vegetation and planktons. As a combined impact, an infested water body experiences reduced sub-surface photosynthetic activity, lower dissolved oxygen concentration, and depletion of nutrient availability for the natural flora and fauna (Mailu, 2001). Water hyacinth infestation hence is a threat to the natural biodiversity of the infested water bodies. Water hyacinth absorbs carbon dioxide from the atmosphere through photosynthesis and the organic carbon gets released from the decaying water hyacinth mat at the end of its life cycle, which increases the biological oxygen demand (BOD) concentration in these ponds. Such high-level BOD concentration adversely impacts pisciculture activities; hence, historically water hyacinth infestation has severely impacted the live-lihood of those dependent on inland fisheries (Honlah, Segbefia, et al., 2019). As water hyacinth mats decay at the end of their life cycle, they release nutrients rapidly into the water. Such in situ release of nutrients fosters the growth of young water hyacinth plants and perpetuates the infestation cycle. It is worth mentioning that water hyacinth can reproduce both sexually and asexually, and its seeds remain viable in the benthic sludge for more than 20 years! Hence, physical removal of the water hyacinth mats does pro-vide only temporary relief as new plants start appearing from submerged seeds under conducive conditions. Water hyacinth infestation of water bodies adversely impacts the livelihoods of those living nearby (Ezama, 2019). Water hyacinth infestation invariably reduces the velocity of the water current, making it a more conducive breeding ground for mosquitoes and other disease-causing pests and vectors (Tewabe, 2015). Water hya-cinth mats increase snails, which serve as a vector for the parasite of Schistosomiasis (Borokini & Babalola, 2012).

Water hyacinth infestation is a major challenge for paddy fields in the lowlands of Vembanand, Kerala. At the onset of each sowing season, farmers undertake physical removal of water hyacinth mats with human labor or chemical control of water hyacinth mats by spraying herbicides. Needless to say, such ad hoc measures provide only tempo-rary relief and of course increase the cost of cultivation as well as the drudgery of these farmers (Janko et al., 2015). Furthermore, the roots of water hyacinth plants make the soil compact and difficult to plow. Many times, boats along the narrow water channels con-necting the low-lying water-logged paddy fields are the only mode of transport (Honlah, Appiah, et al., 2019). Infestation hampers fisheries in many ways. Apart from adverse impact on water quality and damage to the propellers of the fishing boats, the mats make casting fishing nets difficult and often lead to damage of fishing gears (Honlah, Appiah, et al., 2019). The thick mats of water hyacinth increase water loss from the water surface (Sasaqi et al., 2019).

Researchers have reported that the evapotranspiration rate from these mats increases the water loss as compared to evaporation from a free water body (Rashed, 2014). Needless to mention that such water loss will disrupt water-dependent industries such as hydro-power projects (Firehun et al., 2014), irrigation planning, and livelihood opportunities in the catchment area of these water bodies (Arp et al., 2017).

22.3 Track Record of Abatement Strategies

Ever since the weed potential of water hyacinth, which was initially perceived as an ornamental plant because of its lilac color flowers, became apparent, numerous efforts have been made to achieve its eradication from infested water bodies. Physical removal of the mat involves in situ cutting and harvesting using manual or mechanical means. Particularly, this is carried out routinely for navigation channels and in-land surface water bodies to clear up the water surfaces for boat traffic and fishing activities (Moyo et al., 2013). Physical removal of water hyacinth mat may involve drainage of the infested water body or pulling the mat using nets (Patel, 2012). Recently for large swaths of infested stretches, the use of mechanical harvester or crusher boats is becoming popu-lar. Often a significant portion of the mat sinks to the bottom of the water body and its in situ decomposition further deteriorates its water quality (Wassie, 2014). Physical removal methods, though only provide temporary relief and are costly, are often preferred when immediate cleaning of the water surface is desired. It is also preferred for the removal of water hyacinths by hand pulling from shallow parts of an infested water body where people can easily walk in (Moyo et al., 2013). Physical removal of water hyacinth is preferred in locations where manual labor is inexpensive (Gutiérrez et al., 2001). Generally, harvested mats are left near the water body, and the decomposition of the harvested biomass causes odor nuisance in its vicinity. However, large-scale utilization of water hyacinth biomass harvested from infested water bodies for making nutrient-rich compost has recently been reported in the Puri district of Odisha, India. Application of herbicides such as glyphosate is common to curb water hyacinth infestation in paddy fields of Kerala. Such chemical control methods can control the spread of the water hyacinth quickly and efficiently over a large area at a relatively lower cost compared to physical removal methods. However, chemical control methods remain effective for a short period and often result in adverse impacts on the aquatic environment (Oyedeji & Abowei, 2012). The potential adverse impact of herbicides and other poisonous synthetic chemical compounds on marine life often prohibits their application in coastal water bodies or estuaries (Villamagna & Murphy, 2010). Application of biological control methods has been reported for water hyacinth in recent decades (Coetzee et al., 2017). These methods explore the potential use of natural enemies of water hyacinth to suppress the rapid growth of water hyacinth mats (Bownes et al., 2013). Biological control measures involve the release of moths, fungi, and weevils into the ecosystem, which feed off water hyacinth plants (Jernelöv, 2017). The long gestation period has been a major bottleneck for such control measures as it can take many years to reach a substantial predator population in a non-native ecosystem (Villamagna & Murphy, 2010). It is worth mentioning that the release of a non-native species of moth or weevil needs careful scientific planning and careful assessment to eliminate the risk of any potential adverse impact on the entire ecosystem. The release of any new species must not lead to a new environmental challenge in itself. In South Africa, a weevil, *Neochetina eichhorniae* Warner, which was released to provide biological control of water hyacinth infestation, has shown moderate success in periodic yearly assessments conducted recently (Cilliers, 1991). However, the effectiveness of biological control is often linked to the nutrient status of the lake and other ambient factors such as water temperature. Some researchers reported that a combination of low-nutrient waters with higher temperatures would hamper the efficacy of these agents (Bownes et al., 2013). Their results suggest that the negative impact of the herbivorous insects on the aquatic weed would be most effective on rapidly growing water hyacinth mats associated with mesotrophic and eutrophic levels of nutrients in water particularly in temperate areas. Biological control methods that use water hyacinth-specific highly selective predators can efficiently eliminate an existing water hyacinth mat. However, such predators tend to get eliminated along with the water hyacinth mats. As water hyacinth mats keep remerging from the benthic seed deposits under a conducive environment, the biological control measures may require repeated inoculation. In recent decades, it has become increasingly apparent that apart from the physical or chemical or biological abatement strategies there has been an emphasis on the social abatement strategy as well. Involving the local stakeholder and effective awareness generation will help to optimize long-term sustainable abatement strategies taking into account their traditional know-how. Researchers studying aquatic weed infestation in Lake Victoria highlighted the contributions of the various agencies involved in the control process in an inclusive approach (Honlah et al., 2022; (Figures 22.1 and 22.2).

FIGURE 22.1
Water hyacinth-infested canals in Alappuzha, Kerala, India.

FIGURE 22.2
Clogging of water channels by water hyacinth mats in Alappuzha, Kerala, India.

22.4 Potential Use of Water Hyacinth Biomass

The challenges associated with different water hyacinth abatement methods outlined in the previous section highlight that its complete eradication may not be a sustainable long-term strategy. Efficient harvesting and utilization of biomass by adopting a financially self-sustaining model instead should be the strategy adopted (Prabhu, 2016). Periodic manual harvesting and valorization of the harvested biomass as a business model involving rural youth offers an effective low-cost and long-term abatement strategy. Such waste-to-wealth initiatives can be suitably aided by relevant government schemes and would provide alternative livelihoods in the rural hinterlands of India. The nutrient-rich harvested water hyacinth will be amenable to composting as cellulose and hemicellulose constitute 58.6% of the biomass (Datta et al., 2022). The compost prepared would be a good soil supplement particularly for sandy soil by maintaining high residual moisture concentration due to its hygroscopic nature and moisture retention capacity (Agarwal et al., 2016). The use of this biomass has been reported for paper making, biofuel production, and fish feed fodder production. Potential use as feed for ruminants was highlighted by Akinwande et al. (2013). The nutrient-rich biomass has reuse potential as creature feed particularly in developing countries suffering from sufficiently diverse dietary supplements (Jafari, 2010). Freshwater hyacinths cooked with rice grain, vegetable waste, and copra cake are utilized as feed for pigs, ducks, and lake fish in Southeast Asian countries such as Thailand, Malaysia, and the Philippines (Malik, 2007a). It is to be noted that water hyacinth has bioaccumulation potential for several common heavy metals from polluted water bodies. Hence, the water hyacinth harvested from water bodies receiving industrial effluent should not be considered for reuse as a soil conditioning agent. However, a vast array of handicrafts can be made using such biomass in suitable combinations with coconut coir, jute, or other materials. Recently, this biomass has been used for preparing colorful handbags in Assam with support from the Assam Livelihood Mission (Barua et al., 2018). The colors from the water hyacinth flowers can be extracted and used as organic dyes (Gopika et al., 2018). The high growth rate of water hyacinth triggered research on its potential use for biofuel production. This being grown on water surface, unlike terrestrial macrophytes, does not compete with food crops for agricultural land (Bhattacharya & Kumar, 2010). Water hyacinth biomass can also be used as mushroom cultivation media (Chen et al., 2010; Kumar et al., 2014). Utilization of water hyacinth biomass has been reported for preparing special cements as superplasticizer (Alagu et al., 2019). Cellulase production by native bacteria using water hyacinth as substrate under solid-state fermentation has also been reported (G. N. Prabhu & Kurup, 2012; Suresh Chandra Kurup et al., 2005). The benefits of water hyacinth for Southern Africa and its potential for the production of energy through anaerobic digestion have been extensively reviewed by Ilo et al. (2020, 2021).

22.5 Factors Affecting Scale-Up of Water Hyacinth Biomass Utilization

Despite the known potential of water hyacinth biomass and wide-scale recognition of it being a major contemporary global environmental problem, large-scale efforts to utilize water hyacinth biomass are scarce. The following are the main reasons that contribute to this situation.

22.5.1 Lack of Awareness

There is a real lack of awareness about the possible usage of water hyacinth biomass. The wealth of knowledge available at academia in this regard has not been transmitted to relevant stakeholders effectively enough. Particularly, the population living near large water hyacinth-infested surface water bodies all their life often remain unaware of the potential use of this biomass.

22.5.2 Absence of Focused Capacity Building

Many of the potential uses of water hyacinth biomass are simple and do not require high-skill, chemical, or energy-intensive technology. Appropriate capacity building can make rural communities self-reliant on these waste-to-wealth interventions. The absence of focused training and workshops has hindered the realization of the usage potential of nutrient-rich water hyacinth biomass.

22.5.3 No Incentivization

Water hyacinth provides a good substrate for making plates, cups, portraits, egg crates, pens, etc. Such initiatives need incentivization from appropriate authorities along with adequate publicity. Rampant use of plastic-based products is seen all around us. There is a need to put in place appropriate and effective restraining measures such as the ban on single-use plastic items to boost the sale of these eco-friendly alternatives.

22.5.4 Lack of Applied Multi-disciplinary Research

Handicrafts and art-crafts are made with many natural fibers such as jute, coconut coir, paddy straw, etc. Often specialized organizations working on any of these fibers work in silos and suffer from tunnel vision. As a result, the potential of handcrafts and art-crafts which can be made by suitably mixing these natural fibers remains unexplored. The valorization potential of water hyacinth-based plant parts, natural dyes, fibers, etc., can be greatly complemented when used in fusion with other natural fibers mentioned above. There is a need for convergence among researchers working on all eco-friendly fibers to explore ideas on the use of such fusion fabrics to develop suitable alternatives to plastic-made common household items.

22.5.5 Inefficient Market Linkage

There is a lot of interest in the emerging domain of ethical buying. Consumers today are more attracted to brands that adhere to sustainable practices and products. Often such brands don't get easy access to authentic craftsmen working in the hinterlands of India. A closer connection between such corporate brands and craftsmen would help them to understand each other's desired quality standards and capacities respectively. Hence, there is a real need to establish a suitable platform to foster efficient market linkages that can connect the craftsmen and rural enterprises with large corporate brands as well as consumers. Improved backward and forward linkage would increase their net income and foster alternate livelihood-based job creation in the hinterlands of the country.

TABLE 22.1

Different Types of Machine Learning Models Which Are Applied for Weed Mining and Monitoring of Different Varieties of Weeds and Plants

Aim of Study	Target Crop	Methodology of Experiment	Major Findings	Dataset	Author
To estimate water loss due to aquatic weeds	Water hyacinth, common reed, and torpedo grass	The study was done on identified areas of infection of aquatic weeds utilizing techniques like GPS and Satellite imagery (Landsat-8) to determine its location and field visits to estimate water losses through evapotranspiration. The data was collected and unsupervised classification was performed.	Over 90% of the floating weeds were classified as water hyacinth. A total of 92%, 3%, and 5% of evapotranspiration from water hyacinth, common reed, and torpedo grass was observed, respectively.	Satellite imagery (Landsat-8) from https://lv.eosda.com (From Dec 2015 to Nov 2016)	(Ali & El-Din Khedr, 2018)
To develop early weed detection using image processing and machine learning	Chili	The study is based on the potential of machine learning algorithms for weed and crop classification. Here various machine learning algorithms like random forest (RF), support vector machine (SVM), and k-nearest neighbors (KNN) were used with images collected from chilly crop fields in Australia.	In weed detection from RGB images, RF resulted better than the other classifiers in terms of accuracy of 96%. SVM gave 94% accuracy, while KNN had only 63% accuracy.	RGB images were captured by RGB cameras mounted in a drone using a Phantom 3 Advanced drone-mounted camera with a 1/2.300 CMOS sensor.	(Islam et al., 2021)

(Continued)

TABLE 22.1   CONTINUED

Different Types of Machine Learning Models Which Are Applied for Weed Mining and Monitoring of Different Varieties of Weeds and Plants

Aim of Study	Target Crop	Methodology of Experiment	Major Findings	Dataset	Author
To identify and classify weed species	8 weed plants	The study uses a recognition method based on Grabcut and local discriminant projections (LWMDP) algorithm for weed species detection in a crop field. Background is removed using Grabcut. Weed segmentation from the whole image is done by K-means clustering (KMC). Low-dimensional discriminant features are extracted using LWMDP. Lastly weed species are identified using the support vector machine (SVM).	Local weighted maximum margin discriminant analysis and Grabcut and local discriminant projections algorithm outperform other algorithms. A 99% identification rate was observed with CNN when the dataset was augmented 20 times by affine transformation, perspective transformation, and simple image rotations. The average recognition rate for all algorithms with 50 runs was 95% confidence as recognition results.	1600 weed images were taken from South China crop field.	(Zhang et al., 2019)
To detect weed in polyhouse grown bell peppers	Bell Pepper	The study evaluates deep learning-based techniques like Alexnet, GoogLeNet, Inception V3, and Xception to identify weeds from RGB images of bell pepper fields. Different epochs values of 10, 20, and 30 and batch sizes of 16 and 32 were performed for models with hyperparameters tuned to get optimal performance.	An accuracy of 94.5% to 97.7% was observed for various models. Inception V3 had the best performance at 30-epoch and 16-batch size of 97.7% accuracy, 98.5% precision, and 97.8% recall., with type 1 error of 1.4% and type 2 error of 0.9%.	ICAR-Central Institute of Agricultural Engineering, Bhopal, Madhya Pradesh (longitude 77°24′11.28″E and Latitude 23°18′35.67″ N)	(Subeesh et al., 2022)

(Continued)

TABLE 22.1 CONTINUED

Different Types of Machine Learning Models Which Are Applied for Weed Mining and Monitoring of Different Varieties of Weeds and Plants

Aim of Study	Target Crop	Methodology of Experiment	Major Findings	Dataset	Author
To monitor water hyacinth in Kuttanad, India, using Sentinel-1 Sar data	Water hyacinth	The study analyses the use of Synthetic Aperture Radar (SAR) Sentinel-1 to detect water hyacinth at early stages of its life cycle. They compared different methods of change detection based on dual polarimetric data and showed the use of Sentinel-1 for aquatic weed monitoring in Vembanad Lake in Kuttanad, Kerala.	Results of pixels from regions of lake show backscattered intensities between clean sites and infested sites. Using which basic detection masks are established to facilitate the presence of water hyacinth within lake Vembanad.	Dual-polarimetric Sentinel-1 Sar data, provided by the European Space Agency (ESA)	(M. Simpson et al., 2020)
To monitor spread of water hyacinth.	Water hyacinth	The study reviews and evaluates the latest developments in the use of remote sensing for water hyacinth monitoring. They also propose a potential combination-based multi-modal approach for better results.	They are working to design and test prototypes of a multi-modal system that can continuously monitor the presence of water hyacinth using a mix of SAR, and optical imaging, drone-mounted multispectral cameras, Internet-of-Things (IoT)-enabled ground sensor network and citizen science.	SAR and optical imaging by European Satellites	(Datta et al, 2021)

(Continued)

TABLE 22.1 CONTINUED

Different Types of Machine Learning Models Which Are Applied for Weed Mining and Monitoring of Different Varieties of Weeds and Plants

Aim of Study	Target Crop	Methodology of Experiment	Major Findings	Dataset	Author
To use deep convolutional neural networks for weeds and crop discrimination from UAS imagery	Sugar cane	They study tests and analyze these deep learning models: (1) U-Net Model, (2) SegNet, (3) FCN (FCN-32s, FCN-16s, FCN-8s), (4) DepLabV3+ for weed monitoring on USA databases. These deep learning models have been fine-tuned to classify the UAS datasets into three classes, namely background, crops, and weeds, hence facilitating weed identification and monitoring.	An average classification accuracy achieved by U-Net was 77.9%, SegNet 62.6%, FCN-32s 68.4%, FCN-16s 77.2%, FCN-8s 81.1%, and DepLab v3+ 84.3%. These results showed that ResNet-18-based segmentation model DepLab v3+ has the best precision.	UAS datasets: Crop/Weed Field Image Dataset (CWFID) (Haug and Ostermann, 2014) and the Sugar Cane Orthomosaic datasets (Monteiro and Von Wangeheim, 2019).	(Hashemi-Beni et al., 2022)
To detect weeds using convolutional neural networks	Not specified	The study proposes a method for weed detection using convolutional neural networks. There are two primary phases in CNN methodology. Image collection and labeling being first. The second phase involves building the convolutional neural network model of 20 layers to detect the weed.	Here the accuracy of the training set is improved when the number of epochs increases.	1000 weeds and crops images from Kaggle database.	(Hema et al., 2022)
To develop weed classification for site-specific weed management	Rice fields rice cultivar (Tarom Mahali) (Narrow-leaf weeds and wide-leaf weeds)	This study aims to develop a stereo-vision system for identifying and differentiating between rice crops and weeds. Moreover, this method can detect two types of weeds in a rice field by utilizing artificial neural networks (ANNs) and two metaheuristic algorithms.	The proposed ANN-BA classifier had accuracies of 88.74% and 87.96% for right and left channels.	The data was collected in the form of stereo videos by a stereo camera with different channels of each frame extracted.	(Dadashzadeh et al., 2020)

(Continued)

TABLE 22.1 CONTINUED

Different Types of Machine Learning Models Which Are Applied for Weed Mining and Monitoring of Different Varieties of Weeds and Plants

Aim of Study	Target Crop	Methodology of Experiment	Major Findings	Dataset	Author
To detect water hyacinth using coarse and high-resolution multispectral data.	Water hyacinth	This study aims to detect water hyacinths using multispectral data with different spatial resolutions. High-resolution data (<0.1 m) is acquired from an unmanned aerial vehicle (UAV) and coarse-resolution data (10 m) from Sentinel-2 MSI is used.	UAV-based multispectral data, when analyzing OA, had satisfactory results with all classifiers rechecking more than 85%, with the lowest being 87% for SVM, while the highest was reached in the RF, with 94%.	The study area is located in the Mondego River basin, between the cities of Coimbra and Figueira da Foz (Portugal). Three areas with a high prevalence of water hyacinth were selected to be surveyed by UAV.	(Pádua et al., 2022)

22.6 Weed Management

In agricultural production, weeds are the most important biotic constraints all over the world. Plants that grow in places where they are not desired are called weeds. A weed is a plant in the wrong place. A particular plant species may be useful in one place but an undesired weed in another place. Weeds that grow in water bodies are called aquatic weeds. Four general categories of aquatic weeds are algae, floating weeds, emerged weeds (foliage above water), and submerged weeds (majority of foliage below water). Apart from water hyacinth, other commonly found aquatic weeds include duckweeds (*Lemnoideae* sp.), water lettuce (*Pistia* sp.), water thyme (*Hydrilla* sp.), water milfoils (*Myriophyllum* sp.), etc. Weeds in the absence of appropriate control measures can cause significant loss in crop yield. Weeds grow along with other microorganisms such as fungi and bacteria and may harbor pests such as insects, rodents, nematodes, mites, and birds. Weeds compete with crop plants for sunlight, nutrients, space, and water, which adversely impact plant productivity. The severity of weed's impact on overall crop productivity or crop loss depends on several factors such as agro-climatic conditions, growing period, growth rate, weed plant population, and types of weeds and crops. For example, a shallow-rooted weed may cause less damage compared to a deep-rooted weed species for a deep-rooted crop. Improper weed management can result in total crop loss. Weeds can be managed in several methods. In small farms, nominal weed infestation can be adequately addressed by manual clearing. For larger scale or degree of infestation, a wide variety of chemical or nature-based herbicides are generally used (Chauhan, 2020). It is important not to harm the fish, other aquatic animals, and useful plants while herbicides are used. Therefore, it is a crucial task to select suitable herbicides for particular areas and weed types. Improved agricultural practices are appropriate land preparation, fallow management, suitable crop rotation, etc. Relatively low-cost techniques such as solarization and mulching can help in restricting weed infestation. Preventive methods, mechanical methods, biological methods, and chemical methods can be applied to weed management. In mechanical methods, different kinds of machines such as brush rakes, angle blades, shearing blades, rolling brush cutters, and shredders are used to remove the weeds. Hand-pulling of weeds is also one traditional method for removing weeds in small areas. Biological control of weed is using living organisms, such as fish, insects, snails, nematodes, bacteria, or fungi, to reduce weed populations. Plants are controlled biologically by naturally occurring organisms. Biological control research and implementation are even more relevant today. It is required to identify and evaluate foreign and native organisms for use as biological control agents to attack the weeds. Compared to other methods, biological control is an environmentally friendly approach. Some types of weeds become familiar and resistant to particular types of herbicides. In such cases, biological control is the better way to manage the weeds. Apart from this, biological methods have less side effects on applicants and consumers. Several other advanced techniques can be used for weed management such as direct flaming, microwaves or laser radiations, application of steam, and electrical pulses. Excessive weeding may be detrimental as it may increase the cost of cultivation and loss of soil moisture. Hence, a scientific weed management approach is important to optimize net farm income. It is thus essential to integrate manual, agronomical, biological, mechanical, or chemical weed abatement techniques to provide cost-effective and adequate weed management. Such an approach is called integrated weed management (IWM). Prevention is always better than cure. It is easier to prevent aquatic weeds rather than controlling them when they develop. Crop rotation, cover crops, tillage systems, seedbed preparation, soil solarization, and management of drainage and irrigation systems and of crop residues are prevention methods that can be used for weed control (Figures 22.3–22.5).

22.7 How Can AI Help in Real-Time Water Hyacinth Monitoring?

Periodic data gathering about a natural system such as a river or a lake often is not adequate to understand how anthropogenic or other factors impact that natural system. Nature and natural processes are all continuous, flow of a river may be fast, and the increase of ocean surface temperature may be slow. Hence, a continuous series of data at meaningful and practical time intervals is important for policy-makers. Pollution source apportionment and diurnal and seasonal variation of pollution are often important to understand. Water hyacinth infestation is a global challenge, so it is imperative to develop a global data repository (Datta et al., 2021). Though widespread, the nature of water hyacinth infestation, the properties of the water hyacinth mat, and the period of infestation vary a great deal across the globe. A global data reservoir would help to foster cross-learning. Large data sets across different geographical locations would in turn help generic AI tools with global applicability. Industrial scale utilization of water hyacinth would require data on the nature of infestation, quantity of biomass, availability of biomass around the year, etc., to evaluate the commercial merit of such a proposition for a given location. Spatial and temporal availability of water hyacinth biomass availability at a regional scale on a real-time basis can only be captured through AI-based tools using suitable remote sensing and GIS tools (M. D. Simpson et al., 2022). Using satellite-based multi-spectral remote sensing data, drone-based image capturing and field-level data gathering together would help to develop artificial intelligence (AI)-enabled monitoring techniques. Moreover, suitably developed AI tools can help in forecasting the period of emergence as well as the extent of

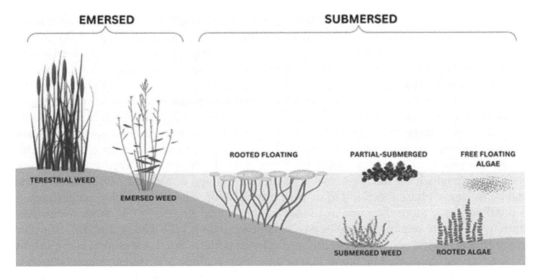

FIGURE 22.3
General types of aquatic weeds present in water bodies.

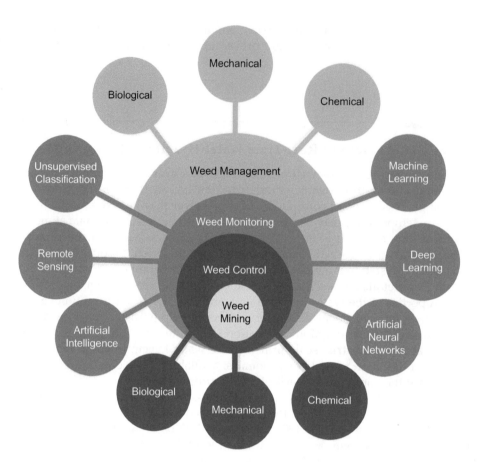

FIGURE 22.4
Weed management, monitoring, and mining.

emergence of water hyacinth mats in large water bodies based on past data, water quality information, and assessing local ago-climatic conditions. Such information would help in advance planning and scientific scheduling of harvesting at specific areas of a lake over a specific period of time enabling optimal use of resources. Water hyacinth mat broadly has four phases. During the early growth phase sexual reproduction takes place from the seeds deposited in the benthic sludge of an infested lake, small plants appear on the water surface and disjointed small patches of mats are formed. This early phase is followed by a rapid growth stage during which asexual growth predominates and dense mats are formed covering entire patches of a water body. While flowering does not occur under all ago-climatic conditions, generally the rapid growth phase is followed by a flowering boom during which the mat gets covered with lilac-colored flowers. The final phase of the mat is the decay phase when old mats turn brownish or yellowish in color. Sometimes, it is possible to see more than one of the above-mentioned phases in one large water hyacinth mat. Remote sensing technology-based tools can detect the different phases of water hyacinth mats based on changes in their reflectance pattern. Such assessment is important to plan harvesting as well as reuse. Harvesting may be done at different phases depending on the intended reuse of the harvested biomass. For example, the reuse of biomass for compost-making would require green biomass as water hyacinth starts releasing

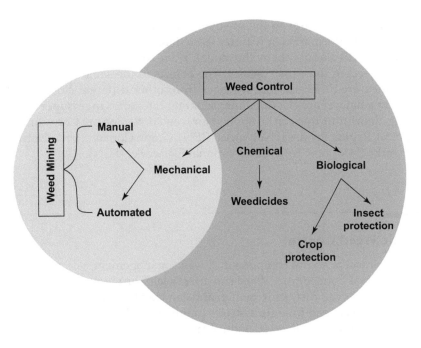

FIGURE 22.5
Weed control and mining.

ammoniacal-nitrogen rapidly as it enters the decay phase. Furthermore, the establishment of a commercial scale unit for extraction of the color for organic dye-making from water hyacinth flowers would find data related to the flowering period, average size of the mat during the flowering stage, etc., most relevant. Choice of location, scale of operation, and the availability of local logistics in terms of electrical supply, transport infrastructure, proximity to potential market, or complimentary industrial presence all can be packaged together using AI for a given water body or a group of water bodies in a region using AI tools. This will greatly help to make rational and scientific decision-making at the policy level.

22.7.1 Different Machine Learning Models Can Be Applied for Weed Monitoring

For weed monitoring, different types of machine learning models can be applied. General categories of machine learning techniques that can be used for weed detection and monitoring are categorized as supervised learning, semi-supervised learning, and unsupervised learning. Supervised learning is the one in which datasets are labeled prior to training and validation. In supervised learning, based on the known data set, the model is trained for mapping input and required output. For solving classification and regression problems, this method is widely accepted. Semi-supervised learning is the one that is between supervised and unsupervised methods. One example of semi-supervised method is the Graph Convolutional Network (GCN) (Kipf & Welling, 2017). The input data structure of input data is the main difference between CNN and GCN. For regular structured data CNN is used, while graph data structure is used in GCN (Mayachita, 2020). In the case when the training dataset is not labeled, it is called unsupervised learning. There is no label in the input dataset in the unsupervised model. The structure of the data is learned and distinct information or features from data are extracted. In this way, the input is mapped to the particular output by the model. Then, different groups or clusters are created from the objects in the whole dataset. The objects in the same cluster have the same features, and they are different from the ones from other different clusters. In this way, the objects from a dataset are classified into separate categories in unsupervised learning. Deep learning algorithms that can be applied for weed detection are Convolutional Neural Network (CNN), Region Proposal Networks (RPN), Graph Convolutional Network (GCN), Hybrid Networks (HN), and Fully Convolutional Networks (FCN).

22.8 Aquatic Weed Control

Aquatic weed control is a vital component of weed management, which is important for agriculture as well as aquaculture. Weed can affect yield, product quality, and production cost. Moreover, weeds can distract irrigation and can lead to ineffective application of pesticides. Weed may even lead to some diseases in the crop.

Three different approaches to weed control are:

(a) Mechanical: Removing weed by uprooting, by hand, or by using trowel
(b) Chemical: Destroying weed by spraying chemical – weedicide
(c) Biological: Keeping some kinds of insects and crop plants to prevent the growth of weeds.

For managing and controlling weeds, it is necessary to identify the types and coverage of weeds in particular farms or any other agricultural area. Weed monitoring and weed mining play crucial roles in weed management. The most useful and effective ways for weed monitoring are applying artificial intelligence and machine learning models. Remote sensing and GIS methodologies are also effective ways of monitoring weed data. Specifically to monitor live data and real-time monitoring, remote sensing provides the accurate data. Marco Esposito, Mariano Crimaldi, Valerio Cirillo, Fabrizio Sarghini, and Albino Maggio applied drone and sensor technology for sustainable weed management. They provided an overview of the most practical sensors in the market. Types of sensors that can be applied are RGB (Red, Green, Blue) or VIS (Visible) sensors, multispectral sensors, and hyperspectral sensors. One of the most successful technologies applied in precision agriculture is unmanned aerial vehicle (UAV). A combination of UAV and machine learning techniques can identify weed patches in a cultivated field with accuracy and can improve weed management sustainability (Craig, 2022).

22.9 Way Forward

Less awareness about water hyacinth-related problems and their economic impacts is not properly evaluated, and large-scale utilization of the biomass is still challenging as when?

Where? How much biomass data is not available in real time? It is difficult to make a bankable business proposal involving rural entrepreneurs or small and medium enterprises (SMEs).

Aquatic weeds like water hyacinth (scientifically, *Pontederia crassipes*) have hardly a recorded history of 100 years. The initial phase of research considered it as another aquatic vegetation with blue flowers; however, its extensive growth pattern and capability to drastically change the habitat of aquatic life and ecosystem make it a notorious aquatic vegetation (Mcdonald & Wolverton, 1980). In the recent past, a number of solutions were proposed for the utilization of the water hyacinth plant and its parts. The solutions mostly comprise low-cost products, less technology involvement, and higher human involvement (Harun et al., 2021; Malik, 2007b). The challenges in the water hyacinth-related problem are not in the translation of biomass into useful materials but in its ability to sustain business models and economic activities (Ajithram et al., 2021; Guna et al., 2017). Although a sustainable supply of raw materials is one of the important limiting factors for all industry and business activities directly or indirectly dependent upon natural resources. In the case of an alternative solution, this becomes more decisive. In the case of *Pontederia crassipes*, this is a valid reason for its slow and insignificant demand from rural entrepreneurs as well as Small and Medium Enterprises (SMEs). There is very little data available for the spread and growth of water hyacinths; also no authentic information is yet available regarding the presence of biomass in the form of water hyacinths. The research work where the growth pattern is monitored, the presence of water hyacinth using advanced techniques like GIS, remote sensing, and drone technology has noticeably broken the ice of this quantifiable question of the availability of aquatic weed in the lakes/pond or other water bodies. This is the first step toward bringing some sustainable economic model from these biological resources that has tremendous potential in varied dimensions. The monitoring of the weed opens new avenues of weed mining in the coming future.

References

Aerobic composting enhances the value of water hyacinth biomass – ICRISAT. (n.d.). Retrieved September 23, 2022, from https://www.icrisat.org/aerobic-composting-enhances-the-value-of-water-hyacinth-biomass/

Agarwal, D., Tongaria, K., Pathak, S., Ohri, A., & Jha, M. (2016). Soil erosion mapping of watershed in Mirzapur district using RUSLE model in GIS environment. *International Journal of Students' Research in Technology & Management, 4*(3), 56–63. https://doi.org/10.18510/ijsrtm.2016.433

Ajithram, A., Winowlin Jappes, J. T., & Brintha, N. C. (2021). Investigation on utilization of water hyacinth aquatic plants towards various bio products – Survey. *Materials Today: Proceedings, 45,* 2040–2045. https://doi.org/10.1016/j.matpr.2020.09.498

Akinwande, V. O., Mako, A. A., & Babayemii, O. J. (2013). Biomass yield, chemical composition and the feed potential of water hyacinth (Eichhornia crassipes, Mart. Solms-Laubach) in Nigeria. *International Journal of Agriculturalscience, 3*(8), 659–666.

Alagu, K., Venu, H., Jayaraman, J., Raju, V. D., Subramani, L., Prabhu, A., & Dhanasekhar, S. (2019). Novel water hyacinth biodiesel as a potential alternative fuel for existing unmodified diesel engine: Performance, combustion and emission characteristics. *Energy, 179,* 295–305. https://doi.org/10.1016/j.energy.2019.04.207

Ali, Y. M., & El-Din Khedr, I. S. (2018). Estimation of water losses through evapotranspiration of aquatic weeds in the Nile River (case study: Rosetta Branch). *Water Science, 32*(2), 259–275. https://doi.org/10.1016/J.WSJ.2018.08.002

Arp, R. S., Fraser, G. C. G., & Hill, M. P. (2017). Quantifying the economic water savings benefit of water hyacinth (Eichhornia crassipes) control in the Vaalharts Irrigation Scheme. *Water SA, 43*(1), 58–66. https://doi.org/10.4314/wsa.v43i1.09

Barua, V. B., Goud, V. V., & Kalamdhad, A. S. (2018). Microbial pretreatment of water hyacinth for enhanced hydrolysis followed by biogas production. *Renewable Energy, 126*, 21–29. https://doi.org/10.1016/j.renene.2018.03.028

Bhattacharya, A., & Kumar, P. (2010). Water hyacinth as a potential biofuel crop. *Electronic Journal of Environmental, Agriculture and Food Chemistry, 9*(1), 112–122.

Borokini, T., & Babalola, F. (2012). Management of invasive plant species in Nigeria through economic exploitation: Lessons from other countries. *Management of Biological Invasions, 3*(1), 45–55. https://doi.org/10.3391/mbi.2012.3.1.05

Bownes, A., Hill, M. P., & Byrne, M. J. (2013). The role of nutrients in the responses of water hyacinth, Eichhornia crassipes (Pontederiaceae) to herbivory by a grasshopper Cornops aquaticum Brüner (Orthoptera: Acrididae). *Biological Control, 67*(3), 555–562. https://doi.org/10.1016/j.biocontrol.2013.07.022

Chauhan, B. S. (2020). Grand challenges in weed management. *Frontiers in Agronomy, 1.* https://doi.org/10.3389/fagro.2019.00003

Chen, X., Jiang, Z., Chen, X., Lei, J., Weng, B., & Huang, Q. (2010). Use of biogas fluid-soaked water hyacinth for cultivating Pleurotus geesteranus. *Bioresource Technology, 101*(7), 2397–2400. https://doi.org/10.1016/j.biortech.2009.11.045

Cilliers, C. J. (1991). Biological control of water hyacinth, Eichhornia crassipes (Pontederiaceae), in South Africa. *Agriculture, Ecosystems and Environment, 37*(1–3), 207–217. https://doi.org/10.1016/0167-8809(91)90149-R

Coetzee, J. A., Hill, M. P., Ruiz-Téllez, T., Starfinger, U., & Brunel, S. (2017). Monographs on invasive plants in Europe N° 2: Eichhornia crassipes (Mart.) Solms. *Botany Letters, 164*(4), 303–326. https://doi.org/10.1080/23818107.2017.1381041

Dadashzadeh, M., Abbaspour-Gilandeh, Y., Mesri-Gundoshmian, T., Sabzi, S., Hernández-Hernández, J. L., Hernández-Hernández, M., & Ignacio Arribas, J. (2020). Weed classification for site-specific weed management using an automated stereo computer-vision machine-learning system in rice fields. *Plants, 9*(5). https://doi.org/10.3390/PLANTS9050559

Datta, A., Maharaj, S., Prabhu, G. N., Bhowmik, D., Marino, A., Akbari, V., Rupavatharam, S., Sujeetha, J. A. R. P., Anantrao, G. G., Poduvattil, V. K., Kumar, S., & Kleczkowski, A. (2021). Monitoring the spread of water hyacinth (Pontederia crassipes): Challenges and future developments. *Frontiers in Ecology and Evolution, 9.* https://doi.org/10.3389/fevo.2021.631338

Datta, A., Rajesh, P., Mishra, P. K., & Dixit, S. (2022, March 23). Sustainable valorisation of water hyacinth biomass through aerobic composting. *International Conference on Circular Economy for Sustainable Water Management (SuWaM2022) at IIT Madras.*

Ezama, D. (2019). Impact of water hyacinth infestation in Nigerian inland waters: Utilization and management. *World Maritime University Dissertations.* https://commons.wmu.se/all_dissertations/1132

Firehun, Y., Struik, P. C., Lantinga, E. A., & Taye, T. (2014). Water hyacinth in the rift valley water bodies of Ethiopia: Its distribution, socioeconomic importance and management. *International Journal of Current Agricultural Research, 3*(2), 67–75. https://doi.org/10.2/JQUERY.MIN.JS

Gopika, G., Kumar, A., & Nagendra Prabhu, G. (2018). Extraction of natural dye from the flowers of Eichhornia crassipes. *Indian Journal of Scientific Research, 20*(1), 63–67. https://www.researchgate.net/publication/350458049

Guna, V., Ilangovan, M., Anantha Prasad, M. G., & Reddy, N. (2017). Water hyacinth: A unique source for sustainable materials and products. *ACS Sustainable Chemistry and Engineering, 5*(6), 4478–4490. https://doi.org/10.1021/acssuschemeng.7b00051

Gutiérrez, E., Huerto, R. n., Saldaña, P., & Arreguín, F. (1996). Strategies for Waterhyacinth (Eichhornia crassipes) Control in Mexico. *Hydrobiologia, 340*, 181–185. doi:10.1007/BF00012752

Harun, I., Pushiri, H., Amirul-Aiman, A. J., & Zulkeflee, Z. (2021). Invasive water hyacinth: Ecology, impacts and prospects for the rural economy. *Plants*, *10*(8), 1613. https://doi.org/10.3390/plants10081613

Hema, M. S., Abhilash, V., Tharun, V., & Reddy, D. M. (2022). Weed detection using convolutional neural network. *BOHR International Journal of Intelligent Instrumentation and Computing*, *1*(1), 46–49. https://doi.org/10.54646/bijiiac.007

Honlah, E., Appiah, D. O., & Segbefia, A. Y. (2019). Coping strategies to water hyacinth invasion among riparian communities in Ghana. *American Journal of Environment and Sustainable Development*, *4*(1), 12–25. https://www.researchgate.net/publication/337759908_Coping_Strategies_to_Water_Hyacinth_Invasion_Among_Riparian_Communities_in_Ghana

Honlah, E., Segbefia, A. Y., Appiah, D. O., & Mensah, M. (2019). The effects of water hyacinth invasion on smallholder farming along river Tano and Tano Lagoon, Ghana. *Cogent Food and Agriculture*, *5*(1), 1567042. https://doi.org/10.1080/23311932.2019.1567042

Honlah, E., Segbefia, A. Y., Appiah, D. O., & Mensah, M. (2022). Responses of institutions and communities to environmental problems of water hyacinth invasion in Jomoro Municipality, Ghana. *Social Sciences & Humanities Open*, *6*(1), 100289. https://doi.org/10.1016/j.ssaho.2022.100289

Ilo, O. P., Simatele, M. D., Nkomo, S. L., Mkhize, N. M., & Prabhu, N. G. (2020). The benefits of water hyacinth (Eichhornia crassipes) for Southern Africa: A review. *Sustainability*, *12*(21), 9222. https://doi.org/10.3390/su12219222

Ilo, O. P., Simatele, M. D., Nkomo, S. L., Mkhize, N. M., & Prabhu, N. G. (2021). Methodological approaches to optimising anaerobic digestion of water hyacinth for energy efficiency in South Africa. *Sustainability*, *13*(12), 6746. https://doi.org/10.3390/su13126746

Islam, N., Rashid, M. M., Wibowo, S., Xu, C.-Y., Morshed, A., Wasimi, S. A., Moore, S., Rahman, S. M., Islam, N., Rashid, M. M., Wibowo, S., Xu, C.-Y., Morshed, A., Wasimi, S. A., Moore, S., & Rahman, S. M. (2021). Early weed detection using image processing and machine learning techniques in an Australian chilli farm. *Agriculture*, *11*(5), 1–13. https://EconPapers.repec.org/RePEc:gam:jagris:v:11:y:2021:i:5:p:387-:d:543131

Jafari, N. (2010). Ecological and socio-economic utilization of water hyacinth (Eichhornia crassipes Mart Solms). *Ecological and Socio-Economic Utilization of Water Hyacinth (Eichhornia Crassipes Mart Solms)*, *14*(2), 43–49. http://www.bioline.org.br/request?ja10025

Janko, A. M., Zemedu, L., Assefa, C., & Janko, M. (2015). Fishermen's willingness to pay for fisheries management: The case of lake Zeway, Ethiopia. *International Journal of Fisheries and Aquatic Studies*, *2*(6), 320–325. www.fisheriesjournal.com

Jernelöv, A. (2017). *The Long-Term Fate of Invasive Species*. Springer International Publishing. https://doi.org/10.1007/978-3-319-55396-2

Kipf, T. N., & Welling, M. (2017). Semi-supervised classification with graph convolutional networks. *5th International Conference on Learning Representations, ICLR 2017 - Conference Track Proceedings*.

Kumar, V. A., Sreelakshmi, T. P., Azmi, T., Bindu, P., Pillai, P. R. U., & Prabhu, G. N. (2014). Mushroom cultivation using aquatic weeds of Kerala. *Mushroom Cultivation Using Aquatic Weeds of Kerala. Proceedings of National Symposium on Emerging Trends in Biotechnology*.

Mailu, A. M. (2001). Preliminary assessment of the cocial, economic and environmental impacts of Water Hyacinth in Lake Victoria basin and status of control. *Biological and Integrated Control of Water Hyacinth, Eichhornia Crassipes. ACIAR Proceedings 102*, *102*, 130–139. https://aquadocs.org/handle/1834/1292

Malik, A. (2007a). Environmental challenge vis a vis opportunity: The case of water hyacinth. *Environment International*, *33*(1), 122–138. https://doi.org/10.1016/j.envint.2006.08.004

Malik, A. (2007b). Environmental challenge vis a vis opportunity: The case of water hyacinth. *Environment International*, *33*(1), 122–138. https://doi.org/10.1016/j.envint.2006.08.004

Mayachita, I. (2020). Training graph convolutional networks on node classification task. *Towards Data Science*. https://towardsdatascience.com/graph-convolutional-networks-on-node-classification-2b6bbec1d042

Mcdonald, R. C., & Wolverton, B. C. (1980). Comparative study of wastewater Lagoon with and without water hyacinth. *Economic Botany*, *34*(2), 101–110. https://doi.org/10.1007/BF02858625

Moyo, P., Chapungu, L., & Mudzengi, B. (2013). A proposed integrated management approach to the control of water hyacinth: The case of Shagashe River in Masvingo, Zimbabwe. *Greener Journal of Physical Science, 3*(6), 229–240. https://doi.org/10.15580/GJOMS.2013.1.170913843

Oyedeji, A., & Abowei, J. (2012). The classification, distribution, control and economic importance of aquatic plants. *International Journal of Fisheries and Aquatic Sciences, 1*(2), 118–128.

Pádua, L., Antão-Geraldes, A. M., Sousa, J. J., Rodrigues, M. Â., Oliveira, V., Santos, D., Miguens, M. F. P., & Castro, J. P. (2022). Water hyacinth (Eichhornia crassipes) detection using coarse and high resolution multispectral data. *Drones, 6*(2). https://doi.org/10.3390/DRONES6020047

Patel, S. (2012). Threats, management and envisaged utilizations of aquatic weed Eichhornia crassipes: An overview. *Reviews in Environmental Science and Bio/Technology, 11*(3), 249–259. https://doi.org/10.1007/S11157-012-9289-4

Prabhu, G. N., & Kurup, R. S. C. (2012). *Bacterial Cellulase Production under Solid State Fermentation – Eichhornia crassipes as Substrate.* Lambert Academic Publishers.

Prabhu, N. (2016). Economic impacts of aquatic WEEDS-A Third World approach. *Journal of Aquatic Biology & Fisheries, 4.*

Rashed, A. A. (2014). Assessment of aquatic plants evapotranspiration for secondary agriculture drains (case study: Edfina drain, Egypt). *Egyptian Journal of Aquatic Research, 40*(2), 117–124. https://doi.org/10.1016/J.EJAR.2014.07.001

Sasaqi, D., Pranoto, P., & Setyono, P. (2019). Estimation of water losses through evapotranspiration of water hyacinth (Eichhornia crassipes). *Caraka Tani. Journal of Sustainable Agriculture, 34*(1), 100. https://doi.org/10.20961/CARAKATANI.V34I1.28214

Simpson, M. D., Akbari, V., Marino, A., Prabhu, G. N., Bhowmik, D., Rupavatharam, S., Datta, A., Kleczkowski, A., Sujeetha, J. A. R. P., Anantrao, G. G., Poduvattil, V. K., Kumar, S., Maharaj, S., & Hunter, P. D. (2022). Detecting water hyacinth infestation in Kuttanad, India, using dual-pol Sentinel-1 SAR imagery. *Remote Sensing, 14*(12), 2845. https://doi.org/10.3390/RS14122845

Simpson, M., Marino, A., Nagendra Prabhu, G., Bhowmik, D., Rupavatharam, S., Datta, A., Kleczkowski, A., Sujeetha, J. A. R. P., & Maharaj, S. (2020). Monitoring water hyacinth in kuttanad, india using sentinel-1 sar data. *2020 IEEE India Geoscience and Remote Sensing Symposium, InGARSS 2020 - Proceedings*, 13–16. https://doi.org/10.1109/INGARSS48198.2020.9358977

Subeesh, A., Bhole, S., Singh, K., Chandel, N. S., Rajwade, Y. A., Rao, K. V. R., Kumar, S. P., & Jat, D. (2022). Deep convolutional neural network models for weed detection in polyhouse grown bell peppers. *Artificial Intelligence in Agriculture, 6*, 47–54. https://doi.org/10.1016/J.AIIA.2022.01.002

Suresh Chandra Kurup, R., Snishamol, C., & Nagendra Prabhu, G.* (2005). Cellulase production by native bacteria using water hyacinth as substrate under solid state fermentation. *Malaysian Journal of Microbiology.* https://doi.org/10.21161/mjm.120504

Tewabe, D. (2015). Preliminary survey of water hyacinth in lake Tana, Ethiopia. *Global Journal of Allergy, 1*(1), 013–018. https://doi.org/10.17352/2455-8141.000003

Villamagna, A. M., & Murphy, B. R. (2010). Ecological and socio-economic impacts of invasive water hyacinth (Eichhornia crassipes): A review. *Freshwater Biology, 55*(2), 282–298. https://doi.org/10.1111/j.1365-2427.2009.02294.x

Wassie, A. (2014). Water hyacinth coverage survey report on Lake Tana, *Technical Report Series 1.*

Zhang, S., Guo, J., & Wang, Z. (2019). Combing K-means clustering and local weighted maximum discriminant projections for weed species recognition. *Frontiers in Computer Science, 1.* https://doi.org/10.3389/FCOMP.2019.00004

Index

access 2, 5, 12, 18, 19, 21, 22, 24, 31, 35, 36, 41, 45, 46, 49, 50, 53, 54, 59, 74, 81, 82, 87, 88, 106, 122, 125, 127, 134–140, 143–148, 150, 151, 155, 158, 166, 179, 184, 186, 190, 197, 202, 204, 206, 214, 220, 222, 225, 252
accident 6, 15, 18, 45, 167, 168, 173
account 11, 37, 38, 40, 44–47, 50, 51, 78, 79, 81, 89, 129, 158, 191, 205, 223, 249
accountability 37, 38, 40, 44, 46, 47, 50, 51, 75, 81, 89, 158, 191
accounting 78
act 1–11, 13–16, 18–23, 26, 27, 30–33, 35–50, 52–56, 58–87, 89–101, 109–122, 126–131, 133, 134, 136, 138, 139, 141, 143–149, 154–165, 167–173, 175–187, 190, 191, 193–197, 203, 204, 210–213, 216, 217, 222, 223, 225, 237, 239–242, 244, 246–249, 251, 252, 254, 256–259, 261–266
adaptation 155
adaptive 56, 119, 139, 176, 190, 197
adaptive robotics 176
adoptions 73
advancements 22, 138, 179, 221
adversarial 92, 116
against 5, 40, 71, 102, 109, 186, 190, 197
ageing 2, 7, 52, 53, 154, 164, 166
    populations 52, 164, 166
agencies 3, 40, 42, 77, 89, 200, 249
agile 176
    manufacturing 176
agriculture 1, 34, 45, 55, 122, 158–162, 178, 180, 184, 185, 262, 266
AI 1–35, 37–135, 137–152, 154–169, 171–200, 202–205, 207–217, 219, 222, 223, 225, 238–249, 251, 252, 256–259, 261–266
algorithm 2, 6, 9–15, 21, 31, 35, 38, 40, 45, 55, 59, 63, 64, 70–73, 75, 76, 79, 87–92, 97, 98, 109, 110, 112–117, 139, 140, 144, 146, 151, 167, 169–174, 185–188, 190, 191, 210, 212–215, 239, 253, 254, 256, 262
algorithmic 63, 89, 90
    trading 89
algorithms 2, 6, 9–15, 21, 31, 35, 38, 40, 45, 70, 72, 73, 75, 76, 79, 87, 88, 91, 92, 97, 98, 100, 109, 110, 112–116, 139, 140, 144, 146, 151, 169, 171–174, 185–188, 190, 191, 193, 195, 217, 218, 239, 241, 243, 253, 254, 256, 262
allocation 52, 103, 213, 214, 217

ambiguity 44, 239
analysis 10, 16, 17, 23, 29–32, 36, 39, 55, 59, 60, 66, 70, 72, 73, 75, 76, 82, 84, 97, 101, 115, 116, 128, 140, 141, 146, 155, 156, 161, 165, 167, 169–173, 177, 181, 183, 188, 195, 196, 206, 210, 211, 218, 219, 225, 237–244, 246, 254
application 8–11, 13, 15, 21, 22, 30, 32, 36, 37, 42, 51, 58–61, 67, 68, 73, 74, 76, 78–81, 86, 87, 90, 94, 95, 98, 101, 105, 114, 127, 128, 133, 136, 138, 140, 141, 145, 146, 148, 149, 155, 156, 158, 159, 161, 162, 167, 178–186, 192–196, 202, 203, 208, 209, 219, 222, 225, 237, 238, 241, 246, 258, 262
applications 8–11, 13, 15, 21, 22, 30, 32, 36, 37, 42, 54, 56, 58–61, 67, 68, 73, 76, 78–81, 87, 94, 95, 98, 101, 105, 114, 128, 136, 138, 141, 145, 146, 148, 149, 155, 156, 158, 159, 161, 162, 178–186, 192–195, 202, 208, 209, 219, 222, 225, 241
architectures 9, 10, 15, 19, 20, 23, 28, 33, 56
artificial 1, 3, 9, 17, 48, 56, 61, 65–69, 78, 81, 91, 98, 100, 101, 114, 116, 119, 133, 134, 141, 149, 162–167, 174, 176, 178, 186, 190, 211, 213, 215, 216, 239, 240, 243, 244, 247, 256, 259, 262
    intelligence 1, 3, 9, 17, 48, 56, 66–69, 78, 81, 91, 94, 96, 101, 114, 116, 119, 133, 134, 141, 162–167, 174, 176, 186, 190, 193, 194, 215, 216, 239, 243, 244, 247, 259, 262
    neural network 9, 98, 101, 116
assessments 14, 62, 105, 208, 210, 249
asset 54, 75, 82, 95, 120, 121, 143, 198, 200, 222
assistants 2, 10, 21, 61, 138
association 41, 98, 165, 221, 237
attack 5, 7, 12, 22, 45, 55, 71, 75, 83, 86, 92, 107–117, 124, 127, 128, 145, 150, 190, 191, 196–205, 208, 258
    detection 55, 92, 102, 117
augmented 13, 61, 88, 176, 254
    reality 13, 61, 176
auth 5, 16, 22, 42, 43, 49, 54, 69, 74, 75, 80, 81, 86, 93, 105, 106, 110, 114, 119, 137, 140, 146, 147, 155, 156, 158, 159, 178, 179, 181, 182, 184, 186, 189, 190, 193, 197, 198, 200, 204, 209, 219, 220, 222, 252, 263
auth0 81
authentication 74, 75, 80, 81, 93, 137, 189, 193

automation 1, 21, 33, 35, 49, 52, 54, 69, 78, 83, 89, 92, 119, 132, 164, 165, 185, 192
autonomous 9, 10, 21, 32, 34, 40, 41, 57, 71, 97, 103, 165, 188, 190, 221
 weapons 9
availability 13, 21, 32, 70, 77, 81, 91, 100, 110, 157, 186, 211, 247, 259, 261, 263
awareness 46, 50, 54, 102, 150, 190, 249, 252, 262

banking 37, 71, 73, 76, 77, 83, 87–90, 96
base 5, 7–12, 16, 27, 29–32, 40, 43, 45, 48, 51, 52, 55–61, 63, 64, 69, 71–96, 100, 102, 105, 114–117, 123, 128–133, 136, 139–142, 146, 147, 152, 156–159, 165, 172, 173, 177, 178, 181–184, 188, 190, 192, 194, 195, 203, 205, 209–214, 217–222, 224, 237–240, 242, 252–261
bias 35, 38–44, 47, 52, 75, 88, 145, 147, 157, 173, 188, 191
biased 13, 88
 data 40
big 3, 5, 13, 17, 21, 27–36, 39, 42, 44, 53, 71, 77, 82, 83, 98, 101, 105, 115, 116, 121, 127, 133, 146, 154, 158, 163, 166, 174, 186, 195, 210, 219, 239, 245
 data 3, 5, 17, 21, 27–36, 39, 88, 98, 101, 115, 116, 133, 163, 166, 174, 186, 195, 210, 219, 245
big data analysis 17
blockchain 4, 7, 19, 20, 24, 55, 76, 91, 128, 129, 131, 132, 140, 141, 154–162, 191, 194, 219
brain 56, 57, 61, 67, 69, 244
buildings 5, 6, 52, 53, 101, 121, 144, 185
business 2, 7, 15, 16, 24, 27, 32, 40–45, 49, 50, 52, 53, 71, 73, 80, 82, 83, 88, 90, 119, 123, 130, 146, 176, 179, 182, 185, 194, 195, 199, 204, 206, 208, 221, 251, 263
 models 2, 53, 130, 263

calculation 59, 73, 75, 112, 156, 222, 223
carbon 7, 18, 19, 23, 120, 124, 144, 159, 161, 167, 247
care 1, 2, 9, 10, 15, 18, 20, 21, 28, 34, 37, 38, 43, 45, 49, 51–54, 64, 66, 74, 75, 83, 93, 95, 122, 131, 133–155, 161, 164, 177, 184, 185, 187, 190, 194, 200, 203, 204, 211–219, 239, 249
cash 73, 77, 78, 89, 90
 flow predictions 73
chain 4–7, 24, 26, 33, 55, 76, 91, 94, 96, 101, 105, 128, 129, 131, 132, 138, 140, 141, 145, 146, 154–163, 175, 185, 191, 194, 195, 200, 219
challenges 3, 8, 10, 19, 20, 23, 24, 27, 28, 34, 35, 47, 48, 51, 53–56, 66, 67, 71, 83, 88, 93, 101, 104, 116, 123, 139, 141–152, 162, 167, 173, 185, 190–196, 216–219, 251, 263, 264

change 2, 3, 7, 14, 15, 23, 37, 45, 57, 67, 71, 72, 76, 83, 88, 90, 93, 95, 100, 103, 104, 108, 109, 112, 118, 120, 121, 123, 127, 130, 136, 143, 144, 146, 154, 155, 159, 160, 165, 167, 174, 176, 179, 180, 184, 185, 188, 204, 223, 246, 255, 260, 263
chargeback 71
cities 5–8, 11, 20, 34, 52, 53, 121, 141, 144, 164, 166, 184, 185, 210, 218, 252, 257
city 3, 8, 20, 27, 28, 31, 33, 42, 49, 54, 56, 72, 96–100, 102–106, 108, 109, 116, 122, 124–129, 131, 145, 158, 194, 210, 237, 248, 251, 252
civil 54, 154, 176, 239
classification 16, 31, 48, 55, 81, 90, 92, 97, 100, 102, 112, 113, 116, 117, 172, 196, 211, 212, 240, 253, 256, 261
 technique 100
climate 2, 37, 45, 118, 120, 144, 154, 155, 159, 223, 224, 246
climate change 2, 37, 45, 118, 144, 154, 155, 159, 246
cloud 4, 5, 19, 21, 50, 75, 88, 101, 105, 133, 136, 141, 156, 163, 165, 169, 170, 173, 176, 185, 192, 205, 211, 212
 computing 19, 21, 101, 133, 165, 185, 192, 211, 219, 220
clustering 11, 31, 98, 117, 187, 219, 239, 242, 243, 254, 266
 algorithm 11, 219
cognitive 56, 64, 66, 70, 128, 131, 240, 244
 architectures 56
collaboration 3, 12, 37, 133, 134, 146, 149, 159, 163, 164, 166, 218
collection 1, 35, 40, 70, 84, 103, 112, 113, 122, 127, 140, 147, 155, 156, 169, 172, 176, 180, 187, 197, 208, 218, 256
colonies 213, 217
color 40, 44, 243, 248, 251, 260, 261
commercial 56, 61, 62, 70, 94, 120, 178, 239, 259, 261
communication 5, 13, 23, 25, 96, 97, 101, 103, 104, 118, 119, 123, 127, 129, 131, 132, 136, 137, 139, 154, 162, 180, 181, 186, 188, 189, 192, 198, 200, 201, 219
communities 3, 17, 18, 22, 38, 252, 265
comparison 78, 88, 97, 108, 111, 114
complexity 29, 35, 50, 76, 108, 118, 188, 213
composition 176, 248, 263
computing 5, 7, 13, 18, 19, 21, 30, 31, 50, 60, 91, 95, 101, 107, 109, 128, 131, 133, 145, 162, 165, 188, 191, 192, 199, 211, 244
concerns 1, 7, 12, 34, 37–40, 44, 51, 54, 75, 101, 106, 109, 115, 122, 123, 144, 145, 147–150, 152, 157, 159, 168, 177, 190, 196, 215, 239

considerations 3, 9, 11, 12, 14, 15, 37, 38, 44, 45, 47, 145, 152
constraints 43, 72, 88, 95, 163, 183, 216, 258
content 8, 11, 13, 32, 59, 61, 62, 87, 122, 161, 200, 204, 205, 211, 239
  ambiguity 239
control 5, 7, 9, 10, 18, 21, 41–45, 54, 71, 87, 88, 96, 97, 102, 105, 108, 110, 115, 116, 120, 121, 123, 124, 126, 129, 130, 135, 138, 143, 146, 147, 149, 151, 153, 158, 161, 162, 165, 170, 179, 182, 191, 199, 200, 204, 210, 211, 219, 258, 259, 261, 262
convolutional 92, 95, 256, 265, 266
  neural networks 95, 256
corporation 1, 44, 45, 54, 56, 129, 130
corporations 1, 44, 45, 54, 56
corruption 3
credit 72, 74, 75, 83, 86, 87, 89, 90, 93, 95, 159, 205, 212
  records 87
  risk 72
  scoring 87, 95
credits 87, 159
crop 9, 34, 45, 91, 122, 154–162, 181, 183, 247, 251, 253, 254, 256, 258, 259, 262, 264
cultural 3, 16, 45, 52, 91, 143, 154–161, 163, 179, 181, 183, 251, 254, 258
customer 11, 21, 27, 33, 40, 70–75, 77, 79, 87, 90, 91, 96, 99, 100, 103, 105, 119, 121, 124, 126, 127, 130, 162, 181, 195
  base 71
  profiles 87
customers 21, 27, 33, 40, 70–73, 75, 87, 90, 96, 100, 103, 124, 126, 127, 130
cyberattacks 5, 7, 12, 22, 49, 50, 83, 108, 109, 116, 124, 127, 145, 150, 190, 191, 196, 197, 200, 203, 204
cybersecurity 22, 49, 50, 54, 75, 116, 119, 123, 127, 130, 146, 150, 193, 196–203, 205
cyberspace 18, 143, 144, 163, 176, 196, 198, 199

damage 22, 46, 49, 54, 159, 191, 247, 248, 258
data 1–13, 15, 17, 19–23, 27–36, 38–42, 49–55, 57, 59–64, 66, 67, 70, 72–76, 80–84, 87, 88, 90–95, 97, 98, 100–103, 105, 106, 108–118, 120, 121, 123–128, 135–140, 143–147, 150, 151, 154–163, 165–174, 176–198, 200, 204, 210, 211, 239–246, 253–257, 259–263, 265, 266
  analysis 17, 36, 39, 59, 73, 87, 97, 140, 167, 169–172, 177, 239
  availability 81
  collection practices 40
  integration 53, 197

mining 31, 59, 60, 93, 95, 98, 113, 239, 240, 243, 244
privacy 7, 28, 34, 39, 88, 138, 147, 159, 189
quality 35, 173
security 2, 75, 143, 146, 159, 186, 187, 190
sources 30, 105, 172, 191
transmission 110, 221, 223
databases 5, 27, 31, 32, 163, 256
decentralized 103, 106, 146
decision 2–7, 10–15, 21, 37, 38, 40, 43, 52, 53, 56, 57, 63, 65, 68–71, 79, 84, 88, 96, 100, 113, 114, 127, 128, 131, 144, 145, 151, 157, 160, 169, 172, 181, 185, 186, 188, 190, 191, 214, 215, 239–243, 246, 261
  support systems 56, 63, 65, 68, 246
  tree 128, 131, 172, 188, 239
decisions 3, 33, 34, 38, 40, 57, 70, 84, 88, 96, 100, 114, 127, 145, 151, 157, 160, 172, 186, 190, 191, 214, 215, 239, 240
deep 14, 15, 17, 25, 26, 37, 57, 83, 92–95, 97, 98, 105, 108, 123, 131, 143, 152, 154, 157, 192, 194, 196, 218, 220, 254, 256, 258
  learning 14, 15, 57, 83, 92, 95, 97, 98, 105, 154, 157, 192, 194, 256
defence 41, 102, 190, 197, 200, 208, 221
  objectives 221
delay 105, 111, 167, 213, 215, 222
delivery 7, 64, 75, 76, 83, 90, 103, 105, 133, 135, 136, 139, 143, 145, 147, 148, 150, 151, 182, 197, 217, 218, 224, 225, 228, 236, 237
demand 2, 5, 7, 54, 72, 82, 116–121, 127, 130, 131, 134, 145, 176, 177, 208, 210, 211, 214, 217, 218, 222, 237, 247, 263
depletion 52, 154, 164, 166, 221, 247
deployment 12, 41, 43–47, 71, 81, 123, 129, 194, 219, 221
deposit 71, 87, 249, 260
destination 168, 171, 172, 174, 221–224
detection 1, 11, 50, 55, 58, 61, 63, 70, 77, 81, 83, 84, 97, 102, 112, 114–117, 128, 131, 136, 143, 185, 187, 188, 190–195, 197, 210, 211, 219, 246, 253–256, 261, 262, 265, 266
deterioration 2
developers 15, 46, 52, 54, 149, 203
development 2, 3, 5, 8, 12, 13, 15, 17, 19, 20, 34, 37, 38, 41–45, 47, 50–53, 56, 57, 65, 66, 68, 70, 82, 88, 96, 101, 109, 112, 113, 118, 120, 121, 123, 128, 131, 140, 143, 145–152, 161, 162, 166, 173, 180, 183, 184, 190, 192, 196, 210, 221, 223, 239, 246, 255
  practitioners 3

devices 2, 4, 5, 7, 18–21, 23, 27, 34, 43, 49, 50, 54, 59, 74, 75, 118, 121–127, 129, 133, 137–141, 143, 147, 150, 155, 156, 159, 165, 184–192, 197, 200, 205, 210, 213, 217, 224
digital 1, 2, 4, 5, 19, 24, 27, 34, 48, 49, 51–55, 60, 66, 67, 71, 76, 77, 79, 80, 82, 83, 88–91, 93, 96, 97, 119, 120, 122, 133, 134, 136–143, 147, 154, 155, 163–167, 169, 176, 177, 182, 186, 187, 194, 195
digital banking 79
digital divide 24, 71, 89, 140
digital economy 2, 24, 80
digital infrastructure 89
digital literacy 24
digital payment 77, 83, 90
digital resources 24
digital technology 2, 4, 51, 96, 120, 154, 155, 163–166
digital twin issues 54
digital twins
discourse 176
discovery 5, 70, 210
disease 2, 5, 9, 122, 134, 136, 139, 143, 145, 151, 155, 159, 178, 181, 182, 193, 217, 248, 262
disruptive 17, 20, 151, 152
    technologies 20, 151, 152
distance 121, 148, 171, 181, 222, 223, 237
distributed 20, 29, 30, 95, 119, 129, 130, 146, 162
    energy resources 129, 130
distribution 7, 97, 98, 100, 108, 120, 123, 126, 128, 129, 160, 182, 240, 244, 264, 266
divide 3, 24, 30, 71, 89, 98, 104, 140, 239, 242, 246, 247
DL 2, 27–34, 41, 43, 45, 51, 53, 57, 59, 61, 64, 75, 83, 85, 88, 90, 95, 103, 105, 112, 119, 122, 123, 127, 138, 140, 151, 152, 154, 158, 159, 167, 184, 185, 193, 200, 204, 210, 225, 237, 240, 246–249, 252, 258–261, 263, 265
documents 31, 83, 136
driverless 2
driverless cars 2
drug 5, 6, 11, 133, 185
    development 5

economic 15, 16, 19, 22, 34, 45, 54, 56, 72, 93, 94, 116, 119, 120, 123, 130, 133, 143, 144, 152, 156, 162, 246, 262–266
    development 56, 143
economy 1, 2, 22, 24, 51, 71, 80, 81, 88, 89, 120, 133, 246, 265
ecosystem 29, 48, 85, 87, 119, 141, 150, 152, 177, 183, 191, 194, 246, 249, 263
    transformation 48, 141, 152

education 1, 2, 4, 5, 9, 11, 19, 22, 24, 50, 51, 53, 54, 56, 58–61, 63–68, 73, 76, 131, 138, 139, 142, 143, 149, 151, 152, 155, 184, 239
    programs 14
educational 11, 14, 61, 63, 64, 67
educators 56, 68
effects 4, 38, 46, 50, 51, 54, 67, 89, 118, 120, 127, 176, 193, 196, 258, 265
electric 49, 96–100, 103–106, 108, 109, 111, 114, 116, 119, 120, 122, 124, 126, 127, 129, 131, 258, 261
    grid 96, 103
electronic 10, 11, 71, 101, 103, 114, 118, 133, 137, 148, 150, 162, 165, 168, 169, 186, 192, 197, 219
    health records 11, 140
emergence 8, 121, 246, 259, 260
employees 4, 19, 75, 81, 88, 89
encoder 85, 114, 117
encoding 114, 161
energy 1, 2, 18, 19, 22, 23, 34, 45, 51, 52, 62, 96, 97, 99–105, 108, 111, 114, 116, 118–121, 123–132, 144, 146, 155, 164, 184, 185, 191, 195, 210, 218, 219, 221–225, 236, 237, 251, 252, 263, 265
    infrastructure 127, 129
enforcement 38, 40, 42, 44
engine 10, 46, 55, 59, 87, 90, 92, 107, 113, 117, 141, 169, 200, 204, 205, 263
engineering 10, 55, 113, 141, 200, 204, 205
entertainment 22, 121
environment 1–4, 7, 9, 10, 13, 18, 19, 22, 34, 42, 45, 51, 52, 56, 57, 60, 71, 72, 77, 82, 120, 123, 124, 129, 133, 138, 149, 150, 154–157, 159, 160, 162, 164, 166, 167, 170, 176–180, 182, 190, 194, 197, 200, 209, 210, 216, 219, 239, 246, 249, 251, 258, 263, 265
environmental 1–4, 7, 34, 45, 51, 103, 118, 120, 123, 124, 129, 133, 143, 159, 160, 164, 166, 167, 176, 182, 239, 246, 249, 251, 258, 265
    deterioration 2
    protection 1, 166
    sustainability 51, 129, 143, 159, 239
equitable 9, 15, 19, 23, 24, 34, 35, 140, 143
    access 143
error 40, 45, 57, 96, 99, 111, 113, 133, 135, 147, 149, 151, 172, 173, 178, 188, 196, 215, 223, 241, 254
ethical 9, 11–15, 19, 20, 24, 34, 35, 37–47, 49–54, 68, 143, 145, 147–150, 152, 156, 252
    concerns 12, 38
    considerations 9, 11, 12, 14, 15, 37, 38, 45, 47, 145, 152
    ramifications 37

facial 38, 40, 42, 44, 64, 67, 194
   recognition algorithms 40
failure 33, 47, 54, 85, 86, 88, 89, 96, 100, 104, 114,
      120, 129, 132, 190, 191
fair 3, 4, 7, 37–41, 45, 51, 67, 140, 147, 173
   and impartial application 51
fairness 37–41, 45, 67
farming 11, 36, 158, 265
features 2, 10, 12, 59, 73, 76, 77, 89, 92, 112, 113,
      121, 128, 129, 143, 146, 160, 162, 172, 180,
      196, 203, 209, 222, 224, 239, 254, 262
federated 39, 101, 116, 154
   learning 39, 154, 159, 161
film 239
financial 14, 16, 22, 23, 35, 50, 51, 63, 64, 69–73,
      75, 81, 83, 84, 91, 110, 119, 120, 123, 139,
      158, 184, 190, 199, 251
   instability 87
   organizations 72, 73, 75, 79, 83, 84, 88, 89
   services 14, 69, 70, 72, 91, 93, 158
fintech 48, 93
flow 6, 7, 15, 20, 21, 27, 34, 52, 54, 73, 96, 97, 103,
      115, 119, 120, 122, 123, 129, 147, 148, 167,
      169, 180, 181, 184, 197, 210, 216, 218, 248,
      251, 263, 264
focus 1, 7, 13, 17, 18, 29, 58–63, 70, 73, 87, 96, 100,
      140, 144, 147, 156, 160, 177, 180, 181, 188,
      191, 201, 213, 215, 222, 243, 252
forecasting 81, 97, 98, 116, 117, 123, 259
forum 60
forwarder 223, 224
   hubs 223, 224
fourth 53
framework 4, 5, 13, 22, 29, 30, 37, 41–44, 46, 47,
      50, 66, 67, 89, 108, 109, 123, 128, 129, 132,
      139, 145, 147–150, 152, 161, 209, 211–220,
      224, 225, 237
frameworks 4, 5, 13, 37, 41–44, 46, 47, 50, 53, 54,
      89, 108, 123, 129, 139, 145, 147–150
fraud 49, 70, 71, 73, 76, 77, 83–86, 90, 93, 94, 146,
      158, 159, 201, 212
fusion 8, 113, 114, 176, 177, 244, 252

gadgets 4, 5, 7, 49, 50, 105, 121, 124–127
gated 67, 108, 109, 114, 158, 207
generative 92, 116
   adversarial networks 116
genomic 5, 11, 194
   data 5, 11
geospatial 177–180, 182, 183
   technology 177–180, 182
global 1, 6, 8, 64, 68, 79, 80, 82, 83, 87, 103, 105,
      118, 134, 142, 176, 179, 180, 182, 198, 199,
      246, 251, 259

goals 17, 19, 20, 87, 104, 120, 144, 161, 164, 166, 177,
      179, 246
governance 3, 48, 53, 75, 81, 145, 176, 177
governments 4, 41, 49, 54, 130, 174, 196
graph 31, 44, 61, 95, 108, 114, 139, 141, 144, 196,
      212, 216, 237, 239, 241, 243, 259, 261, 264,
      265
grid 5, 19, 22, 49, 52, 54, 96–121, 123–132, 180, 191,
      210
grids 5, 19, 22, 49, 52, 54, 96, 97, 100–107, 109, 110,
      114–121, 127–132, 191
growth 2, 3, 15, 34, 38, 43, 67, 71, 72, 78, 82, 91,
      121, 134, 143, 157, 158, 176, 179, 184, 206,
      239, 251, 258, 260, 262, 263
guidelines 38–41, 43, 44, 53, 90, 145

handling 28, 29, 31, 32, 83, 90, 221
   power 221
hardware 5, 9, 31, 136, 149, 198, 205
health 1, 2, 4–7, 14, 15, 18–21, 28, 34, 35, 37, 38, 43,
      45, 48, 49, 51–54, 64, 95, 118, 122, 131,
      133–152, 154–157, 160, 161, 177, 178, 184,
      185, 187, 194, 195, 211–219, 239, 247
   risks 11, 21
   status 35, 138, 213, 215
healthcare 1, 2, 9, 10, 15, 20, 21, 28, 34, 37, 38, 43,
      45, 49, 51–54, 95, 122, 131, 133–152, 154,
      161, 177, 184, 185, 194, 211, 213–219, 239
   delivery 135, 136, 143, 145, 147, 148, 151, 217,
      218
   infrastructure 51
   professionals 134, 138, 139, 149, 151, 217
   resources
hierarchical 93, 98, 128, 239, 242
   clustering 239
historical 28, 29, 53, 64, 72, 81, 82, 87, 157, 178,
      186, 246, 248
   data 28, 29, 53, 72, 81, 82, 157, 186, 246
hubs 221–225
human 1–4, 10, 12, 13, 16–19, 22, 25, 34, 36,
      38–45, 47, 48, 50–57, 59, 61, 69, 70, 83,
      92, 97, 104, 118, 133, 140, 141, 143, 144,
      147, 148, 151, 154, 155, 161, 163–167,
      176, 177, 179, 182, 184, 200, 239, 241,
      248, 263
   brain 56, 69
   rights 47, 50, 51
   supervision 40

identity 49, 71, 194, 210, 215
illiteracy 71
images 14, 27, 93, 141, 182, 244, 253, 254, 256
immune 146, 213, 217
   systems 213, 217

impact 3, 13, 14, 19, 22, 33, 35, 38–41, 45, 46, 58, 67, 75, 76, 93, 101, 105, 118, 119, 121, 126, 129, 133, 143, 145, 146, 155, 157, 158, 161, 184, 197, 204, 206, 210, 212, 225, 239, 246–249, 258, 259, 262, 265, 266
impartial 40, 51
  algorithms 40
implementation 5, 22, 24, 37, 48, 53, 55, 75, 101, 123, 133, 134, 241, 243, 258
  challenges
inclusive 2, 7, 12, 15, 19, 23, 24, 46, 47, 50, 51, 54, 140, 143, 163, 164, 166, 249
inclusivity 15, 53, 154
independent 32, 33, 59, 72, 79, 89, 91, 120
  agencies 89
individuals 3, 17, 18, 21, 22, 24, 35, 38, 44, 49, 51, 54, 62, 64, 89, 122, 124, 139, 143, 145, 159, 174, 185, 199, 207, 213, 214
industrial 16, 17, 19, 21, 52, 54, 119, 121, 132, 155, 163, 184, 185, 251, 261
  productivity 54
industry 4, 8, 18, 36, 43, 66, 69, 72, 79, 88, 114, 120, 122, 127, 128, 130, 133, 138, 141, 145, 147, 154, 164, 166, 177, 185, 263
  4.0 1, 8, 25, 33, 36, 40, 48, 52, 55, 60, 73, 76, 91, 93, 94, 101, 102, 114, 115, 117, 131, 140, 141, 143, 152, 159–167, 174–177, 182, 183, 189, 192–195, 208, 212, 228, 231, 233, 236, 238, 240, 243, 245, 250–259, 263, 264, 266
inequity 2
inflation 81
information 5, 10, 12, 20, 28, 34, 35, 39, 41, 42, 44, 45, 48, 52, 56, 60, 62, 63, 67, 70, 90, 97, 98, 105, 108–114, 120, 121, 124, 127, 128, 130, 133, 135–141, 143, 149–152, 154, 156, 163, 167–170, 172, 173, 176–185, 187, 190, 192, 193, 197, 199–202, 204, 205, 215, 237, 240, 241, 260, 262, 263
  security 187
infrastructure 4, 6, 11, 23, 24, 33, 49–54, 89, 97, 116, 119, 120, 122, 123, 126–131, 136, 140, 151, 170, 173, 178, 191, 206, 208, 210, 261
innovation 7, 12, 17, 18, 23, 32, 42, 43, 47, 48, 52, 90, 133, 141, 152, 164, 166, 176, 177, 179, 239
innovations 17, 23, 90, 177, 239
insight 14, 23, 27, 28, 33–36, 45, 52, 53, 62, 66, 68, 123, 137, 144, 145, 185, 186, 190, 213, 215
instability 3, 87
insurance 72, 82, 84, 146
integration 9, 24, 47, 49, 53, 65, 71, 75, 78, 119, 120, 128–131, 139, 143, 144, 147, 148, 163, 164, 196, 197, 243
intellectual 184, 185

property 184, 185
intelligence 1, 3, 9, 17, 18, 21, 37, 48, 49, 65–69, 75, 77, 78, 81, 91, 94, 101, 114, 116, 119, 133, 134, 141, 154, 155, 162–167, 174, 176, 184, 186, 190, 192–195, 200, 211, 239, 240, 243, 244, 246, 247, 259, 262
intelligent 10, 11, 17, 21, 22, 41, 56, 58–61, 63, 65, 94, 95, 97, 103, 108, 115, 121, 123, 131, 141, 152, 175, 177, 190, 192, 195, 197, 210, 214, 239, 241
interaction 5, 8, 9, 64, 83, 105, 106, 139, 144, 158, 165, 177, 207
interactive 14, 22, 30, 66, 139, 149, 182
interconnectedness 88
interest 1, 43, 56, 78, 90, 103, 174, 222, 243, 252
interface 53, 136, 137, 171, 188, 244
internet 8, 48, 121, 128, 131, 132, 137, 150, 152, 162, 163, 169, 173, 193, 196, 200, 204, 219, 220
  of things 48, 131, 132, 152, 162, 193, 220
interoperability 23, 53, 129, 147, 148, 158, 215
IoT 115, 144, 160, 193, 195, 219, 258, 265
irrigation 159, 160, 248, 262
issues 7, 8, 13, 37–40, 46, 49–54, 64, 71, 75, 103, 104, 110, 120, 122, 128, 130, 139, 145, 152, 154–159, 164, 166, 167, 174, 176, 185, 187, 189, 190, 192, 195, 196, 211, 219

land 22, 25, 33, 66, 90, 161, 162, 179, 183, 192–195, 206, 247, 248, 251, 252, 258, 264
  and water use 22
language 9, 10, 13, 15, 32, 45, 57, 58, 67, 69, 77, 79, 82, 88, 149, 152, 183, 193, 243
law 7, 35, 38, 40–46, 50, 51, 53, 130, 200, 201, 205
  enforcement agencies 40, 42
learning 2, 5, 19, 31, 33, 35, 39, 45, 53, 57–67, 69, 71, 78–81, 83, 84, 87, 90–95, 97–102, 105, 112–117, 128, 132, 142, 151, 154, 156–163, 165, 169–174, 176, 183, 185–188, 190–195, 208, 215–218, 237, 239, 240, 242–245, 247, 253, 254, 256, 259, 261, 262, 265
legal 2, 37, 41, 42, 46, 91, 158, 196, 200
  concerns 54
  issues 37, 46
level 4, 15, 16, 45, 65, 79, 80, 82, 88, 89, 92, 98, 104, 108, 109, 113, 119, 122, 126, 128, 147, 148, 151, 159, 160, 163, 176, 179, 200, 221, 224, 237, 247, 249, 259, 261
lifecycle 81
lifespan 125, 126, 221
limitations 3, 47, 106, 114, 128, 145–149, 191, 197, 211, 215, 221
linear 81, 108
  regression 81

linked 3, 7, 50, 108, 123, 129, 249
  gadgets 50
liquidity 73, 75, 88
literacy 24, 45, 56, 71, 151
lives 1, 3, 5, 7, 12, 21, 24, 34, 37, 38, 40, 49, 118, 119,
    121, 122, 131, 135, 143, 154, 156, 160, 174,
    177, 184, 185, 196, 239, 241
load 30, 50, 62, 63, 83, 89, 96, 97, 109, 111, 116, 119,
    161, 200, 204, 224, 225
loan 64, 70, 73, 79, 87, 91, 94, 158, 159
  management 79
loans 64, 73, 87, 158, 159
logic 1, 3–7, 15, 17, 22, 25, 33, 35, 36, 38, 43, 50, 54,
    65, 67, 83, 90, 93, 98, 105, 113, 122, 123,
    129, 131, 139, 141, 157, 158, 179, 183, 185,
    192, 194, 200, 247, 249, 258, 260–266
loss 23, 35, 55, 72–75, 83, 84, 110, 112, 113,
    120, 148, 191, 223, 247, 248, 253, 258,
    264, 266

machine 2, 5, 10–13, 21, 27, 31, 33, 35, 45, 48, 49,
    57, 59, 62, 64, 65, 78–81, 83, 84, 87–90,
    92, 93, 105, 107, 109, 112–117, 121, 133,
    144, 154, 156–161, 165, 169–174, 185–188,
    190–195, 197, 210, 212, 215–219, 239, 240,
    247, 253, 254, 258, 261, 262, 264, 265
  learning 2, 5, 13, 31, 33, 35, 45, 49, 59, 62, 64,
    65, 69, 71, 83, 84, 87, 90, 92, 93, 97, 98,
    105, 107, 109, 113–117, 154, 156–161,
    169–174, 185–188, 190–195, 210, 212,
    215–218, 239, 247, 253, 261, 262, 265
  learning algorithms 45, 79, 92, 107, 156, 157,
    171, 172, 174, 190, 191, 193, 195, 217
maintenance 52, 58, 63, 119–122, 125, 126, 132,
    155, 168, 185, 191
manage 2, 6, 7, 15, 16, 19, 22, 27, 28, 30, 32, 49, 62,
    68, 75, 77, 79, 81, 82, 84, 88, 91, 96, 97,
    100, 103, 104, 106, 108, 116–130, 132, 135,
    140, 141, 151, 152, 158–162, 177–181, 183,
    185, 186, 192, 195, 196, 199, 206, 210, 211,
    219, 256, 262
management 2, 6, 7, 15, 16, 22, 27, 30, 32, 53, 62,
    68, 75, 77, 79, 81, 82, 84, 88, 91, 96, 97,
    100, 104, 106, 108, 120–125, 132, 135, 140,
    141, 143, 144, 151, 154, 155, 158–162, 177,
    178, 180, 181, 183, 185, 192, 195, 206, 210,
    211, 256, 262
manufacturing 1, 7, 10, 18, 21, 33, 52, 54, 55, 101,
    105, 114, 115, 176, 177, 184, 185, 195, 197
market 2, 27, 32, 66, 70–73, 75, 77, 79, 80, 124, 127,
    133, 134, 142, 158, 159, 252, 261, 262
  demand 72
  risk 72

mass 1, 2, 6, 22, 27, 28, 48, 49, 73, 88, 89, 97, 98,
    221, 240, 244, 249, 251, 252, 259, 260
  adoptions 73
mean 7, 10, 24, 52, 53, 56, 59, 60, 81, 97, 98, 110,
    133, 139, 140, 181, 192, 196, 239, 248, 254,
    259, 266
media 5, 27, 34, 66, 68, 75, 92, 93, 96, 119, 122, 128,
    139, 141, 156, 201, 205, 225, 237, 249, 251
medical 6, 11, 12, 14, 19, 43, 45, 50, 93, 105, 137,
    138, 145, 149–152, 164, 195, 217, 219
  images 11, 14, 93, 141
medication 5, 134, 137, 138, 147, 160
  development 5
memory 30, 31, 101, 205, 221, 222
  limitations 221
meters 57, 72, 87, 96, 101, 103, 112, 115, 123, 124,
    126, 127, 175, 181, 187, 197, 205, 247, 254
micro 32, 33, 36, 64, 103, 117, 120, 129, 210, 258
microgrids 103, 120
mindsets 3
mining 31, 59, 60, 63, 93, 95, 98, 113, 114, 146, 222,
    223, 239, 240, 243, 244, 246, 247, 260–263
ml 11, 13, 16, 18, 23, 29, 67, 88, 135, 138, 140, 143,
    144, 175, 219
mobile 19, 50, 60, 75, 79, 89, 133, 138, 139, 143, 156,
    169, 177, 181, 192, 213, 237, 244
  devices 50, 75, 138, 213
  services 89
models 2, 9, 21, 53, 54, 67, 69, 70, 72, 81, 83, 87, 88,
    91, 95, 105, 106, 108, 110, 111, 114, 130,
    138, 146, 147, 157–160, 172, 181, 191, 193,
    197, 211, 237–240, 243, 254, 256, 266
modern 1, 3, 50, 60, 98, 104, 154, 168, 177, 196, 211
  technology 1, 3, 50, 154
monitoring 7, 32, 33, 41, 42, 44, 58, 61, 63, 64, 90,
    111, 119, 120, 123, 125, 128–134, 136–141,
    143, 146, 147, 161, 162, 177, 179, 183, 190,
    195, 208, 244, 246, 255, 256, 259–263
mortgage 79
multicast 223, 237

named 8, 69, 72, 79, 91, 121, 176
  data networking 8
natural 10, 13, 15, 22, 45, 69, 82, 88, 120, 178, 193,
    213, 217, 243, 246, 247, 249, 252, 258, 259,
    263, 264
  environment 22
  language processing 13, 15, 82, 88, 193, 243
navigation 166–174, 182, 247, 248
needs 2, 3, 5, 12, 17, 18, 22, 24, 31, 33, 41, 43, 54, 57,
    60, 61, 63, 79, 87, 96, 98, 99, 123, 130, 133,
    139, 159, 166, 181, 198, 202, 208, 217, 249
  of individuals 17, 18

network 4, 5, 7–10, 21, 22, 36, 47, 49, 50, 57, 60,
        62, 81, 89, 91, 92, 98, 101, 114, 116, 117,
        120, 121, 123, 126–129, 131, 132, 136, 146,
        153, 156, 161, 163, 167, 168, 179, 181, 182,
        190–193, 197–202, 204, 205, 207–211, 223,
        224, 237, 238, 244, 255, 256, 265, 266
    effects 89
    security 50, 110
networked 81, 184, 210
    intelligence 184
networking 8, 53, 60, 131
networks 4, 5, 7–10, 22, 36, 47, 49, 50, 52, 54, 57, 91,
        92, 94, 95, 98, 101, 103, 105, 110, 116, 120,
        128, 131, 132, 146, 153, 156, 167, 172, 185,
        186, 197, 199, 204, 207, 208, 219, 221, 223,
        237, 238, 244, 256, 265
neural 9, 10, 57, 67, 91, 92, 94, 95, 98, 101, 116, 128,
        156, 256, 265, 266
noncompliance 89
nonlinear 81
    regression 81
norms 3, 4, 41

online 19, 27, 50, 60, 61, 66, 71, 74, 75, 77, 81, 82,
        88, 95, 108, 109, 113, 114, 121, 139, 163,
        176, 196, 204, 209, 245
    transactions 27, 71, 77, 82
open 8, 25, 30, 37, 40–43, 45, 46, 50–53, 65, 67, 88,
        91, 105, 106, 112, 119, 121, 123, 152, 192,
        194, 195, 198, 208, 209, 223, 263
openness 37, 40–43, 45, 46, 50, 51, 91
operational 27, 28, 64, 93, 102, 111, 114, 121,
        129, 181
operations 21, 28, 33, 50, 71, 72, 80, 82, 87, 88, 90,
        121, 155, 186, 190, 196
optimization 11, 13, 21, 70, 72, 73, 83, 88, 89, 95,
        100, 108, 113, 131, 185, 219
organization 15, 16, 21, 27, 28, 31, 40–43, 45, 47,
        61, 67, 70–73, 79–84, 145, 146, 150, 152,
        185, 190, 191, 193, 196–201, 208, 210, 214,
        215, 221–224, 252
organizations 15, 21, 27, 28, 31, 34, 35, 45, 47, 61,
        75, 77, 79–84, 88, 89, 145, 146, 150, 185,
        190, 191, 193, 196, 198, 201, 214, 215, 221,
        222, 252
OTP 167, 202

paradigm 13, 17, 93, 101, 115, 210, 217
    shift 210
parcel
payment 71, 77, 78, 82, 83, 87, 90, 91, 146, 158
penetration 88, 120, 196, 205–211, 247
    testing 196, 205, 207–211

testing tools 203
people 1–5, 7, 18, 19, 21, 22, 34, 37, 40, 41, 44,
        48–52, 54, 71, 73, 77, 89, 106, 133, 134,
        139, 140, 143, 154, 155, 161, 163, 176, 177,
        179, 181, 183, 186, 196, 199, 200, 210, 216,
        247, 249
    of color 40
performance 6, 7, 16, 21, 32, 53, 60, 61, 63, 64, 101,
        113, 118, 121, 122, 137, 168, 173, 187, 188,
        190, 191, 204, 205, 224, 225, 237, 243, 254
personalized 9, 14, 18, 21, 34, 60, 66, 87, 133,
        136–140, 143, 145, 146, 151, 167–174, 185,
        213, 215, 217, 218, 239
    care 138, 140, 213, 215, 218
    navigation system 167, 169, 170
physical 1, 4, 5, 10, 13, 17, 18, 21, 34, 49, 56, 102,
        108, 117, 121, 124, 126, 138, 143, 144, 146,
        147, 150, 151, 163, 169, 170, 176, 177, 181,
        184, 185, 189, 196, 197, 211, 216
    technologies 1
ping 3, 4, 7, 11, 12, 14, 19, 24, 30, 32, 37–40, 43, 50,
        53, 54, 62–65, 72, 74, 76, 91, 100, 104, 110,
        112, 119, 122, 124, 127, 129, 138, 145–149,
        156, 157, 162, 167, 169, 171, 175, 178, 179,
        182, 183, 185, 190–193, 208, 210, 239, 246,
        251, 265
point 3, 22, 32, 42, 46, 50, 52, 60, 67, 80, 81, 89, 98,
        102, 114, 126, 129, 134, 136, 138, 139, 171,
        180, 187, 195, 208, 223, 224, 239, 242
policies 3, 4, 19, 24, 41, 42, 46, 81, 83, 88, 197,
        208, 210
    and strategies 24
policy 6, 7, 10, 16, 46, 47, 68, 79, 81, 83–86, 99, 181,
        259, 261
political 3, 4, 22, 35, 39, 44, 56, 200
populations 52, 134, 140, 143, 158, 160, 164, 166,
        258
PoS 4, 14, 20, 25, 28, 30, 41–47, 53, 54, 56, 57, 63,
        64, 66, 67, 69–77, 80, 81, 83, 87–90, 93, 94,
        96, 98, 103–106, 108, 122–126, 128–133,
        138, 143, 157, 168, 176–179, 181, 182,
        185–188, 191, 192, 199, 200, 202, 203, 206,
        221–225, 237, 239, 248, 249, 251, 252, 255,
        256, 259, 260, 262–266
power 2–6, 11, 19, 29, 34, 38, 42, 45, 50, 54, 83,
        88, 91, 96–100, 102–105, 111, 113–116,
        122–126, 138, 139, 143–146, 154, 179, 188,
        191, 196, 215, 218, 221, 223, 239, 248
    transmission 104, 120
powered 4, 6, 11, 14, 15, 34, 38, 45, 91, 130, 138,
        139, 144, 184, 239
practices 14, 16, 37, 44, 45, 47, 62, 97, 127, 143, 181,
        183, 201, 252, 258

practitioners 3
prediction 11, 53, 57, 60, 69, 73, 80, 81, 87, 88, 91, 94, 95, 100, 115, 116, 128, 138, 161, 171, 172, 186, 188, 194, 195, 243, 244
predictions 11, 53, 57, 73, 80, 95, 138, 186, 188
prejudice 4, 37, 40, 41, 44, 51
prevention 70, 76, 83, 108, 127, 136, 143, 156, 211, 259
price 72, 80, 81, 90, 91, 95, 98, 120, 125, 126, 130, 211
privacy 1, 2, 4, 7, 23, 28, 34, 35, 41–47, 49–54, 71, 82, 83, 88, 106, 109, 116, 128, 137, 138, 140, 143, 159, 161, 173, 174, 183, 195, 196, 210, 219, 239
    and security 1, 7, 23, 28, 46, 51, 52, 54, 109, 122, 147, 173, 195
    protection 39, 41, 128
process 1, 2, 10–13, 15, 20, 21, 27–39, 41, 43, 50, 56, 63, 64, 69, 70, 72, 74, 76, 77, 82, 84, 88, 89, 98, 99, 105, 108, 110, 126, 128, 154, 155, 163, 165, 169–173, 177, 180, 182, 183, 185–188, 190, 193, 195, 197, 199, 208, 210, 216, 219, 222, 242, 243, 249, 253, 259, 265
processing 1, 4, 5, 10, 13, 15, 20, 27–33, 36, 41, 50, 53, 59, 63, 69, 74, 82, 84, 88, 98, 110, 112, 113, 128, 145, 146, 154, 155, 165, 169, 170, 172, 173, 177, 180, 183, 193, 195, 219, 243, 253, 265
production 1, 5, 7, 18, 34, 54, 91, 96, 99, 114, 116, 127, 129, 154, 155, 160, 161, 181, 211, 223, 247, 251, 258, 260, 262, 264, 266
productivity 6, 7, 12, 21, 54, 122, 154, 157, 160, 164, 258
professionals 20, 42, 46, 134, 135, 138, 139, 149, 151, 152, 156, 213–217
profile 73, 74, 76, 82, 87, 95, 103, 146
profiles 87, 103
programs 14, 46, 139, 148
property 184, 185
prosperity 2
protection 1, 28, 35, 38, 39, 41, 49, 128, 145, 166, 209, 261
protocol 4, 5, 23, 49, 53, 86, 121, 137, 146, 150, 154, 194, 208, 209, 219, 221–225, 237, 238, 244
protocols 4, 5, 23, 49, 53, 121, 137, 146, 150, 154, 219, 237
public 17, 38, 43, 46, 51, 52, 114, 129, 133, 165, 166, 178, 180, 182, 184, 196, 210, 244, 247, 252, 264, 265
    safety 178, 182, 184

quality 7, 10, 13, 14, 19, 21, 35, 49, 54, 62, 65, 75, 88, 96, 100, 101, 108, 109, 114, 115, 119, 126, 133, 139, 140, 144, 145, 149, 154, 156, 157, 160, 163–167, 173, 179, 181, 183, 185, 211, 242, 244, 246, 248, 252, 260, 262

quantum 7, 212
    computing 7

racially 40
radio 76, 108, 128, 131, 180, 221
    transmissions 221
ramifications 2, 37, 42
rate 1–6, 10, 13–18, 21–24, 27–30, 32–35, 37–40, 42, 44–47, 50–54, 56, 57, 59, 61, 62, 64, 65, 73–78, 83, 87, 88, 90, 91, 98, 100, 101, 104, 105, 111–114, 116, 118, 121, 123, 127–130, 138–141, 146–151, 154–161, 163, 170, 177, 179, 194–197, 199, 200, 207–214, 216–219, 221–224, 237, 239, 246–249, 251, 252, 254, 258, 262
ratings 239–244
ratio 1–5, 9–12, 14, 15, 19, 21, 22, 24, 27, 28, 33, 41, 47, 53, 54, 56, 57, 61, 62, 69–76, 78–84, 87–90, 93, 95, 99, 102, 103, 105, 108, 110–114, 116, 119–126, 128–131, 133, 134, 139, 143–152, 155, 158, 159, 161, 163–166, 173, 178, 181, 185–190, 192, 194, 200–203, 205–211, 218, 221–225, 236, 237, 243, 244, 251, 253, 258, 259, 261, 264, 266
reality 13, 58, 60, 61, 66, 88, 138, 139, 149–152, 176, 247
realm 17, 176
recognition 10, 38, 40, 60, 64, 67, 98, 101, 211, 237, 251, 254, 266
recommendation 31, 37, 41, 43, 45, 46, 53, 57, 64, 71, 77, 87, 139, 167, 170–174, 206
recommendations 37, 41, 43, 45, 46, 53, 57, 64, 87, 139, 167, 170–174, 206
records 11, 12, 45, 70, 76, 87, 105, 133, 138, 140, 145, 158
recruiting 40
recurrent 91, 94, 116
    neural networks 91
reduction 78, 83, 111, 181
regression 31, 81, 98, 113, 116, 240, 242, 244
regulation 4, 19, 28, 37, 39, 43, 44, 47, 48, 51, 89, 90, 95, 106, 130, 137, 145, 146, 150, 155, 159, 174
regulations 19, 28, 37, 39, 44, 51, 89, 137, 145, 146, 150, 155, 174
regulatory 37, 41–44, 46, 47, 50, 53, 123, 129, 139, 147, 148, 158, 194
    frameworks 37, 46, 47, 50, 123, 129, 139, 147, 148, 150
reinforcement 9, 15, 87, 94, 95, 99, 100, 108, 109, 116, 117
    learning 9, 15, 87, 94, 95, 99, 100, 108, 116, 117
remittances 71

report 19, 69, 71, 72, 75, 77–83, 86, 155, 159, 172,
        175, 199, 202, 206, 209, 212, 251, 266
request 13, 32, 190, 204, 219, 221, 223, 237, 265
research 8, 15, 22, 24, 46, 47, 49, 52, 56, 57, 60, 62,
        63, 65, 66, 78, 81, 83, 89, 91, 93, 97, 100,
        101, 106–109, 114, 116, 128–131, 140, 141,
        148–152, 159, 178, 179, 181, 182, 185, 187,
        188, 191, 193–196, 208, 221, 222, 237, 244,
        246, 249, 251, 252, 258
resource 2, 3, 16, 21, 22, 24, 30, 42, 45, 52, 53, 59,
        71, 75, 81, 83, 98, 101, 103, 105, 119, 123,
        124, 129, 130, 140, 150, 151, 154–157, 160,
        164, 166, 173, 179–182, 191, 197, 204,
        213–217, 219, 239, 246, 260, 263, 264
    allocation 52
    management 22, 30, 53
resources 3, 24, 30, 42, 45, 53, 59, 71, 75, 81, 103,
        105, 119, 123, 124, 129, 130, 140, 150, 151,
        155, 160, 166, 173, 179, 180, 191, 197, 204,
        217, 246, 260, 263
response 10, 50, 60, 71, 74, 116, 120, 124, 126, 131,
        185, 191, 199, 210, 218, 246, 264
responsibility 3, 4, 15, 16, 40, 41, 43, 46, 51, 53,
        81, 97
responsible 13–16, 22, 24, 32, 37, 38, 40, 41, 43, 51,
        89, 145, 146, 169, 178
    development 37, 41
    use 22, 24, 43, 51, 145, 146
resumes 40
retail 80, 185
    operations 80
revolution 9, 13, 54, 90, 120, 121, 123, 130, 133,
        146, 155, 160, 179, 185, 194, 218, 222
rights 4, 34, 37, 38, 41, 42, 47, 50, 51, 81, 145, 202
risk 4, 5, 7, 11, 14, 15, 21–24, 35, 38, 43, 45, 54, 64,
        67, 70–73, 75, 76, 79, 84, 87, 88, 91, 92,
        100, 108, 110, 112, 116, 120, 121, 135,
        138, 139, 145–151, 161, 167, 168, 174, 180,
        186, 190, 191, 193, 196, 201, 208, 210, 214,
        215, 249
    assessments 208, 210
    calculation 73
    profile 76, 87
risks 4, 7, 11, 15, 21, 22, 24, 35, 43, 54, 67, 72, 84,
        88, 120, 121, 145, 150, 168, 174, 186, 190,
        191, 193, 196, 201, 215
robotics 10, 21, 24, 34, 57, 61, 133, 143, 144, 147,
        148, 165, 166, 174, 176
robots 1, 5, 9, 18, 19, 50, 51, 53, 54, 66, 121, 154,
        155, 164, 165
route 6, 32, 52, 167–170, 172, 173, 223, 224, 237
    request 32, 223, 237
routing 167, 169, 171, 173, 221–225, 244

protocols 223, 237
tables 221, 222

safety 5, 7, 11, 12, 14, 15, 34, 40, 42, 43, 45, 51, 97,
        100, 114, 121, 123, 133, 137, 139, 140, 147–
        151, 155, 167, 172, 178, 182, 184, 203, 209
    and security 14, 133, 137
schemes 42, 193, 251
scoring 63, 87, 93, 95
secure 5, 7, 20, 28, 45, 46, 50, 51, 54, 74, 75, 101,
        105, 113, 116, 117, 127, 131, 135–138, 146,
        147, 151, 156, 158, 159, 186, 189, 190, 197,
        204, 208, 210, 211, 215, 220
    authentication 137
security 1, 2, 12, 14, 16, 22, 23, 28, 32, 34, 35, 43,
        46, 49–52, 54, 55, 71, 74, 75, 82, 83, 96,
        106, 112, 115, 116, 119–124, 127–131, 133,
        137, 138, 140, 143, 150, 151, 154, 173, 174,
        179, 184–193, 195–203, 205, 207–212, 215,
        219
    analysis 196, 202, 211
segmentation 238, 254, 256
sensor 4–8, 11, 18, 20, 27, 33, 34, 45, 47, 53, 105,
        118, 119, 126, 127, 129, 131, 137, 138, 147,
        153–158, 161–165, 167, 169, 172, 173, 176,
        177, 181, 184, 185, 188, 193, 195, 211, 213,
        219, 221–224, 237, 238, 244, 253, 255, 262
    data 6, 33, 53, 244
    hubs 221, 222
sensors 4, 5, 7, 11, 18, 20, 27, 34, 45, 118, 119, 126,
        129, 137, 138, 147, 154–158, 162–165, 167,
        169, 172, 176, 181, 184, 185, 188, 193, 213,
        221, 223, 262
services 2, 6, 11, 14, 15, 32, 33, 36, 69–73, 79, 80, 87,
        93, 120, 121, 133, 134, 136–141, 143, 148,
        150, 158, 163, 165, 166, 171, 176, 184, 192,
        197, 199, 200, 212–215, 217, 218
shift 17, 18, 22, 70, 108, 138, 154, 210
signals 168, 194, 221, 222
simulation 14, 53, 60, 65, 108, 111, 138, 165, 224
single 80, 89, 108, 113, 170, 209, 222, 243, 252
    point of failure 89
skills 24, 48, 63, 65, 88, 140, 148, 149
smart 5–8, 11, 17–21, 34, 36, 49, 50, 53, 61, 65, 70,
        80, 91, 100–110, 112–121, 123–132, 137,
        138, 141, 143, 145–148, 154–157, 164, 166,
        169, 170, 177, 184, 185, 188, 192–195, 205,
        210, 213, 218
    agriculture 156, 161, 162
    buildings 53
    cities 5, 7, 8, 20, 34, 121, 130, 131, 141, 164, 166,
        184, 185, 210, 218
    city 128, 131, 194

farming 36, 154, 155, 161, 162
grids 5, 19, 104–107, 109, 110, 114, 116–121, 127–132
healthcare 145–148, 213
meters 101, 103, 123, 126, 127
social 7, 19, 27, 34, 37, 38, 44, 50–54, 60, 66, 92, 93, 95, 133, 139, 149, 152, 154, 163, 164, 166, 176, 177, 200, 204, 205, 211, 249
change 2, 15
media 27, 34, 66, 92, 93, 139, 205
realm 17
responsibility 15, 16, 51
societal 3, 10, 15, 20, 22, 34, 35, 41, 42, 51, 52, 144, 148, 174, 176, 239
development 239
society 1–9, 11, 13–19, 34, 35, 37, 38, 41, 43–48, 50–56, 96, 118, 122, 133, 134, 140, 141, 152, 154, 155, 161, 163–167, 174, 176, 177, 184, 191, 195, 213, 216, 239
software 30, 32, 44, 49, 62, 67, 71, 88, 111, 127, 136, 138, 149, 165, 179, 181, 185, 189, 198, 200, 204
applications 138, 208
solution 2, 7, 18, 21, 28, 30, 33, 44, 45, 50, 53, 54, 60, 61, 75, 77, 100, 103, 116, 118, 122, 124, 128, 129, 134, 141, 150, 151, 156, 169, 172, 177, 178, 180, 182, 190, 192, 193, 195, 221, 246, 257, 263, 266
solutions 2, 7, 18, 21, 28, 44, 45, 50, 53, 54, 60, 75, 116, 118, 122, 124, 128, 129, 134, 141, 150, 151, 172, 177, 178, 180, 190, 192, 193, 195, 246, 257, 263
sources 3, 11, 19, 23, 24, 27, 30, 34, 42, 45, 53, 59, 68, 71, 75, 81, 89, 96, 97, 99, 101, 103, 105, 107, 118–121, 129, 130, 140, 150, 151, 155, 160, 166, 169, 172, 173, 179, 180, 186, 191, 197, 200, 201, 204, 217, 246, 260, 263
space 18, 60, 62, 143, 144, 163, 169, 170, 173, 180, 196, 258
square 247
stability 3, 81, 87, 88, 96, 114, 115, 124, 191
stakeholder 4, 15, 37, 46, 47, 53, 73, 87, 135, 136, 148, 160, 168, 176, 177, 239, 249, 252
standard 3, 15, 23, 37, 40–43, 46, 49, 71, 90, 128, 130, 140, 146, 163, 176, 186, 209, 224, 252
standards 3, 15, 23, 37, 40, 41, 43, 46, 49, 90, 128, 146, 176, 186, 209, 252
status 32, 35, 113, 138, 144, 201, 213, 215, 222, 249, 265
steering 221–225, 237
stock 79, 80, 89, 91, 156, 160, 162

strategies 10, 14, 18, 24, 27, 52, 54, 59, 108, 128, 186, 195, 197, 212, 218, 246, 249, 265
stress 7, 41, 75, 89, 119, 155, 156, 167, 169, 172
level 89, 119
strict 3, 46, 51, 89, 108, 174, 182, 204, 222, 247, 249, 258, 263
structured 27, 31, 60, 83
data 27, 31
study 22, 37, 40, 55, 58, 61, 62, 69, 72, 73, 80, 88, 91, 93, 95, 101, 107, 108, 114, 116, 128, 131, 141, 142, 158, 159, 162, 172, 179, 186–190, 192, 193, 195, 211, 223, 225, 237, 241, 243, 249, 253–257
success 2, 22, 37, 41, 47, 58, 72, 83, 88, 108, 123, 144, 173, 191, 224, 239, 240, 244, 247, 249, 262
rate 239
supervised 11, 92, 103, 108, 187, 240, 242, 253, 265
learning systems 114
supervision 40
support 19, 21, 22, 27, 30, 40, 45, 53, 56, 58–61, 67, 68, 70, 74, 75, 79, 81, 83, 88, 94, 98, 110, 120, 124, 129, 131, 135, 136, 139, 148, 149, 156, 164, 169, 172, 173, 176, 178, 183, 200, 201, 216, 222, 224, 240, 246, 251, 253, 254
sustainability 1, 3, 4, 11, 15, 16, 22, 50, 51, 53, 122, 129, 130, 140, 143, 146, 154, 155, 159, 160, 176, 184, 214, 239, 262
standards 176
sustainable 2, 4, 5, 15, 17, 19, 20, 34, 38, 50–54, 118, 127, 130, 143, 144, 152, 154, 155, 160, 161, 163–167, 174, 176, 177, 195, 213, 246, 249, 251, 252
agriculture 154
development 8, 17, 19, 20, 53, 152, 161, 176, 177
development goals 17, 20, 161
innovation 176
system 2, 4–7, 9–18, 20–23, 25, 29–34, 37–54, 56–65, 67, 68, 70, 71, 74, 77, 78, 85–89, 96, 97, 100–103, 105, 107–114, 116–133, 144–152, 154–159, 161, 162, 165–174, 181–188, 190–202, 204–217, 219, 221, 224, 225, 244, 246, 249, 255, 256, 259, 263, 264
systems 2, 4–7, 9–15, 17, 18, 20–23, 29, 31, 33, 34, 37–47, 49–54, 56–65, 67, 68, 70, 71, 74, 77, 78, 86, 87, 89, 94, 96, 97, 100–103, 113, 114, 116–126, 128–133, 135, 136, 140, 141, 144, 146–151, 154, 155, 161, 162, 165, 167–174, 178, 179, 181–186, 194–201, 207–213, 224, 225, 246, 259, 264

technical 7, 11, 12, 34, 35, 74, 91, 98, 120, 145, 183, 212

technique 11, 27, 28, 33, 46, 48, 57, 59, 60, 63, 65, 69, 83, 92, 93, 95, 97–100, 103, 107, 108, 113, 114, 128, 131, 137, 141, 161, 167, 169, 171, 172, 178, 179, 181, 186, 187, 196, 204, 207, 219, 222, 223, 225, 246, 247, 253, 254, 258, 259, 265

technological 1, 3, 5, 7, 17, 22, 36, 38, 43, 50, 54, 65, 90, 105, 122, 123, 129, 139, 174, 176, 183, 185, 192

technologies 5–11, 15, 17–20, 27, 30, 32–35, 41, 42, 49, 59, 71, 75, 76, 80, 83, 84, 88–91, 96, 101, 103, 105, 106, 109, 119, 120, 123, 128, 130, 131, 133, 134, 137, 147–152, 154–158, 160, 161, 164, 166, 169, 174, 176–179, 186, 188, 189, 191, 192, 194, 197, 204, 213, 215–218, 262

technology 1–7, 10, 17–20, 27, 37–54, 56, 57, 63, 65, 67, 70, 72, 77, 78, 94, 96, 108, 110, 118, 120–124, 130, 133–136, 138–141, 143, 145–152, 154–167, 169, 176–186, 192, 194, 196, 197, 200, 201, 208, 210, 211, 213, 214, 216, 218, 239, 246, 252, 260, 262, 263, 265
    automation 78
    developers 149
    solutions 50, 54

term 10, 27, 28, 31, 34, 40, 56, 73, 75, 80, 82, 88, 91, 93, 96, 98, 100, 103, 110, 113, 114, 116, 122, 140, 143, 145, 146, 165, 168, 176, 177, 186, 187, 197, 204, 208, 210, 223, 224, 237, 241, 249, 251, 253, 256, 261

terminal 80

testing 46, 77, 112, 196, 205–211, 221

theft 22, 49, 54, 85, 86, 102, 108, 109, 111, 116, 120, 184, 215

things 3, 6, 17, 48, 55, 57, 121, 131, 132, 141, 142, 152, 161, 162, 174, 207, 212, 219, 220

throughput 29, 71, 223, 225, 236, 237

timely 45, 73, 75, 84, 90, 213, 214

tools 11, 15, 21, 23, 24, 27, 28, 59–62, 64, 66, 72–75, 80, 81, 97, 137, 141, 143, 154, 169, 177, 181, 199, 203, 207–210, 239, 243, 246

trading 80, 82, 89, 91–95, 127, 159, 161

traditional 17, 27, 31, 32, 34, 73, 76, 82, 96, 99, 133, 192, 258
    data management tools 27

traffic 6, 7, 11, 15, 18, 20, 21, 34, 52, 54, 96, 109, 121, 127, 144, 167–174, 184, 185, 190, 192, 204, 221, 222, 237, 248
    signals 221

trained 13, 15, 45, 52, 65, 75, 88, 89, 108, 109, 163, 187, 215, 261
    employees 75, 89

training 4, 9, 14, 22, 46, 53, 57, 75, 76, 98, 100, 101, 108, 138, 139, 148–152, 183, 187, 188, 190, 216, 252, 256, 261
    data 98, 100, 112, 187, 188, 261

transaction 20, 27, 70, 71, 74, 77, 79, 80, 82, 83, 90, 112, 128, 129, 146, 158, 159

transactions 20, 27, 70, 71, 74, 77, 80, 82, 83, 90, 128, 129, 146

transformation 22, 48, 94, 122, 141, 152, 182, 216, 241, 242, 254

transition 103, 124, 152, 165, 169, 176, 180, 182, 199

transmission 5, 100, 103, 104, 110, 119, 120, 126, 128, 131, 139, 182, 221, 223, 225

transmissions 221

transparency 5, 12–15, 37, 38, 44, 47, 52, 88, 96, 146, 158, 188, 193, 196

transportation 1, 2, 11, 14, 15, 21, 22, 34, 37, 38, 49, 51–54, 139, 154, 177, 184, 185, 191, 239
    infrastructure 6

tree 68, 80, 94, 117, 122, 128, 131, 156, 172, 175, 179, 188, 211, 237, 239

trustworthy 43, 51, 52, 188, 204

tutoring 56, 58, 61, 67, 68
    systems 56, 67, 68

twin 6, 52–55

twins

unauthorized 22, 106, 140, 147, 184, 186, 190, 197, 198, 204, 220
    access 22, 140, 147, 184, 190, 197, 220

unicast 223

universal 19
    access 19

unstructured 27, 31
    data 27, 31

unsupervised 11, 98, 103, 113, 187, 242, 253, 261, 262
    learning 11, 98, 187, 242, 261, 262

urbanization 133, 144

user 2, 21, 28–31, 39, 40, 42, 44, 46, 52, 53, 59, 70, 71, 73, 74, 77, 79, 81–84, 87, 96, 110, 111, 136–139, 149, 151, 168–174, 178, 182, 190, 194, 200, 204, 205, 210, 211, 241
    account lifecycle management 81

utilization 17, 105, 131, 190, 223, 237, 246, 249, 251, 259, 262, 263, 265, 266

value 2, 12, 16, 31, 35, 39, 51, 53, 76, 80, 82, 98, 99, 128, 133, 134, 152, 157–160, 172, 184, 205, 210, 240, 254, 263

variety 11, 22, 27, 28, 30–33, 35, 46, 73, 87, 91, 96, 98, 104, 107, 108, 111, 118, 130, 136, 138, 157, 163, 172, 185, 196, 203, 215, 239, 258 vector 98, 112, 113, 156, 172, 180, 182, 183, 200, 237, 240, 248, 253, 254

velocity 27, 28, 31, 33, 248

virtual 2, 10, 13, 21, 53, 54, 57, 58, 60, 61, 88, 104, 134, 138, 139, 149, 151, 163, 169, 170, 173, 176, 219

    assistants 2, 10, 21, 138

    reality 58, 88, 139, 151, 176

vision 5, 10, 11, 17, 19, 20, 40, 41, 49, 52, 53, 57, 88, 133, 143, 144, 154, 155, 163, 165, 184, 216, 219, 239, 252, 256, 264

voice 67, 170, 204

volume 2, 5, 6, 31, 33, 34, 50, 71, 82, 100, 185

vulnerabilities 50, 186, 191, 196, 200, 201, 203, 207–210

vulnerability 75, 109, 199, 202, 204–207, 209, 211

vulnerable 50, 74, 89, 140, 150, 184, 186, 197, 199, 200, 202

water 11, 22, 54, 93, 122, 154, 157, 159, 181, 183, 210, 211, 246–253, 255, 257–266

wearables 5, 18, 121, 133, 137, 213, 217

weather 9, 91, 105, 123, 129, 156, 157, 159, 160, 169, 246

wireless 4, 5, 47, 104, 128, 153, 161, 185, 188, 219, 221, 237, 238, 244

    sensor networks 4, 5, 47, 153, 219, 221, 238, 244

workforce 78

world 1, 5, 13, 18, 19, 22, 27, 34, 35, 38, 47, 49, 52, 53, 56, 58, 69, 74, 76, 78, 82, 83, 111, 118, 120, 121, 129, 138, 143, 149, 154, 163, 177, 179, 181, 187, 188, 196, 221, 243, 247, 258

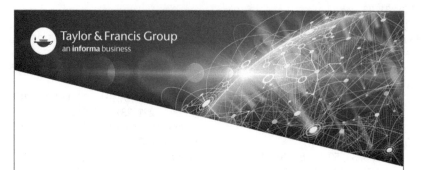